The Other Side of Paradise

The Other Side of Paradise

FOREIGN CONTROL IN THE CARIBBEAN

BY

Tom Barry, Beth Wood, and Deb Preusch

THE RESOURCE CENTER

The Grove Press Latin America Series

Grove Press, Inc./New York

Contents

Tables

ACKNOWLEDGMENTS

Several people deserve special mention for their valued assistance in the preparation of this book: Chuck Hosking for donated time and for comments on the manuscript, Lou Baldwin for his careful reading of the manuscript, and Kit Tremaine and Michael Kelley for their support, which made this book possible. We appreciate the many comments we received from experts who read portions of the book: Marc Herold, Cathy Sunshine, John Cavanagh, Michael Hooper, Tim Draimin, Richard Charles, Michael Kaufman, Alex Stepick, Josh DeWind, Tim Smith, Fred Goff, Steve Hellinger, Robin Broad, Robert Girling, and Phil Brenner.

Deserving of many thanks for performing with a smile the nitty-gritty work on the book are: Lee McCormick, Joani Quinn, Barbara Bush-Stuart, Denise Doughtie, and Steve Blake; also Chrys Seanna, Jean Shepherd, and Bill Cocke.

We are also grateful to Lisa Rosset of Grove Press, whose assistance and encouragement have made the publication of *Dollars and Dictators* and *The Other Side of Paradise* possible.

CARIBBEAN COUNTRY STATISTICS*

Country	Population (000s)	Density (per square mile)	Infant mortality (per 1000)	Life expectancy (years)	Literacy (%)	Population access to piped water (%)(urban/rural)
United States	24,193	64	14	74	99	—
Puerto Rico	3,240	943	18	72	88	—
US Virgin Islands	103	780	22	—	—	—
Anguilla	7	191	—	—	—	—
Bermuda	72	3,496	14	73	98	—
British V.I.	13	225	37	70	98	—
Cayman Islands	20	201	14	—	93	—
Montserrat	12	304	40	68	76	—
Turks & Caicos	8	42	43	—	100	—
French Guiana	77	2	29	70	73	92/60
Guadeloupe	312	454	19	67	70	—
Martinique	303	713	13	68	70	—
Neth Antilles	247	645	—	—	95	—
Antigua-Barbuda	77	715	32	62	88	—
Bahamas	235	44	32	68	93	—
Barbados	254	167	23	70	98	88/100
Cuba	9,858	224	19	73	96	93/—
Dominica	74	257	20	58	80	—
Dominican Rep	6,280	334	73	62	68	47/34
Grenada	111	834	15	63	98	30/40
Guyana	803	10	45	69	86	69/60
Haiti	5,186	484	130	48	23	21/3
Jamaica	2,228	505	16	69	82	40/73
St Kitts-Nevis	45	429	53	68	88	—
St Lucia	119	500	30	69	80	—
St Vincent	128	853	60	67	80	—
Suriname	376	6	39	69	80	—
Trinidad	1,076	543	24	66	97	43/64

* years vary for the figures, but are as close to 1982 as possible
Sources: Annual Report, IDB 1982; *Economic and Social Progress in Latin America*, IDB 1983; *Countries of the Caribbean Community: A Regional Profile*, AID 1982; *The World Factbook*, CIA 1983; *CCAA's Caribbean Datebook*, Caribbean/Central America Action, 1983; U.S. Embassies; *Statistical Yearbook for*

Unem-ployment (%)	Foreign debt ($ million)	GNP/GDP ($ million)	Per capita income ($)	Largest exports (#1/#2/#3)
10	—	3,080,700	13,154	machinery/chem/trans/equip
25	8,200	12,617	3,918	chem/petro prod/pharm
9	—	542	4,743	petro prod
40	—	3	420	salt/lobster/livestock
2	—	598	10,894	drugs/bunker fuel
—	—	31	2,540	fresh fish/gravel & sand/fruit & veg
—	9	72	4,800	turtle shell/trop fish/dried fish
6	2	20	1,736	poly bags/trop plants/elec parts
—	—	15	2,000	conch shells/crawfish/salt
10	—	120	1,935	shrimp/timber/rum
—	—	957	3,040	bananas/sugar/rum
21	—	1,169	3,559	petro prod/bananas/rum
20	—	864	3,472	petro prod
18	54	126	1,649	manufac goods/machinery/chem
19	228	1,353	5,756	petro prod/pharm/crawfish
11	332	603	2,373	sugar/elec components/clothing
2	3,200	14,000	1,410	sugar/nickel/citrus
23	58	59	798	bananas/laundry soap/toilet soap
25	2,063	5,999	955	sugar/dore/coffee
14	17	97	883	cocoa/bananas/nutmeg
21	933	560	697	sugar/bauxite/rice
12	464	1,380	266	coffee/bauxite/sugar
26	2,060	3,181	1,428	alumina/bauxite/sugar
20	11	52	1,062	sugar
14	18	131	1,071	bananas/coconut oil/cocoa
20	16	73	657	bananas/arrowroot/coconut
15	27	1,080	3,042	alumina/bauxite/aluminum
12	1	2,986	2,776	petro prod/crude petro

Latin America, ECLA/UN 1980; *Quarterly Economic Review: Cuba, Dominican Republic, Haiti, Puerto Rico,* Bank of London and South America, March 1983; *Caribbean Overview,* Canadian Govt Department of External Affairs, 1982; *Statistical Abstracts of the U.S.,* Department of Commerce, December 1982

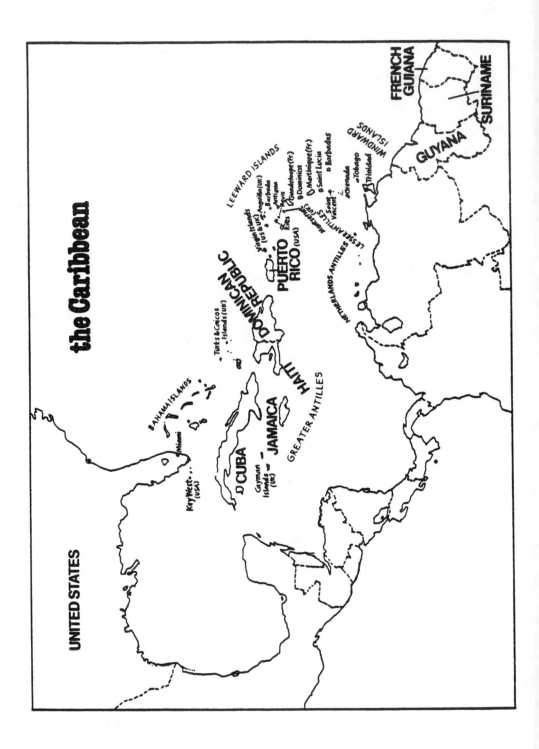

the Caribbean

UNITED STATES

BAHAMA ISLANDS

Miami

KeyWest... (USA)

CUBA

Cayman
Islands (UK)

JAMAICA

Turks & Caicos
Islands (UK)

HAITI

DOMINICAN REPUBLIC

GREATER ANTILLES

PUERTO RICO (USA)

Virgin Islands
(US & UK)

LEEWARD ISLANDS

Anguilla (UK)
Barbuda
Antigua
Guadeloupe (Fr.)
Dominica
Martinique (Fr.)
Saint Lucia
Barbados
Saint Vincent
Grenada
Tobago
Trinidad

Saba
St. Kitts
Nevis
Montserrat

WINDWARD ISLANDS

LESSER ANTILLES

NETHERLANDS ANTILLES

GUYANA

SURINAME

FRENCH GUIANA

Glossary of Terms

Caribbean: The islands in the Caribbean Sea plus the Bahamas and Bermuda, as well as South American countries of Guyana, Suriname, and French Guiana.

Caribbean Basin: The nations of the Caribbean and the seven countries of Central America, a geographical demarcation popularized by the Reagan administration.

West Indies: The islands between North America and South America, often including all the countries of the Caribbean.

Commonwealth Caribbean: The nations and territories in the region that belong to the British Commonwealth of Nations: Anguilla, Antigua, Bahamas, Barbados, Bermuda, British Virgin Islands, Dominica, Grenada, Guyana, Jamaica, Montserrat, St. Kitts, St. Lucia, St. Vincent, Trinidad, and Turks and Caicos.

British Caribbean: The Caribbean islands that remain colonies of Great Britain: Anguilla, Bermuda, British Virgin Islands, Cayman Islands, Montserrat, and Turks and Caicos.

Eastern Caribbean: The English-speaking islands in the eastern Caribbean Sea: Anguilla, Antigua, Barbados, Dominica, Grenada, Montserrat, St. Kitts, St. Lucia, and St. Vincent.

Antilles: The Caribbean islands. The Greater Antilles are Cuba, Hispaniola (Haiti and the Dominican Republic), Jamaica, and Puerto Rico; the Lesser Antilles are all the islands southeast of Puerto Rico including the islands off the coast of Venezuela.

Leeward Islands: The northern group of islands in the Lesser Antilles, those that extend southeast of Puerto Rico to the Windward Islands.

Windward Islands: The islands that lie south of the Leeward Islands, extending from Guadeloupe to Grenada, usually excluding the eastern island of Barbados.

Introduction

I come from the nigger yard of yesterday, leaping from the oppressor's hate and scorn of myself. I come to the world with scars upon my soul, wounds upon my body, fury in my hands. I turn to the histories of men and the lives of peoples. I examine the shower of sparks, the wealth of the dreams. I am pleased with the glories, and sad with the sorrows, rich with the riches, poor with the loss.

—Martin Carter, from "I Come from the Nigger Yard of Yesterday"

The same clear sea washes the shores of the islands and the continental states of the Caribbean, but diversity and distance are key characteristics of the region.* The Bahamas are farther from Guyana than London is from Leningrad. Neither ITT satellites, jet travel, nor television hookups can close the awesome communications gap that separates the Caribbean countries. Linguistic, political, and economic differences keep the Caribbean people apart more than do ocean waters. Only 90 miles away from the United States, Cuba has closer economic and political ties to the Soviet Union, half the world away. Puerto Rico, another Spanish-speaking island, does not communicate with Cuba and carries on more trade with most of the 50 U.S. states than it does with its neighboring islands.

Many Caribbean people know more about events and places in the United States, Canada, and Great Britain than on islands only a few hundred miles away. At least six political and economic centers of gravity pull on the Caribbean. Depending on what country you are in, you can expect to get most of your consumer goods, news, and entertainment from cities as far away as Brussels, Moscow, Paris, Miami, Toronto, or London.

The Caribbean is a hodgepodge of nationalities, languages, and cultures. Its racial and color groupings include black, mulatto, white, Asian,

*Included in this study by virtue of their proximity and similar economic and political conditions are the Bahamas and Bermuda. Because the Resource Center examined Belize in its book on Central America, this mainland country has been excluded, although definitions of the Caribbean frequently include Belize.

Amerindian, and East Indian. Despite the region's diversity, the shared history of sugarcane and slavery as well as common economic difficulties have given the Caribbean a single identity. The islands arch southeast from the tip of Florida along the Caribbean Sea to the mainland of South America, where three countries known as the Guianas form the southern reaches of the Caribbean region. So tiny are some of these islands that the six British dependencies could fit into New York City. Cuba, by far the largest, occupies half the area of the other Caribbean islands combined, yet even this relatively large island is smaller than the state of Ohio. The home of 31 million people, the Caribbean encompasses 27 political entities, of which 12 are still colonial dependencies of the Dutch, French, British, and the United States.

Although there are only three Spanish-speaking states, over 19 million (61 percent) of the Caribbean people speak Spanish. English predominates in 19 states, but English-speakers make up only 20 percent of the region's population. French is the official language in three French overseas departments (with a population of almost 700,000) and in Haiti. Most of the 5.7 million Haitians, however, speak a distinctive Creole* and cannot speak French. Dutch and its derivatives are spoken by about 250,000 people in the Caribbean.

Most Caribbean people are descended from slaves brought to the region from West Africa in the dark and fetid holds of slave ships. Many others trace their ancestry back to East Indians who left their homes as indentured servants to British masters. A creole class of plantation managers, merchants, and colonial administrators directed this mass exploitation of slaves and servants. The slave trade brought over ten million Africans to the Caribbean—the largest forced migration in history. Fully a third of those who were dragged in chains from their villages never completed the Atlantic passage, their sick or dead bodies thrown overboard like spoiled cargo. A daily routine of 12 to 18 hours in the canefields was the miserable fate of those who arrived at what were essentially labor camps established by the Spanish, Dutch, French, and British. Slave gangs built the impressive stone walls and forts that protected the islands from competing colonizers and internal slave revolts.

The colonial conquest of the Caribbean began in the 1500s with the Spanish. As Spanish power declined, the Dutch, English, and French rushed into the lower Caribbean in the 17th century, and a period of interimperialist conflict ensued. At the end of the 19th century, yet another imperial power, the United States, started to carve out its domain in the Caribbean. The United States gained control of the four major countries—Haiti, Cuba, Puerto Rico, and the Dominican Republic—

---

*Creole refers to people of European heritage born in the West Indies, and to the language resulting from the mixture of the different languages in the region.

that make up two-thirds of the Caribbean population. Frequent U.S. Marine invasions and gunboat diplomacy marked early U.S. influence, but dollar diplomacy eventually secured the United States a firm position in the Caribbean. Except for Spain, all the original European colonial powers still hold a piece of the Caribbean.

THE MODERN CARIBBEAN

The Caribbean nations emerged in the 1960s from a grim history of colonialism and dictatorship that stretches back through the mists of three centuries. Then the old order started to break up: Cuba had a revolution against Batista and U.S. imperialism, the Dominican Republic finally was free of dictator Rafael Trujillo, and the colonies of the Commonwealth Caribbean began the process of obtaining independence from Britain. The transition to independence was remarkably smooth: conflict occurred only during Guyana's shift to independence. The 1960s were a formative period, a time of vision and hope. West Indians were saying "Massa Day Done": the time had run out for the old masters. The habits of slavery were being cast aside for a new dignity and for a new future.

For a while it looked as if the Caribbean nations were indeed making the transition from preindustrial and colonial times to become modern, developed countries. The economic structures started to open up to include the modern sectors of mining, petroleum, banking, tourism, and manufacturing. Reacting to popular pressure, Caribbean political leaders took some measures to ensure that more of the benefits of the economy stayed at home. After a short period of rising commodity prices in the 1970s, their high ambitions for economic progress and an escape from the underdeveloped past began to crumble. The Caribbean nations faced rising interest rates, sinking prices for exports, shrinking markets, and increasing costs of oil and other imports. Their industrialization plans were stalled, and the problems of unemployment, debt, and poverty raced on. Despite political independence and some degree of economic diversification, the Caribbean nations found themselves still teetering on the edges of the world market.

The Caribbean nations face a choice between three broad economic development strategies. (1) They could commit themselves to nationalist programs that would promote regional economic integration and more local ownership of resources and industries (nationalism). (2) They could follow Cuba in its revolutionary break with the international capitalist system (socialism). (3) They could further open up their economies to foreign trade and investment in the hope that the benefits from the foreign-owned operations would trickle down into the local economy (dependent capitalism). Having seen the strategies of economic nationalism fail in Jamaica and Guyana because of either foreign pressure or internal problems, the Caribbean governments have steered away from that option. Not wanting to risk internal upheaval and international pressure, most Caribbean countries have discarded the socialist approach to development and have chosen or resigned themselves to a dependent and capitalist path of economic development.

Many Caribbean leaders have completely opened up their countries to foreign investment and trade, partly because of pressure from the Reagan administration and partly because they could formulate no other economic strategy. Jamaica, the most ardent nation of this new embrace of dependent capitalism, was held up by Washington as a showcase for the rest of the third world. Unable to construct a lasting network of fruitful cooperation among themselves and other third world nations, the Caribbean nations have increased their traditional reliance on the developed countries and their corporations. Politicians now discuss building national links with the U.S. economy more than they talk about working together as a region. It is the sad lot of the Caribbean nations to compete with each other for the crumbs of investment, aid, and trade that fall their way.

The Caribbean is also becoming one of the world's areas most penetrated by transnational corporations (TNCs).* Both the process and the result of this continuing foreign domination are known as "underdevelopment." The developed nations and their corporations wring the economic surplus out of the Caribbean states and block any transition to a condition of internally propelled economic growth. The developed nations keep developing, and the third world countries stay underdeveloped.

ECONOMIC CONDITIONS

If stripped of their many imported goods—the cars, video sets, and latest fashions all common in the Caribbean cities—the countries of the region would remain essentially what they were a hundred years ago: plantation societies with sugarcane, bananas, cocoa, and a few mines scattered throughout the region. Describing the evolution of the foreign-controlled Caribbean economy, Trinidadian economist Lloyd Best said it was a transition from "pure plantation" to "modified plantation" and finally to its present state of "plantation even further modified."

In the Dominican Republic, most of the people are peasants who live in oppressive poverty in rural areas where unemployment is over 50

---

*Transnational corporations are firms that have business outside their home country. TNCs are also known as multinational corporations.

percent, illiteracy is 80 percent, and many are malnourished. Six percent of the population controls 40 percent of the wealth, and a handful of foreign companies control every major area of the economy.[1] The Caribbean, as a whole, has little to show for 20 years of attempted economic development. Two of the six poorest nations in the hemisphere are Caribbean countries, including Haiti, one of the most destitute places in the world. The Gross Domestic Product (GDP) of most Caribbean nations has either stayed the same or declined in relation to that of the world's large capitalist nations. The region is hopelessly in debt to the developed world, unemployment has grown to depression levels, the cost of imports is rising much more rapidly than the value of exports, and no signs herald an economic turnaround in this decade.

A Sinking Trade Balance

The value of goods imported by the Caribbean nations far outweighs the value of their exports. Their consumption of imported products exceeds their ability to pay. In 1976, the Caribbean nations suffered a trade deficit of $3.5 billion. Six years later, in 1982, the trade deficit had more than doubled, to $8.7 billion. In the Dominican Republic the deficit grew almost 10 times in those six years. Nearly a hundred years ago, Cuban *independista* José Marti said the system of international trade whereby the industrial nations import cheap unprocessed goods and export expensive manufactured goods meant that the industrial powers "command" and the underdeveloped countries "serve." He warned: "It is necessary to balance trade in order to assure freedom."

Four main factors contribute to the Caribbean's trade imbalance: (1) unequal (unjust) terms of trade, (2) world recession, (3) dependence on a few exports, and (4) liberal government import policies. Advocates for the United Nations–sponsored New International Economic Order have criticized the unequal terms of trade endured by the Caribbean and other third world nations and have called for higher international prices for basic commodities produced by underdeveloped nations. Unprocessed products like coffee, bauxite, sugar, and tobacco earn relatively less on the world market than in the past, and the market for these goods is shrinking because of recessionary trends in the developed nations. Because Caribbean nations rely on one to three main exports for over 75 percent of total export income, their economies often experience sudden drops in revenue when world prices fall.[2] Generally, the Caribbean governments have failed to adopt restrictions on the imports of nonessential items. Rather than use foreign exchange* productively within the econ-

---

*Foreign exchange, or foreign currency, refers to the holdings by one country of the currency or bonds of another country. Countries need to maintain reserves of foreign exchange to pay for imports.

omy, the governments have allowed scarce funds to leave the countries for luxury goods. The region needlessly imports not only expensive consumer goods but also basic items like food and clothing—most of which could be supplied by local producers.

New Tropical Plants

The Caribbean states originally had hoped that industrialization would guarantee them a place in the modern, developed world and provide work for their unemployed. There have always been two parts of the industrialization strategy in the Caribbean. One plan, called import substitution, was to establish industries that would locally produce goods that traditionally have been imported. The other plan was to attract foreign corporations to the region through tax incentives. Using the Caribbean's cheap labor, the TNCs would assemble goods for export to industrial markets. This second plan was called industrialization by invitation.

As in other third world areas, the import-substitution strategy was only partially successful. More industries were created, and more goods were manufactured and marketed in the region under this plan. But the industrialization was only superficial, since most of the machinery and components needed in the manufacturing process had to be imported. Import substitution failed to reduce the overall need for imports. The most profitable import substitutions, such as food processing and the manufacture of home-care products, came to be owned by TNCs and not by a local industrial class. The locally owned import-substitution industries that did develop often could not compete with the higher quality and lower prices of foreign manufactured goods.

The Caribbean nations looked to the success that Puerto Rico had in attracting assembly plants, and wanted to do the same. In their attempt to emulate Puerto Rico's Operation Bootstrap, however, the Caribbean nations failed to appreciate that it was Puerto Rico's special relationship with the United States that allowed the U.S. possession to attract so many TNCs. They have also failed to recognize the many problems associated with this model of development, which was based on the attraction of companies to the cheap and unorganized labor in the third world. The original advocates of this industrialization-by-invitation strategy of development said that once the region initially succeeded in luring foreign investors to their shores, wages would gradually rise and linkages with the local economy would start to flourish. These promised benefits, however, have not been realized. The foreign-owned assembly plants, which are grouped together in industrial zones, have remained isolated from the other economic sectors. Wages have stayed at their original low levels. In Haiti, for instance, the government is reluctant to raise daily wage rates above $2.64 for fear of driving investors away.

Neither strategy has succeeded in pulling the economies out of their condition of underdevelopment. Unemployment has grown, wages have stagnated, and the number of locally owned businesses has diminished. Industrialization has failed to create the huge number of jobs promised by optimistic planners and economists. In Haiti, the assembly sector accounts for 12 percent of the country's gross domestic product and 35 percent of its exports, but employs only 5 percent of its workers. In Jamaica, the percentage employed in industry grew only 2 percent between 1960 and 1977, while agricultural employment fell from 40 to 15 percent.[3] The Caribbean has generally experienced growth in employment only in unproductive sectors like tourism, domestic work, trade, and government services.

You Can't Eat Paradise

Street hawkers sell Washington apples in Haiti, tissue-wrapped pears in Trinidad, and Georgia peanuts in Barbados. Yet, it is often difficult to find yams, fresh vegetables, or fresh fish for sale in the street markets of the Caribbean cities. One of the unfortunate trends in Caribbean life is the stagnation of agriculture. Less and less land is under production, fewer people work in agriculture, and more food imports are needed for local consumption. Most of the agricultural production is oriented to exports rather than to providing food for the local market. The Caribbean is a net importer of food: a paradise that can't feed its people. Agriculture as a percentage of the GDP in the Caribbean is on a rapid decline. Twenty years ago, over 30 percent of the GDP in the Dominican Republic came from the agricultural sector, but today it hovers at only 16 percent. The percentage has dropped from 43 to 32 in Haiti, and from 25 to 10 in Barbados. Not one Caribbean nation has increased its agricultural output in the last two decades. (Source excludes Cuba.)[4]

The same system of agriculture for export that prevailed under slavery, which was abolished 150 years ago, still structures rural life in the Caribbean. The best Caribbean land produces sugarcane, bananas, tobacco, cocoa, pineapples, flowers, and spices. While the former colonial sugar companies, like Tate & Lyle and Booker McConnell, no longer directly own large Caribbean sugar estates, they have retained their interest in export agriculture in the form of management contracts, rum manufacture, shipping agreements, and technological services. Conglomerates from the United States, like United Brands and RJ Reynolds, have Caribbean operations in bananas, tobacco, and pineapples. This emphasis on privately controlled export agriculture in the Caribbean has driven small farmers off their land into the already overcrowded cities, burdened the nations with high import bills for food, and led to widespread malnutrition throughout this tropical region.

Dependence on export agriculture to the exclusion of production for local consumption plagues the Caribbean economies, but at the root of the problem is the question of who controls and who benefits from agricultural production. Both Cuba and the Dominican Republic depend on sugarcane as their largest source of foreign exchange. In contrast to the Dominican Republic, however, Cuba experiences virtually no malnutrition. Cuba has no shantytowns and no destitution in the countryside. The difference is that the foreign exchange earned in Cuba from sugarcane production goes to the national treasury, while in the Dominican Republic it goes to Gulf + Western and other private producers.

It is easier and politically safer to rely on the traditional export crops and historic patterns of land ownership than to tackle the difficult issue of agrarian reform. Clearly, the Caribbean needs a new approach to the countryside that promotes a form of internally motivated growth in the agricultural sector. Foreign aid and foreign investment push Caribbean nations away from agrarian reforms and local food production. Instead, traditional rural economic structures and export production are emphasized. The Caribbean people are left eating imported canned food and using most of their land to grow coffee, bananas, and sugar for export.

"Going Foreign"

As dreams fade in paradise, Caribbean people have searched for a better life in the developed nations where there are more jobs and opportunities. About 20 percent of the Caribbean people live in the United States,[5] and many islanders regard Brooklyn as their country's second-largest city because of all their relatives and friends living there. West Indians can be found around the world, working as farmworkers in Florida, bus drivers in London, kitchen help in Toronto. The Caribbean also loses its professionals in a "brain drain" to the wealthier nations. West Indian doctors, engineers, and professors take their skills out of the region when they cannot find high-paid work. The United States is now the home of one of six Barbadians, one of five Jamaicans, one of ten Cubans, and two of every five Puerto Ricans.

But "going foreign"—the Jamaican term for migrating to an industrial nation—is no longer a viable option for Caribbean people. As economic conditions worsen, Canada, Great Britain, the Netherlands, and the United States have all turned off the traditional escape valve for the Caribbean by enforcing stricter immigration regulations. This lack of migration opportunities has contributed to the unemployment crisis that wracks Caribbean society. "The gravity of the unemployment situation, especially as it affects young people, is the most explosive problem facing the region today," concluded the authors of *The Caribbean Community* [Caricom] *in the 1980s*.[6] While unemployment has jumped to over 40 percent in some Caribbean nations, new government austerity programs limit the amount of public assistance available to the growing mass of men and women without the means to support themselves.

POLITICS OF TRANSITION

Politics is a lively, often violent affair in the Caribbean. In Barbados and Trinidad & Tobago, calypso singers bring poetry, sarcasm, and an upbeat tempo into the political arena. Politicians fear criticism from the calypsonians as much as they fear nasty editorials or a public scandal. In the last several years, a couple of Caribbean governments have banned certain calypso songs because of their sharp words about the ruling party. In Jamaica, reggae songs explore the difficulties the nation is having with the International Monetary Fund, and speakers on radio talk shows lash out with sharp Caribbean wit at the "big men" of politics.

At the beginning of the decade, Caribbean scholar Gordon K. Lewis said, "The Caribbean of the 1980s will witness a massive escalation of violence, both social and political."[7] In Jamaica, 800 people died violently during the 1980 election campaign, mostly at the hands of political gunmen. Terrorist bombs in Puerto Rico and the French Caribbean regularly give vent to some of the bitterness about continued colonial rule. Haiti's security forces still go about their dread business of repression. Many Haitian exiles say the only difference between "Baby Doc" and "Papa Doc" is that the young dictator prefers to kill his opponents with less fanfare than his macabre father. Feuding between parties results in firebombings in St. Kitts, and brutal human rights violations are on the rise in Guyana under the dictatorship of Forbes Burnham. In Grenada, a revolution collapsed when the army killed the island's popular prime minister. Supplied and trained by Washington, many of the police forces of the English-speaking Caribbean have become soldiers ready to crush internal or external foes. In the Dominican Republic, soldiers stand ominously on street corners, prepared for a new round of repression. Throughout the region, the escalating economic crisis is reflected in the spread of random urban violence. In the 1980s, the Caribbean is losing whatever remained of its reputation for tranquility in a rising tide of repression and violence.

Prime Minister Maurice Bishop of Grenada, killed in October 1983, labeled as a "five-second democracy" the revered Westminster parliamentary form of government adopted by countries of the Commonwealth Caribbean. He called it a system of government that caused disunity and senseless bickering while providing no year-round vehicle for popular power. Bishop and other members of the New Jewel Movement said that in Grenada they were creating a new kind of democracy that directly involved poor people and workers. A book published by the revolutionary government, entitled *Is Freedom We Making,* described this new democracy of popular assemblies, workplace meetings, and national budgetary discussions. Events proved, however, that the New Jewel Movement had not moved fast enough to establish institutions that guaranteed popular participation. The turmoil in the New Jewel Movement and the subsequent U.S. invasion were bitter blows to the region's radical parties, which saw Grenada as a viable alternative to the dead end of traditional economics and politics. In addition, the U.S. invasion of Grenada reminded all politicians that the United States will not tolerate nationalist challenges to its hegemony in the region.

While the colonial and externally dominated past was certainly responsible for the isolation of the Caribbean states from one another, neither the queen nor Yankee imperialism can be totally blamed for the current divisiveness in the region. The assertion of nationalism in the Caribbean comes now in the form of intraregional rivalries and micronationalism. Jamaica often takes stands against the rest of the English-speaking Caribbean, Barbados against its poorer neighbors in the Eastern Caribbean, Nevis against St. Kitts, Tobago against Trinidad, Aruba against Curaçao, and so on. The economic and political federation of all these ministates—the obvious solution to many of the region's problems—has not made much progress.

Despite its problems and divisions, the Caribbean is a highly diverse and creative region that has contributed more than its share of authors, poets, scholars, and musicians. Aimé Césaire of Martinique raised black consciousness throughout the world with his poetry of inspiration. Other literary notables include Derek Walcott, V. S. Naipaul, George Lamming, and Roderick Walcott. Joan Armatrading, Silvio Rodríguez, Willie Colón, Harry Belafonte, Bob Marley, Peter Tosh, and Mighty Sparrow have come from the Caribbean, the birthplace of calypso, reggae, steel drum, and *nueva trova* music. Such renowned scholars as C. L. R. James, Clive Thomas, and Arthur Lewis have given the Caribbean a reputation for high scholarship and insightful analysis. In addition to creative excellence, the masses of Caribbean people have demonstrated an admirable persistence and resilience in the fight against colonialism and imbedded class structures. Its resistance leaders—José Marti, Pedro Albízu Campos, Uriah Butler, Maurice Bishop, Walter Rodney, and, of course, Fidel Castro—have provided inspiration for many colonized, oppressed people all over the world.

A crucial part of Caribbean politics concerns race. In the 1960s, the Jamaican government expelled historian Walter Rodney after he made speeches addressing the explosive but usually ignored issues of racial stratification. The black power movement, which swept through the Caribbean in the 1960s and 1970s, has now subsided, and many of its leaders have become the theoreticians of socialist parties in the English-speaking Caribbean. Frantz Fanon, a native of Martinique, explored the depth and intensity of racial problems in his books *Black Skin, White Masks* and *The Wretched of the Earth.* "The juxtaposition of the white and black race," wrote Fanon, "has created a massive psycho-existential complex." The racial protests and riots in the Caribbean did result in a greater awareness by government and business of the need to integrate blacks visibly in the regional economy and politics. The partial replacement of white administrators, however, has done little to change many of the conditions of discrimination and exploitation in Caribbean life.

TO THE WORLD OF TOMORROW

"Flags, national anthems, local legislatures, black cabinets and boards of directors don't, by themselves, say anything about whether real decolonization has been effected," commented economist Trevor Farrell of the University of the West Indies.[8] The dominant trend in Caribbean politics has been to strive for political independence while remaining economically dependent on trading relationships and on the operations of transnational firms. Cuba was the first in the latter half of this century to challenge this economic dependence; and then, in the 1970s, Guyana, Jamaica, and Grenada also tried breaking away from the neocolonial stranglehold. Guyana turned to state capitalism and, because of economic difficulties, has begun to reestablish ties with TNCs. Jamaica stood up to aluminum corporations and promoted democratic socialism but was driven to economic and political ruin by international forces. Grenada, the English-speaking nation that moved the furthest toward socialism, became the target of harsh U.S. criticism and U.S. economic destabilization. Grenada's experiment with socialism eventually fell victim to personal and political infighting, and was finally crushed by heavy-handed U.S. military intervention.

The Caribbean nations came into the 1980s from the "nigger yard" of yesterday. But they have not escaped it. The region still consumes what it does not produce, and produces what it does not consume. Throughout the Caribbean, the conditions of underdevelopment still fester and swell. Sadly, those Caribbean people who have managed to achieve their independence and set out on a course of development have found themselves out of colonialism's nigger yard but in the backyard of their powerful northern neighbor. Some nations, like Edward Seaga's Jamaica and the Dominica of Eugenia Charles, became willing pawns of the United States and have laid out the welcome mats for the TNCs, while others like Cuba and Grenada became outlaws in the empire.

The Other Side of Paradise examines how foreign corporate and government control has shaped the contemporary Caribbean economy and politics. It looks at a dark and different side of the Caribbean—not the Caribbean of smooth sailing, carnival fun, and paradise vacation spots. Part I deals with foreign influences on the major sectors of the economy and presents an overview of regional finances and international aid programs. The last two chapters of Part I concentrate on the expanding role of the United States in the Caribbean. Part II presents profiles of all the Caribbean states and nations. *The Other Side of Paradise* explores the burden of both past and present foreign domination in the Caribbean.

> From the nigger yard of yesterday,
> I come with my burden;
> to the world of tomorrow,
> I turn with my strength.[9]

—Martin Carter, from "I Come from the Nigger Yard of Yesterday"

Transnational Corporations:

THE STRANGERS IN PARADISE

The brain is housed in steel and glass slabs located in or near a few crowded cities: New York, London, Frankfurt, Zurich, and Tokyo. The blood is capital, and it is pumped through the system by global banks assisted by a few governments. The financial centers, New York, London, Frankfurt, Tokyo, and their fictional extensions in such tax havens as Panama and the Bahamas, function as the heart. The hands are steadily moving to the outer rim of civilization. More and more goods are now made in the poor countries of the southern periphery under the direction of the headquarters in the north, and most are destined to be consumed in the industrial countries.

—Richard Barnet, author of *Global Reach*

Transnational corporations—firms that have business outside their home countries—have penetrated the Caribbean more than other regions of the world. Foreign capital dominates all the leading sectors of the region's economy: banking, tourism, mining, manufacturing, petroleum, and export agriculture. Many foreign corporations doing business in the Caribbean have sales and assets larger than the gross national products of the Caribbean countries in which they operate. Shell, for instance, in 1981 had 46 times more in annual sales than Suriname's annual exports. The Caribbean business of some of these large TNCs does not even merit mention in their annual reports, even though their investment may be one of the most important economic activities of the country.

The Caribbean's long colonial history, its proximity to the world's largest capitalist market, and the postwar globalization of production and marketing all contributed to the present occupation of the Caribbean by foreign corporations. A TNC's main office makes decisions about its subsidiary operations and seldom takes the country's welfare into consideration. The former prime minister of Trinidad & Tobago, Eric Williams, once remarked, "The decisions of these corporations can make nonsense of the economic plans in the developing countries." The TNCs have created a global network that organizes the development of third world countries in such a way as to maximize their own profits. Foreign corporations use the Caribbean in the following five ways: (1) as a source of raw materials; (2) as a center for low-wage assembly industries; (3) as a haven for offshore insurance, corporate finance, and banking; (4) as a marketing outlet for their products; and (5) as a market for products of TNC-controlled import-substitution industries.

Because of inadequate government statistics, it is difficult to quantify the economic involvement of TNCs in the Caribbean region. Incredibly, only a few of the Caribbean governments even keep up-to-date lists of the foreign corporations doing business in their countries. In Jamaica, the government does not enforce the requirement that foreign corporations check in annually with the Registrar of Companies, and many of the largest TNCs have lagged five or more years behind in registration. The Caribbean governments often do not know the real identity of the TNCs, only the name of the affiliate or subsidiary. In order to better understand the economic forces at work in the Caribbean, the Resource Center staff visited foreign embassies, company offices, and a variety of business associations to determine the extent of corporate operations in the Caribbean.

STRENGTH IN NUMBERS

Tables 1A and 1B list the major foreign TNCs with extensive direct investment in the Caribbean. Dominating the transnational scene in the region are U.S. corporations, which have more than 1,740 branches, subsidiaries, or affiliates in the Caribbean.* More than 560 companies hail from foreign nations other than the United States. TNCs from the U.S. outnumber non-U.S. corporations except in the French departments and in several of the small English-speaking islands. Many of the largest TNCs in the world operate in the Caribbean, including 77 of the top 100 U.S. industrial corporations, the three largest U.S. banks, and 47 of the 500 largest non-U.S. corporations.[1] The numerical presence of TNCs in a Caribbean country is not always the best indicator of their influence in that country. While there are only 32 TNCs in Suriname, two of them, Alcoa and Shell, exercise a determining influence in that country. In islands like Dominica and St. Lucia the activities of just one agribusiness and shipping company, Geest Industries, have a greater effect on the economy and life of those islands than the combined operations of all the other TNCs doing business there. The impact of an office

---

*The calculation of the number of TNCs in the Caribbean does not include TNC presence in Puerto Rico, where there are more than 2,000 U.S. TNCs.

of Royal Bank of Canada or Barclays far outweighs the presence of a foreign-owned hotel or even an assembly plant. The economic sectors with the largest number of TNCs in the Caribbean are manufacturing and services. The TNCs in agriculture, finance, and mining and petroleum, however, while not as numerous, exercise a far greater degree of control.

Retailing of consumer goods, small farming, and some professional services like law are the only sectors of the Caribbean economy that transnational corporations do not dominate. The TNCs even own or manage most of the Caribbean's utilities, a sector controlled by governments in other parts of Latin America. Jamaica and the Dominican Re-

TABLE 1A
SELECTED U.S. CORPORATIONS IN THE CARIBBEAN
(6 or More Subsidiaries)(Excluding Puerto Rico)

Corporation	Number of Subsidiaries	Main Business
Alcoa	8	mining
Beatrice Foods	7	food
Bristol-Myers	7	home products
Castle & Cooke	6	agriculture
Chase Manhattan	11	banking
Citicorp	18	banking
Coca-Cola	13	bottling
Colgate-Palmolive	7	home products
Continental Telephone	6	communications
Esmark	21	manufacturing
Exxon	16	oil
Gulf + Western	26	manufacturing/agriculture
Holiday Inn	13	travel
ITT	14	communications
RJ Reynolds	13	agriculture
Reynolds Metals	8	mining
Texaco	11	oil
Trans World	7	travel
United Brands	9	agriculture
WR Grace	15	chemicals
Warner Lambert	8	pharmaceuticals
Wometco	9	bottling

Source: The Resource Center, Compilation of Corporations, 1984

TABLE 1B
SELECTED CANADIAN & EUROPEAN
CORPORATIONS IN THE CARIBBEAN
(3 or More Subsidiaries)(Excluding Puerto Rico)

Home	Corporation	Number of Subsidiaries	Main Business
Canada			
	Alcan	9	mining
	Bata	3	shoes
	Canadian Pacific	6	travel/food
	Scott's Hospitality	8	travel
	Seagram	5	liquor
	Canadian Imperial Bank	10	banking
	Royal Bank of Canada	35	banking
	Bank of Nova Scotia	40	banking
France			
	L'Air Liquide	3	gas/chemical
	Club Méditerranée	8	travel
	Banque Nationale Paris	5	banking
	PLM	5	travel
Netherlands			
	Algemene	5	banking
	Amro	5	banking
	Heineken	5	liquor
Switzerland			
	Nestlé	13	food
United Kingdom			
	BAT Industries	6	tobacco
	Barclays	88	banking
	Berger, Jenson, & Nicholson	4	paint
	BICC	3	communications
	Booker McConnell	17	agriculture
	Cable & Wireless	13	communications
	Commonwealth Development	9	utilities
	Geest Industries	6	agriculture
	Kier International	4	construction
	Grand Metropolitan	7	travel
	Rowntree Mackintosh	3	food
	Tate & Lyle	9	agriculture
	Taylor & Woodrow	5	financial
	Trust House Forte	11	travel
UK/Netherlands			
	Unilever	4	food
	Royal Dutch Shell	18	oil

Source: The Resource Center, Compilation of Corporations, 1984

public are the Caribbean nations with the most TNC subsidiaries. In considering TNC influence in the Caribbean, it is also important to recognize the role of TNC commodity brokers, which do not directly invest in a country but exert pervasive influence in some sectors of the economy, particularly agriculture. By purchasing and reselling coffee, tobacco, and other crops, these buying groups act as intermediaries between producers of the Caribbean nations and the sellers in the industrial countries.

There are conflicting trends in foreign direct investment in the Caribbean. In several economic sectors—namely, mining, local banking, agriculture, and utilities—many TNCs have transferred their stock ownership to Caribbean governments but usually have retained their interest in those industries through management contracts, technology transfer agreements, and marketing. In other areas—particularly in services, manufacturing, and offshore finance—there has been a marked increase in the number of TNCs doing business in the Caribbean. In recent years, foreign direct investment in light manufacturing has been rising steadily, as seen in the increasing numbers of TNCs that have located in the industrial free-trade zones in the Caribbean. Many of the assembly plants are owned not by large TNCs but by small foreign investors. Frequently, the Caribbean is the only area where these small companies have foreign investment. This trend has been encouraged by Caribbean nations that hope to develop their economies by attracting foreign investors to set up assembly operations on their islands. If certain contributions are made to local development efforts, however, they are usually incidental and small in comparison to the money saved by the investors.

In addition to the TNCs with active business, many thousands of "brass-plate" corporations are registered in the major tax havens of the Caribbean: Bermuda, the Bahamas, the Netherlands Antilles, and the Cayman Islands. In these and other smaller islands, corporations set up subsidiaries simply to take advantage of secrecy regulations and lack of corporate taxes. There is often little more to these corporations than a plate with the firm's name on the door of a one-room office. Most TNCs have at least one of these Caribbean brass-plate subsidiaries through which they can transfer company sales and investments, thereby saving millions of dollars in taxes and fees. These corporations include Talres Development (Tate & Lyle), Greyfin (Greyhound), New Company (Pillsbury), Transtrading Overseas (Castle & Cooke), and Risk Resources (Esmark).

Value of TNC Investment

The most complete data on foreign direct investment in the Caribbean come from the U.S. Department of Commerce, which supplies investment figures for U.S. corporations with over $500,000 in investment abroad. Figures from the Department of Commerce do not include U.S. investment in Puerto Rico and the U.S. Virgin Islands. The Resource Center, however, estimates that there is $2.9 billion in direct U.S. investment in the U.S. Virgin Islands and $16.1 billion in Puerto Rico.[2] In 1982, U.S. corporations or individuals had $29.1 billion in direct investment in the Caribbean—16 times the 1970 figure of $1.8 billion (Table 1C). An overwhelming amount of this direct investment ($25 billion) was in banking and finance, reflecting the importance of offshore financial centers in the Caribbean. About 35 percent of all U.S. finance-related investment outside U.S. borders is located in Bermuda, the Bahamas, and the Netherlands Antilles.[3] Petroleum, the second largest category of U.S. direct investment in the Caribbean, reached $1.6 billion (Table 1C). From 1977 to 1982, the U.S. nonfinancial investment jumped 70 percent, from $2.4 billion to $4.1 billion.

The investment figures presented by the Department of Commerce fall short of quantifying the full extent of U.S. investment in the Caribbean for the following reasons: (1) it reports only the book value or historical costs of U.S. investment, not the resale value of the business; (2) it only identifies direct investment as 10 percent or more of voting securities; (3) the $500,000 minimum investment standard does not include the many hundreds of small-business operations or ventures like tourist shops and restaurants owned by U.S. citizens in the region; (4) it excludes the value of management, licensing, and technology contracts; and (5) the figures include only direct investment, not the assets of foreign affiliates.

The book value of foreign direct investment is usually only a fraction of its true value. While the Department of Commerce reports the book value of U.S. investment in Jamaica as $373 million, the U.S. Agency for International Development (USAID) estimated the investment as being close to $1 billion. The distinction between book value and assets becomes critical when a corporation is being nationalized by a foreign government. For instance, in the cases of Reynolds Metals in Guyana and Exxon and Revere Copper in Jamaica, the corporations demanded and received compensation considerably above the book value of their investments. The Dominican Republic compensated Rosario Mining for an amount over 7 times the book value of its property.

Another factor to consider when determining the value and influence of foreign direct investment is the value of assets. These refer to the total value of a corporation's equity, including the interests of both U.S. direct investors and other persons. Increasingly, TNCs do not require that their foreign investment be in wholly owned or majority-owned businesses. To control a corporation, small minority interest often suffices, especially when it includes contracts to supply technology and management services. In the Caribbean, the assets of businesses (in petroleum, mining,

TABLE 1C
U.S. DIRECT INVESTMENT IN THE CARIBBEAN*
BY CATEGORY
($ millions)

Category	1970	1977	1982
Mining	447	336	482
Petroleum	395	945	1,591
Manufacturing	314	290	522
Trade	174	574	873
Banking	290	862	2,131
Finance (including insurance, real estate)	**	8,879†	22,860†
Other	237	269	637
CARIBBEAN TOTAL*	1,857	12,155	29,096

* does not include French Guiana, Guyana, or Suriname
** in 1970, the banking category included finance
† investment figures for the Netherlands Antilles was corrected by the authors to eliminate the effects of transfers through financing affiliates
Sources: Survey of Current Business, U.S. Department of Commerce, August 1983; Selected Data on U.S. Direct Investment Abroad 1950–1976, U.S. Department of Commerce, February 1982

and manufacturing) affiliated with U.S. owners in 1977 (latest available figures) had a book value of nearly 4 times the value of direct investment in these same sectors.[4]

While the largest (nonfinance-related) U.S. direct investment in the Caribbean is in the petroleum industry, U.S. investment in manufacturing creates 3.4 times as many jobs. Affiliates of U.S. corporations employ about 100,000 workers in the Caribbean. U.S. affiliates employ the most workers in the Dominican Republic, which has large mining operations and the diverse investments of Gulf+Western in agriculture, tourism, and manufacturing (Table 1D).

The rate of return from U.S. investment in the Caribbean is substantially higher than in other regions. In 1980 the rate of return in the Caribbean was 30.5 percent, considerably higher than either the international average of 14.3 percent or the Latin American average of 15.8 percent. The Bahamas and the Cayman Islands have extremely high rates of return, which is hardly surprising, since the very purpose of offshore profit centers is to allow corporations to funnel their profits through their brass-plate affiliates.

Like U.S. investment, other foreign economic interest in the Caribbean is largely in banking, insurance, petroleum, and mining. Neither

TABLE 1D
U.S. DIRECT INVESTMENT BY COUNTRY, 1977
($ millions)

Country	Number of Companies	Total Assets	Total Income	Number of Employees	US Direct Investment
Bahamas	228	61,095	6,453	8,234	997
Barbados	20	220	117	2,366	26
Bermuda	350	17,513	14,584	2,486	7,708
Dominican Rep	82	1,270	711	47,171	243
French Antilles	11	95	142	479	12
French Guiana	5	(D)	(D)	(D)	(D)
Grenada	3	(D)	(D)	(D)	(D)
Guyana	7	(D)	(D)	(D)	3
Haiti	21	74	67	4,243	14
Jamaica	88	995	986	11,124	378
Neth Antilles	152	6,407	2,190	4,715	1,430*
Suriname	12	316	308	6,498	(D)
Trinidad	69	1,589	1,417	15,914	971
UK Assoc States	23	75	30	450	45
UK Dependencies	102	13,582	1,330	1,302	336
CARIBBEAN TOTAL**	1,173	103,231	28,335	104,982	12,163

(D) means the data was suppressed by the Department of Commerce for reasons of confidentiality, and was not included in the Caribbean total
* investment figure for the Netherlands Antilles was corrected by the authors to eliminate the effect of transfers through financing affiliates
** the totals presented for the Caribbean are lower than the actual reported direct investment because the Department of Commerce has not published all country figures for reasons of confidentiality
Source: US Direct Investment Abroad, 1977, US Department of Commerce, April 1981

European nor Canadian investors have nearly as much investment in manufacturing industries as do U.S. companies, but they do have substantial interests in trade, tourism, and utilities. Canadian direct investment in the Caribbean, which is concentrated mainly in banking, mining, and transportation, is estimated at $850 million.[5] No regional direct investment figures are available for investment from Great Britain, which has had the longest and broadest involvement in the region. Non-U.S. TNCs tend to invest in import-substitution industries more than in operations for export. Overall non-U.S. corporations doing business in the Caribbean want to secure raw materials and maintain outlets for their goods rather than use the Caribbean as a platform to export assembled products.

TABLE 1E
U.S. DIRECT INVESTMENT 1977 AND 1981
($ millions)

Country	1977	1981
Bahamas	997	2,987
Barbados	26	41
Bermuda	7,708	10,353
Dominican Rep	243	373
French Antilles	12	18
Guyana	3	10
Haiti	14	31
Jamaica	378	385
Neth Antilles*	1,430	6,652
Trinidad & Tobago	971	932
UK Associated States	45	61
UK Dependencies	336	585
CARIBBEAN TOTAL**	12,163	22,428

* investment figures for the Netherlands Antilles were corrected by the authors to eliminate the effects of transfers through financing affiliates
** totals presented for the Caribbean are lower than the actual reported direct investment figures because the Department of Commerce has not published all country figures for reasons of confidentiality
Sources: "U.S. Direct Investment Abroad, Yearend 12–29–82," Department of Commerce; Marc Herold, "Worldwide Investment and Disinvestment by U.S. Multinationals: Implications for the Caribbean and Central America," February 1983

Variety of Corporate Activity

Foreign direct investment refers to investment in company stock (equity). Indirect, sometimes called portfolio, investment refers to private capital flowing from one country to another that does not involve the purchase of equity in a foreign affiliate or subsidiary. An increasingly common type of indirect foreign investment involves the use of loans rather than equity to finance new operations. Rather than selling shares, a company will often arrange for loans to finance overseas investment. Recently, investment houses like Morgan Guaranty have been moving more of the funds they manage into foreign financial markets. Because these loans do not come from the U.S. parent company, the capital flow is not categorized as direct foreign investment. Falconbridge's nickel mine in the Dominican Republic, for example, was financed almost entirely through this indirect means of loan capital. The purchase of bonds is another form of indirect foreign investment that has been on the increase in the 1980s.

Before the growth of TNCs and foreign direct investment, lending by banks and investment houses to foreign governments and corporations was the typical form of capital flow overseas. While this form of investment did not initially involve direct control over the management of the borrowing company or government, foreign lenders (with the help of their governments) were often successful in controlling the borrower's finances. Such was the case in the Dominican Republic in 1904, when the U.S. government took control of the port authority of that country to collect customs revenues in order to guarantee the repayment of private U.S. financiers.

Another type of investment that does not show up in foreign investment figures is settler investment, which finances a new business established by foreigners who are residents of a Caribbean nation. Small businesses like restaurants, gift shops, and modest hotels are examples of settler investments common in the Caribbean. After several generations, these settler investments are usually considered to be local operations. Many British investments in the Caribbean Commonwealth have become so integrated into the fabric of the country that it has become difficult to categorize their nationality.

TNCs make profits in the Caribbean from another practice called transfer pricing. This term refers to the prices assigned by a TNC to the transfers of goods, services, capital, and technology between its subsidiaries and affiliates in different countries. Because so many TNCs are conglomerates, a substantial portion of world buying and selling is merely a movement between divisions of the same company. The TNCs regularly manipulate prices to transfer profits to low-tax countries, like the Bahamas, to reduce their overall tax burdens. Transnational corporations operating in the Caribbean often overprice their imports and underprice their exports among their own subsidiaries to reduce taxes on profits and sales.

Payments of fees and royalties to the TNCs for marketing, technology, and management services also enhance TNC profits. Although many TNCs are reducing their direct investment in the Caribbean, they continue to receive steady flows of income from service contracts they arrange with foreign corporations. Figures from the U.S. Department of Commerce show that income to U.S. corporations from fees and royalties in the Caribbean doubled between 1977 and 1981.[6]

Similarly, payments to TNCs for freight and insurance drain the Caribbean economies. Because the Caribbean nations cannot rely on their own shipping and insurance firms, they have to turn over their scarce foreign exchange to TNCs like Nedlloyd, Sealand, and Booker Shipping. From 1975 to 1980, the cost of freight and insurance for eight Caribbean nations (members of the Inter-American Development Bank, IDB) increased 50 percent, amounting to a net outflow of almost $700 million.[7] Reported foreign capital flows do not include other important sources of income for foreign corporations like reinvested earnings, investment incentives, depreciation allowances, and local borrowing.

The profits earned by TNCs are either repatriated to company headquarters or reinvested in the subsidiary operations. Only rarely does the surplus generated by foreign investment enter the local capital market. Rather than adding capital to the host countries, TNCs increasingly borrow from local capital markets, a practice that diverts local savings into foreign hands. In terms of direct capital flows, foreign investment generally results in more money being taken out of the Caribbean than is being put there. From 1976 to 1981, the amount of investment income (profits) leaving eight Caribbean nations increased from $585 million to $1,310 million.[8] For each of those six years, foreign corporations withdrew more profits from the Bahamas, Barbados, the Dominican Republic, Guyana, Jamaica, and Trinidad than they invested in those years. The total foreign investment income that left these six Caribbean countries between 1976 and 1981 was 4 times as much as new foreign investment in those countries. These figures support the decapitalization and dependency theories of many leftist economists who say that the penetration of foreign investment results in a net disinvestment for the country.

Despite the long history of foreign investment in the Caribbean, few examples exist where this foreign control has given a boost to the local economy on a long-term basis. Once they gain a niche in the economy, foreign investors undermine local business because of the formidable competition presented by their superior technology and financial resources. In the Caribbean, foreign capital did not supplant a national bourgeois class, since the Caribbean societies were entirely the creation of colonial powers from the beginning. The unrelenting foreign control of the economy over the centuries also explains the stunted growth of a national and regional entrepreneurial class in the Caribbean.

LOCAL vs. FOREIGN

In the early colonial days, the economies of the Caribbean dependencies were part and parcel of the foreign economies of the colonizing countries. Gradually, there arose small local entrepreneurial classes that established locally owned businesses and trade operations. Because of the predominance of foreign trade and investment, which was unusually high compared with other colonized regions, the formation of a local entrepreneurial class in the Caribbean has been very restricted. The local businesses that did develop were not owned by former slaves or imported laborers, but mainly by the descendants of white settlers from the colonizing countries or from immigrant groups from Europe and the Middle East.

In the last 30 years, there has been a trend of disinvestment by the

TABLE 1F   TNCs IN THE CARIBBEAN*

Country	Manufacturing					Services			Finance		Minerals		Ag	Sales	U.S.	TOTAL Non-U.S.	Combined U.S. and Non-U.S.
	Drug & Home Products	Garment	Food	Chemical	Other	Travel	Construction	Other	Banking	Real Estate & Insurance	Mining	Oil					
US Virgin Islands	4	–	6	3	8	10	4	23	3	15	1	4		11	92	9	101
UK Dependencies	–	1	3	1	1	6	1	13	7	17		1	1	5	57	44	101
French Antilles	–	1	4	1	–	5	–	1	2	9		2	3	3	22	43	65
Neth Antilles	7	3	5	2	12	13	2	10	7	2		6	7	4	87	34	121
Antigua-Barbuda	–	2	4	–	1	8	1	7				3		3	31	9	40
Bahamas	7	–	11	4	19	26	5	19	21	26	2	8	7	14	169	29	198
Barbados	4	8	5	2	27	11	1	21	4	10		3	1	6	103	48	151
Dominica	1	–	1	–	1	–	1	2		3			6	1	16	7	23
Dominican Rep	42	57	34	14	60	8	6	31	9	27	5	4	24	19	340	22	362
Grenada	1	1	3		1			8		2				1	15	4	19
Guyana			1				1	1	1	4	1	2	1	9	23	27	50
Haiti	8	41	11	3	53	16	3	28	4	5	1	4	13	7	197	31	228
Jamaica	14	13	21	11	43	19	11	38	12	33	10	4	24	27	280	143	423
St Kitts-Nevis		2	1	1	3	1		3	1	1				2	14	7	21
St Lucia		3	3		4	3		2		4		3		3	25	19	44
St Vincent		2	2		2	1		3	1					2	16	11	27
Suriname	1			1				2	1	3	1	1	2	2	14	18	32
Trinidad	13	9	13	13	41	11	18	41	5	17	1	41	2	21	246	61	307
U.S. TOTAL	102	143	129	56	276	138	54	253	77	180	22	86	91	140	1,747		
NON-U.S. TOTAL	3	7	54	27	58	63	17	40	123	54	14	22	42	42		566	
COMBINED U.S. & NON-U.S. TOTAL	105	150	183	83	334	201	71	293	200	234	36	108	133	182			2,313

Source: The Resource Center, Compilation of Corportions, 1984

* The Resource Center included the subsidiaries and affiliates of foreign-based (outside of the Caribbean) corporations that have business operations in the Caribbean. Not included were brass-plate companies, financing affiliates (in the Netherlands Antilles), offshore insurance firms, commodity brokers, offices of trading agents and sales representatives, and companies that had shipping as their only line of business in the Caribbean. We defined Services as the travel industry and construction. The sub-category of other services includes advertising, communications, restaurants, publishing, and schools. Manufacturing includes garments (shoes and sporting goods included), chemicals, food processing (including beverages), and other industries (such as electronics and equipment manufacturing). The category of Sales includes retailing operations but not distributors. Finance includes both banking (not including offshore) and other financial services, which include insurance, real estate, and accounting firms. Under the category Minerals, oil refers to oil and gas production and refining but not exploration.

TNCs, particularly in banking, utilities, mining, and agriculture. Most disinvestment has come at the initiation of the TNCs and not the host governments. The TNCs have divested in certain sectors to reduce their risks and get rid of unprofitable enterprises. But rather than leave the region completely, the TNCs have tried to maintain and increase their flow of profits through management and technology agreements. Several governments—notably Jamaica, Trinidad, and Guyana—sought to achieve a degree of national control over industries owned by TNCs. The governments became part or full owners through joint ventures with the TNCs or through nationalizations. But ownership, as the Caribbean nations have found out, does not necessarily mean control.

University of Guyana economist Clive Thomas, writing about joint ventures and nationalized companies, said that the reorganized companies tend to be simply "plants," not real "firms." "It is true that there are titles such as Directors, Managers, Managing Directors, et cetera. But the local [plant] makes no decisions regarding prices . . . output . . . levels of investment, or markets. All these are done at the head office, where decisions which normally define a firm are made. The apparatus which exists locally is just a participant in a multi-plant firm."[9]

BETTER WAYS NEEDED TO CONTROL TNCs

The underdeveloped nations of the Caribbean, if they are to stay in the capitalist world economy, need the TNCs. They need TNCs for technology, capital to expand existing local operations, capital for large projects such as mining, and access to world markets. But the possible benefits of foreign investment are often overshadowed by adverse results if a government does not impose a measure of control and regulation. Practical examples of regulations of TNCs include:

- Limited repatriation (or return) of profits to guarantee some local investment
- Investment only in certain areas of the economy where local ownership is unlikely
- Prohibition of land or resource ownership
- Full transfer of technology and know-how associated with companies' operations
- Restricted payments for services of foreign management and consultants
- Emphasis on the use of local materials and appropriate technology

If left completely uncontrolled, investment by TNCs obstructs locally owned economic development (private and public), increases the flow of imports, raises the external debt, and discourages regional economic integration. The strong presence of TNCs in the Caribbean nations has had the further result of tying the economy and politics of each country to those of the large industrial nations, particularly the United States. If and when a country tries to restructure its economy along nationalist or socialist lines, it automatically has to contend with the awesome power of the developed world. For all these reasons, the penetration of TNCs diminishes the long-run capacity of the Caribbean economy to transform itself.

Agriculture:

THE NEW PLANTATION

"'Give us this day our daily bread' shouldn't be a prayer to Shell Oil."
—Third world spokesperson at a conference of the
UN Food and Agriculture Organization

Agricultural development in the Caribbean resembles the pattern of royal succession. "The king is dead, long live the king." The brutal system of slavery and colonial plantations that dominated life in the West Indies for two and a half centuries may be dead, but its legacy lives on.

The islands still depend on exports to the colonizing nations. Sugar, cocoa, coffee, and bananas continue to define the economies of the Caribbean. Gone for the most part are the colonial masters, but company agents, consultants, advisers, and financiers remain. No longer do West African slaves cut cane under the persuasion of the master's whip, but throughout the Caribbean their descendants cut cane, gather coffee beans, and pick bananas for as little as three dollars a day. The plantation is dead; but almost anywhere you go in the Caribbean, you can hear the persistent refrain and see plantations being reborn time after time.

The Caribbean economies unfortunately have been unable to break the bonds of the plantation economy. Despite the abolition of slavery, the achievement of political independence, and the rise of national consciousness, there have been no essential changes in the heavily export-oriented, import-dependent structure of the Caribbean economy. Widespread popular revolt in the late 1930s was the first important challenge to the plantation system. As Gordon K. Lewis noted in his *Growth of the Modern West Indies*: "[It was] a revolt of West Indian peasants and workers against a society in which, despite formal emancipation, they were still regarded merely as suppliers of cheap labor to sugar kings and oil barons in search of quick profits."[1]

Partly as a reaction to Caribbean nationalization, foreign companies have reduced their direct investment in agriculture and have tried to maintain a low profile so as not to agitate the West Indians. Caribbean politicians have made a show of confronting the colonizers, but only rarely has local leadership seriously considered the possibility of breaking out of the plantation economy. Many have sidled up to the United States, the new foreign overseer of the plantation, which has dispatched its development agents, agricultural experts, commissions, and investors to ensure U.S. command of agricultural development in the Caribbean.

PRECARIOUS DEPENDENCE

Despite their acceptance of the need to diversify their economies, the Caribbean nations still rely on only a few agricultural crops. Even Cuba, the exception to many generalizations about Caribbean life, depends on sugarcane for over 60 percent of its total export earnings.[2] About 40 percent of the Caribbean exports are in a completely raw form and serve as inputs to downstage production in the industrial world.[3] An absurd case in point is the export of Grenadian nutmeg nuts to Holland, where they are ground and packaged. The worldwide recession of the 1980s has exacerbated this lopsided exchange as consumer demand shrinks and prices sink below the costs of production. The UN Food and Agriculture Organization (FAO) reported an across-the-board decline in the prices of 15 leading agricultural commodities over the last two decades.[4] Bananas and cocoa, for example, were selling in 1980 at prices 20 to 40 percent lower than in 1960. A pound of coffee sells for about half the price it commanded five years ago, and sugar sells for 20 percent of its price of only several years ago.

Box Lunch in Paradise

This steady decline of world commodity prices is a principal reason for growing political and economic instability in the region. But it is only part of the story for the underdeveloped countries of the Caribbean. They get it coming and going. Their colonized history has made them dependent on both exports and imports. The Caribbean hardly fits the category of a tropical paradise where all your food is there just for the picking. You need to pack a box lunch for the reality of this paradise. On the street corners of Port of Spain, vendors sell Washington State apples and imported pears, not the mangoes or papayas one would expect. At the bus stations in Barbados, almost everyone munches on raw peanuts imported directly from Georgia and sold by Rastafarian street hawkers. Most Caribbean countries import over 50 percent of their food, with some, like Trinidad, Barbados, and Antigua, importing over 80 percent.[5] Even when the countries host food-processing firms, these companies import about 80 percent of the food ingredients for their processed products.[6]

The total domination by export crop production of cultivable land set the stage for the current tragedy of inadequate food production. In 1647, an observer in the West Indies reported: "Men are so intent upon planting sugar that they had rather buy foode at very deare rates than produce it by labour, so infinite is the profit of the sugar workes."[7] The Caribbean islands at that time depended on the continental colonies' exports of dried fish, grain, beans, and vegetables. This reliance on imported food brought disaster when the North American Revolution and birth of the United States interrupted supplies. Between 1780 and 1787, more than 15,000 plantation workers in Jamaica died of famine. Two centuries later, the primacy of export-crop production, combined with the omnipresence of foreign foods on the shelves of even the most remote rural stores, effectively hinders the development of self-sufficiency in basic food production. Foreign food items also tend to have better access to retail and wholesale networks and advertising facilities than do the small number of local products. The average annual per capita food import bill has risen to over $200, and the region is paying 60 percent more for food imports than it was ten years ago.

Psychohistorical factors also contribute to the sorry state of the production of food for local consumption. Tinged with memories of slavery, farming is not a prestigious occupation. Despite the severity of the food crisis in the region, fewer and fewer Caribbean people are choosing agriculture for their life's work. Per capita food production has dropped steadily. In Haiti, agriculture's share of the economy has dropped about 10 percent in the last ten years.[8] This widespread decline in agriculture has reduced available jobs and hastened the ugly process of urbanization. Those Caribbean people living in cities have increased from 24 percent in 1960 to over 40 percent in 1980. By the year 2000, over 70 percent of the Caribbean population will be living in overcrowded cities like Kingston and Port of Spain. Dr. Robert E. Culbertson from Florida International University told a congressional committee: "The average Caribbean farmer's age is over 50 and not enough youth are entering farming careers."[9] The only exception to this is Cuba, where farming cooperatives are increasing in popularity among young people.

The Caribbean people suffer from an increasing problem of nutritional deficiency because of the region's inability to feed itself. The relatively recent consumer preference for foreign-produced goods certainly contributes to this problem. The diet of more than 50 percent of the population is lacking both protein and calories.[10] Nutrition-linked ills include energy and protein deficiency, iron-deficiency anemia, obesity, and related health problems like hypertension and diabetes. A study by the Caribbean Food and Nutritional Institute found that reliance on imported food for daily energy requirements increased from 65 percent to 92 percent from 1977 to 1980. Anemia is widespread among children under five and in pregnant and lactating women.[11]

The United States directly benefits from the import dependence of the Caribbean, which buys over $800 million of food from the United States every year.[12] The foreign exchange necessary to purchase U.S. food represents roughly one-half the current-accounts deficit of the region. Assistance from the United States to the region amounts to only about 20 percent of the food bill the Caribbean pays each year to U.S. companies.[13] Agriculture expert Robert A. Pastor from the University of Maryland told the Joint Hearings on Agricultural Development in the Caribbean and Central America: "If our purpose is to promote agricultural development in the region and to assist these small nations to become self-sustaining and viable members of the Caribbean Basin community, we are clearly failing. In fact, we are contributing to the region's agricultural dependence rather than to its development."[14] Pastor used Puerto Rico as an illustration of how U.S. policies have failed to promote self-sufficiency in the Caribbean: "Puerto Rico, a classic example, was a major exporter of sugar before World War II and now imports sugar from the United States. Its industrialization program—Operation Bootstrap—created only half as many jobs in manufacturing as it lost in agriculture."[15] A lush, fertile island capable of feeding its population, Puerto Rico nevertheless imports over 80 percent of its food from the U.S. mainland. The island territory produces only 4 percent of its own tomatoes and none of its own rice.[16]

A 1982 United Nations report found that serious environmental problems associated with agriculture in the Caribbean stem from the use of unsuitable soils.[17] "The problem has arisen," the report stated, "partly because of the land tenure situation in which the bulk of farmers are forced onto marginal lands because the best farmlands are being occupied by comparatively few farms." In the West Indies, local farms feed only one-third of the population, and 70 percent of the children are malnourished. Those who argue that there are too many people on the islands overlook figures on Caribbean land use showing that over half of the arable land has been turned over to the production of crops and cattle for export. The Institute for Food and Development Policy points out that the Dominican Republic and Haiti have a longer growing season and only slightly less cultivated land per person than Italy—a country where there is less export crop production and people eat much better. Arguments against dividing large plantations are often based on U.S. experiences in which large farms have proven more efficient than small ones. But given the available technology in the Caribbean, the productivity per unit of land can be higher on small farms.[18]

Unfortunately, recession and falling terms of trade have caused most Caribbean nations to stress agricultural export production rather than building a local agricultural market. Pressured by international development agencies and financial institutions, the Caribbean governments are inviting the old plantation companies back and welcoming new foreign agribusiness concerns like the Latin American Agribusiness Development Corporation, United Brands, and Gulf + Western. The colonial plantation is dead, but the neocolonial plantation lives on in the Caribbean.

SUGAR: THE BITTERSWEET HARVEST

For three and a half centuries, unrefined sugar has been the main export crop of the Caribbean. In the 1630s the Dutch introduced sugarcane cultivation to the West Indies. Soon afterwards, the British, Spanish, and French started their own cane plantations, and spread the sugar business from Guyana on the coast of South America to Belize in Central America and to most islands in the West Indies. The legacy of colonial sugar plantations worked by slaves in chains lingers in the Caribbean: the moss-covered stone walls of the old sugar mills, the names of early plantations (now the names of private estates), the stories of rebellious slaves who burned the fields and homes of the plantocracy, the cane juice sold in the streets of Kingston, the tales of the slaves who fled to the hills of Jamaica and to the bush in the Guianas. The colonial past is more than a memory; it is the determining part of the present reality of the Caribbean, where sugar is still the leading export of Barbados, Cuba, the Dominican Republic, Guadeloupe, St. Kitts, and Guyana. The Caribbean has not escaped its plantation history; it is still sadly dependent on those canefields. Sugar is the lifeblood of so many Caribbean countries, said one regional development expert, that "it's a touchstone of poverty, part of the history of slaves . . . all caught up together. It's a very emotional thing."[19]

The World Sugar Market

The Caribbean sugar industry is facing crisis and disarray. In 1982, world sugar prices dropped to eight cents a pound from a peak of 45 cents a pound in 1980.[20] Hardest hit is Cuba, which in 1982 had a record-breaking sugar harvest of 8.2 million tons, including 3.2 million tons sold on the world market. Rainy weather, labor problems, and organizational difficulties have also plagued the sugar industry in the Commonwealth Caribbean. Barbados in 1982 left 40,000 tons of cane in its fields; Trinidad's state-owned sugar company Caroni is losing more money than any other state enterprise; and, according to a May 8, 1981 LARR report, the Jamaican government is considering handing over the sugar cooperatives to Tate & Lyle or some other TNC. The high prices of the late 1970s encouraged world sugar producers to raise output, but world demand has stagnated because of the recession and a growing use of other sweeteners. Health-conscious consumers have cut down on their coffee consumption, and diet-watchers are searching grocery shelves for sugar-free items.

The three major arrangements for the purchase of Caribbean sugar are the International Sugar Agreement (ISA), the sugar protocol attached to the Lomé Convention, and the contract Cuba maintains with the Soviet Union. Parties to the ISA are members of the International Sugar Organization (ISO) and include the major sugar-trading countries like Cuba, the United States, the Dominican Republic, and the Soviet Union. The ISO monitors free market prices and production of sugar not covered by protective agreements. The sugar protocol of the Lomé Convention protects the agricultural production of the Commonwealth Caribbean. Under this convention, the European Economic Community (EEC) agrees to purchase most or all of the sugar produced in former colonial regions of the EEC members. Sugar from Jamaica and Barbados, for example, goes to this guaranteed European market. The third major agreement affecting the Caribbean is the special arrangement under which the Soviet Union and the Council for Mutual Economic Assistance (Comecon) socialist nations buy about one-half of Cuba's sugar at a guaranteed price.

The other important factor in the Caribbean sugar trade is the quota system set unilaterally by the United States that determines the maximum amount of sugar each Caribbean country can export to the United States. After Castro took power in Cuba, the United States parceled out quotas to other nations to substitute for Cuban sugar. All the agreements and quota systems have advantages and disadvantages, but all place the producing nations of the Caribbean in an inferior position because these countries depend more on their sugar sales to the industrial nations than the industrial nations depend on them for sugar purchases.

The Commonwealth Caribbean nations have a love/hate reaction to the provisions of the Lomé Convention that grant them "privileged access" to the European market. Without that access, they would have a difficult time finding outlets for their sugar. But resentment is building among these "privileged" countries toward the ability of the European nations to determine the price levels and the rules that govern the convention countries. Critics of the Lomé Convention point out that the producing countries consistently receive the lowest possible prices. Prices set by the Lomé Convention often do not cover the costs of production, insurance, or freight from the distant Caribbean ports to Europe. The real beneficiaries, say the critics, are the processing companies like Tate & Lyle and the European shipping companies who profit from guaranteed EEC business. The Lomé Convention, by operating outside the International Sugar Organization and by pushing five million tons of unwanted sugar back onto the world market, has contributed to falling world sugar prices. An ISO official called the EEC's refusal to join ISO "the biggest single factor prejudicing the operation of the agreement."[21]

Caribbean Basin sugar producers are experiencing not only falling prices but also sugar import quotas from the United States. To protect U.S. sugar producers from the slump in world prices, the Reagan administration lowered the import quotas from most Caribbean countries. The reduced quotas have undercut many of the benefits of the Caribbean Basin Initiative (CBI), especially for major sugar producers like the Dominican Republic, which has traditionally exported over 80 percent of its sugar to the United States. Robert Pastor told a congressional committee that a system that treated Caribbean producers like U.S. producers— with no quotas, no fees, and no duties—would channel $200 million more into the Caribbean regional sugar industry. He predicted that the restricted entry of Caribbean sugar will in many ways negate the positive effects of the CBI. "It is impossible," said Pastor, "to predict how this will affect the economies and the politics of these countries, but given the fragility of both at this time, one can probably expect riots and a widening of the violence in Central America."[22] For the countries of the Caribbean Basin, President Reagan's announcement of sugar quotas demonstrated the United States's concern for its own narrow interests in the region.

The International Sugar Workers Conference in 1983 called the policies of both the European Economic Community and the United States "protectionist and at times expansionist."[23] The International Sugar Workers concluded that rather than exhibiting concern for the world market, the EEC and the United States continue to subsidize their own production and exports, thereby create market instability and a gross excess of supply.

In the arrangement between Cuba and the Soviet Union, the USSR reimburses Cuba for its sugar at a rate much higher than the current low prices. This agreement works to the disadvantage of Cuba in times of exceptionally high world prices, because then the Soviet Union pays below the market price. But the arrangement at least partially insulates Cuba from the wide market fluctuations that can easily destabilize a small country. The accord with the Soviet Union is a barter arrangement that gives Cuba goods valued at 3 to 4 times the 1982–83 sugar prices.[24]

Tate & Lyle

Tate & Lyle, which has nine Caribbean subsidiaries, is the world's largest independent sugar company. This sugar firm, which has been producing and refining sugar since 1903, imports 95 percent of EEC sugar for refining in its two refineries in England. Tate & Lyle has entered into contracts with all the Lomé Convention countries for up to 100 percent of their sugar production.[25]

Having sold its canefields, Tate & Lyle retains influence through consulting and purchasing contracts. In 1971, the Jamaican government purchased the firm's 65,000 acres, together with all machinery and improvements, for a price highly favorable to Tate & Lyle. Immediately thereafter the company leased all the land back. But the Sugar Industry Authority, which the Jamaican government set up to regulate the Tate & Lyle operations, became more than the paper tiger the company had expected. Tate & Lyle pulled out and the government instituted a system of cooperatives to manage the sugar estates.

In Trinidad & Tobago, Tate & Lyle's Caroni controlled about 90 percent of the country's sugar crop in the pre-independence era. By tradition, the chairperson of the Sugar Manufacturers Association was a Caroni official. Nationalist sentiment persuaded the government to buy 51 percent of Caroni in 1971. This joint venture allowed the company to benefit from government-guaranteed loans and other government support. In 1976, however, Tate & Lyle invited the government of Trinidad to buy its remaining shares and signed a lucrative contract to provide the publicly owned firm with a wide range of technical and advisory services. Typical of other Trinidadian nationalizations, the agreement resulted from the initiative of the private sector. Although it gained an ownership position, the government still experienced a loss of foreign exchange because of the fees and payment for technical services that continued to go to Tate & Lyle.

Gulf + Western

The huge U.S. conglomerate of Gulf + Western entered the Caribbean in 1967 when it bought the South Puerto Rican Sugar Company, which owned the Dominican Republic's largest sugar mill at La Romana and the surrounding canefields. Now the largest private landowner, Gulf + Western is also the largest taxpayer and the largest employer in the Dominican Republic. The town of La Romana clusters around the monstrous smokestack of the world's biggest sugar mill, which spews out dense, particle-laden smoke that deposits a layer of black soot over the town and fills the air with the sickly-sweet smell of burning sugarcane. Within several blocks of the mill, the smoke and smell are so intense as to choke the lungs and numb the brain. La Romana's residents regularly complain of lung and heart ailments from the ash-filled air, but little is being done to combat this obvious threat to public health.

The Gulf + Western mill accounts for about 400,000 tons of sugar each year. The company also produces sugar in Florida and has extended its agricultural activities beyond sugarcane to include cattle ranching, citrus production, and vegetable farming.²⁶ In 1983, Gulf + Western acquired almost 8 percent of United Brands, which began as a banana company and is now a huge agricultural business conglomerate. At least six of Gulf + Western's 26 Caribbean subsidiaries involve agribusiness.

Booker McConnell

Until Guyana nationalized its sugar industry in 1976, Booker McConnell's Guyanese subsidiaries sustained the corporation's sugar industry worldwide. The company maintains an ongoing relationship with Guyana through technical service contracts, sale of equipment, international marketing of sugar, and the purchase of bulk rum. The principal interests of the British firm are engineering services and food distribution. Other important activities include liquor manufacture and distribution, health products manufacturing, poultry breeding, shipping, and management services for agriculture. In 1980 the conglomerate began the process of acquiring International Basic Economy Corporation (IBEC), a Rockefeller company with long-time interests in Latin America. A representative for the newly formed Booker McConnell subsidiary said: "The merger brought together two companies with complementary strengths in agribusiness and long histories of involvement in the developing world."²⁷ Booker McConnell also has 17 Caribbean subsidiaries with consulting contracts in the sugar industry in Jamaica and the Dominican Republic.

Sugar: Work of Slaves

Two Haitians cutting cane in the Dominican Republic stopped for a moment to pose for a picture. They had worked for many years in the Dominican Republic, they said, and had learned elementary Spanish. The elderly men said they were working every day now, but were never told at what rate they were being paid; they just accepted whatever they received from the bosses. In the Dominican Republic, cutting cane is "slave work," thought to be fit only for Haitians or the lowest elements of Dominican society.

These men are paid not by the hour or by the piece, but by each ton of sugarcane they cut. They live by the strength of their arms, the blade of their machetes, and their ability to endure a way of life that has hardly changed for hundreds of years. They trudge into the forests of ten-foot cane, repeatedly bending down to swing their machetes; at the end of the day, they load their two to four tons of sugarcane into a waiting bin. Back home in their wooden shacks by the edge of the canefields, they see railroad car after railroad car full of the burned, brown stalks rumble by on the way to the sugar mill. Cutting cane is the only life these Haitians know, it was the work of their parents and grandparents and the work of slaves before them.

The Dominican Republic relies on the backbreaking work of the Haitians to harvest its largest export crop. In 1982, the Anti-Slavery Society of Great Britain reported to the United Nations that "harassment and forced labor remain at unacceptably high levels" in the Dominican Republic. Of the 110,000 permanent residents in the country's work camps (bateys), 85,000 are Haitians. An additional 30,000 Haitians cross the border each year to cut Dominican cane, of whom 15,000 to 20,000 are undocumented immigrants.

According to the Anti-Slavery Society, Haitians work seven days a week during the six-month sugar harvest and receive about $1.50 for each ton cut. They cut about two tons in a day that lasts from four o'clock in the morning to six o'clock in the evening. Haitian canecutters live in small, crowded, dark rooms furnished only with iron bedframes, often without mattresses. Discrimination is another part of the harsh life that Haitians endure in the Dominican Republic because the Dominicans who cut cane have segregated and slightly better accommodations. The latrines, one per 200 workers, are also segregated. The ethnic barriers are so intense that Dominican prostitutes will not usually go to bed with Haitian cane workers.

Other Caribbean workers, mostly from Jamaica, travel to Florida to cut cane for Gulf + Western, the U.S. Sugar Company, and the Sugar Cane Growers Cooperative of Florida. The U.S. Department of Labor allows Florida cane growers to contract about 15,000 West Indians to temporarily work cutting cane under the H–2 Program. One Jamaican canecutter described the pressures of contract work: "If the supervisor sees us talking to a white man, we get sent home. We complain about food here, we get sent home. We say we want more money for the cane, we get sent home. Anything we do the supervisor don't like, we get sent home."[28] The cane companies contract West Indians rather than hiring local workers because they can pay the Caribbean workers less and have more control over them.

A Future for Sugar

To a great degree, the course of Caribbean history has followed the ups and downs in the sugarcane industry. Many of the countries have been unable to escape this dependency on sugar, making their future path toward development uncertain. Rather than free themselves from the TNCs, several cane-growing countries have asked Tate & Lyle, Booker McConnell, and Gulf + Western to take hold of the reins of the floundering industry.

Nowhere is this trend so pronounced as in Jamaica, where, after a brief experiment in sugar cooperatives, the Jamaican government under the administration of conservative Edward Seaga began to consider handing over the industry lock, stock, and barrel to the TNCs. Once regarded as the world's best sugar-producing country, Jamaica is now producing half the amount that it did in the early 1970s. Jamaican sugar production is beset by labor conflicts, a $200 million deficit, and an inefficient bureaucracy.[29] So depressed is the industry that Jamaica has begun to import sugar from the United States.

More than an economic problem, the sugar crisis is a sensitive political issue in Jamaica. The sugar workers have a radically different view of the crisis than the Seaga administration. They feel that the industry has never truly been nationalized and turned over to the cooperatives. The voice of sugar employees, The Workers Times, charged in January 1983 that the field and factory workers have never had a say in the operations of the industry. They blame some of the current problems in the industry on the halfway approach to nationalization and the lack of workers' participation that characterized the government of Michael Manley. According to the newspaper, "Inefficient and corrupt managers"—not the cooperative workforce—make the decisions. Instead of the workers, "foreign experts from Gulf + Western, Tate & Lyle, and Bacardi are the ones who are consulted and courted endlessly."[30]

The conservative Seaga government has turned from the workers to the TNCs. Following the advice of his foreign consultants, Seaga tried to enforce a moratorium on wage increases in the industry and wants the government to sell publicly owned sugar mills. Tate & Lyle has offered to take over the National Sugar Corporation, which, sugar workers reported in The Workers Times, would be a "return to the colonial system." As part of the trend toward turning the sugar industry over to private owners, a task force was set up by the U.S. Business Committee on Jamaica to make recommendations to Seaga. Task force spokesperson Alvaro Carta, chief of Gulf + Western's Food Products Company, said that the report—which recommended the restructuring of the industry—"is a very important part of what will be taken into consideration to make their [Jamaica's] final decision."[31]

Other producers—like St. Kitts, Trinidad, and Barbados—face similar problems. The labor supply is diminishing despite the severe unemployment crisis. Native workers refuse jobs in the canefields because of the stigma of slavery and the comparatively low wages. But wages in the Commonwealth Caribbean, accounting for about 50 percent of production costs, are already high compared with those in many other producing nations like those of Central America. In Barbados, an estimated 28 percent of the workers—whose average age is 45—will retire in the next four years with little prospect of replacement, since the youth of Barbados prefer to seek employment in the tourism industry.[32]

For the first time in a hundred years, Puerto Rico in 1982 had to import sugar from the United States.[33] In the early 1900s, U.S. investors like Rockefeller's Eastern Sugar Company considered Puerto Rico an ideal place to grow sugar because no tariffs protected the territory's sugar exports to the United States. Sugarcane occupied 44 percent of the island's cultivated area and employed almost half the agricultural laborers. But in the 1950s investors started to take land out of agricultural production and to speculate in the booming real estate market.[34] By emphasizing the Bootstrap industrialization program, the government discouraged investment in agriculture, and in doing so contributed to its decline.

In contrast to the unhealthy state of the industry in other Caribbean nations, the production of sugar and related products in Cuba is flourishing. An 8.2-million-ton sugar crop in 1982 exceeded expectations, and prospects are good for coming years. The world's largest sugar producer, Cuba has profited from its mutually beneficial arrangements with the Soviet Union and the Comecon nations, which purchase about one-half the island's sugar crop. Cuba has ambitious plans to reach an output of ten million tons by 1985—a 50 percent increase from 1980. The U.S. State Department has considered a secondary boycott on products using Cuban sugar, which could exclude from the U.S. market hundreds of processed foods, including Swiss chocolate and Canadian Club whiskey. Despite difficulties, Cuba has moved to the forefront of the development of cane byproducts such as plastics, detergents, fuel, and chemicals. Cuba's sugar industry, although a victim of world market fluctuations that have shaken the other sugar-producing nations, is less affected and still thrives while continuing to modernize.[35]

THE BANANA ISLANDS

> Work all night, and a drink of rum.
> Daylight come, and me want to go home.
> Stack banana 'til the morning come.
> Daylight come, and me want to go home.
> Come, Mr. Tallyman, tally me banana.
> Daylight come, and me want to go home.
> Lift six-hand, seven-hand, eight-hand bunch.
> Daylight come, and me want to go home.
> —Banana boat song

Since the early days of United Fruit's operations in Jamaica, hurricanes, hard work, and the presence of foreign corporations have characterized the Caribbean banana industry. United Fruit left Jamaica after a hurricane destroyed its plantation in 1932, and it was not until the arrival of Geest Industries from England in the 1950s that the industry started to thrive again. The business of growing, picking, and shipping bananas has not changed much since it began in the Caribbean a hundred years ago. In St. Lucia, the men and women who go out to the fields in bare feet and ragged shirts to pick the bunches of bananas get paid barely enough to support themselves. Just before the banana boat comes to port, they often work through the night sorting and stacking bananas. What has changed is that the banana companies have become conglomerates with their own shipping fleets and diversified investments throughout the globe. In their early days, the banana companies of United Fruit and Geest Industries depended almost entirely on the banana market for the health of their businesses. Today, however, only the banana worker and the banana farmer depend so totally on bananas.

At the beginning of this century, Jamaica was one of the world's leading banana-producing countries and the prime supplier of the entire European community. But hurricanes, droughts, and a declining labor supply due to emigration reduced the country's banana production. The tiny island of Dominica now exports almost as many bananas as Jamaica, although the Jamaican government is trying to revive the industry. The Caribbean as a whole exports about 450,000 tons of bananas a year. The banana industry employs, directly or indirectly, half the working population of the Windward Islands.

Because of its departments of Martinique and Guadeloupe, France is Europe's only banana producer. A government agency closely regulates the production and sale of bananas from the French Antilles. Its strict monitoring of the supply-and-demand balance has given the French consumer the best relationship between banana production prices and consumer prices. U.S. consumers buy bananas at prices 10 times the plantation sale price, while French consumers buy them at only 6 times the plantation prices.[36]

The Banana Companies

The leading banana companies in the Caribbean continue to be Geest Industries and United Brands (the parent of United Fruit). Through its British subsidiary, Fyffes, United Brands buys bananas from three nations in the region: Belize, Jamaica, and Suriname. Fyffes buys Suriname's entire banana crop of 34,000 tons, loaded 3 times a month, through the year, onto Fyffes's ships. Another United Brands subsidiary, OLEP Bananas, entered an arrangement with the government of the Dominican Republic to grow bananas on that country's north coast. United Brands's La Compagnie des Bananes in Paris coordinates banana production in Martinique and Guadeloupe. United Brands conveniently maintains these autonomous subsidiaries in Europe to benefit from the banana protocol of the Lomé Convention and the trade conventions established by England and France.

Fyffes began as an importer and distributor of bananas in the United Kingdom but has expanded into distributing fruit, vegetables, and flowers. When the ships of this subsidiary of United Brands set off to the Caribbean, they fly the flag of the United Kingdom. Rather than owning banana plantations, the company contracts banana production from cooperatives and farmers. In addition, it has started managing banana projects for a fee and a purchase guarantee. In British parliamentary hearings, the chief executive officer of Fyffes stressed that the company will provide assistance and managerial skills, but not capital, to banana projects. "I think it is much easier for the Caribbean Development Bank or the World Bank or government agencies to talk to those governments rather than a commercial company," he said. "We should manage the projects and have all the responsibility of good management, but we shouldn't be investing shareholder capital."[37]

Geest and Its Bananas

Geest Industries purchases the entire banana crop of four Eastern Caribbean islands: St. Lucia, St. Vincent, Grenada, and Dominica. Founded as Geest Horticultural Products by two brothers in 1936, the company is now the largest wholesale produce company in the United Kingdom. Geest International is the company division responsible for the procurement of fresh fruit from the Caribbean. In addition to bananas, Geest buys limes, grapefruit, and coconuts from Dominica; mangoes, pineapples, and ginger root from St. Lucia; and coconuts, mangoes, and eggplant from St. Vincent. Throughout England, Geest has marketing centers, each with its own banana-ripening center. The privately owned firm is branching out into processed, health, and convenience foods.

Geest Industries came to the Caribbean in 1952 with the promise to buy every banana of export quality from the Windward Islands. Eventually the farmers' associations and the colonial governments of the four banana-producing countries signed an exclusive production contract with Geest and diverted the entire export production system from sugar and spice to bananas. The company, having acquired large estates in St. Lucia and Dominica to increase production on the islands, has since sold back most of its estates to local farmers and cooperatives. For the last three decades, Geest has dominated the agricultural sector of these Windward Islands.

When it began its banana business in the Caribbean, Geest had to hire boats to ship the bananas to England, but it now owns a fleet of huge white 3,500-ton ships that include other profitable cargo business in their regular shipping runs to the Caribbean. Two other export agents, Volton Brothers and John Bâptiste Ltd., in addition to Geest's own trading company, handle the export arrangements for all the Windwards' bananas. Banana farmers sell their produce to each island's banana growers' association (BGA). A regional organization set up by growers called WINBAN (Windward Islands Banana Growers Association) coordinates and advises the BGAs, which contract with Geest Industries for all their bananas. Geest sets the price for the green bananas and has the right of rejection based on quality. The two main problems with this system are the monopoly control exercised by Geest and the inefficiency of the growers' associations.

The late 1970s and early 1980s were rough years for the Caribbean banana industry. Hurricane David in 1979 and Hurricane Allen in 1980 flattened the Caribbean banana plantations. Then came the decline of the value of the pound against the dollar, bringing losses in 1983 to over $10 million in the Windwards alone.[38] The market in the United Kingdom could accommodate substantially more duty-free bananas from the Caribbean islands, but England has purchased an increasing amount of what are known as "dollar-market bananas" because of the low production of the Caribbean nations. Dollar-market bananas are those bought from outside the European Economic Community, from producers in South and Central America. Although the countries selling dollar-market bananas pay a hefty duty to enter the United Kingdom, they account for about half the UK market. Lower wages, higher productivity, and greater efficiency allow these bananas from outside the preferred market to compete effectively with protected suppliers.

Theoretically, Geest pays for the green bananas from the Windward Islands at prices negotiated with the growers. Geest's monopoly, however, gives the company a far superior bargaining position and forces the islands to accept the contract and price set by Geest. The price that the BGAs receive from Geest has fallen below their operating costs and has left the BGAs unable to pay the smaller growers enough to cover production costs. A British Development Division study found that, at the prices offered by Geest, all types of farmers are losing money. Large farmers are losing one to three cents per pound of bananas exported while the "income left for the small and medium farmers is considerably less than they could earn as manual farm laborers."[39] As one Dominica banana grower said, "Whenever the banana farmer picks up his cutter, he is losing."[40]

In contrast, Geest is pulling a higher and higher percentage of the retail market price of bananas. In recent years, their percentage has jumped from 35 to 45 percent, meaning that the BGAs and the growers receive an ever-lower percentage of the consumer price.[41] The *Geest*

Star or one of the company's other mighty ships arrives each week at the island's port, loads up in a day, and then is on its way back to England. Left behind are the BGAs and WINBAN, which have taken the brunt of criticism for the industry's problems. In effect they are the middlemen for Geest: they are the ones who reject a farmer's bananas and hand out the meager paychecks. There is no denying that the BGAs have not been very effective in that role. The farmers' disaffection with the BGAs began when their managers squandered the aid and development assistance sent to the islands after Hurricanes David and Allen. The BGAs also failed to provide promised services for the banana farmers and have in some cases run up extraordinary debts. In 1982, the total debt of the Dominica Banana Growers Association amounted to an unmanageable $25 million, while St. Lucia's BGA had a debt of $11 million with no resources to pay back the loans.[42]

Because Geest controls the purchasing, shipping, ripening, distribution, and sale of bananas and because it enjoys a protected source of bananas, it can jack up the price of bananas at each stage. Overall, Geest Industries clearly deserves at least part of the blame for the banana crisis. Geest has in recent years pulled itself further away from the exigencies of banana production and has drastically reduced its land ownership on the islands to avoid risks like hurricanes and banana diseases. The company says it is also trying to avoid the negative image associated with foreign ownership, which it says is often politically unacceptable.

"The farmers don't seem to identify the main enemy in the banana market as Geest," says Richard Charles, a leader of the Dominica Farmers Union.[43] Charles feels the lack of adequate education and the influence of outside aid organizations have meant that the finger of blame has been pointing in the wrong direction. "Nobody has ever seriously challenged Geest," he says. "Geest is sucking the blood out of both the banana workers and farmers. The banana contracts the islands regularly sign make us slaves to Geest."

The 1981 study by the British Development Division suggested that the banana contracts be revised and the islands' bargaining position be strengthened. It reported that the contracts are currently cost plus—a situation in which "Geest takes few, if any, risks." Furthermore, "the overall structure of the industry, the traditionally limited role of the [British] government in the price negotiations and the relative power of the marketing agents [Geest] have all contributed to the traditionally weak bargaining power of the producers in the trade negotiations." The development agency recommended that Geest share the risks of banana production. It warned that if the Windwards' banana industry were to collapse, Geest would lose its guaranteed market and would then "have to compete on an equal basis with other international companies." Finally, the agency said that the situation in the islands is critical and that if the banana industry falls, "there will be substantial economic disloca-tion in the Windward Islands and this is likely to have hefty political implications."

Privatizing Dominica

The U.S. Agency for International Development (USAID) stepped into this crisis in the Windward Islands by using grants and loans as leverage to restructure the banana industry on the islands. Without con-sulting the growers of Dominica, the Dominican BGA, or WINBAN, Prime Minister Eugenia Charles signed an agreement in 1982 with USAID to institute the following reforms: restructure the growers' association into the Dominica Banana Company to be managed by officials from is-land banks and businesses; turn the boxing plants over to the private sector; and "privatize" other subcomponents in the industry such as dis-ease control, distribution of inputs, and the provision of technical and administrative assistance. The agreement also required all loan and pur-chase decisions by the Dominica Banana Company to be reviewed by USAID.

Another part of the covert agreement was the stipulation that the grant money be used to purchase farm inputs, like fertilizer and machin-ery, that are manufactured by U.S. firms. Seventy-five percent of the grant to the banana industry, or $1.3 million, will be used to buy speci-fied disease-control materials from Texaco and DuPont. The balance of the grant will pay U.S. advisers to develop private enterprise in Dom-inica's banana industry. As part of its restructuring program, USAID sponsored a series of meetings about the situation in Dominica with rep-resentatives from Geest Industries, the Royal Bank of Canada, and Bar-clays.[44]

A copy of the USAID agreement was leaked to the Dominica Farm-ers Union, which then called together the island farmers to discuss it. The farmers' union objected that the agreement was signed without their consultation and that the privatization program would put the industry into the hands of USAID, the foreign banks, and the island's business elite. Union representative Richard Charles admitted that the BGA had management problems, but pointed out that the farmers had started to solve those problems before the USAID accord with the prime minister. He said the plan for a banana company was an attempt by the United States to further weaken WINBAN and to obstruct a unified approach by the four islands. According to the farmers' union, an all-too-obvious omission of USAID's plan is its failure to address the monopoly power of Geest Industries. Because of the explosive popular opposition, USAID subsequently withdrew, at least temporarily, its signed proposal for the creation of a new banana company to replace the BGA. But USAID and the foreign banks remain intent on privatizing the island's banana production. Yet another threat to Dominica's banana farmers came when Peter Johnson of Caribbean/Central American Action (CCAA) stated that the CCAA had asked Gulf+Western "to go down and do something in Dominica" in the way of recommendations for privatization of banana production.[45]

An opposition party in Dominica called the Dominica Liberation Movement warned that islanders should not be lured by the public relations efforts of Geest nor the offers of assistance by USAID. "At each level," it said, "we must demand our fair share of the cake and not depend on a Christmas gift from the boss or a $5,000 gift from Geest to the hospital or a toilet from USAID."[46] David Dimark of the Ministry of Agriculture in St. Lucia feels that the islands should band together and invest in their own ripening and distribution network in England while simultaneously trying to diversify production.[47] "Other production has been neglected because of bananas," he said. "Banana growing is a continuation of the plantation system of economy where domestic food production is ignored and there is no linkage with the rest of the economy, only with England."[48]

CARIBBEAN COFFEE

The hills of Haiti, the Dominican Republic, and Jamaica produce some of the world's best coffee crops. Farmworkers handpick the orange-red coffee beans and drop them into the straw bags they carry over their shoulders. The beans then dry in nearby coffee sheds and are subsequently shoveled into burlap bags for shipment to foreign markets. Because of its ability to earn foreign exchange, Caribbean coffee rarely sells in the local market. Successful advertising by the instant-coffee producers has replaced home-grown coffee with processed products like Nescafé. In Jamaica, only the expensive restaurants serve their customers the famous coffee grown in the Blue Mountains that lie outside Kingston.

Coffee beans pass through a long line of middlemen before they finally reach the consumer. Growers sell their beans to a trader or broker, who then passes the coffee through customs, after which the coffee is sold to a processor or roaster. It often changes hands again, going to a wholesaler, who distributes the coffee to the retail market. In the Caribbean, the governments themselves commonly perform the function of trader. Caribbean coffee beans leave the region unprocessed, thus depriving the coffee-producing countries of further earnings that would come through coffee processing and marketing. The oligopolistic control by the major coffee companies, however, makes it unlikely that the Caribbean nations could independently develop their own connections within the industry.

The United Nations Commission on Trade and Development (UNCTAD) noted that the "concentration in ownership of processing and distribution is actually a result of major coffee firms' strategy to merge and/ or to acquire their rivals to increase their market shares."[49] Nestlé and General Foods control 20 percent of the world market; these two companies, together with Consolidated Foods and Jacobs, control 90 percent of coffee sales in Europe and Japan. Just four corporations dominate the world trade in roasted coffee: General Foods, Procter & Gamble, Consolidated Foods, and West Germany's Jacobs.[50] Four firms also control the instant-coffee market: Nestlé, General Foods, Procter & Gamble, and Consolidated Foods. Some companies, like General Foods, handle their own brokering.

Like other raw agricultural exports, coffee is commanding lower and lower prices. Economic and health considerations have led to a stagnant market. To counter this drop in coffee consumption, in 1983 the National Coffee Association launched a $24 million advertising campaign to promote coffee drinking among young people.[51] Coffee growers are generally small farmers squeezed by buyers and sellers who stand between them and the market. One-third of the Haitian population depend on the coffee market, but most of them are victims of a vicious system of speculation and government taxation. Haiti's dictator Duvalier has imposed a 30 percent export tax on coffee that takes the surplus from the impoverished countryside and puts it in the pockets of the Duvalier family and the ruling elite.[52] The coffee tax drastically reduces the income of the peasant cultivators, forcing them to allocate still more land to their coffee crop and reduce the land available to grow their own food. Coffee production in the Dominican Republic relies on the hard work of undocumented Haitian laborers who receive below subsistence wages. In Jamaica, about 90 percent of the coffee goes to Ueshima Coffee, Japan's largest coffee company, which has established the Blue Mountain Coffee Company. Ueshima finances the Jamaican farmers to produce coffee for the expanding Japanese market.[53]

TOBACCO: MAKING THE CARIBBEAN MARLBORO COUNTRY

The paved road ends an hour west of Santo Domingo. Only horses, mules, and motorbikes travel in this rugged, isolated hill country. The *campesinos* of the Yamasa region survive by tobacco. Alongside the dusty road, they spread the leaves out to dry; and inside their two-room homes, families sort and pack them. The community leaders met one Saturday morning to discuss their economic predicament. "The tobacco isn't for us *Dominicanos*," said one weathered peasant. "It's for companies like Philip Morris from the United States. All our lives we labor to produce tobacco for Philip Morris."[54]

Caribbean tobacco-producing countries are Jamaica, Cuba, and the Dominican Republic. Cigars are the common form of tobacco export, while the cigarettes produced in the Caribbean stay within the region. Female workers, paid $2 to $3 a day, roll cigar after cigar six days a week for the major tobacco firms. The Dominican Republic and Jamaica are respectively the fourth- and fifth-largest exporters of cigars to the United States. In Jamaica, the one TNC cigar manufacturer is larger than the three local cigar companies. The foreign corporations also monopolize the cigarette market. The Cigarette Company of Jamaica is really a subsidiary of BAT Industries—the largest cigarette concern in the world and Britain's third-largest industrial corporation. The E. León Jiménez Company is not a locally owned firm in the Dominican Republic but a subsidiary of Philip Morris. Other TNC tobacco firms in the Caribbean are RJ Reynolds, Culbro, Consolidated Cigar, and Rothmans (UK).

Tobacco companies rationalize expanding their business in third world nations by saying they indirectly provide the technical advice, marketing assistance, and cash necessary to increase food production. They reject the charge that growing tobacco is a colossal waste of acreage badly needed to feed the hungry. The tobacco corporations say their presence and example in third world nations stimulate modern agricultural production. As Sir Richard Dobson, the chairperson of BAT, said, "I believe it is safe to say that more food is produced because of the presence of tobacco than would be grown in its absence."[55] Not only does the growth of the tobacco industry in the Caribbean take away land needed for food production, but advertising by the cigarette companies has induced increasing numbers of third world people to spend their scarce money on cigarettes rather than food. Another adverse effect of the tobacco industry is its contribution to the deforestation of the region. The drying or curing of tobacco is one of the heaviest single demands on the wood supplies of the producing countries, since it requires about six acres of trees to cure one ton of tobacco. One of every eight trees felled in tobacco-growing countries like the Dominican Republic is burned to dry tobacco.[56] Some 400 of the country's rivers and streams have permanently dried up in the past 25 years because of uncontrolled tree felling.[57]

GANJA: THE UNDERGROUND ECONOMY

Cultivated on the rolling hills of Jamaica, ganja (marijuana) is easier and more profitable to market than any other crop. As one Jamaican peasant farmer told the leading daily newspaper, the *Daily Gleaner*, "Even if you plant one thousand banks of yam, you can't get from it the money you would get from one acre of ganja." In Jamaica, ganja is widely consumed, popularized by the Rastafarian* religious cult, which calls it "the weed of wisdom," and by the reggae music of Peter Tosh and the late Bob Marley. The first Caribbean ganja users, however, were not the Afro-Caribbeans but the East Indians who brought the "holy plant" with them in the mid-19th century. Although the consumption and sale of ganja is illegal, its use is widespread. On the streets of Kingston and at rural bus stops on the winding mountain roads, Jamaicans pass each other loosely rolled, cigarlike "spliffs." Ganja tea is a popular drink among all age groups in the country, although frowned upon by the middle and upper classes.

Jamaican ganja consumption has been rapidly increasing in the last five to ten years. High unemployment and the consequent boredom among city youth have contributed to ganja's continuing appeal, but smoking ganja is also a popular workplace pastime. Some Jamaican employers complain that ganja lowers productivity, but others say ganja improves performance by reducing rough handling of delicate products and by alleviating the drudgery and boredom of arduous, repetitive jobs like canecutting.

More than a cultural habit of Jamaicans, ganja is probably the nation's largest private business. *Newsweek* reported in 1981 that Jamaica was the second-largest supplier to the United States after Colombia. It is a $1.1-billion business, of which about $200 million gets back to the Jamaican economy. Although the weed has been illegal for over a hundred years, an estimated 8,000 farmers cultivate ganja. A list of Jamaicans who have been involved in the ganja trade reads like a guest list to the Governor's Ball. Mostly foreign dealers broker this major export crop. One back-country farmer said he preferred not to do business with Jamaican buyers: "Them too cheap, sah. We prefer the plane man them, the white man them."

Foremost among the ganja dealers, according to the *Daily Gleaner*, is the Ethiopian Zion Coptic Church, which considers ganja both a sacrament and a good business proposition. The country's largest private landowners, the Coptic Church operates many of the estimated 120 illegal airstrips in the country. The Coptic Church owns posh residences, aircraft, deep-sea fishing boats, a supermarket, a gas station, a furniture store, productive food farms, rice fields, and a hauling company. Its police connections and wealth have protected the organization's top echelon from prosecution for drug trafficking. The marijuana church is the

---

*Rastafarianism is a religious and cultural sect in the Caribbean that rejects the white society of "Babylon." Many Rastafarians look to Ethiopia (the only African land that was not subjugated by Europeans) for political, spiritual, and cultural guidance. Smoking ganja is for Rastafarians a sacramental act.

informal but effective social services center in many rural areas. Although the Coptics normally operate outside the traditional system, they represent an increasing political power because of their wealth and their national network of protection and business contacts.

The U.S. Bureau for International Narcotic Matters has targeted Jamaica because it is both the major regional producer of marijuana and an important transfer point for drug traffickers. The agency budgeted $1 million in 1983 to block Caribbean drug traffic and set up a training program for Jamaican police. Prime Minister Seaga is reluctant to cooperate with the Reagan administration's campaign against Jamaican ganja because of its recognized importance to the economy as a producer of foreign exchange. The prime minister also cannot ignore a 1981 newspaper poll that found 62 percent of the populace opposed to the U.S.-sponsored campaign to halt the ganja trade.

FERTILE GROUNDS FOR TNCs

Fertilizers and pesticides may be considered essential to modern agriculture, but the price of these petroleum-based inputs has dramatically increased the cost of farming. All over the third world, billboards advertising the latest chemicals now compete with the familiar messages from Coca-Cola and Pepsi. Dow Chemical, Shell, Amoco, and Grace are common names in the rural areas of the Caribbean. In 1980, 40 percent of the $2.6-billion U.S. pesticide production was destined for export markets.[58] Because of their high levels of toxicity, many of these exported pesticides have been banned by the USDA for use in the United States.

Trinidad is a major world producer of nitrogen fertilizers; and although the country has its own natural supply of hydrocarbons, TNCs control the entire industry. Three of the four firms that control over two-thirds of the world's nitrogen-production capacity have operations in Trinidad: WR Grace, the Williams Companies, and Amoco. In 1965, WR Grace established Federation Chemicals as its first ammonia plant. Any visitor to Port of Spain will see the slogan "Nationalize Fedchem" painted everywhere, evidence of the enmity that has grown between WR Grace and Trinidadians. The workers have battled continually for increased wages but have met steadfast company resistance. The union has pointed out that WR Grace can well afford to increase the workers' paychecks, since wages constitute only 4 percent of total production costs.[59] Grace, which also owns 49 percent of Trinidad Nitrogen, has fertilizer plants in Jamaica, the Netherlands Antilles, St. Lucia, the Dominican Republic, and Puerto Rico. Other foreign fertilizer companies do not actually produce fertilizer in Caribbean countries but simply mix and bag chemical imports in order to evade tariffs on imported finished goods.

Organizations of foreign industrial countries have contributed to the expanded use of chemical fertilizers in the Caribbean. Most of the aid to agricultural projects specifies the purchase of fertilizer from corporations of the donor country. Farmers have to purchase fertilizers, pesticides, and other farm implements with credit from the aid organization; this leads to an increased indebtedness of the small farmers and an expanded market for the TNCs. USAID has also directly bought fertilizers for its projects from WR Grace, Stoller Chemical, Texaco, Mobil Chemical, and DuPont Latin America.

FEEDLOTS AND FORESTS

Cattle raising for export is not the large business in the Caribbean that it is in Central America and other parts of the third world. But several foreign corporations do have cattle ranches in the region: Bookers in Jamaica, Reynolds Aluminum in Jamaica, Servbest Foods of Chicago in Haiti, and Gulf + Western in the Dominican Republic. A Dutch company, Enginieursbureau HN Van Kijk, has cattle ranches in Suriname, poultry hatcheries in the Dominican Republic and Barbados, poultry- and egg-processing plants in Trinidad and Jamaica, and a meat-packing plant in Puerto Rico. In the Dominican Republic, Gulf + Western has its own extensive milk-cow herd called the Romana Red after the center of its operations in La Romana. Nowhere is there such misuse of scarce Caribbean land as in Haiti, where Servbest Foods produces beef and pork for sausage destined for U.S. consumers while many Haitians never taste fresh meat.

Plantation agriculture, wood gathering, and peasant hillside farming have depleted the forests throughout the Caribbean. The devastation is unparalleled in Haiti. Flying into Port-au-Prince, one immediately sees the denuded mountains that tell a story of waste, plunder, and desperate living. The sugar plantations and the coffee farms use the best valley land, while the four million rural Haitians scratch out a living on the barren mountainsides. The Haitian peasants scatter their seeds before an April storm, hoping that it will not wash away the seeds and the negligible topsoil. Haitians use wood, in the form of charcoal, as the heating and cooking fuel. They scavenge the land for pieces of wood, dead or alive, that are then put into a pit and smoked into charcoal for their own use or for sale in the cities. Experts predict that unless there is a massive replanting campaign, Haiti will be devoid of trees in less than ten years. Despite the magnitude of deforestation, the Haitian government continues to grant permits for the cutting of the few remaining forested areas. In many of the Caribbean islands, the destruction of the tropical forests for plantations has increased the potential for damage by hurricanes, which leave banana and cocoa plantations flattened.

The largest tropical forests of the Caribbean lie in the southern reaches of Guyana, French Guiana, and Suriname. Forests cover 72 percent of Guyana while 20 million acres of French Guiana's forests are virtually untouched, and the vast interior of Suriname is entirely primitive forests. As many as 90 different tree species grow in a single four-acre patch of these immense forests. The countries are trying to open the forests for commercial exploitation but the lack of good roads limits, at least temporarily, the possibility of extensive logging. Two TNCs active in the timber and paper business in the Caribbean are Weyerhaeuser, through its subsidiary West Indies Pulp and Paper, and International Paper, which has operations in the Dominican Republic, Martinique, and Guadeloupe. Other businesses are looking to the Caribbean as a market for U.S.-produced wood. U.S. exports of southern pine lumber to the Caribbean constitute more than one-third of U.S. overseas sales.

CARIBBEAN FOOD MARKET ALL WRAPPED UP

A "Made in Jamaica" label on a bag of macaroni or a "Made in Trinidad" label on a package of margarine may mean nothing more than that those products are packaged in the Caribbean. Most of the food value comes from overseas. Food processing in the Caribbean is import-intensive, meaning that more than half the food processed in the Caribbean uses agricultural products imported from foreign countries. Transnational corporations establish finishing-touch industries in the Caribbean to slip under the tariff barriers and to gain a competitive edge in the local market. One study revealed that 81 percent of the value of the agricultural inputs for the food-processing industry in Barbados and the Eastern Caribbean came from sources outside the Caricom market.[60] For some products, like bread, spaghetti, corn products, and animal feed, the imported food value is 100 percent.

The top ten world food processors have diverse operations in the Caribbean, although a couple, like Greyhound, have Caribbean subsidiaries in other than food processing (Table 2A). Products of the Swiss-owned Nestlé show up everywhere: the tea in the restaurants, the liquid in the baby bottles, the chocolate milk many children drink, and in television advertisements. So successful has been the promotion by the food processors that the demand for high-cost, luxury-food products in the third world is growing 3 to 4 times faster than the population.

Other major food processors operating in the Caribbean include RJ Reynolds, United Brands, IC Industries (Pet), Procter & Gamble, HJ Heinz, International Multifoods, Kellogg, Stokely-Van Camp, Esmark, Norton Simon, Gerber Products, Quaker Oats, Florida-based Pantry Pride, Castle & Cooke, Rowntree Mackintosh (UK), and Beatrice Foods. Beatrice, the largest food-processing company in the United States (ranking number 35 on *Fortune*'s list of the 500 largest corporations), has extensive operations in the Caribbean. While the conglomerate formerly kept its corporate presence quiet, Beatrice now publicly promotes its many well-known brand names: La Choy, Dannon, Swiss Miss, Fisher Nuts, Culligan water purifiers, and Samsonite. Rowntree Mackintosh, another large corporation with a little-known name, is the world's largest confectionery exporter and has a licensing and technical agreement with Highgate Foods, a Jamaican-owned company. The urbanization of the Caribbean has opened up a vast new market for the TNC food processors who produce canned meals and sell fast food to the millions of new urban denizens. The McDonald's, Pizza Hut, and Kentucky Fried Chicken franchises have promoted new eating habits throughout the Caribbean.

TABLE 2A
CARIBBEAN OPERATIONS
OF LEADING FOOD PROCESSORS

World Rank	Company	Number of Caribbean Subsidiaries
1	Unilever (Netherlands/UK)	4
2	Nestlé (Switzerland)	13
3	Kraft	1
4	General Foods	3
5	Esmark	21
6	Beatrice Foods	7
7	Coca-Cola	13
8	Greyhound	6
9	Ralston Purina	5
10	Borden	5

Source: The Resource Center, Compilation of Corporations, 1984

The Beverage Business

The TNCs began their domination of the food-processing industry with the beverage business. Through massive advertising, manufacturers of American soft drinks have changed the definition of refreshment from fresh lemonade and fresh fruit *batidos* to bottles of sugar, caffeine, artificial coloring, and patented syrup. And the national beer is often a transnational brew. Cervecería Nacional Dominicano may look Dominican, but it is owned by United Kingdom's BAT Industries. From their bottling plants and breweries scattered around the Caribbean, the beverage firms can cover the entire region. The major U.S. TNCs in the Caribbean beverage business are Coca-Cola, Wometco, PepsiCo, and Philip Morris.

Other leading TNCs that provide drink to the region are Heineken, Guinness, and Booker McConnell.

The Grain Merchants

An extreme case of dominant TNC control of food processing in the Caribbean is in the grain industry. Because the region has very little capacity to grow wheat or other grains (except rice), it is almost completely dependent on the few giants of the world grain trade like Pillsbury, Canadian Pacific (Maple Leaf), General Mills, and Seaboard.

The Caribbean Community (Caricom) Secretariat is attempting to tackle the foreign control of grain supply and milling in the English-speaking Caribbean through a joint buying and shipping service. As it stands now, the milling companies generally buy grain from their own affiliate companies in the United States or Canada, an arrangement that Caricom considers a conflict of interest. In Barbados, even though the government owns 60 percent of the flour mill, its partner Maple Leaf controls all decision-making and retains a practical monopoly on grain supplies. In Grenada, the local management of the joint venture with Continental Grain has no input into the purchasing decisions, which are all made in the United States. In most cases, instead of publicly bidding for the grain contracts the TNC buyers purchase through cost-plus, intracompany agreements that increase the cost of flour for the Caribbean people.

A study by Caricom found that the value of its grain imports was $140 million in 1980, in addition to a $35-million shipping bill.[61] It calculated the region could save at least $22 million if the countries instituted competitive buying and joint shipping of the grain. Not only have the Caribbean nations been paying more than the market price because of monopoly pricing practices, but the grain companies have been selling them a higher grade of wheat than necessary for general purposes. The region now suffers high freight rates as a consequence of the fragmented market, but bulk purchases and chartered shipping could save $10 million a year. Outside the Commonwealth Caribbean, TNC control is just as concentrated. A United Nations survey found that in the Dominican Republic, two foreign firms controlled 100 percent of the flour milling, 95 percent of the bread and manufactured pastry business, and 100 percent of the animal-feed production.[62]

In the feed-milling industry, TNCs have set up joint ventures with local firms but control all the purchasing and shipping decisions. Because the country markets are so limited, prices are high. In addition to flour milling, many of the grain companies control feed milling. These companies include Central Soya, Ralston Purina, I.S. Joseph, Larro, Lipscomb, and Biotech. Foreign animal-feed producers regularly depend on a higher percentage of imported inputs than do locally owned and locally operated firms.

Rather than alleviate the Caribbean's dependence on imported food, the TNC food processors aggravate the problem by inducing desire among the Caribbean people for new foods composed mainly of imported ingredients. This change in eating habits has impeded the improvement in production and marketing of indigenous staple foods. One survey showed that many Caribbean residents are not concerned about the decline of local food production because they have developed imported tastes: "They regard it something of a status symbol to prepare a meal which consists of foreign foods from tins and boxes. In many cases, they even hesitate to admit to eating such things as sweet potatoes and breadfruit; and will never offer them to anyone they wish to impress."[63]

PROSPECTS FOR CARIBBEAN AGRICULTURE

When economists and politicians discuss agriculture in the Caribbean, the problems of providing land to small farmers, jobs for farmworkers, and low-cost food for the rural and urban poor are seldom mentioned. Instead, too many discussions and plans stress increasing export-crop production, earning more foreign exchange, and attracting foreign investment. This emphasis has been encouraged by the international financial institutions, the commercial banks, and foreign-aid organizations, as well as the TNCs that dominate world agribusiness.

Undoubtedly, most Caribbean nations will continue to rely on a few major export crops because they lack other resources. But it does not make good economic sense to ignore production for the local food market. The almost exclusive attention given to the export sector has resulted in huge food-import bills and the consequent loss of foreign exchange earned by export crops. Other reductions of net foreign-exchange earnings are the purchase of fertilizers, pesticides, and new farm machinery and the payment for management and consultancy services.

Haiti's Duvalier once said that he doubted there was a serious hunger problem in Haiti. After all, he said, the island had plenty of papaya trees for the picking. While hunger in the Caribbean has not reached the proportions it has in other parts of the third world because of the tropical climate and the abundant fruit, people cannot live by papayas alone. An astounding lack of official concern about rural issues in the Caribbean is causing serious problems in both the country and the city. The poor from the country are streaming into densely populated areas, escalating the urban crisis and exacerbating the problem of insufficient food production. With this alarming increase in urban population, malnutrition and hunger are becoming ever more serious in the Caribbean. The large number of disenfranchised still living in the rural areas represents an untapped potential that could increase agricultural production through better land distribution. Local capital and resources should also be used to build agricultural processing industries to feed the local population.

Island Factories:

INDUSTRY AND COMMERCE IN THE CARIBBEAN

They work more minutes per hour at 10 percent higher labor productivity than in the United States, and at wages one-tenth those in the United States.
     —TNC assembly plant manager in St. Kitts

The West Indies are no longer the rum islands and calypso colonies of the past, but neither have they become industrialized and developed. Caribbean economies have changed markedly during the last two decades. Most of the islands now have one or more industrial zones, an industrial development agency, a detailed investment code, and a large urban workforce ready for the assembly line. In the past, the Caribbean produced little more than plantation crops like sugar, bananas, and coffee. But now consumers around the world have jeans, shoes, calculators, bras, and baseballs that were manufactured in the Caribbean.

Caribbean leaders started to chart the course of the modern Caribbean in the 1950s and 1960s. They hoped a diversified economic base would eventually move the nations out of their underdeveloped state. As it was first conceived, Caribbean industrialization had two key elements: import substitution and assembly manufacturing for export. Both strategies were intended to increase participation in the international capitalist system rather than turn toward socialist planning. One of the early Caribbean development economists, W. Arthur Lewis, admitted that at first the industrialization plans of the Caribbean would entail "a period of wooing and fawning" of foreign capitalists, but predicted that this period of supplication would be short and lead to the Caribbean nations' becoming equal associates of the capitalist countries.

IMPORT SUBSTITUTION: PRODUCING FOR THE CARIBBEAN MARKET

Import substitution—the encouragement of industries to produce goods that were formerly imported—sounded like a sensible development

strategy, but it has not succeeded in creating strong and diverse industrial development in the Caribbean. The Caribbean nations embarked
on their import-substitution plans by imposing high tariffs on the entry
of foreign goods in order to encourage the growth of an industrial capacity based in the region. The main drawbacks of the strategy were the
following:

• Increased domination of the region's economy by the TNCs
• Protection of inefficient and uncompetitive local industries that
  produced under monopoly conditions
• Reliance on a high percentage of imported materials, equipment,
  and machinery, thereby not reducing the dependence on industrial nations
• Few requirements that local materials and labor-intensive methods be used

The import-substitution industries that have contributed the most to
regional economic development use materials available locally, such as
companies that produce cement, fertilizer, canned fruit, cotton yarn, and
furniture. Other industries manufacturing products like shoes, plastic
goods, clothing, metal items, paints, and pharmaceuticals have little interaction with other sectors of the economy. Rather than pay the high
tariffs to ship their goods to the Caribbean market, the TNCs have set
up "finishing touch" plants within the Caribbean to assemble goods for
the local market. A company that produces toothpaste, for example, will
not send shipments of commercially packaged toothpaste into the Caribbean but only the various components of the product, the paste and the
tubes. The company then hires low-paid Caribbean workers to mix up
the toothpaste components and put the paste into tubes for regional distribution. This widespread practice by TNC manufacturers runs contrary
to the purposes of the import-substitution strategy. Because the Caribbean is not industrialized, the rise of foreign-owned industries has also
caused increased importation of machines and equipment, thereby draining
foreign exchange reserves.

ASSEMBLY INDUSTRIES: PRODUCING FOR
THE U.S. MARKET

Operation Bootstrap in Puerto Rico was the model for the second
element of the industrialization strategy in the Caribbean. Like Puerto
Rico, which had started promoting itself in the 1950s as an ideal spot for
assembly industries, the other Caribbean islands thought they could attract TNCs with their cheap labor and investment incentives. The TNCs

would manufacture products, not for the Caribbean market, but for the world market, particularly the nearby United States. The rationale for this development strategy, sometimes called "industrialization by invitation," was that the assembly plants would provide jobs and that eventually the plants would establish links with the local economy.

The type of manufacturing plants that have come to the Caribbean through this industrialization-by-invitation strategy are often called offshore industries because their products are shipped "offshore" and do not enter the local market. These offshore factories generally locate in industrial zones, constructed by the host country, that have the factory shells and infrastructure in place and ready for TNC investors. In most cases, the assembly plants import duty-free all the assembled products. Under this system of production, Caribbean workers assemble a large variety of products, such as Rubik's Cube® puzzles, cassette tapes, sports equipment, and apparel.

Generally, four government and corporate entities combine to create assembly industry enclaves in the Caribbean.

- The TNC, which wants to internationalize its production and reduce assembly costs
- The segment of the local business elite, which benefits from increased foreign presence by establishing subcontracting operations and other forms of dependent business
- The home government of the TNC, which gives tariff exemptions on imports of assembled materials and encourages foreign investment with subsidies, tax breaks, and other support
- The government of the host country, which sets low minimum wage rates and passes incentives for export industrialization

Companies assembling goods for export back to the United States benefit from special U.S. tariff provisions that reduce or waive import duties on these products. The most common, the 806.3 and 807 tariff regulations, stipulate that duties will be assessed only on the value added to products by overseas production operations. This means that if Manhattan Industries sends parts of shirts to the Dominican Republic for final assembly, only the value added by the assembling activity will be subject to import duties. The Caribbean Basin has become a favorite spot of U.S. corporations for assembly operations because of the cheap labor and the area's proximity to the United States. To further encourage Caribbean exports to the United States, the Caribbean Basin Initiative permits an expanded category of products to enter the United States duty-free.

Most export-processing industries use only one local input: the labor of Caribbean workers. After a month or less of training, the TNCs can get Caribbean workers to meet the efficiency level of U.S. workers—

TABLE 3A
807 EXPORTS TO THE UNITED STATES

Country	807 exports to US ($ millions)		807 exports as % of manufacturers' exports to US	
	1975	1981	1975	1981
Haiti	54.7	171.3	77.8	75.1
Dominican Rep	15.8	119.7	27.9	52.4
Barbados	9.7	53.2	90.7	91.6
Jamaica	10.4	17.1	80.0	72.0
Leeward/Windward	4.0	11.7	50.0	75.4

Sources: Computed from data from International Trade Commission and Department of Commerce; "Multinational Corporations in Central America and the Caribbean," John Cavanaugh and Joy Hackel, Institute for Policy Studies, August 1983

who are paid as much as 10 times more. Other incentives, like tax exemptions and factory accommodations, put icing on an already attractive cake for the TNC firms with offshore production in the Caribbean.

The workforce gains no lasting benefit because the skills learned are usually specialized and few advanced programs exist to upgrade them. One woman who had worked at a jeans assembly plant in the Dominican Republic for 12 years was doing the same job for which she had been initially hired and could not, after all those years in the factory, even assemble a whole pair of pants by herself. One of the most striking features of assembly industries is their overwhelmingly female workforce. The managers of these assembly plants claim that women are more pliable and passive than male workers.

Government-sponsored repression keeps workers unorganized and low-paid in some Caribbean nations like Haiti and the Dominican Republic. While political democracy ostensibly reigns in the Dominican Republic, workers still suffer from government-sponsored repression when their organizing threatens the investment climate. In Haiti, unions are outlawed and no worker organizations are tolerated. When asked about this lack of labor unions, a director of the Haitian-American Chamber of Commerce gave this oblique reply: "If you were a journalist from the *Miami Herald*, I'd tell you that we don't have labor problems here in Haiti because we treat our workers so well."[1]

"There are no unions in the industrial zones," said Julio de Peña Valdéz, the director of the Dominican Republic's General Confederation of Workers. The governments, which subsidize the free zones, cooperate with the companies to keep unions out of these assembly areas. Not only are unions suppressed, but workers are often fired for any sign of resistance. "These corporations take advantage of the high levels of unemployment here to keep the workforce destabilized by continually laying off old workers and then hiring new ones," said de Peña.[2]

SUBCONTRACTING FOR EXPORT

A variety of export processing that has become very popular in the Caribbean is called international subcontracting. Rather than involving themselves directly in the Caribbean countries, many TNCs have subcontracted their production to other smaller TNCs or to Caribbean-owned businesses. Under this arrangement, the subcontractor usually supplies the factory, the management, and the employees, and contracts to manufacture a product to meet certain specifications—be it pajamas, fancy underwear, or leather handbags.

Garments, toys, furniture, and electronic/electrical products are the most common items assembled by Caribbean subcontractors. The massive growth of subcontracting in the Caribbean increases the ability of TNCs to avoid militant workers, revolutionary upheavals, and economic downturns. When workers go on strike, it is no longer the problem of the corporation but of the subcontractor. If sales slow down, a company can simply reduce or cancel its contract instead of having to close down one of its own plants. If a revolution breaks out, the company just signs another contract with an assembly firm on another island. Many subcontractors are locally owned operations, while others are often small foreign firms that do not have strong operating bases in their home countries and are not willing to take the risks of direct investment. In Barbados, 15 of the 22 firms producing for U.S. corporations have U.S. ownership.

From 1975 to 1981, the dollar value of international subcontracting in the Caribbean increased fourfold. The two leading subcontracting spots in the Caribbean are Haiti and the Dominican Republic. After Mexico, Haiti leads the entire hemisphere in subcontracting. Haitian subcontractors produce over 75 percent of the country's manufactured exports to the United States. A study by ONAPI, Haiti's industrial development agency, reported that over 70 percent of the country's garment and stuffed-toy industries were run by partially Haitian-owned firms, predominantly subcontractors.[3] An estimated 150 U.S. and 40 other foreign corporations have subcontracting arrangements in Haiti. Most U.S. firms that subcontract production to Haitian firms expect to pay less than a third of the production costs that they would pay in the United States.

Currently, over 50 percent of the Dominican Republic's manufactured exports to the United States are products assembled by subcontractors. Subcontracting operations have gone beyond traditional garment sweatshops. Barbados has several data-processing subcontractors, like the U.S. firms Dataram and Satellite Data Corporation. In these new office-work factories, Caribbean workers receive information via satellite. They process the data and then transmit it by computer back to the United States. Why send data to faraway Barbados for processing? For the same reason that toys are stuffed and baseballs are stitched in the Caribbean: cheap wages. Barbadians receive $1.50 an hour for work that earns their U.S. counterparts $4 to $12 an hour.[4] The Caribbean nations may be underdeveloped, but they certainly are not isolated from the latest trends in the transnational economy.

Caribbean Sweatshops

The Caribbean is a haven for runaway garment companies that have set up labor-intensive operations. Workers in the island factories earn $20-$50 a week and use old Singer sewing machines. Foreign garment companies have more activity in the Caribbean than any other manufacturing sector. Some of the largest apparel corporations in the world, like Esmark's Playtex and Consolidated Foods's Hanes and L'Eggs, have assembly plants in the Caribbean. Only a relatively small number of non-U.S. firms have apparel operations in the region, and most are in Haiti, where West German companies have recently set up assembly operations. Most of the apparel assembly comes not from the direct operations of TNCs, but from subcontracting firms that piece together garments for larger corporations. The Dominican Republic, Haiti, and Barbados have the most garment business in the Caribbean. In the English-speaking Caribbean, an estimated 20,000 people, mostly women, work in 750 garment factories producing primarily for the U.S. market.[5]

Garment factories in the Caribbean export bras, shoes, underwear, pajamas, gloves, dresses, and playsuits to the United States. If you wear a bra, chances are it was made in the Caribbean. More bras are supplied by Caribbean Basin countries to the U.S. market than any other manufactured product. In 1980, Haiti and the Dominican Republic supplied the U.S. market with about 3 million brassieres. The Caribbean bra industry is an extension of U.S. business: companies like Maidenform ship the straps, the hooks, and the cups to Caribbean assembly plants, where low-paid women workers stitch together the pieces into bras for U.S. women. Caribbean nations supply the United States with 20 percent of its playsuits, 23 percent of its hosiery, 15 percent of its dresses, and 19 percent of its cotton nightwear.[6] Shoe uppers (shoes without the soles) are another leading Caribbean export. After South Korea, the Dominican Republic and Haiti are the top U.S. suppliers of leather shoe uppers, and the two Caribbean countries follow Taiwan as the leading suppliers of cotton and fiber shoe uppers.

Jamaica not only has ambition to become the electronics center of the

Caribbean, but it has also set out to become the most advanced Caribbean apparel center. It launched a major campaign to train hundreds of workers and to build a complex of 20 factories to house the new investors. A USAID grant funded the international consulting firm, Kurt Salmon Associates, and Singer Company to provide pretraining for sewing-machine operators and to promote the growth of the garment industry in Jamaica. Currently, the island hosts only a few garment factories, including a subsidiary of Gulf + Western.

Next to the Gulf + Western shirt plant in the Kingston Free Zone is a jeans factory. In a recent interview the manager of the plant said that he never has any trouble with his workers: "If one of the girls is a couple of minutes late for work, she is locked out; if any of them start squawking about anything, we show them the door." Floor bosses walk the aisles to make certain productivity is kept up and talking is kept down. "We pay them a fraction of what we have to pay at our plant in Mississippi," the manager said. "Of course, our workers are all black there too. I don't mind too much. The situation is different here than in Mississippi where you can always get away from it, but here in Jamaica the blacks are everywhere."[7]

The employees of the garment factories work under highly regimented conditions and remain low-paid and unorganized mainly because of the many antilabor practices that characterize this industry. In the Dominican Republic, labor leaders have charged that Karolin, a subsidiary of Gulf + Western, regularly fires its female workers shortly before the termination of their probation periods. During probation, workers in Caribbean assembly plants receive less than permanent workers even though they usually can meet production quotas within the first few weeks of employment. More than 100 women workers at the Karolin plant in 1983 elected a committee to ask management for a raise of ten cents an hour. Fearing the slightest evidence of worker unity, Gulf + Western temporarily closed down the assembly plant, fired the workers, and requested that the Dominican military clear out the factory. The women responded by occupying a church and the National Congress to publicize their grievances. At the La Romana free zone in the Dominican Republic, the Karolin workers, who were not rehired, have become a symbol of what happens when workers raise their voices against the employment practices and low wages of foreign corporations.

CARIBBEAN COMMUNITY (Caricom)

A central part of the industrialization strategy in the English-speaking Caribbean has been the regional integration of the markets of the individual countries. The first attempt to establish such a Caribbean common market came in 1958, when the West Indies Federation was founded at the instigation of Great Britain. The British formed this political and economic federation as a way to manage their colonies better and keep them within the economic orbit of Great Britain. The West Indies Federation disintegrated shortly afterward owing to interisland rivalries and the withdrawal of Jamaica. Still recognizing the need for a regional economic union, the four largest English-speaking countries—Barbados, Trinidad, Guyana, and Jamaica—created the Caribbean Community (Caricom) in 1973. Nine other states (Antigua, Belize, Dominica, Grenada, Montserrat, St. Kitts, St. Lucia, St. Vincent, and, most recently, the Bahamas) later joined the regional union.

The principal economic objective of Caricom has been to increase the size of the Caribbean market in order to encourage new investment and the growth of profitable industries. The leaders of the Caricom nations felt industrialization by import substitution would only succeed if there was one large regional market. Caricom created a common market that liberalized trade (little or no import duties or tariffs on regional trade) between members. It also set up a high tariff wall to protect Caribbean manufacturers from the flow of competing goods produced outside the region. Besides implementing the regional common market, Caricom also was authorized by its members to support institutions and projects that improved the region's infrastructure and encouraged new private investment. Working alongside Caricom is the Caribbean Development Bank, the other leading regional economic institution. The regional integration plan formulated by Caricom was, in many ways, designed to create a framework for the development of capitalism in the region. This was in direct contrast to the visions of early trade union leaders like Grantley Adams of Barbados and T. A. Marryshow of Grenada, who had favored a socialist union of former British colonies. "We make no secret of our belief," said Adams, "that there is no hope for the West Indies unless they become a socialist commonwealth."

The industrialization program of Caricom was hardly socialist and not even nationalist. Instead, it opened the English-speaking Caribbean market to penetration by foreign investors who benefited from the expanded market. To encourage the purchase of local materials, Caricom trade guidelines established a local value-added criterion that allowed goods with a certain percentage of local inputs (about 40 to 50 percent) to circulate duty-free within the common market. However, the appendix to the Caricom treaty listed 12 pages of goods that qualified as local inputs because they were not easily produced within the region. The listed exemptions ranged from apples, grapes, rye, barley, oats, semolina, and wheat to paper, silk, wool, iron, steel, copper, and other minerals.[8] To qualify under the value-added criterion, a firm could include any of the listed exceptions, plus padded overhead expenses for transport, power, and other local services. The many exemptions allowed such products as canned tomato juice to be considered local because the metal, paper, and imported concentrates are all treated as local, even when only the tomatoes were locally produced. Even apple juice could be a local product in this tropical region under the expansive standards of the common market. This ability to include imported components in the assembly of "local" products opened the market to many finishing-touch industries. Not only was the established value-added criterion absurdly loose, but it was also not enforced. The Caricom agency established to monitor the value-added regulation now concentrates on promoting industrial development, not regulating it. In 1982, Caricom introduced slightly better regulations to encourage the use of more Caribbean inputs into manufacturing.

As a result of Caricom's hesitancy to control and direct the flow of foreign investment, the region is still not economically integrated. Most nations have stronger connections to the United States, Great Britain, and Canada than to each other. Rather than promoting new local industrialization, Caricom protected already existing Caribbean companies and opened up the region for investment by transnational firms. As a consequence of Caricom's failure to take control of economic development, there has been further polarization between the more- and less-developed nations. Foreign and regional capital, in the absence of any restrictions, flowed to the more developed nations, thus increasing their dominance in regional affairs.

Foreign firms have set up assembly operations in the Caribbean, mainly in Jamaica and Trinidad, to take advantage of the wider Caribbean market. After a decade of regional integration, the less-developed nations of the community still drag economically behind the four more developed nations. Ninety-five percent of the exports within Caricom come from Guyana, Barbados, Jamaica, and Trinidad, the latter two benefiting the most from the Caricom market.

Economist Clive Thomas, while critical of Caricom policies that have opened the region to foreign corporate penetration, said the true weakness of Caricom comes from the economic structures of the individual country members. He has argued for a socialist alternative at the national level.

> If at a national level the multinational corporations dominate, at the regional level they cannot but do otherwise. If at a national level feudal relations dominate in the countryside, how can it be otherwise at the regional level? If we are seeking to promote capitalist advance at the national level, at the regional level the same must happen. The fact of operating regionally cannot itself resolve the basic national issues of ownership and control by the people

over the means of production, of the struggle to develop a just, human and socialist society, or the need to effectively secure the development of social and political life.[9]

Caricom by and large failed to create a regional economy: the Caribbean's most important economic sectors—tourism, transport, export-agriculture, bauxite, energy—remain unintegrated and in the control of TNCs. Each country still produces what it does not consume and consumes what it does not produce. Regional trade as a percentage of total trade has not increased since the founding of the common market, and imports from outside the region constitute more than 90 percent of total imports to the Caricom nations. The lack of unity among Caricom nations could not have been illustrated more clearly than by the U.S. invasion of Grenada. Trinidad—only 90 miles away from Grenada—was not even consulted by the other Caribbean nations before the invasion.

The invasion of Grenada caused a severe split in Caricom between Guyana and Trinidad, who criticized U.S. intervention, and the organization's other members. Jamaica and Dominica, the two close U.S. allies in the region, are pushing for Caricom to set political standards for membership and increase the emphasis on foreign investment. Interregional trade wars, attempts to ostracize pre-invasion Grenada, and bilateral alliances with the United States all constitute the dog-eat-dog mentality that has characterized Caricom relations since 1980. "The politics of regional integration has disappeared from the agenda of most Caribbean leaders," observed Clive Thomas. "It is as if we have forgotten that no single territory can have a future on its own."[10]

Although Caricom has made some notable achievements, such as its support for the University of the West Indies, the Caribbean Food Corporation marketing and distribution arrangement, and the West Indies Shipping Corporation, Caricom has had very limited success in developing an integrated Caribbean economy and in improving the well-being of the Caribbean people.

CORPORATE CARIBBEAN HOLIDAYS

Each island has its own industrial promotion agency that tries to lure foreign companies with promises of profit. The promotion agents proudly hand out glossy brochures with varieties of the same come-ons: cheap labor, stable governments, tax holidays, and factory shells ready for occupancy. What used to be regarded as incentives for investment have become an expected part of investing in the Caribbean. Nowadays, a foreign firm probably would not consider a location that did not offer unrestricted remission of profits, tax holidays of ten years or more, duty-free imports of machinery and raw material, and training programs for its workers. The tiny Caribbean islands compete among one another and other third world countries to offer the most attractive package of incentives for prospective investors. "Incentives are an integral part of the Haitian posture as a nation of unlimited business opportunities," noted an official of Haiti's industrial development agency. Some extend the tax holiday to 25 years, others offer to waive all licenses and fees, and many now compete to offer the lowest rents and utility rates.

If the foreign company does not have enough ready capital, no matter, because most Caribbean nations make local financing available even for initial investment costs. A prominent part of the export-oriented industrial development strategy is free-trade zones, where imports enter and exports leave duty-free. The approximately 16 free zones that now exist in the Caribbean generally have no unions. The World Bank, Caribbean Development Bank, Inter-American Development Bank, and many bilateral agencies like USAID subsidize the cost of these incentives for investment by building the industrial zones, paying for promotional brochures, providing loan capital, and underwriting training programs. All the money and effort spent on offering the best investment deal, however, probably does little to influence a decision by an investor, because the incentives are much the same the world over. Political stability, availability of water and electricity, wage differentials and the level of worker organizing, transportation costs, and the general living conditions for company managers are long-term factors that most countries can do little to change overnight.

Finding a Cheap Twin

Puerto Rico, which has been losing factories to islands with even cheaper labor, is promoting the "twin-plant" concept in the Caribbean. José Madera, the administrator of Puerto Rico's industrial development organization, said, "Our position is that, if certain labor-intensive processes are not profitable in Puerto Rico, then it is in our interest that they be performed near Puerto Rico."[11] Under the twin-plant program, factories will use Puerto Rico as the base for their Caribbean operations. In the U.S. territory, the companies will concentrate on the more capital-intensive portions of manufacturing. Then, for the routine labor-intensive phases, the companies will open assembly plants in Haiti, the Dominican Republic, or other Caribbean islands that offer low wages. Among the corporations that have such twin-plant arrangements are GTE, Esmark's Playtex, Intel, Dwyer Instruments, and Honeywell. Many corporations involved in twin plants take advantage of Puerto Rico's special tax breaks

TABLE 3B
TNC MANUFACTURERS IN THE CARIBBEAN
(Selected Listing) (Excluding Puerto Rico)

Product	Company
Cosmetics	Chesebrough Ponds, Eli Lilly, Esmark (Max Factor), Mennen, Revlon, Sterling Drug
Electronics	Becton Dickinson, Bendix, Digital, GTE, Hitachi (Japan), Intel, Microdata, Motorola, Pico Electronics, Thompson Brandt (France), TRW
Fertilizer	Amoco, Union Commercial, Williams Companies, WR Grace
Garments	Bata (Canada), Consolidated Foods (L'Eggs), Esmark (Playtex), Gulf+Western (Kayser Roth), Interco (Florsheim), Lovable, Maidenform, Manhattan Industries
Home Products	Colgate-Palmolive, Gillette, Johnson & Johnson, Procter & Gamble, Unilever (UK-Netherlands)
Industrial Products	American Can, Continental Screw, Crown Cork & Seal, Cutler Hammer Eaton, Hagemeyer (Netherlands), Metal Box (UK), Ray-O-Vac, Royal Packaging, Van Leer (Netherlands), Swedish Match (Sweden)
Industrial and Agricultural Products	Bayer (West Germany), Dow Chemical, DuPont, Henkel (West Germany), Mobil Oil, Molson (Canada, Diversey), Monsanto, Sophus Berendensen (Denmark, Rentokil), Shell, Standard Oil of California (Chevron's Ortho), Velsicol (Northwest Industries)
Paints	Berger Paint (UK), Brandram-Henderson (UK), Rohm & Haas, Sherwin-Williams
Pharmaceutical	Abbott, Bristol-Myers, Cooper Labs, Pfizer, Sterling
Tires	Dunlop (UK), Firestone, General Tire, Goodyear, Uniroyal

Source: The Resource Center, Compilation of Corporations, 1984

under the 936 program, which exempts firms from federal income taxes. Other twin-plant companies in Puerto Rico subcontract assembly work to other firms in islands with cheap labor.

One large subcontractor, Haiti's General Assembly, owned by one of Haiti's wealthiest families, assembles products for a number of U.S. corporations with operations in Puerto Rico. In exchange for the contract, General Assembly pays for all overhead, supervision, social security, and training. Rudy Thomasson, general manager of Power Parts of Haiti, said that the twin-plant system between Puerto Rico and Haiti allowed the U.S. territory to compete effectively against countries like Taiwan and Korea.[12] At the industrial park in Port-au-Prince, manager George Elies remarked: "Puerto Rico is dying of attrition and is no longer competitive because of its high wages. I told the industrial development people in San Juan: 'You need Haiti now, and Haiti needs Puerto Rico.'" Elies noted that plants are closing down in other parts of the world, such as the Philippines, to come to Haiti, and, with the twin-plant arrangement with Puerto Rico, Haiti can attract yet more assembly business.[13]

In addition to its connections with Haiti, Puerto Rico has been working closely with Jamaica to develop a twin-plant system in line with U.S. government efforts to use Puerto Rico to keep the Caribbean economically tied to the United States. Proposed twin-plant industries include the molding of plastic dolls in Puerto Rico, with the sewing of doll dresses done by the cheap labor in Jamaica, and the manufacture of raw printed-circuit boards in Puerto Rico while Jamaican workers assemble and place the electronic components onto the boards.

THE PRIVATE LOBBY

The Caribbean business community is getting organized—"American style." As part of the U.S. emphasis on the Caribbean, the U.S. government and the U.S. private sector are working to ensure that the interests of business, not necessarily local business, are in the forefront of regional political and economic decisions. This is not a new focus for U.S. Caribbean policy, but the magnitude of the campaign has escalated since Ronald Reagan entered the White House.

U.S. TNCs have always been conscious of the need for a strong lobbying and public relations effort to represent their concerns in Latin America and the Caribbean. The two main organizations of this type have been the Council of the Americas and the Association of Chambers of Commerce in Latin America (ACCLA). Many corporate sponsors of the Council of the Americas have operations in the Caribbean: Citibank, Merck, RJ Reynolds, Alcoa, Johnson & Johnson, BankAmerica, Southeast First National Bank of Miami, International Basic Economy Corporation, and Bechtel.

Chambers of commerce are as much a feature of most American cities as city hall. U.S. businesses thought it was a good idea to establish similar organizations throughout the hemisphere. Representing all these U.S. chambers in the region, ACCLA plays a powerful lobbying role in the corridors of the U.S. Capitol. Alexander Perry, Jr., the president of AC-CLA, explained: "Our opinion is sought after in Washington on many issues. We get involved not only in the relationship between the United

States and Latin America but in their relationship with our administration in the United States."[14] Stanley Urban, the president of a prominent U.S. business organization in the Caribbean, the Haitian-American Chamber of Commerce, has expressed strong opinions on the relationship between the people of Haiti and its government. At an ACCLA conference in 1982, Urban said: "I honestly believe that a dictatorship is the best form of government for these people [Haitians]. There are six million illiterates on that island. Think what the Ruskies could do there."[15]

During the Carter administration, the founding of the Committee for the Caribbean indicated special attention by the U.S. corporate community to the Caribbean Basin. The Committee for the Caribbean turned out to be the forerunner of a more powerful and better-funded organization called Caribbean/Central America Action (CCAA). The chairperson of Tesoro Petroleum, Robert West, had been the main organizer of the committee and became the first president of CCAA. In 1979, the Committee for the Caribbean, together with the American Enterprise Institute and the Council of the Americas, sponsored the first Miami Conference to promote foreign investment in the Caribbean Basin. At that conference, Robert West said that the U.S. private sector was "an untapped resource that can provide far more investment capital than all the aid the U.S. government can ever offer."[16]

All 56 of the original corporate contributors to CCAA have identifiable interests in the Caribbean (Table 3C), and the large majority have interests in Central America. The business organization receives a portion of its funds from the federal government and coordinates its own programs with the activities of the Overseas Private Investment Corporation (OPIC), USAID, and the Department of Commerce. The CCAA has two chief functions: to promote new foreign investment in the Caribbean Basin, and to build a network of private-sector organizations in the region. Both functions operate in conjunction with the overall strategy of the Caribbean Basin Initiative. CCAA promotes foreign investment by publishing a series of expensive booklets that advertise the opportunities for profit in the region.

Executive director Peter Johnson described the role of CCAA as a broker arranging deals between U.S. firms and local business owners in the Caribbean Basin. Johnson said, "Although multinational corporations account for much of the foreign investment in the region, CCAA will be emphasizing investments by small- to medium-sized U.S. businesses." Each year the organization sponsors the Miami Conference to put U.S. investors in touch with Caribbean Basin politicians and business owners. It also cohosts telemission conferences that provide direct television communication between U.S. corporate representatives and the private sector in the Caribbean.

TABLE 3C
CORPORATE SUPPORTERS OF CCAA

Aluminum Company of America	IBM World Trade Americas Far
Amerada Hess	East Corporation
Amoco Foundation	Grand Metropolitan
Amoco International Oil	InterNorth
Arnold & Porter	Litwin Engineers & Constructors
Arthur D Little International	Maidenform
Ashland Oil	Miami Herald Publishing
Atlantic Richfield	Mobil Oil
Consolidated Foods	Occidental Petroleum
Bank of America National Trust	Pan American World Airways
and Savings Association	Peoples Energy
Caribbean Holidays	PepsiCo
Charter Company	IC Industries
Chase Manhattan Bank	Procter & Gamble
Citibank	Reynolds Metals
Coca-Cola	Rosario Dominicana
Continental Telephone	Santa Fe Industries
Control Data	RJ Reynolds
EF Hutton	Shrimp Culture
Eastern Airlines	Southeast First National Bank of
Exxon	Miami
General Electric	Tenneco
General Foods	Tesoro Petroleum
Grace Foundation	Texaco
Gulf + Western	Touche Ross
HB Fuller	Tropical Shipping and
Hvide Shipping	Construction
	United Brands

Source: CCAA Fact Sheet, 1981

To increase the connections between the private sectors in the U.S. and the Caribbean, CCAA has created a system of twin chambers. Throughout the United States, from Houston to Providence, chambers of commerce have linked up with Caribbean private-sector organizations as twins. Business people from New Haven, Connecticut, now go on "get-acquainted" tours of Montserrat. Chamber members from Richmond, Virginia, are attempting to establish a free-trade zone in the U.S. Virgin Islands that will work with Richmond's free zone, and the Houston chamber now hosts a Jamaica Day each year. In another part of this chamber communication program, CCAA's computer data base, Caribbean Basin Information Network, provides current investment information to the U.S. and Caribbean private sectors.

David Rockefeller, the chairperson of CCAA, also helped organize the CBI Coalition and the U.S. Business Committee on Jamaica. He formerly served as chairperson of Chase Manhattan, which is the leading U.S. bank in Central America and has 34 commercial branches in 11 Caribbean states. Rockefeller also founded the Council of the Americas, which now functions under the aegis of the Americas Society, another Rockefeller-supported organization.

Technology Contracts—A Questionable Deal

A recent and rapidly expanding form of TNC control in the Caribbean industrial sector comes under the broad category of technology contracts. The lack of capital is only a symptom of underdevelopment in the Caribbean. The Caribbean nations also lack the machines and equipment necessary for modern agricultural and industrial production. They also do not have the know-how to use this new technology or the production methods that make business competitive. Rather than directly invest in the region, a corporation will sell its technology, its patented production methods, and its advisers to locally owned firms. Sometimes these contracts between TNCs and third world companies are called "transfer of technology" agreements.

Many foreign firms have discovered that they can arrange contracts that allow locally owned firms to use their technology for a high price or in exchange for equity participation in the company. Transnational corporations favor direct ownership when technology is more difficult to control. TNCs fear that once the local firms copy the technology, they will cancel the contract with the corporation. When the technology cannot be easily copied or transferred, however, the TNCs are often content with a contract without any direct ownership.

Examples of technology contracts include a dairy-processing firm in Trinidad that operates under a license from Nestlé, a welding company in Jamaica that has a license from a large Swiss corporation, and a soap factory in Dominica that produces according to a formula supplied by Lever Brothers (Unilever). Almost all engineering consultants hired by Caribbean governments come from North America or Europe. The Barbados Industrial Development Corporation has found that promises by foreign investors that they would transfer technology and train local managers have been largely unfulfilled. As its recent Development Plan admits: "The Barbados economy is still wedded to an imitative technology and a foreign managerial elite."[17]

Jamaican economist Norman Girvan notes, "Much of what is called technology transfer is not genuine transfer but transfer of artifacts, not knowledge."[18] What the Caribbean nations receive are operating instructions for technology but never a transfer of the knowledge to create technology appropriate to their particular requirements. The Caribbean nations have grown dependent on technology that often is not applicable to their real needs. Highly capital-intensive technology does not tap the large numbers of unemployed, and it strains the foreign-exchange supply to buy expensive foreign machinery. In the cases of both the sugar and the petroleum industries, technological advances have caused severe cutbacks in the workforce.

Rather than starting from the premise that development should fully employ the land and labor of a country, technology-led economic development has benefited only the narrow interests of the local business elite and the foreign investors. "The forms in which technology is imported into the Caribbean tend to frustrate local technological development and perpetuate technological dependence," maintains Girvan. He explains that he is not arguing "against the use of foreign technology but rather against passive, undiscriminating importation where critical decisions are all taken externally."[19]

TRANSNATIONAL SERVICES

Hundreds of TNCs operate in the Caribbean in the service sector. Although they have little direct investment in the region, these TNCs pervade the Caribbean and dominate the following businesses: construction, agricultural equipment sales, financial services, shipping, and office equipment sales. The major TNCs in transportation rentals—Hertz (RCA), Avis (Esmark), and National Rent-A-Car—appear in almost every Caribbean airport. Retail sales is one section of the service sector that is relatively free of TNCs, except for an occasional Woolworth's or a sales outlet for Westinghouse. TNCs, however, own most of the region's communications industry. The communications giants—ITT, RCA, GTE, and Cable & Wireless (UK)—can be found throughout the Caribbean, as can others like Anglo Canadian Telephone, BICC (UK), and Commonwealth Development (UK).

Because just about everything the Caribbean nations import or export is handled by foreign firms, shipping services constitute a major loss of Caribbean foreign-exchange reserves. Although Jamaica and Guyana have nationalized their sugar industries, they still rely on the shipping subsidiaries of Tate & Lyle (Sugar Line and Anchor Line) and Booker McConnell (Booker Steamship). Geest Line of Geest Industries is another major shipping company in the region, while all the major bauxite TNCs have their own shipping companies.

The changing habits of the Caribbean are encouraged by advertising agencies in Miami or New York, as well as by U.S. subsidiaries scattered throughout the Caribbean, especially in Puerto Rico. Of the world's 11 top advertising firms, seven have offices in the Caribbean: J. Walter Thompson; Young & Rubicam; Interpublic/McCann-Erickson; BBDO; Leo Burnett; Foote, Cone & Belding; and Norman, Craig & Kummel. The world's fourth-largest agency, the Interpublic Group, has offices in Puerto Rico, Barbados, Jamaica, and Trinidad.

The Business of Financial Consulting

The world's largest accounting firms not only provide financial services for the TNCs throughout the Caribbean but also do the accounting for all bilateral and multilateral programs, as well as for the Caribbean governments themselves. The four major firms and the number of countries in which they have offices are: Touche Ross (12), Peat, Marwick, & Mitchell (10), Price Waterhouse (8), and Coopers & Lybrand (6). Others doing business in the Caribbean include Arthur Young, Taylor & Woodrow (UK), Ernst & Whinney, Arthur Anderson, and Merrill Lynch. Like the other companies, the TNC accounting firm Coopers & Lybrand extends its activities far beyond providing accounting services for businesses. It has a major contract with USAID to study the investment potential of several Caribbean countries and the possibilities of establishing joint ventures with Caribbean businesses. Because of that arrangement Coopers & Lybrand has obtained other contracts with Caribbean governments to advise them on industrial promotion for foreign investment. The company often serves corporations that decide to invest in the Caribbean. So widespread are its activities in this sector that one USAID official in Barbados commented, "Sometimes I wonder if AID isn't really working for Coopers & Lybrand rather than the other way around."[20]

In the Dominican Republic, the eight largest accounting firms are all foreign companies, of which all but one started doing business in the country after the U.S. military occupation in 1965. They came to the Dominican Republic to offer financial services to the many foreign corporations that were investing in the country. No government agency regulates or sets standards for accountants, but the Institute of Certified Public Accountants has a commission that sets operating standards. Representatives of six large foreign corporations serve on this standards commission, which has no representatives from the much smaller local accounting firms.

The accounting TNCs have penetrated every private and government sector in the Dominican Republic. Because all bilateral and multilateral contracts require the use of "internationally recognized accounting firms," the foreign accounting companies and their affiliates gain access to the country's national accounts. In the Dominican Republic, these firms serve as the accountants for the State Sugar Council, the Dominican Electricity Corporation, and the State Corporation of Public Enterprises, as well as having contracts with the Central Bank. Through their involvement in the national accounts, foreign accounting firms learn a great deal about the country's economy, knowledge that can be put to profitable use by their transnational clients. The accounting companies also exercise great influence over the state to direct its finances in ways that are more acceptable to the objectives of foreign corporations and international agencies than to the Dominican people.

INDUSTRIALIZATION BY IMITATION

The two key elements of the Caribbean development strategy, import substitution and industrialization by invitation, have both failed to develop the economy of the region. Plans for the creation of import-substitution industries have promoted the duplication of high-cost industries and led to the domination of regional trade by TNCs and a few Caribbean industrialists. The industries have tended to rely more on imported inputs than on the use of local materials.

Despite the lack of evidence that the strategy has made any lasting contribution to the economy in the last 20 years, industrialization by invitation has, once again in the early 1980s, become the economic-development fad of the Caribbean. The Reagan administration promised to aid the friendly Caribbean nations, like Jamaica and Dominica, in their efforts to attract investment from the United States. Commenting on this trend in Jamaica, its former prime minister Michael Manley said:

> Seaga, during the campaign, committed himself to a resurrected Puerto Rican model. He didn't like to use the word 'Puerto Rico,' because it's been discredited, so he preferred to talk about the countries of the Far East. But essentially the model is the same. In Puerto Rico, after the most massive foreign-investment program in the world over the last thirty years, it has produced 25 to 30 percent unemployment, with 50 percent of the people on food stamps and a massive migration to the United States. The model does what all models of a colonial nature do—it increases dependence. Seaga began with the very essence of a dependent capitalist strategy of development—consumer satisfaction, massive foreign capital, deregulation of the economy. We believe completely in the reverse, in inviting people to face self-restraint so as to provide the internal basis for a self-reliant economy.[21]

The promotion of industrialization by attracting assembly plants to the region has led to competition between the islands and to internal economic policies that favor foreign investors over the rights of workers to a decent wage. State funds are not directed toward projects that directly satisfy basic needs but go instead to print fancy promotional materials, construct expensive infrastructure, and build industrial parks for prospective investors. Industrialization is a "misnomer," says Felipe Vicini, a member of the Dominican Republic business elite. "We are just getting packaging work. And do you know what the industry will do when it finds a cheaper source of labor somewhere else?" he asks. "Just what they did in coming here: They take a wrench and undo four bolts, remove their equipment, crate it up and ship it off."[22]

The focus on the need for foreign investment has reduced emphasis on regional economic strategies and on the need to build industries that process local materials. For the time being, however, most Caribbean nations have eschewed other development strategies in favor of the premise of dependency capitalism. Show us how capitalism works, pleaded Prime Minister Eugenia Charles of Dominica. "We are all mimics at heart and imitative of the things we see and associate with."[23]

Tourism:

THE SUN-LUST INDUSTRY

*Visit a plantation with its original 18th century splendor
and running much the same way for hundreds of years.*
—Jamaican tourist promotion brochure

Every night the same songs are requested in the lounge of the British
Colonial Sheraton in Nassau. The newly arrived, sunburned batch of
tourists drink rum punches while listening to the standard Harry Belafonte rendition of the Caribbean banana-boat song "Day-O" and popular
calypso or reggae tunes. Outside, the hustlers on the street "pssst" pass-
ersby with whispered offers of "ganja," "white nose candy," and "black
pussy." In St. Lucia, amused little kids stand on the beach staring onto
the terrace of the Couples resort where rows of visiting white women are
learning to sway their hips and shoulders as the natives do.

In Jamaica, you can stay at any number of hotels, such as the Royal
Caribbean with a choice of superior or deluxe accommodations. Or you
can "experience complete freedom" at the Hedonism II resort, where
you pay for your drink with a plastic shark's tooth. On the beaches at
Ocho Rios, the Caribbean beach boys in their swim briefs make the rounds
of female sunbathers to sell their bodies to white women for a day of
drinks and food, and maybe more. Native craftswomen in the straw markets patiently pose to have their pictures taken again and again, while
the tourists bargain for their straw baskets and hats in the manner ad-
vised by their tourist manuals. In Haiti, you can sign guest registries that
include the names of the Rolling Stones, Barbara Walters, and other jetsetters. Would-be voodoo priests earn $5 a night swallowing burning coals
and eating glass at the nightclubs. Everywhere artists try to sell paintings
and carvings that evoke all the tragedy and the vitality of the Haitian
people.

Tourists traveling to Cuba and preinvasion Grenada received warnings that the U.S. State Department would not be responsible for their
safety. Yet the State Department seemed unconcerned about the gun
battles waged in the streets of Kingston during the 1980 elections. In
Barbados, young black men wearing "Beach Attendant" T-shirts and
practiced smiles tend sunburning tourists, and in the evening black-tied

waiters serve piña coladas and coconut crushes. Throughout the Caribbean (but unseen by the tourists) oil refineries, hotels, restaurants, and Bacardi rum distilleries spew waste into emerald waters. Each day, cruise ships pass by on their weekly tours of paradise.

"Sun-lust tourism" is the label the travel industry has for the Caribbean tour business. Eastern Airlines advertises Caribbean vacations with billboards showing a half-clad woman discarding her clothes with the words, "Take off . . . for the Caribbean." Lower air fares and chartered tours brought the Caribbean within the financial reach of the middle class, but the DuPonts, Mellons, and Rockefellers still maintain their own tradition of elite and secluded Caribbean vacations. Every year about 11 million tourists travel to the Caribbean (including those in cruise stops).

TOURING WITH THE TRANSNATIONALS

If you are a tourist in the Caribbean, it is easy to feel at home. For the U.S. tourist, there are thirteen Holiday Inns, nine Hiltons, and nine Sheratons throughout the area. A traveler from Great Britain can lodge in any one of eight Trust House Fortes or at any one of the five hotels owned by Grand Metropolitan. The Club Méditerranée of Paris offers seven resort hotels throughout the Caribbean for those who want a French flavor to their vacations.

Tourism is big business—the second largest international business after petroleum.[1] Because tourism is so geographically scattered, the tourism industry makes perfect transnational business sense. A diversified company can profit from many different aspects of the industry. Transworld Airlines (TWA), for example, not only flies passengers around the globe but also can arrange all their vacation plans through its subsidiaries, Getaway Tours and Hilton Tours. If you are traveling on business, you may go to a convention center managed by another TWA subsidiary and stay at the nearby Hilton Inn. And when hunger strikes, TWA's Sparton Food System will be there to serve you.

ITT can make you feel at home in a Sheraton Inn and bring you closer to home through its international communications system. Trust House Forte has its own travel service, hotel management company, and airport service firm, and a restaurant subsidiary named Colony Foods. Holiday Inns can easily set up a new hotel in the most remote location by relying on the services of its subsidiary Inn Keeper Supply Company, which designs, engineers, and furnishes new Holiday Inns. Another subsidiary, called Inn Care, will take care of the day-to-day needs of the inn. The Dohrmann Company, another Holiday Inns firm, distributes restaurant supplies; and tagging along are the two restaurant companies, Pipers and Perkins. In the Dominican Republic, Gulf + Western built up a fully integrated tourism industry around its company town of La Romana in the center of the Dominican sugarcane belt. It has its own transportation company and airstrip to guarantee the arrival of its hotel guests, who dine on steak from a G + W cattle ranch and vegetables from a G + W farm.

In the Caribbean, TNCs have controlled the development of the tourism sector and have reaped the bulk of the industry's profits. Large foreign firms are invariably present in four phases of the industry: airlines, hotels, services, and tour operators. The Caribbean islands depend on the foreign airlines for most of their tourist traffic; yet the decisions regarding flight destinations and scheduling remain almost totally beyond the control of these small nations. Not only do the major airlines transport the tourists, but they also frequently profit from other parts of the tourist trade, such as the tour operating business (Table 4A). While two-thirds of TWA's revenue comes from its airline business, two-thirds of its *profits* come from its hotel and food business.[2]

The TNC innkeepers have opened their doors around the globe. All of the following travel TNCs have at least five hotels in the Caribbean: Club Méditerranée, Commonwealth Holiday Inns of Canada (Scott's Hospitality), Hilton International, Holiday Inns, Intercontinental Hotels (Grand Metropolitan), Sheraton Hotels (ITT), and Trust House Forte.[3] Another important hotel company is Gulf + Western, which has numerous hotels and assorted travel services in the Dominican Republic. The prevailing presence of the TNCs in the Caribbean is a relatively recent phenomenon: 60 percent of the TNC hotels have set up operations in the region since 1970.[4] Like other TNCs, the hotel companies have diversified into other businesses, many of which directly complement their travel accommodations operations.

Alternative Forms of Control

Many Caribbean hotels are owned by small foreign firms or by individual foreigners. Generally, however, the executive hotels in the cities and the luxury resorts have larger corporate owners. The average number of rooms for the TNC hotels in the Caribbean varies from 117 rooms per hotel in Barbados to 379 rooms in Jamaica. Direct equity ownership is a fading form of transnational arrangement, especially in the Caribbean. Becoming ever more common are contract management agreements, licensing, franchises, and technical service arrangements. A United Nations survey found that only 20 percent of the TNC-associated hotels had TNC ownership, while 8 percent were franchises, 22 percent had licenses, and 49 percent had management contracts.[5] These alternative forms of investment allow the corporation to free itself from the risks of direct ownership and to concentrate on selling its name, trademarks, and

TABLE 4A
AIRLINE AND RELATED TRAVEL BUSINESS

Company	Caribbean Operations
American Airlines	Flagship International (hotel food and management services), Sky Chefs (inflight catering)
Air Canada	Venturex (tour operator), Air Jamaica (26% owned)
Air France	Sotair (tour operator), Tourisme France International (tour operator), Hotels Meridien, Air Guadaloupe (45%), Air Charter International, Servair (catering affiliated with Marriott), Sodetair (forwarding agent)
British Airways	Tour operators: Alta Holidays, Enterprise Holidays, Martin Rooks, Silver Wing, Airway Holidays, Trust House Forte Travel (30%). Other interests: British Overseas Air Charter, International Aeradio (51%) (T&T), Aircraft Services (35%) (Bermuda), Caribbean Telecom Ltd (42%) (T&T), Corntech (100%) (Jamaica), Airport Catering, Engine Overhaul
Eastern	Dorado Beach Estates (PR), Dorado Beach Development (PR), ETC Travel Club
KLM	Holland International Travel Group (tour operator), Curacao Plaza Hotel, Hilton Hotel (Netherlands Antilles), Torarica Hotel (Suriname)
Pan American World Airways	Pan Am's World Tours (tour operator), charter operations including Caribbean, Hadrian (Bermuda), International Aeradio (T&T)
Transworld Airlines	Getaway Tours (tour operators), Hilton International, Convention Center (operator) (PR), Sparton Food Hotel Equipment, Hilton Tours

Source: The Resource Center, Compilation of Corporations, 1984

services. Often, as has happened in Jamaica, foreign corporations suddenly withdraw their investments, forcing the government to assume ownership of the hotels. Later the companies return to offer their management services after the government has failed to make a go of the hotel business.

To receive a Holiday Inns license, a hotel owner pays an initial fee of $300 a room and a 4 percent royalty on gross room revenues. In return, the corporation trains management, inspects the hotel, and provides manuals and training films for the staff. Another 2 percent royalty permits the hotel to hook into Holiday Inns' international reservation service.[6] A more expensive and more common plan is the management contract, whereby the hotel owner hires an international firm to do everything but hold equity in the hotel. The responsibilities of the corporate management team range from designing the hotel to managing daily operations. Cost overruns caused by spendthrift managers frequently plague management contracts because management decisions are no longer made by the more cost-conscious owners.

One study of these indirect forms of control found that in almost every case in which a TNC operation had been unsatisfactory in the Caribbean, the TNC had no direct financial involvement in the hotel. In contrast, in all cases where the hotel-keeping experience was satisfactory, the TNC had direct financial input.[7] Caribbean governments that have sought an ownership position in the tourism industry to increase foreign-exchange earnings often find that foreign-exchange reserves are being drained by a steady flow of fees, royalties, and commissions to the transnational corporations.

Tour Operators

An important part of the tourism industry cannot even be found in the Caribbean phone books, but its influence is decisive in the region's development. This is the business of the tour operators, who design wholesale package vacations that include air fare, ground transportation, accommodations, meals, and entertainment. Virtually all the companies that package Caribbean tours have their offices outside the Caribbean. From Great Britain, Thomson Travel controls one-fifth of the international tour market; Silver Wing, Cosmos Holidays, and Horizon Midland also control substantial portions of the market.[8] The increasing cost of chartering tours and the prohibitive expense of advertising have forced many smaller firms out of the competition. The two largest British tour operators charter tours with their associated airlines: Thomson Travel with Britannia Airways and Silver Wing with British Airways. The hotel chain Trust House Forte also has associations with British Airways. Canada's Suntours, which is partially owned by Royal Bank of Canada, has its own charter air service as well as several Caribbean hotels. In any given year Suntours handles more Caribbean tourists than any single Eastern Caribbean island.[9] The wholesale tour business in the United States is less concentrated, although most of the major airlines have affiliated tour-operator companies. Pan American has Pan Am's World, TWA has Getaway Tours, and Eastern has ETC Travel Club.

Tour operators also have ties with the financial sector. Cartan Tours is part of AVCI Financial Services, which promotes the Carte Blanche credit card. If you have American Express, you are fully covered in the Caribbean. Both Haley Travel and American Express Travel belong to American Express. The company's regional subsidiaries include Shearson/ American Express (Puerto Rico) and American Express Travel Services (T&T, USVI, and Jamaica). Barclays Bank of London owns Thomas Cook and Sons, a company that conveniently both arranges tour plans and sells travelers' checks.

The capability to direct the flow of the tourist trade puts the tour operator in a powerful position relative to local interests. The tour operators can pressure local hoteliers to drop their rates or face a loss of business. Particularly vulnerable to this type of commercial blackmail are regions like the Caribbean, where room occupancy rates are already dangerously low. The domination of the industry by the foreign tour operators damages the chances of small islands or new locations to develop a new tourism business, because operators tend to stick to time-proven tours. Conversely, a local hotelier may one day find that the flow of tourists has suddenly dried up simply because one tour operator in London, Montreal, or New York decided to switch the destinations of the tours.

Tour operators contribute to the foreign-exchange crisis in the Caribbean through their prepayment policies. Tourists, particularly those on prepaid tours, spend almost all their vacation allowance in their home country before ever leaving for the Caribbean. Owing to the transnational nature of the business, payments for services actually delivered in the Caribbean go directly to the New York headquarters of Sheraton or Hertz, never even passing through agency offices in Jamaica or the Dominican Republic.

Cruising the Caribbean

A growing number of tourists experience the Caribbean from the deck of an ocean liner. Berths on these immense white Love Boats cost from $100 to $300 a day, and they depart regularly from Miami, Port Everglades, San Juan, and New York on their island-hopping cruises through the Caribbean Sea. The major lines cruising the Caribbean are: Norwegian Caribbean, Carnival Cruise, Royal Caribbean, Princess, Costa, Holland America, and Cunard.

Cruising is a deluxe holiday, but hardly an ideal way to see the islands. The cruise ships linger for only a few hours at each port, giving the passengers just enough time for some quick shopping. The ships are self-contained vacations. One cruise company, the Norwegian Caribbean, boasts that its flagship, SS *Norway*, is the "Playground of the Caribbean." "There's never been a cruise ship like her," says the company's brochure. "She's taller than most buildings and longer than six city blocks. You'll find a variety of bars, continental cafes, even an old fashioned ice cream parlor, and the most modern space-age electronic games room at sea. Here too is a beautiful duty-free shopping arcade with a two-story drug store and boutiques specializing in goods from around the world." On the SS *Norway* you can eat eight times a day if you so desire, meet NFL football stars on Sundays, and enjoy entertainment by the greatest names in show business.

The cruise ships feature golfing greens, casinos, exercise clinics, and classes in art, financial planning, and home computers. In its brochure, Royal Caribbean Cruise Line says, "One of the greatest compliments passengers can pay us is when we come into port and they don't leave the ship." There is little interaction between the passengers and the economy and population of the islands they visit. Most of the money spent goes to duty-free shops specializing in imports from around the world. According to one cruise ship promotion: "You will enjoy shopping for English bone china, Irish linen, Scottish tweeds, antiques, and exotic liqueurs." The center of duty-free shopping is St. Thomas in the Virgin Islands, which attracts more cruise-ship spending than the combined amount received by seven other major Caribbean destinations. A study of Guadeloupe found that 20 percent of the cruise visitors never went ashore, and that those who did leave ship spent an average of only $9 when in port.[10] One of every three Caribbean tourists arrives in a cruise ship, but the cruise business contributes only 5 percent of the foreign-exchange earnings of the region's tourism industry.[11] Harbor dues, dock labor, and taxi services are often the only direct benefits of the cruise-ship arrivals. Most cruise passengers return home without ever having tasted local cooking or talked to an islander, with the exception perhaps of a waiter working aboard the cruise ship.

Although the cruise business, like the rest of Caribbean tourism, has suffered from the effects of world recession, visiting the Caribbean in *Love Boat* style is still a popular alternative to air travel. Along with the total entertainment atmosphere offered by the cruises, tourists like the security of the ships and the isolation they offer from the stark realities of Caribbean poverty. At nightfall, the gaily lit ship, like a floating carnival, weighs anchor and heads out to sea, with snatches of party music drifting back to the darkening island.

AID FOR TOURISM

Tourism is a subsidized business. Foreign and local governments and multilateral institutions like the World Bank build roads for the tourism industry, expand airports, train hotel workers, and offer generous tax incentives for investment in tourism. Caribbean governments place more emphasis on infrastructure investments than would normally be provided, since tourists have higher expectations for all the modern conveniences. Island residents certainly take advantage of improvements in roads, utilities, and municipal services, but it is these residents who pay for the services, not the tourism industry.

Many of the islands have what is known as a Hotels Aid Ordinance, which grants investors in hotel construction duty-free entrance for needed materials, equipment, and furniture. Governments also provide low-interest investment capital and guarantee capital loans. Hotel investors are exempt from corporate income taxes for 5 to 15 years—the bigger the hotel the longer the exemption. In Jamaica, hotels with more than 350 rooms enjoy a 15-year exemption from income taxes. Puerto Rico's governor Carlos Romero Barceló in 1983 announced a "new era" for Puerto Rican tourism. Heralding the new era are numerous incentives to the tourism industry that include a 90 percent exemption from property and inventory taxes for hotels. The tax incentives and duty-free import clearances granted to the tourism industry are a tremendous drain on government revenues and must be counted against the benefits of Caribbean tourism. "The problem with international tourism in the Caribbean," observes tourism expert Herbert Hiller, "is it demands an image of paradise, and the fiction has become too costly to maintain."

In travel agencies around the world, colorful brochures with slight pictorial variations of bikini-clad women, black waiters serving rum punches, and natives in colorful array lure the prospective vacationer to the Caribbean. Most of these brochures, even those advertising individual hotels, are paid for by each country's bureau of tourism. As much as $70 million each year goes to public-relations firms, located mainly in New York, to promote the islands in the sun.[12] In just one year Jamaica spent $12 million to advertise its better features.[13] A representative of the Jamaica Tourist Board complained that the country had to spend an average of $17 to attract each Canadian tourist to Jamaica.[14] Another expense for Caribbean governments is the maintenance of about a hundred overseas tourist offices, including 60 in the United States. Hotel chains and tourists are always demanding better standards of service from those in the tourist trade. The burden of upgrading skills and attitudes of workers has fallen on the Caribbean governments. The director of the Grand Bahamas Promotion Board noted that before the commencement of government-sponsored training programs the lack of proper hospitality was a serious problem, but the Bahamian people are "very service-oriented now."[15] In Jamaica, the training program has graduated close to a thousand hotel staff, taxi drivers, craftspeople, and car-rental clerks—all of whom received "attitude-development" courses.

Multilateral institutions and foreign governments often finance projects in the tourism industry on the grounds that tourism aids economic development. Critics, however, suggest that insuring a resort hotel in Haiti or financing a golf course and a Holiday Inn in the Dominican

Republic probably is not the most appropriate and beneficial way to foster the development of the Caribbean economies. Washington often directs its aid for the Caribbean tourism sector to the most friendly governments. Its OPIC insurance programs promote U.S. ownership of tourist
hotels and resorts. International aid programs poured hundreds of millions of aid dollars into Jamaica after the election of conservative Edward
Seaga as prime minister. Following the lead of Washington and the IMF,
tourists had shied away from Jamaica during the Manley years. Seaga's
free enterprise government, which, when it took power in 1980, was
backed by bountiful international financial support, made tremendous
progress in rebuilding Jamaica's tourism industry. A television advertising campaign in the United States focused on a game of polo in Jamaica
with a voice-over saying: "Come back to gentility. Come back to Jamaica."

The Reagan administration was primarily responsible for a decline in
the tourism industries in Cuba and Grenada. It prohibited U.S. tourists
from traveling to Cuba and warned that the State Department would not
be responsible for the safety of visitors to Grenada. The number of visitors to Maurice Bishop's Grenada dropped drastically because of the negative publicity from Washington, but the People's Revolutionary Government forged ahead with its plan for an expanded tourism industry. The
country's former director of tourism, Angela Bishop, said, "Tourism must
be linked to other sectors of our economy and must provide an effective
stimulus for agriculture and agro-industrial production. It cannot be viewed
in isolation but must provide an outlet for indigenous cultural expression
of our people."[16] Cuba has experienced some success in attracting Canadian and European visitors with a brand of import-free tourism, which it
calls "un turismo sano," or "healthy tourism." "Be the first on your block
to go to Cuba," advertised Suntours of Canada in 1975. "When you come
back you can hand out the same cigars Castro smokes and talk of how
you walked the Bay of Pigs."

THE BACKSIDE OF TOURISM

Emerald waters, sugar-white beaches, turquoise skies, and the peace
of a tropical island rate among the leading attractions of the Caribbean.
Club Med advertises its Caribbean resorts as an "antidote to civilization."
But tourists trying to escape the industrial world are discovering all the
evils of the civilized world encroaching upon and in some cases engulfing
their Caribbean hideaways. Gazing from the balconies of the Holiday Inn
in Barbados, vacationers can appreciate the lingering sunsets and the
easy breeze of the trade winds, but a more discriminating look around
the oceanfront reveals a Mobil Oil refinery, with the smell of oil hanging
in the evening air. Sewage from the hotel and the crowded city of Bridge-

town flows into the famously clear Caribbean Sea. Warm water from sea-side power plants is killing off the nearby aquatic life and ruining the attractions of snorkeling. An article in *Time* magazine observed, "Sadly, in recent years less enticing images have begun to intrude. They show thick plumes of exhaust spilling from new oil refineries; bubbling, dark cesspools of untreated wastes only a hop away from beaches jammed by tourists; mountainsides scarred by open-pit mining and hardscrabble agricultural plots. The vacation paradise now faces the spread of environmental blight at an alarming rate." [17]

The rush to development by Caribbean governments and the tourism industry is threatening the regional environment. Vacationers from North America and Europe have overrun some of these Lilliputian countries. The number of annual stopover visitors to the U.S. Virgin Islands is 7 times the local population figure. [18] One of every five persons in Bermuda during the eight months of the tourism season is a tourist. Foreign visitors heavily tax the infrastructure of the islands. In the case of Barbados, vacationers use water and sewers 1.6 times more than the native population and use over 27 times as much electrical power. [19] Nine-tenths of the sewage generated by the 30 million Caribbean residents and 7 million stopover visitors is dumped directly into the Caribbean. Many of the hotels discharge their waste into the very waters where their guests swim. In addition to this filth, the Caribbean absorbs the uncounted tons of waste dumped at sea by cruise ships and yachts. Sewage and vandalism endanger the fragile coral reefs. Some entrepreneurs go as far as to attack the reefs with sledgehammers and dynamite to collect pieces of coral and other reef life like starfish and sea urchins. The evidence of environmental destruction caused by uncontrolled tourism is rapidly mounting, but Caribbean officials still tend to regard the short-term benefits of new marinas and hotels more highly than the long-term rewards of a clean and healthy environment.

COSTS AND BENEFITS

Along with light manufacturing and mining, tourism in the post-World War II years has become a major part of the Caribbean economies. Government planners and multilateral aid organizations promote tourism because of its potential to provide jobs, to earn foreign exchange, and to spur the development of the local economy. But the seasonal nature of the industry, its high import content, its foreign control, and its damaging psychological effect all substantially reduce the benefits of tourism to the Caribbean islands. Planning and finance ministers in the Caribbean tend to look more at growth charts of tourist arrivals than at unemployment and literacy rates as indicators of their countries' economic progress.

Caribbean governments rely on tourist dollars to balance their budgets, buy their imports, and keep their economies afloat. In 1981, visitor expenditures in the region totaled $3.5 billion, distributed in the following manner: 19.5 percent to the English-speaking nations of Caricom, 25.9 percent to Puerto Rico and the U.S. Virgin Islands, 19.9 percent to the Bahamas, 10.9 percent to the Netherlands Antilles, 7.9 percent to Bermuda, and 4.0 percent to the French departments.[20] Four out of five of the 11 million tourists come from either North America or Europe.[21] As large as the tourism business is in the Caribbean, it fades in comparison with the U.S. tourism industry. In 1982, visitors in Florida spent about 6 times what non-cruise ship visitors spent in all the Caribbean islands combined.[22]

Tourism contributes about a quarter million jobs to the Caribbean, ranging from a meager 2 percent of the workforce in Jamaica to 70 percent in Bermuda. Although the tourist service jobs are eagerly sought, the work is generally low-paid and unskilled. For some, tourism jobs are a chance to escape the drudgery of canecutting and other arduous agricultural work; but for most West Indians, these service jobs are the only alternative to a dead-end life of unemployment. Working either as maids, waitresses, or kitchen help, women fill as many as 75 percent of jobs in the tourism sector.[23] One attraction of sun-lust tourism, only hinted at in the glossy brochures, is the availability of native women for male tourists either explicitly as prostitutes or in the roles of hospitality girls, massage and bath attendants, strip-tease performers, and hostesses. Hardly any of the money generated by the sex industry ends up in the hands of the women themselves; it goes instead to the tourist agencies, hotels, club owners, and pimps.

Tourism is a leading earner of foreign exchange for Jamaica, Barbados, Antigua, St. Lucia, and many other Caribbean islands. But not all the tourist dollars spent on the islands stay there to benefit local economic development. Baltron Bethal, tourism director for the Bahamas, estimated that 81 cents of every tourist dollar "finds its way back to the United States."[24] Undeniably, the tourism industry economically benefits the Caribbean islands, but as with every other TNC-controlled industry in the region, the primary benefits go to the foreign hotel chains, airlines, and suppliers of imports for the tourists. In Antigua, 90 percent of the tourism sector is under the control of the predominantly foreign private sector.

The wining and dining Caribbean tourists are likely to enjoy food and beverages from their home countries. The less diversified an economy, the higher the import content of the tourism industry. Menus of the

Pegasus Hotel in Kingston and the Hilton in Santo Domingo cater to the tastes of their clientele, not to the constraints of local food supply. Most tourists do not want and are not offered local dishes like baked yam or kalalloo soup. Along with the food, all hotel equipment and furniture comes from foreign distributors. Frequently a hotel company will import a U.S. construction firm to build a hotel, even when local construction companies are available. In Guadeloupe, imports account for about 80 percent of the total cost of hotel supplies.[25]

According to the Organization of American States (OAS), tourism provides a benign form of interaction between the developed and under-developed worlds. "Millions of tourists traveling from country to country not only help to raise the standard of living of the host country but also encourage integration of peoples through the interchange of ideas, drinking and eating habits, and styles of clothing," states the OAS.[26] Apart from government ministries and local owners of the tourism industry, how-ever, favorable sentiment about tourism in the Caribbean is not easy to find. Officials and business people lament the negative attitude with which many of their compatriots view tourist-service jobs. "Service with a snarl" is what too many tourists receive in Martinique, complained one cham-ber of commerce representative.[27] Governments have mounted "smile for the tourists" campaigns to encourage better service and treatment of the tourists. St. Vincent has a program to "inform residents of the social, cultural, and economic benefits of tourism" while St. Lucia has launched an awareness campaign to help St. Lucians better appreciate the value of tourists. In Jamaica, the government has posted signs in public trans-portation reminding working-class Jamaicans that tourism is also "their" business. But for many West Indians tourism seems an unlikely path toward economic development, and they would prefer a way of getting ahead that does not require kowtowing to white tourists. "It is com-pletely unacceptable that the poor of the world are ordered to put on their Donald Duck suits and smile mindlessly at their own reduced con-dition," commented one authority on Caribbean tourism.[28]

"The industry was never really designed as part and parcel of Jamai-ca's development," noted sociologist Rex Nettleford of the University of the West Indies.[29] "Everything which has been done in that industry has been done for someone else and never for us. Instead of building our house and decorating it for ourselves and having our visitors welcome to share it with us, we have decided to put up monstrosities which we think they would want." The natural beauty of the Caribbean has been trans-formed into visions of Miami Beach, Honolulu, and Atlantic City. Speak-ing of the invasion of the Caribbean by the foreign tourist industry, a local tour operator acidly commented, "They rearranged the environ-mental harmonies and left the stink of pollution and decay. They bom-barded innocent people with unrealistic promises of a new standard of living, and plunged them deeper than ever into ill-tempered privation."[30]

Tourism has become a trap for the Caribbean people. It has deepened the economic dependency of the region, chiefly on the United States, and has caused deep psychological and cultural damage. Caribbean tourists generally have come not to share the local culture, ambience, and cuisine, but to model the island communities in the image of themselves and their own foreign culture. Caribbean parents complain that their children grow up with values of a consumer and disco culture that are especially inappropriate for such underdeveloped societies. Fred Bean, Bermuda Police Commissioner, lamented: "Too many people want to live and socialize like the tourists on a daily basis without working."[31]

The industry has caused far-reaching damage to the national psyche by rewarding obsequious behavior with employment and tipping and by withholding those rewards from, and thereby effectively punishing, those islanders who lack the talent for servile behavior. Caribbean journalist Alister Hughes remarked, "We made special efforts to maintain the image. But nobody warned us of the danger and, in the interest of attracting the tourist dollar, we overdid the effort and offered more than service. We offered servility. We acted, in the worst sense of the word, as unspoiled 'natives' of the Caribbean isles, and in the process developed an outsized inferiority complex."[32] Summing up the worst side of the industry, William Demas, president of the Caribbean Development Bank, said: "We welcome foreigners, we ape foreigners, we give away our national patrimony for a pittance to foreigners, and, what is worse, we vie among ourselves in doing all these things. It is a state of psychological, cultural, and intellectual dependence on the outside world."

A printed statement by the Caribbean Hotel Association confirmed this trend: "People who speak against the chain hotels are just not viewing the situation objectively. Without the large hotels, most of the islands would dry up and blow away. Hilton is probably doing more to further local island cultures than anyone else, including the islanders themselves." Tourism has grown to become the largest single industry in the Caribbean. But it is an industry out of control, where the costs often outweigh the benefits and where the benefits of the businesses often go to foreign firms. Being somebody else's playground has meant that the Caribbean's fishermen have become beach boys, its farmers have turned into waiters, and the TNC hotels are defining the local culture.

Oil And Mining:

CONTROL OF NATURAL RESOURCES

We have always been externally propelled, so that when somebody else says "grow sugar," we grow sugar. When somebody says "grow bananas," we grow bananas. That's what has happened in Trinidad. Sure we have oil, but there is no attempt to link the needs of the people with the output of this industry.
—David Abdulah, Education Officer for the Trinidad & Tobago Oilfield Workers Trade Union

The region's bauxite reserves and petroleum industry are often cited by Washington to explain the strategic importance of the Caribbean. North America has long relied on the Caribbean for its supply of bauxite, the mineral ore used to produce aluminum. The Caribbean also serves as a principal oil refining and transshipment center. One-sixth of the oil consumed in the United States is refined in the Caribbean, and one-half of U.S. oil imports pass through Caribbean shipping lanes. The mining and petroleum industries constitute the bulk of North American investment in the Caribbean. To emphasize the seriousness of its strategic concern, the Reagan administration in 1983 staged combined sea, land, and air military war games in the Caribbean to protect, by means of a simulated threat, the flow of oil to the United States and U.S. access to the region's bauxite.

CARIBBEAN OIL-REFINING AND OIL-PRODUCING CENTERS

There are three parts of the oil industry in the Caribbean: production, refining, and transshipment. Only Barbados and Trinidad & Tobago produce crude oil and natural gas. Barbados does not produce enough petroleum to cover its own needs, but Trinidad & Tobago is an important oil- and gas-producing nation. The Caribbean is one of the world's major refining centers not because of oil production within the region but because crude petroleum is shipped there from around the world for refining. The Caribbean has been highly regarded as a refining center because of its political stability, its deep harbors, its lack of environmental regulations, and its proximity to major shipping lanes and the Panama Canal. However, all sectors of the oil industry in the Caribbean have come on hard times in the last several years. The world recession has cut into the demand for petroleum and petroleum-based products. Oil production peaked and is now steadily declining in Trinidad, but the production of natural gas is picking up.

In the United States, new regulations concerning oil imports and new incentives for domestic production have made the refining business less attractive, particularly for non-U.S. companies like Shell. Refineries were built in the 1960s in the Bahamas and in the U.S. Virgin Islands to evade import restrictions on fuel oil to the U.S. eastern seaboard. For many of the same reasons that refineries were placed in the Caribbean, the oil corporations have located major transshipment terminals in the region. The terminals are used to unload crude oil from supertankers and transfer the load to smaller tankers, which, unlike the new supertankers, are allowed to enter North American harbors.

NETHERLANDS ANTILLES

The origin of the Caribbean as an oil refinery center dates back to the early part of this century. The petroleum corporations that were producing oil in Venezuela did not want to make large investments in Venezuela because they feared nationalization. Instead, the companies decided to build their refineries for Venezuelan oil off the coast in the Dutch and British colonies, which they considered much safer. In 1917, Shell built a refinery in Curaçao to handle 80 percent of its Venezuelan crude. It was followed by Standard Oil of Indiana, which constructed its own giant refinery on the Dutch island of Aruba. Later, Standard of Indiana sold its operations in the Netherlands Antilles to Standard Oil of New Jersey (now Exxon).

The refineries in the Netherlands Antilles today are among the largest and most modern in the world. By modernizing and mechanizing the refineries in the last 25 years, Shell and Exxon have been able to reduce their workforce by over two-thirds. Crude oil continues to come from Venezuela and the Middle East to be refined and shipped, mostly to North American markets. In these Dutch colonies, petroleum refining accounts for nearly 20 percent of the gross national product and about 5 percent of the employment. The government of Venezuela has expressed interest in buying the two refineries and in exploring for offshore oil near Aruba. Besides the two refineries, there are three transshipment terminals in the Netherlands Antilles: one owned by Shell, another owned by Exxon, and the third owned jointly by Northville Industries and Paktank (West Germany), located in Bonaire.

TRINIDAD & TOBAGO

Before 1907, the year black gold started spurting in commercial quantities from exploratory drilling, Trinidad was a British colony not unlike the other islands of the Commonwealth Caribbean. Its main economic activity was the sugarcane business, which was then almost completely controlled by the company Tate & Lyle of Great Britain. During both world wars, crude oil from Trinidad fueled the British war machine. Today, most of Trinidad's refined petroleum goes directly to U.S. markets.[1]

Unusual in the Caribbean, Trinidad both produces and refines petroleum. Oil has made the country into a regional power, but it has also created an inflated economy and an array of environmental problems. The petroleum industry has also given rise to a militant workforce that presents a constant challenge to TNC investors and the government. The backbone of the economy, the petroleum business employs about 20,000 workers and accounts for half the national product.[2] Between 1970 and 1980, the country increased its earnings from the petroleum industry 30 times, making Trinidad & Tobago one of the wealthiest nations in the hemisphere. The government's plans to use this income to build an industrial sector have been threatened by falling oil prices and pressure by the petroleum companies for reduced taxes. The unions and other critics have called for the industry to be taken out of the hands of the TNCs, while the government fears that a confrontation with the foreign petroleum firms will isolate the country and destabilize the economy. The industry is already partially nationalized, but the main refining capacity and production are controlled by TNCs.

British Move Out, U.S. TNCs Move In

British Petroleum and Shell dominated the industry for almost a half century before voluntarily selling their increasingly unprofitable operations to Trinidad in 1968 and 1974, respectively. From the nationalized British Petroleum holdings, the government, at the suggestion of the Oilfield Workers Trade Union, created the National Petroleum Corporation. However, Prime Minister Eric Williams then turned around and invited the little-known Tesoro Petroleum of Texas to manage and jointly own the new government corporation. The government signed a contract with Tesoro that gave it control over finance, production, and marketing. In effect, it turned over the newly created National Petroleum Corporation (which controlled one-third of the country's total oil production) to a foreign corporation. The new company, called Trinidad-Tesoro Petroleum Company, became the base that allowed Tesoro to expand from a struggling oil company to what was five years later called "the fastest growing energy company in the United States."[3] Helping the company expand were a 100 percent exemption from income taxes and substantial financial assistance under the government's Guarantee of Loans Act.

The nationalization of Shell followed years of the corporation's neglect of its facilities and oilfields. Workers complained of deplorable conditions in the fields, poor maintenance of flow lines, oil losses, and severe pollution problems. Shell had stopped replacing old machinery and equipment and had fired hundreds of workers. Nonetheless, Shell received a highly favorable purchase price and payment terms, besides maintaining a supply agreement with the government. The Shell facilities were incorporated into the government's Trinidad and Tobago Oil Company (Trintoc), which has a technical assistance contract with Tesoro.

Although Trinidad-Tesoro Oil is a major part of Tesoro's operations, the joint venture is small when compared with the operations of the two main TNCs in the country. Amoco, otherwise known as Standard Oil of Indiana, controls most of the country's offshore oil and gas production. Amoco, which does not own a refinery on the island, ships its crude oil from Trinidad to its own refineries elsewhere in the world. The other dominant TNC is Texaco, which produces mostly from offshore wells and owns two-thirds of the country's refining capacity. Trintoc owns the balance of the nation's oil-refining business. The operations of Amoco and Texaco are both wholly owned by the two TNCs. Oil production has been declining, and no new major fields have been discovered in the last decade. Major discoveries of natural gas deposits have occurred, however, and proven reserves may last 40 years. A spectacular discovery of a large deposit of offshore gas by Amoco Trinidad in 1983 bodes well for expanded natural-gas production and the country's plans for an industrial complex based on gas consumption. Amoco will develop the new gas field in accordance with an agreement that commits Amoco to produce all the natural gas necessary for local consumption.

The Texaco Trinidad complex at Pointe-à-Pierre forms an almost autonomous enclave. It comprises the refinery, the oil storage and transshipment facilities, administrative buildings, and senior staff housing, as well as a dairy farm, a bird sanctuary, and an 18-hole golf course. The company boasts that out of its 6,700 permanent staff, only 9 (including the general manager) are foreigners.[4] While it does maintain a policy of hiring mostly nationals, Texaco does not encourage local control of the complex. All decision-making power resides in the corporate headquarters in the state of New York. According to one report, Texaco does not even keep its Texaco Trinidad financial records in Trinidad for fear the workers could use the information against it.[5]

Texaco got a toehold in Trinidad in 1956 when it bought the operations of a British firm, Trinidad Leaseholds, which also had marketing activity in Jamaica, Puerto Rico, and the Dominican Republic. With the loss of its facilities in Cuba after Fidel Castro's army overthrew Batista, Texaco compensated by expanding its Trinidad plant. Texaco Trinidad, the second largest landowner in Trinidad after the government, has grown to become one of Texaco's major complexes.[6] The Trinidad subsidiary accounts for 8 percent of Texaco's worldwide refining capacity and as much as 14 percent of the company's sales in the Western Hemisphere.

Issues of National Control

Besides the large foreign investments by Amoco and Texaco, scores of foreign contractors and suppliers operate in the petroleum industry. Servicing the industry in Trinidad are companies such as Halliburton, Combustion Engineering, Bechtel, Black & Decker, Turner Construction, Petroleum Helicopters, and Santa Fe International. The continued pervasive presence of foreign contractors hardly supports the notion that the flow of foreign capital into a third world nation encourages the development of local capitalism and is conducive to the transfer of technology. For the last 70 years, the foreign oil companies have been claiming that they have contributed to the process of transferring industrial technology to Trinidad, but local technological capability has not yet been developed.

According to Trinidadian economist Trevor M. A. Farrell, "It is only meaningful to talk about the multinational corporations transferring technology if the country can develop the technical capability to operate its own industry and determine the direction of development." He concluded that this "remains a vain expectation in Trinidad."[7] The education officer for the Oilfield Workers Trade Union, David Abdulah, described the technology gap in his country: "We are one of the oldest oil industries in the world. Our first oil was drilled back in the 1860s. For many years, we were the largest oil producer in the British empire. Yet, we don't have any indigenous oil technology. We cannot design our own oil structures and drilling platforms. We can't produce designs for refineries. We don't even do our own seismic work; we still have to contract that out and send the results to Houston. This is after 130 years of oil activity."[8]

The solution advocated by Farrell and other economists is not to wait year after year for the companies to parcel out training and technology. Rather, he said, Trinidad should assume direct control of its economy by nationalizing the entire production and refining industry. By this strategy the Caribbean oil industry, like that of Mexico, would learn by doing. "We cannot," according to Farrell, "wait in vain for the multinational corporations to teach us the tricks of the trade."[9]

The Oilfield Workers Trade Union has been prodding the government to take firmer steps toward nationalizing Texaco and Amoco, the two major oil companies in the country. It claims that Texaco has gradually been reducing its workforce and intentionally not maintaining its plant because of plans to pull out of the country. While applauding the initial steps toward state control of the petroleum industry, such as the joint venture with Tesoro and the founding of the state-owned National Petroleum Company, the union has relentlessly criticized the government for its failure to challenge the two major foreign corporations. Several years ago, Texaco categorically refused a government request for majority holding, but in 1983, it offered the government 75 percent of its interest in the Pointe-à-Pierre refinery. The government was interested in obtaining equity and some management control in the Texaco refinery so that it could direct its portion of light-crude production to the refinery; it has never shared the strong view held by the Oilfield Workers Trade Union: "Texaco Must Go." Coming at the same time as Texaco's offer to sell most of its refining capacity to the government was a similar offer from Tesoro to sell out its interest in Trinidad-Tesoro.

In the view of the petroleum TNCs, it does not make economic sense to continue to sink money into Caribbean refineries. Texaco explained, "A Caribbean refinery such as the Texaco facility at Pointe-à-Pierre, operating largely on imported crude oil and exporting the bulk of its products to the United States where prices are either controlled or affected by controls, cannot be profitable under present circumstances, and accordingly additional investment is not now justified."[10] The other reason for Texaco's slowdown in refinery maintenance and offshore drilling was undoubtedly an attempt to put pressure on the government to lower taxes and to restrain the militancy of the union. And the strategy worked: the government did reduce taxes on drilling and the union did agree in 1982 to cutbacks in benefits and reduced personnel—matters that both the government and the union had declared to be nonnegotiable.

The slowdown and threatened pullout by Tesoro and Texaco threw the government's ambitious plans for industrialization into disarray, since it had been planning to construct a multibillion-dollar petrochemical and industrial complex based on the petroleum industry's continued good fortune. The government had also been hoping to persuade Texaco to expand its refinery to become the refining and distribution center for the entire Caribbean. The government has neither the money nor the skilled personnel to proceed with both its industrialization plans and more extensive involvement in the petroleum sector. If the government did gain control of both the Tesoro and Texaco refineries, it would face the same market problems about which both corporations have complained. In addition, it would be left without a guaranteed source of crude oil unless it nationalized the large production capacity now owned by Amoco. While the government has been interested in increasing its equity participation in the petroleum industry, it has expressed no interest in taking total control of the entire industry—a solution the Oilfield Workers Trade Union has advocated all along.

THE U.S. VIRGIN ISLANDS AND ST. LUCIA

When the Hess Oil Company (now Amerada Hess) started construction on its oil refinery in St. Croix in 1966, the U.S. Virgin Islands were completely undeveloped. Donkeys were still an important means of transportation on the slow-moving, backwater U.S. territory. Leon Hess, the owner of the company, made a deal with the Islands' governor (a presidential appointee) to open a huge oil refinery to process Persian Gulf crude oil into heating oil for the United States. The independent oil company was able to undersell competitors for the U.S. east-coast market, since the other refining companies did not enjoy the extraordinary cost-saving advantages in the Virgin Islands.

In 1965, the legislature of this U.S. territory offered a package deal to Hess if it would build a refinery on St. Croix. The package included exemption from all property and franchise taxes, license fees, import duties, and trade and excise taxes. Another provision of the investment package waived 75 percent of the company's income taxes on the operations of what is now considered the world's largest oil refinery. A third attraction of setting up a refinery in the Virgin Islands was a clause in the Jones Act of 1920 that specifically excluded the Islands from a requirement that all U.S. oil companies were to use U.S.-flag ships in domestic trade. This exemption allowed Hess to save 5 to 40 cents a barrel of oil by using foreign-flag ships to ship oil to markets on the U.S. mainland.[11] Yet another advantage of the Caribbean location was that the Virgin Islands were not subject to the environmental and health regulations that applied to refineries in the United States. Through transfer pricing Amerada Hess has managed to transfer the profits made by other subsidiaries to its subsidiary in the Virgin Islands, where profits are barely taxed under the Islands' generous incentive program. So profitable was the St. Croix refinery that Leon Hess decided in 1974 to close down a large New Jersey refinery and expand operations in the Caribbean, with their substantially lower labor costs.

In 1981, when the Virgin Islands' contract with Amerada Hess expired, the company halted construction of a $250 million expansion project and laid off nearly a thousand workers. The shutdown and layoffs had the desired effect of stirring up the workers to demand that the Virgin Islands government immediately sign a new contract with the company under many of the same terms. Leon Hess repeatedly rejected the government's offers for new terms; and in April 1981 he wrote the governor of the Islands a letter that said Governor Luis "must accept full responsibility" if they failed to reach a settlement, adding that the real victims would be the employees of the Hess refinery. "Insulting and inflammatory" is how Julio Brady, federal program director for the Virgin Islands, characterized the response of Hess to the government's offers. "It virtually threatened that the Governor's political future was done for if he did not agree [with Hess]."[12] But the territorial government didn't yield completely to the pressure from Hess and its workers, and in re-negotiation of the contract managed to remove some of the early exemptions given to the company.

One reason the government could negotiate with some confidence that Hess would not pull out of St. Croix was the new transshipment terminal that the company was building in St. Lucia. Amerada Hess had pressured the government of what was then a British colony to let it build a refinery and a transshipment terminal that would store oil coming into the Caribbean in huge ocean tankers. The company never built the refinery in St. Lucia but did follow through on the terminal, which would be next to useless without the refinery at St. Croix. Supertankers, which cannot go directly to St. Croix, now deposit their fuel at the St. Lucia terminal, and lighter ships transport it to the Virgin Islands for refining.

DEPENDENCY ON OIL IMPORTS

The dependency of the Caribbean nations on imported oil has put a severe strain on their economies in the last decade. Between 1970 and 1981, the combined oil import bill of the Caribbean nations increased almost 20 times. In 1970, oil imports were 6 percent of Jamaica's total import bill, but by 1981 oil imports were 33 percent of the country's imports (Table 5A). One of the main benefits of Cuba's association with the Soviet Union is that Cuba receives 98 percent of its petroleum imports from the Soviet Union as the result of trade agreements between the two nations.[13]

The mining industry is a major consumer of petroleum products. Ironically, in Jamaica, the production of the country's major exports, bauxite and alumina, emphasizes Jamaica's dependence on fuel imports. Alumina production alone consumes half the nation's oil imports. Puerto Rico, the leading gas and oil hog in the Caribbean, consumes more fuel than does any one of the countries of Egypt, Israel, Algeria, or Peru. Partly responsible for the huge fuel intake in the U.S. territory is the gas-consuming car culture on the island. Most of the petroleum, however, goes to generate electricity for the island's petrochemical industry. Three industries in Puerto Rico—chloralkali, electrode, and petrochemical plants—use more electricity than any of 14 Latin American countries.[14]

TABLE 5A
PETROLEUM AS PERCENTAGE OF TOTAL IMPORT COSTS

Country	1970	1981
Barbados	5.1	12.8
Dominican Republic	6.2	32.8
Guyana	8.2	34.1
Haiti	5.6	16.0
Jamaica	6.3	33.0

Sources: *Yearbook of International Trade Statistics*, UN, 1982; *International Financial Statistics*, IMF, 1982

TABLE 5B
OIL IN THE CARIBBEAN
Production, Refining, Transshipment

Location	Company	Ownership	Functions
Antigua St. John's	West Indies Oil (temporarily closed 1983)	National Petroleum Antigua-Barbuda Govt	18,000 bpd* refinery
Bahamas Freeport	Bahamas Oil Refining Co (BORCO)	50% Charter Oil 50% Chevron (SOCAL)	500,000 bpd refinery 60,000 bpd desulfurizer 350,000 bpd crude oil distribution facilities
Freeport	Burmah Oil	Apex Oil Bahamas Govt	transshipment

Barbados			
St. Michael	Mobil Oil Barbados	100% Mobil Oil	4,000 bpd refinery
Bridgetown	Barbados National Oil	100% Barbados Govt (formerly Mobil)	production
Cuba	Instituto Cubano del Petroleo	100% Cuba Govt (formerly Shell, Exxon & Texaco)	3 refineries totaling 68,750 bpd 120,000 bpd refinery under construction
Dominican Republic			
Bonao	Falconbridge Dominicana	100% Falconbridge	16,500 bpd refinery
Haina	Refinieria Dominicana de Petroleo	50% Royal Dutch Shell 50% DR Govt	30,000 bpd refinery
Jamaica			
Kingston	Petroleum Corp of Jamaica	100% Jamaican Govt (formerly Exxon)	33,000 bpd refinery
Martinique			
Fort de France	Societe Anonyme de la Raffinerie des Antilles	24% Royal Dutch Shell 14.5% Exxon 11.5% Texaco 25% CFP 25% Erap	13,000 bpd refinery
Netherlands Antilles			
Aruba	Lago Oil and Transport	100% Exxon	480,000 bpd refinery transshipment
Bonaire	Bonaire Petroleum	Northville Industries Paktank	transshipment
Curaçao	Curaçao Oil Terminal		1.2 million bpd transshipment

Location	Company	Ownership	Facility
Curaçao	Shell Curaçao	100% Shell	370,000 bpd refinery transshipment
Puerto Rico			
San Juan	Caribbean Gulf Refining Corp	12% Gulf Oil 88% others	40,000 bpd refinery
San Juan	Petrolane of Puerto Rico		LP gas producer
Yubacoa	Yubacoa Sun Oil	100% Sun Oil	85,000 bpd refinery
Penueles	Clark Oil (formerly Commonwealth Refining)	Apex Oil	161,000 bpd refinery
Penueles	Peerless Petro-chemicals		10,000 bpd refinery
Guayanilla		PPG Industries	bulk terminal
St. Kitts-Nevis		planned, by Canadian investors	10,000 bpd refinery
St. Lucia			
Cul-de-Sac	Hess Oil	100% Amerada	transshipment
Trinidad			
Point-a-Pierre	Texaco Trinidad	77% Texaco Oil 23% others	355,000 bpd refinery
Brighton	Texaco Trinidad 23% others	77% Texaco Oil 23% others	6,000 bpd refinery
Port of Spain	Amoco Trinidad	Standard Oil of Indiana (Amoco)	oil & gas production
Port of Spain	Trinidad-Tesoro Petroleum	50.1% T&T Govt 49.9% Tesoro (formerly British Petroleum)	oil & gas production
Port of Spain	Trinidad-Tesoro Agriculture	Trinidad-Tesoro Petroleum	

Port Fortin	Trinidad & Tobago Oil (Trintoc)	100% T&T Govt (formerly Shell)	100,000 bpd refinery
	Trinmar	Standard Oil of Indiana (Amoco) Trinidad-Tesoro Trintoc	oil & gas production
Port of Spain	Occidental of Trinidad	100% Occidental Petroleum	production
US Virgin Islands St. Croix	Hess Oil-Virgin Islands	100% Amerada Hess	700,000 bpd refinery (largest in world)

* bpd = barrels per day
Source: The Resource Center, Compilation of Corporations, 1984

MINING IN THE CARIBBEAN

BAUXITE AND ALUMINUM

Aluminum is sometimes considered the "magic metal" because of its strength, formability, and light weight. Since the 1940s, aluminum has been a key material for construction, the manufacture of consumer goods, and packaging. Packaging, represented by the aluminum can, in the last decade has become a major market for the aluminum companies, many of which have their own aluminum can factories. Aluminum made the modern aerospace industry possible, and 30 percent of aluminum production is used for defense-related manufacturing. Traditionally, the Caribbean nations were the main suppliers of the U.S. and Canadian aluminum industries. By the end of World War II, British Guiana (Guyana) and Dutch Guiana (Suriname) were between them supplying over two-thirds of the Western world's requirements of bauxite. But Brazil, Guinea, and Australia have supplanted the Caribbean in the last decade. Less than 50 percent of U.S. bauxite currently comes from the Caribbean.[15]

Bauxite refers to soil that contains more than 30 percent alumina, or aluminum oxide; aluminum is the most common metallic element found in the earth's crust.[16] When mined, bauxite is generally bright red, but the refined alumina is a fine white powder. Five tons of Jamaican bauxite produces two tons of alumina, which in turn produces one ton of aluminum when smelted. Until World War II, the developed nations paid little attention to bauxite reserves outside Europe and the United States. During the war, however, when military demands for aluminum exceeded available supplies, the United States started paying closer attention to the bauxite reserves in Guyana and Suriname. The Dutch government even gave the United States permission to send a thousand soldiers to protect the bauxite mines in Suriname, then Dutch Guiana, and thus to ensure an uninterrupted flow of ore for the United States. Throughout the war, the federal government owned its own aluminum smelters within the United States, but when the war ended, it turned them over to private corporations, mainly Reynolds and Kaiser. The large smelting capacity built up during the war that was then handed over to the private sector is one reason why U.S. corporations have not been interested in building additional smelters in the Caribbean.

Bauxite mining and aluminum production is a highly concentrated business, with six fully integrated companies controlling about 60 percent of the bauxite production and 70 percent of the capitalist world's alumina refining.[17] These top six companies, known as the Six Sisters, are Aluminum Company of America (Alcoa), Aluminum Company of Canada (Alcan), Kaiser Aluminum and Chemical, Reynolds Metals, Pechiney Ugine Kuhlman of France, and Swiss Aluminum. Bauxite is generally mined from open pits, since the bauxite earth lies close to the surface. Because it is soft earth, the mining operations are not as capital-intensive as other mining. The intermediate stage, production of alumina, is twice as capital-intensive as the mining of bauxite. The production of alumina and aluminum is highly capital-intensive and expensive because it requires a great deal of electricity.

Although the underdeveloped nations account for about 75 percent of all bauxite reserves and mined bauxite, they account for only 17 percent of all alumina production and about 9 percent of all aluminum production.[18] Jamaica, Guyana, and Suriname, in that order, are the three major Caribbean bauxite producers. Enjoying attractive tax incentives in the U.S. Virgin Islands is an alumina plant owned by Martin Marietta; and Alcan has a bauxite transshipment terminal in Trinidad. The government of Trinidad & Tobago has contracted with two U.S. firms, National Steel and South Wire Aluminum, to build an aluminum smelter at the Point Lisas industrial park, but the project is on hold until the market improves. In 1982, bauxite production ceased permanently in Haiti and temporarily in the Dominican Republic.

Confrontation with the Aluminum Corporations

A producers' union for countries with bauxite had been in the works since 1967, when the Caribbean Bauxite Mine and Metalworkers Federation Congress called on Caribbean governments to set up a council of bauxite producers. The doubling of petroleum prices in 1973 by the OPEC nations was the impetus needed for the formation of the International Bauxite Association (IBA) in 1974. Prime Minister Michael Manley of Jamaica was the motivating force behind the founding of the producers' association. He said that the future of third world nations lay in a change in the international terms of trade. "We want trade, not aid," declared Manley in his support of the IBA. Realizing that it needed the unity of the other bauxite producers if it was to stand up to the transnational mining companies, Jamaica helped form this union of producing countries shortly after it had levied a sharply increased tax on the bauxite companies. Soon after Jamaica completed its new arrangements with the bauxite companies, a wave of renegotiations began in Suriname, the Dominican Republic, Haiti, and Guyana, as all these countries imposed stiffer bauxite levies following the Jamaican formula. The two main objectives of the IBA were to negotiate with the TNCs to secure a fair return, and to promote an orderly and rational development of the industry.

The IBA, however, has failed to become an important producers' union for three reasons: (1) its failure to include all the producing nations, (2) the weak structure of the organization, and (3) the concentration and integration of the aluminum industry. Brazil, which holds 10 percent of world bauxite reserves, has refused to join the IBA; and Australia, although a member of the association, has not imposed any export levies like the other member countries.[19] The governing body of the association, the IBA's Council of Ministers, serves mostly as an advisory panel, since its resolutions are binding on member countries only if passed unanimously. "It is a harmony born of weakness," wrote one observer.[20] Because of their competitiveness, the IBA countries have not yet even set a minimum price for bauxite ore. "Bauxite isn't oil," noted an article in Forbes; "if you don't like what one member of the IBA is doing, there are plenty of other places where you can get supplies."[21] Because the economies of larger countries like Brazil and Australia are not as dependent on bauxite revenues as the Caribbean nations, they can sometimes offer corporations a better deal.

Also keeping the bauxite countries weak and unorganized is the concentrated power of the TNC producers. The six corporations listed above control each process of the aluminum industry from bauxite mining to aluminum manufacturing. More than 75 percent of bauxite sales and 87 percent of aluminum sales are made by affiliates of the same corporations.[22] The integrated and extremely concentrated nature of the industry has made it difficult for the IBA countries to confront the power of the aluminum giants.

The bauxite industry brings very few indirect benefits to underdeveloped countries like Jamaica. Ripple effects on unindustrialized economies are limited, because the industry requires relatively few inputs that can be purchased locally. The necessary components—heavy earth-moving equipment, 40-ton trucks, petroleum, and caustic soda for alumina refining—are not produced in Jamaica but have to be imported from industrialized nations. Employment provided by the industry is not proportionate to the percentage of the country's foreign exchange provided by the aluminum companies. Even though bauxite is Jamaica's leading export, the industry provides less than 2 percent of the country's employment.[23] In Jamaica, the yearly growth of the labor force is more than 5 times the number of workers employed by the industry.[24]

"I am sure," wrote economist Norman Girvan, "that the managements of Alcoa, Alcan, Reynolds, and Kaiser would like to be in a position to feel that the operations of their companies lead to economic development of Jamaica, Guyana, and Suriname so long as this is consistent with their business strategy. The trouble is that it is not."[25] The groundbreaking efforts of the Manley government have resulted in increased income for the Caribbean bauxite nations, but it is doubtful that they are getting their full share of the profits from the industry. The value of crude bauxite relative to that of its processed form (aluminum) is still lower than that of any other of the third world's 16 most important exports.[26]

Like all corporations, aluminum companies aim to keep their costs down and their profits high. When one country or region seeks a better deal, the transnational corporation seeks another place that can offer it a better investment climate. Bauxite companies are also looking for locations where energy costs are low, a fact that could increase the bauxite/ alumina industries in countries like Guyana and Suriname that have a tremendous hydroelectric potential, but may cause a decline in the Jamaican industry. Although long-term market prospects for bauxite are good, the future for the Caribbean bauxite countries is uncertain as the TNC firms seek other areas of the globe where labor is cheaper, state control is less strict, and taxes are lower. Bauxite has been an important source of foreign exchange and employment for the Caribbean countries, but its economic contribution relative to its potential has been low.

Jamaica

In the 1950s, Jamaica moved from its traditional dependence on Great Britain toward closer relations with the United States. With the start of bauxite production by mainly U.S. firms, the British colony changed to become an economic outpost of the United States. Under the initial bauxite-mining agreements, Jamaica received only 12 cents per ton of bauxite mined.[27] More than 20 years after the start of bauxite mining, the government of Prime Minister Michael Manley took measures to bring the industry under national control and increase its economic contribution to the country. The Manley government received widespread support from all sectors of the public: workers, national bourgeoisie, radical intelligentsia, and government bureaucrats. Standing firmly behind Manley was the local business community, which depended on public investment funds for most large development projects. The large business community felt increased national control of the bauxite industry would directly benefit them by bolstering the nation's investment budget. It would also increase the investment capital that the government made available to national lending agencies such as the Jamaican Development Bank.[28]

The major difficulty that faced Prime Minister Manley in his effort to assert national control over the bauxite industry was the problem of taxing a product that was not sold in a competitive market. The prices for Jamaican bauxite were arranged between divisions of the same company, as in the case of Reynolds Jamaica Mines selling its bauxite to the Reynolds smelter in Louisiana. The companies kept this transfer price low to avoid local taxes and royalties. The Manley government overcame this obstacle by establishing a bauxite levy that was indexed to the price of aluminum sold in the United States. In that manner, Jamaica found an easy way to circumvent the difficulty of determining the true price of bauxite when sold from one subsidiary to another. Fortunately for Jamaica, all the major North American aluminum companies had made large investments in the country, and its bauxite was highly valued because it was unusually close to the surface and consequently inexpensive to mine. Furthermore, the operations of many alumina plants in the United States were geared specifically to the composition of the bauxite from Jamaica, which was then the world's second-largest producer. The Kaiser alumina plant, for instance, was over 80 percent dependent on Jamaican ore.[29] These factors made the aluminum corporations dependent on Jamaica and gave the country great leverage when it decided to bring the industry under tighter national control. Economist Norman Girvan explained, "Alone among the bauxite exporting nations, Jamaica had both the motivation to seek higher returns and the leverage to secure them, even over the opposition of the companies."[30]

In 1974, Jamaica instituted a 7.5 percent levy on the bauxite producers, which resulted in a 60 percent increase in government revenues from bauxite. The government also gained increased control of the industry by nationalizing all bauxite-producing lands and by gaining 51 percent of the equity of the bauxite mining operations. However, it negotiated only a small equity participation in the alumina refineries. After agreeing to the nationalization measures, the companies received a guarantee of a 40-year supply of bauxite from lands that would be leased back to the companies at 7 percent of the purchase price. Another measure introduced by Manley gave the government the right to sit on the managing committee of each mining company. In addition, the government established the Jamaica Bauxite Institute, which gave it a base of information about the industry for the purpose of giving it more clout at the bargaining table. For example, the institute soon found that the island's high-grade bauxite reserves totaled 2 billion tons, not the 600 million tons the companies had been claiming.[31] As then Finance Minister David Coore stated, Jamaica had been "at the mercy of the bauxite and aluminum companies because they knew the facts about their industry and we had only such knowledge as they saw fit to let us have."[32]

Howls of protest and a flood of threats by the aluminum corporations challenged the Manley initiatives. The companies were in the forefront of the economic destabilization efforts aimed at the nationalist politics of Michael Manley and his party. The international capitalist recession was one reason for bauxite production cutbacks after 1975, but that did not explain the disproportionate cutbacks experienced by Jamaica. Efforts by the companies to slow production and thereby sabotage government revenue projections also explain the decline in bauxite production. At the same time they were cutting back bauxite and alumina production, the companies were hiking prices. The new prices had no relation to the levies of the Jamaican government, but simply served to boost profits at a time of low production. In the U.S. press, the aluminum companies conducted a campaign blaming the Jamaican government for the price hikes. Many observers also felt the bauxite corporations provoked and prolonged a number of strikes that occurred after the increased bauxite levies as a way to undermine the Manley government. The U.S. government joined in the destabilization campaign by cutting off its bilateral aid and obstructing multilateral support for Jamaica's development plans.

Seaga and Bauxite

In contrast with its treatment of the Manley government, Washington took extraordinary measures to assist the Seaga government in Jamaica by authorizing several acquisitions of Jamaican bauxite for the U.S. National Defense Stockpile of strategic materials. In his November 1981 letter to the General Services Administration (GSA) requesting 1.6 million tons of Jamaican bauxite, President Reagan said, "While improving our own defense posture, this program will contribute to Prime Minister Seaga's strategy for Jamaica to rely to the maximum extent possible on production and exports to fuel its own economic recovery. The stability and economic strength of Jamaica are important to our national security interests in the Caribbean."[33] The fact that "a substantial portion of our bauxite ore-carrying ships were sunk [during World War II] in the South Atlantic by enemy submarines" pointed to the need for wartime resources of bauxite, said Reagan. In 1983, seeing that Jamaica was still in the economic doldrums, President Reagan requested that the GSA purchase another 2 million tons of Jamaican bauxite.

In making the requests, President Reagan asked the GSA to waive federal laws calling for competitive bidding and use of U.S.-flag vessels. "I follow the directives of the President," said GSA Commissioner Roy Markon, defending the noncompetitive acquisition.[34] The GSA negotiated directly with the Seaga government for the approximately $100 million worth of bauxite, which was mined by two U.S. companies, Reynolds Metals and Kaiser Aluminum. The two GSA purchases directly benefited these two corporations at a time when the worldwide demand for bauxite and aluminum was depressed. In the first purchase, the GSA traded surplus agricultural products like dry milk and milk fat for the 1.6 million tons of bauxite, making the deal the first use of agricultural barter to acquire strategic raw materials in almost 15 years. The Jamaican government, in turn, paid the mining corporations. The second deal, a straight cash transaction, had the maximum beneficial effect on Jamaica's cash flow. The president waived the regulation on the use of U.S.-flag vessels for government purchases because Reynolds Metals registers its ships in Panama. As of January 1984, the United States had 10.4 million metric tons of Jamaican bauxite. These purchases will continue to expand massively because the Reagan administration has set a goal of stockpiling 20 million metric tons of Jamaican bauxite.

In the shadow of these extraordinary purchases was the U.S. Business Committee on Jamaica, a group of corporations organized by David Rockefeller to promote the economic progress of the Seaga administration. The *New York Times* reported that the Rockefeller group lobbied the Reagan administration to aid the aluminum industry by buying Jamaican bauxite.[35] Four of the 24 corporate members of the committee are aluminum companies: Reynolds Metals, Kaiser Aluminum, Anaconda Aluminum, and Alcoa.

President Reagan also persuaded the Overseas Private Investment Corporation (OPIC) to waive its rules concerning the country limit on its insurance coverage. Worried that it might be overexposed in several countries, in the early 1970s OPIC adopted a rule limiting the agency's insurance coverage in any one country to 10 percent of the agency's total coverage. In 1982, however, OPIC exceeded that limit in Jamaica when it authorized a $50 million insurance policy to Kaiser, Reynolds, and Anaconda for their joint venture in bauxite mining in Jamaica. "The president says we want to help the Caribbean and Jamaica, so we can bend the rules," said OPIC's Robert L. Jordan.[36]

Despite his anticommunism, Seaga did not turn down an offer by the Soviet Union in 1982 to buy 1 million tons of Jamaican bauxite over seven years. It was the capitalist world, however, that offered special deals for

Jamaican bauxite. Both General Motors and Chrysler arranged deals that allowed the automobile companies to get Jamaican alumina in exchange for vehicles, parts, and machinery produced by the companies.

Beginning in 1979, the Jamaican government has gradually backed away from its plans for further control and to increase levies on the industry. The Jamaica Bauxite Institute announced it would reduce the levy on the bauxite producers in 1984; and it has also tried to arrange its taxation of the industry so the foreign producers could use the Jamaican levy to offset payments against their home-country taxes. Despite the changes, the bauxite industry is more important than ever to Jamaica, providing 70 percent of the country's exports. This dependence means, said Carlton Davis of the Jamaica Bauxite Institute, that in Jamaica "the companies are still in the driver's seat."[37]

Guyana

In the early 1900s, Alcoa, which owned the Aluminum Company of Canada, started exploring for bauxite and buying bauxite lands in Guyana. The British colonial government had little concern for the long-term welfare of its subjects, and the main bauxite lands fell into foreign hands without any participation of the country's residents. A local affiliate of Alcoa, the Demerara Bauxite Company (Demba) was established in Guyana in 1916, and in 1928 became part of the independent aluminum company, Alcan. Demba paid only 5 cents for each ton it mined on crown lands while paying absolutely no royalties on the bauxite it mined on its own lands.[38] In return for allowing Alcan to mine, the company had promised the government of British Guiana that it would build an alumina plant in the British Commonwealth. British Guiana expected the plant to be built within its boundaries, but Alcan instead built the processing plant in Quebec. In British Guiana, Alcan established an enclave isolated from other economic life in the British colony. It was not until 1968 that its company town, MacKenzie, was even connected by road to the capital. The next foreign bauxite company was Reynolds Metals, which accounted for 20 percent of Guyana's production.

Following the overthrow of the government of Cheddi Jagan in 1953 by the British, Alcan and Reynolds Metals operated in an extremely favorable political climate, but the government of Forbes Burnham, which assumed power in 1964, proved to be not as malleable as the bauxite companies had wished. It became increasingly nationalistic and started pushing Alcan to build an aluminum smelter in Guyana. The company resisted, and then, in 1970, the government declared that it would hold 51 percent of all companies operating in the nonrenewable resource sector. After extensive but unsuccessful negotiations with Alcan, the Burnham government nationalized the entire Alcan complex in 1971. Recalling the negotiations, economist Norman Girvan wrote: "It would be naive to pretend that the attitudes of those present at the negotiating table did not reflect the profound antagonism that exists everywhere between the third world and metropolitan capitalism. From the standpoint of the Alcan representatives, they were dealing with 'natives' for whom they felt deep contempt. Some of the Alcan people did nothing to hide the feeling, while others made heroic efforts that only became increasingly weaker under conditions of exhaustion, fatigue, and provocation."[39]

At the time of the nationalization, bauxite produced in Guyana directly supported two Canadian towns that had Alcan aluminum smelters. As an Alcan official said, "Demba represents a raw material foundation on which much of Alcan's international aluminum superstructure is erected."[40] During the heated negotiations that preceded nationalization, the Guyanese negotiating team charged that Demba Bauxite Company had an investment policy that "was subject to decisions made in the board rooms of Montreal and New York, which are consistent only with the interest of its North American parent and never in the light of the economic interest of Guyana."[41] One aspect of this foreign control became evident only after nationalization, when Alcan said that it was not going to honor the guarantees of the workers' pension fund, which was maintained in Montreal.

Despite the hard feelings engendered by the nationalization debate, Alcan continued to purchase bauxite from Guyana. Under a contract with the Guyana Bauxite Company, the country's bauxite is stored at the Alcan transshipment terminal in Trinidad, and Alcan's Saguenay Lines is one of the shipping companies that ships the bauxite down the Demerara River across the Caribbean to the terminal. Immediately after the nationalization, Alcan sought out sources of bauxite in Australia, Guinea, and Brazil for "a much broader and diversified material base." Neither Alcan nor other TNCs, however, threatened to boycott Guyana's bauxite. Because of its special composition, bauxite from Guyana, unlike most available bauxite, is valued for its role in the production of other chemicals. Over half the U.S. supply of calcined bauxite has come from Guyana.[42] In 1975, Guyana also nationalized the operations of Reynolds Metals. In both cases, it was generally considered that the compensation offered the companies was favorable to them.

In the years immediately following nationalization, the Guyanese workers and managers enthusiastically proved that they could indeed run the bauxite industry. Later, government bureaucracy and political interference in the industry resulted in a serious slowdown in bauxite production. A former manager said that the ruling party started interfering in the management affairs of the industry in 1975, and from then on bauxite production began falling apart as underpaid technicians and others frustrated by President Burnham's political interference started leaving the country.

Under pressure from the World Bank and the IMF, Guyana in 1982 opened negotiations with Alcan, Kaiser, and U.S. Steel over the possibility of resuming some degree of private investment in the national bauxite industry. Technically, Alcan was in a position to take hold of the industry since Guyana had failed to meet the agreed-upon nationalization payments. Alcan, displeased that Guyana was also negotiating with two other companies, withdrew from the negotiations. Guyana contracted U.S. Engineers and Consultants, a subsidiary of U.S. Steel, to study the production problems of the industry, and has hired Kaiser Aluminum Technical Services to overhaul the country's alumina plant. Since 1982, the government has contracted Green Construction of the United States to remove earth and mine bauxite at its principal mine. Other foreign firms hired by the government to help its mining industry include Touche Ross, Australia's Austroplan, and the U.S. firm Geocon.[43] In addition to its substantial compensation debt, the government has obligations to repay several guaranteed loans from the Royal Bank of Canada and U.S. Eximbank for its bauxite operations. The reentry of TNCs into the nationalized mining industry was a clear sign of the weaknesses of state capitalism under Forbes Burnham.

NICKEL

Mined in Cuba and the Dominican Republic, nickel is an element that, when alloyed with other metals, produces a high quality of steel. Its use in weapons manufacturing led the Defense Department to qualify nickel as being the closest to a true "war metal." The United States, the world's largest consumer of the metal, imports about 90 percent of its nickel supply. The main suppliers of nickel to the United States are two Canadian corporations, Inco and Falconbridge. In 1972 Falconbridge, with $200 million in financing from the World Bank and a group of U.S. investors, opened a large nickel mine near Bonao, which lies some 60 miles north of Santo Domingo in the Dominican Republic.

An intricate financing arrangement stands behind the Falconbridge venture in the Dominican Republic. Although Falconbridge is headquartered in Canada, control rests in the United States, mainly with Superior Oil, which holds about 30 percent of company stock. Inco had discovered the Dominican Republic nickel deposits in the 1950s, but decided not to proceed with a mine because, according to one Inco executive, President Trujillo was demanding "too big a bribe."[44] Falconbridge took over the concession but had to delay its mining project in 1965 because of political upheaval and the U.S. invasion. In 1969, Falconbridge incorporated Falconbridge Dominicana (Falcondo), a Dominican corporation, to develop the deposit. Falconbridge owned 65 percent of Falcondo's shares, while Armco, a U.S. steel-equipment company, owned 17 percent, the Dominican government 9 percent, and various local investors the remaining 9 percent.[45] The project was designed not only to produce nickel but also to process the ore into ferronickel ingots for sale to steel manufacturers around the world. Falconbridge is under a long-term contract to handle all Falcondo's marketing.[46]

Most of the capital to finance the Falcondo operation came not from equity financing (stock ownership) but through long-term loans from the following sources: $114 million from three major insurance companies, Metropolitan Life, Equitable, and Northwestern Mutual; $25 million from the World Bank (this was the first World Bank loan authorized for the Dominican Republic); and $41 million in short-term revolving credit from two banks—the Canadian Imperial Bank of Commerce ($20 million) and Citibank ($21 million).[47] The Loma Corporation was set up to manage the private-sector loans to Falcondo and to contract expropriation and political-risk insurance from OPIC.[48] The government of the Dominican Republic guaranteed the World Bank loan to Falcondo.

Financing the project mostly with loans rather than selling shares allows the nickel project to reduce local profits to a minimum through continual repayment of the interest and principal of the loan. Ninety-two percent of the company's original capital consisted of loans from foreign financial institutions. The interest payments on these huge loans are deducted from Falcondo's total income before profits are calculated.[49] In 1982, Falcondo still had a long-term debt of $173 million and had paid out $32 million in interest and amortization payments.[50] That same year, Falcondo declared a loss for tax purposes, even while it continued to repatriate millions of dollars in loan payments to the United States.

Cuba is in the process of significantly expanding its nickel production facilities and could become the third largest mine producer of nickel in the 1980s. The U.S. Department of Defense contracted for all the production from the large nickel industry in prerevolutionary Cuba. The country's nickel deposits at Nicaro were developed originally by the Freeport Sulphur Company under a U.S. government contract to build up nickel supplies during World War II.[51] Cuba currently is developing two new deposits at Nicaro and Moa Bay.

RED MUD AND OIL SPILLS

There is little room to absorb environmental damage in the small Caribbean nations. Oil spills, deforestation, and water and air pollution

TABLE 5C
MINERALS IN THE CARIBBEAN

Location	Company	Ownership	Functions
Bahamas			
	Marcona Ocean Industries	100% Marcona	aragonite mining
Cuba			
Moa Bay	Cubaniquel	100% Cuba Govt	nickel mining
Nicaro	"	100% Cuba Govt	nickel mining refinery
Punta Gorda	"	100% Cuba Govt	nickel mining 30,000 tpy* refinery
Pedro Alba	"	100% Cuba Govt	refinery
Dominican Republic			
Cabo Rojo	Alcoa Exploration	100% Alcoa (temporarily closed 1982)	3,000 metric tpd** bauxite mining
Bonao	Falconbridge Dominicana (Falcondo)	65.7% Falconbridge Nickel Mines 17.5% Armco 9.5% DR Govt 7.3% Individuals	50,750 metric tpy ferro-nickel mining 9,000 tpd refinery
Pueblo Viejo	Rosario	100% DR Govt	10,000 metric tpd gold & silver mining dore refinery
Guyana			
Berbice	Guyana Mining Enterprise (Guymine)	100% Guyana Govt	3,500 long tpd bauxite mining
Linden	Guyana Mining Enterprise (Guymine)	100% Guyana Govt	bauxite mining 300,000 tpy alumina refining
Haiti			
Miragoane	Reynolds Haitian Mines	100% Reynolds Metals (closed 1982)	bauxite mining

Sedren	Sedren		copper, gold, silver mining
Jamaica			
	Jamaica Bauxite	100% Jamaica Govt	bauxite land agriculture land
Ewarton	Jamalcan	93% Alcan 7% Jamaica Govt	5,000 long tpd bauxite 624,000 tpy alumina refinery
Kirkvine	Jamalcan	93% Alcan 7% Jamaica Govt	5,000 tpd bauxite 615,000 tpy alumina refinery
	Alcan Products of Jamaica	100% Alcan	
	Sprostons	100% Alcan	
		100% Alcan	dairy farming
Claredon Parish	Jamalco	94% Alcoa 6% Jamaica Govt	bauxite mining 880,000 short tpy alumina refinery
St. Ann	Kaiser Jamaica Bauxite	49% Kaiser Aluminum & Chemical 51% Jamaica Govt	bauxite mining
		100% Reynolds Metals	cattle
	Jamaica Alumina Security	37% Reynolds Metals	
	Jamaica Reynolds Bauxite Partners	49% Reynolds Metals 51% Jamaica Govt	bauxite mining
St. Elizabeth	Aluminum Partners of Jamaica (Alpart)	36.5% Kaiser 36.5% Reynolds 27% Atlantic Richfield (Anaconda)	bauxite mining 1.3 million short tpy alumina refinery

Puerto Rico			
	Amax		copper exploration
		Kennecott PR Govt	possible joint venture for production & smelter
Suriname			
Onverdacht	Billiton Maatschappij Suriname	100% Royal Dutch Shell	bauxite mining 8,500 metric tpd alumina refinery
Moengo	Suriname Aluminum (Suralco)	100% Alcoa	bauxite mining
Paranam	Suralco	65% Alcoa 45% Billiton	bauxite mining 73,000 tpy aluminum smelter
Trinidad & Tobago			
	Chaguaramas Terminals	100% Alcan	transshipment
	Sprostons	100% Alcan	
	Geddes Grant Sprostons Industries	Alcan	
US Virgin Islands			
		100% Martin Marietta	bauxite mining alumina refinery

* tpy = tons per year
** tpd = tons per day
Source: The Resource Center, Compilation of Corporations, 1984

immediately threaten the fragile island environments, where small impacts are often system-wide. Environmental risks on these small islands have been accepted because their dependent economies so desperately need foreign exchange.

Refining oil in the Caribbean was a convenient answer to rising fears within the United States of oil spills spoiling the shores of the mainland.

The Caribbean offered deep harbors, cheap labor, and no environmental regulations. Each day, oil tankers transport about 5 million barrels of oil through the Caribbean Sea to and from the region's oil refineries and transshipment terminals. At any one time, there are about one hundred loaded oil tankers in the Caribbean Sea.[52] All this oil shipment results in periodic accidental oil spills, and there is also the continual pollution resulting from the operational discharges from the oil tankers. Much of the oil pollution in the Caribbean—about 7 million barrels a year—comes from the regular discharges of oil from tankers while they are cleaning out their tanks.[53] Oil spills often have dramatic results. Large tracts of mangrove along Puerto Rico's north shore have not yet completely recovered from a 1973 oil spill of a tanker passing by the island. Not only do oil spills inevitably damage beaches and coastal vegetation, but they also kill sea life because of toxicity and the stickiness of the oil.

Another constant source of oil pollution of Caribbean waters is off-shore oil drilling around Barbados, Trinidad, Venezuela, and Mexico. It has been estimated that about 7 percent of offshore production ends up in the sea as a result of pipeline accidents, blowouts, platform fires, overflows, and other malfunctions.[54] The UN regards offshore oil production as the major threat to the coastal shrimp industry in the Caribbean.[55] Oil refineries also contribute to regional oil pollution, as in the case of the Guaranara River in Trinidad, which is now a dead river because of liquid wastes from oil refining. Alongside this problem of oil pollution, there is also other environmental damage associated with the construction and operation of oil refineries. When Amerada Hess constructed the port for its refinery at St. Croix in the U.S. Virgin Islands, it dredged a mile-long channel that cut through the coral reefs surrounding the island, thereby destroying the beaches' only protection from erosion.[56] Tons of pollutants are also released into the Caribbean skies from the oil refineries throughout the Caribbean.

Waste is the greatest environmental problem caused by the bauxite/alumina industry. From every two tons of bauxite that are processed into alumina comes more than one ton of waste. In the bauxite mining areas of Jamaica, huge muddy red pools of bauxite tailings lie next to the alumina plants. The International Bauxite Association calls the Jamaican bauxite industry "extremely costly" because of the associated environmental damage. Every decade about 30 square kilometers are covered with the red mud. The IBA reported in 1983 that chemicals from the bauxite waste ponds are contaminating the ground water around the mines—a problem about which nearby villagers frequently complain. In Guyana, there are regular complaints about "the bauxite dust which pollutes the air and finally settles in the most secret parts of the homes."[57] Dead fish can be seen floating in the creeks and rivers of Guyana as a result of the caustic soda that escapes as waste from the alumina process.

PROBLEMS OF NATIONALIZATION

The experiences of Jamaica, Guyana, and Trinidad & Tobago with varying forms of nationalization have underscored the problems of challenging the control of TNCs. The limited nationalization undertaken by the Manley government in Jamaica was met by production cutbacks and an international publicity campaign against the democratic socialist government—measures that contributed to destabilization of the country. Lack of capital, technological know-how, and guaranteed markets have hindered the pursuit of more extensive control over the bauxite/alumina industry. Trevor M. A. Farrell called the nationalization in Jamaica "a farce and a fantasy." He said, "Despite government control of 51 percent of the operations of key companies in the bauxite industry, the agreements guaranteeing decades of bauxite reserves and arrangements with respect to processing and taxation mean that Jamaica has not achieved effective control over its key mineral resource."[58] Ten years after the first bauxite reforms, the government has less bargaining power than before. During this decade, companies have diversified their sources of bauxite, thereby reducing the importance of Jamaican bauxite. Meanwhile, Jamaica remains in the weak position of being a producer of primary commodities with no additional linkages in its economy and no additional technological capability.

In Guyana, the nationalized industry failed primarily because of the inefficient and undemocratic character of the Burnham government. Although its calcined bauxite continued to be in demand by aluminum companies even after nationalization, production failed to meet the market demand because of management problems, worker dissent, and lack of skilled personnel. The decreased foreign-exchange earnings (due to the drop in bauxite sales) combined with the burden of compensation payments to create a severe external public-debt crisis in Guyana.

Nationalization in Trinidad has never been confrontational. The government takes pride that neither foreign governments nor the companies themselves have objected to the terms of compensation, but the friendliness of nationalization is more an indication that the country was cheated rather than that it negotiated well. The government has been willing to step in to buy ailing industries but has not attempted to exercise state control over the most profitable sectors of the petroleum industry. David Abdulah, Education Officer of the Oilfield Workers Trade Union, believes that a firmer and more courageous policy of nationalization is needed in Trinidad & Tobago. Asked about the results of Jamaica's efforts to nationalize their bauxite industry, Abdulah replied: "I think that Manley pussyfooted a lot. He wanted to break the influence of multinationals, and yet tried to play the game at the same time. You cannot do both. You either do one thing or another. You cannot begin to squeeze the multinationals and not begin to line up all the alternatives beforehand."[59]

To a certain degree, nationalization fits in with the global strategies of the TNCs. In some cases, as in Trinidad, nationalization provides a good example of how a company can rid itself of an unprofitable investment. Another case in point was the sale of the Exxon refinery to the Jamaican government in 1982. The government's Petroleum Corporation of Jamaica bought the facilities at the replacement value quoted by Exxon, rather than the book value. What is most important to the TNCs in cases of nationalization is that the third world nations continue to play by and respect the rules of the international capitalist game. Joint ventures, such as those in Jamaica and Trinidad, can actually be in the interest of the corporate investors. A manager of Alcoa in Jamaica said that what really matters is that "Jamaica has a stake in the system."[60] The joint ventures arranged in Jamaica have exactly that result: the interests of the government of Jamaica and the corporations have been brought together in the venture, while the TNCs have preserved their ultimate control. By bringing government capital into their foreign investments, corporations lower the costs and risks of each venture. The government will also be more likely to provide infrastructure for the project and less likely to raise the industry's taxes.

In theory, the nationalization of the mineral sector sets the preconditions for development of an economy along lines that benefit the society. The experiences of all three nations have shown, however, that nationalization does not necessarily mean that the industry will be put to work for the citizens of Caribbean countries. Because the new source of government funds from the bauxite levies in Jamaica injected sorely needed investment capital into the local economy, there has been no talk of pulling the government out of the bauxite companies or repealing the bauxite levy even under the reactionary atmosphere of the Seaga government (although the TNCs did successfully pressure the government to lower the levy). The income generated by the bauxite reforms has not "trickled down" to the common people in Jamaica. The same holds true in Trinidad, where the flood of petroleum dollars never reached the country's poor. Instead of embarking on programs to build desperately needed housing, Trinidad's government has poured hundreds of millions of dollars into capital-intensive industries that provide neither a large number of jobs nor essential products. There was no "pussyfooting around" about nationalization in Guyana, yet there has been no attempt to share the national wealth. Instead, the production is in the hands of a small political/economic class that has proven incapable of efficiently running its own business. Bauxite workers, who originally supported the nationalization of the Guyana bauxite mines, later approved of moves to denationalize the industry because, under the ownership of the Burnham government, the mines were so poorly run that the workers worried about the security of their jobs.

The lesson learned in the Caribbean was that nationalization is not something that by definition aids the course of self-determination and development. It is important to consider the following elements in assessing a nationalization strategy: (1) the beneficiaries of nationalization, (2) the degree of foreign control that remains even after nationalization, and (3) the ability of the government to manage the industry and to secure future markets. Nationalization and the localizing of equity may ease the stranglehold of the TNCs, but the superiority of the TNCs in technology, capital resources, and access to markets seriously limits any challenge to their power.

Caribbean Finance:

LAUNDERING MONEY IN THE SUN

We think of these small countries sometimes in the same
way as we do in handling the affairs of a medium-sized
company.
                                    —Canadian bank manager in Antigua

In the middle of the urban decay of Jamaica's capital city is a modern section called New Kingston. An enclave of glass and concrete, the fancy new neighborhood's tallest buildings are the banks. Throughout Kingston the names of the banks appear everywhere: Royal Bank Jamaica, Scotiabank, Canadian Bank of Commerce, and Citibank. It is the same in almost every part of the Caribbean. The biggest and best buildings on the islands are occupied by one or another foreign bank.

The foreign banks have been in the business of money saving, money dealing, and money lending in the Caribbean for as many as a hundred years. The British-owned Colonial Bank, the first prominent foreign bank, monopolized the financing of the early sugar plantations. Then came David and Alexander Barclay, who, before they decided to expand their London financing business to Jamaica in 1836, were prominent slave traders. Another half century passed before the Bank of Nova Scotia, in 1889, became the first Canadian bank to settle in the Caribbean. The British and Canadian banks spread throughout the islands and monopolized the region's financial sector. The American banks followed other U.S. corporations to the Caribbean in the 1960s, attracting bank customers with their modern approach and liberal lending policies. After establishing themselves, Citibank and Chase Manhattan adopted the more restrictive and traditional credit policies of the Canadian and British banks. Foreign transnational banks dominate banking in the Caribbean. The largest and most geographically diverse of these foreign banks are Barclays Bank, Royal Bank of Canada, Bank of Nova Scotia, Canadian Imperial Bank of Commerce, Citibank, Chase Manhattan, BankAmerica, and First Boston. All but First Boston rank among the 50 largest banks in the world by assets (Table 6A).

When talking about finance in the Caribbean, you need to go beyond the region to Miami, which some people call "the capital of the Carib-

TABLE 6A
WORLD RANK OF TNC BANKS OPERATING
IN THE CARIBBEAN

Bank	World Rank	Number Branches* in Caribbean
BankAmerica	1	17
Citibank	3	23
Barclays Bank	6	98
Chase Manhattan	15	34
Royal Bank of Canada	17	109
Canadian Imperial Bank	31	58
Bank of Nova Scotia	45	143
	TOTAL	482

* refers to number of offices. One subsidiary can have more than one office or branch

bean" because it is the locus of most trade and banking operations of the region. This booming city is the second-largest financial center in the United States after New York. Many of the banks centered in Miami, such as Citizens and Southern National Bank, have no commercial branches in the Caribbean. Instead they concentrate on financing Caribbean trade and attracting new bank deposits by the Caribbean elite. The largest proportion of the savings business of Miami banks involves foreigners. Most of this foreign business is not with foreign governments or official institutions. Rather, private business owners and individual foreign residents, mostly of Latin America and the Caribbean, regularly do their banking in Miami.[1]

Transnational finance in the Caribbean encompasses not only the many foreign banks with branches in the region, but also the business of offshore finance and the financing of external debt by the transnational banks. The section "Debt for Development" examines the increasingly important role of foreign banks in the external-debt financing of the Caribbean. This chapter explores the presence of foreign bank branches in the region and the use of the Caribbean as a center for both offshore financing in the Eurocurrency market and in the insurance industry.

THE TRANSNATIONALIZATION OF BANKING

In the past ten years, the leading banks of the industrial nations have opened offices in the remotest parts of the third world. Some economists call this transnationalization of banking the "second wave." The expansion of the large money-center banks followed the first wave of foreign investment by industrial corporations that hit the shores of the underdeveloped nations in the 1960s. The banks soon followed to meet the financing needs of a worldwide network of factories, assembly plants, and distributorships. The banks also started crossing country borders because of declining rates of return in the industrial economies and to escape government restrictions on the export of capital. The Canadian and British banks had already established a strong regional presence before the postwar boom in international investment and trade. The second wave brought the U.S. banks on the financial scene, while the Canadian banks and Barclays of London intensified their activities. The arrival of the U.S. banks in the Caribbean signaled the advent of American political and economic hegemony in the basin.

Through control of the region's money flow, the transnational banks have gained considerable influence in determining the economic and political development of the Caribbean. Chase Manhattan says its three lending priorities in foreign countries are to finance short-term trade in U.S. exports, the subsidiaries of U.S. corporations, and export-oriented production.[2] Through their lending policies, transnational banks promote a form of economic development more in the interests of their own home countries than in those of the third world. This decision-making by foreign bankers on how to spend local savings presents the most telling case of the extent of foreign economic control in the Caribbean.

Foreign banks are not willing to take the same risks in the Caribbean or in other third world regions as they are with domestic lending. They lend to trade and export production businesses and to TNC manufacturers, rather than to locally based business ventures where the risks are much greater. The transnational banks frequently tie their lending to government programs like the U.S. Export-Import Bank and Export Development Corporation of Canada, which guarantee the loans. After collecting the savings of the local depositors, the banks lend it to foreign corporations that need capital to build a plant or to expand. In this way, the transnational banks in the Caribbean facilitate the flow of national surplus funds into the hands of foreign investors. Particularly attractive to the foreign banks is lending to assembly plants that have low overhead costs because of government incentives and low labor costs. In addition, these foreign-owned assembly plants usually enjoy easy access to world markets and use advanced cost-efficient technology.

The British and Canadian banks have a long history of providing capital to the plantocracy and mercantile class of the islands. Foreign banks prefer to lend for agricultural export production rather than for local consumption, since export crops earn valued foreign currency. In its report on the Caribbean Basin, the Federal Reserve Bank of Atlanta found that while most of the region's commercial banks have ample experience in financing the export of traditional crops like coffee, bananas, and sugar, they are "frequently inexperienced in providing the farmers with working-capital loans or in working with small or medium farmers in isolated areas."[3]

Tobacco farmers who produce for Philip Morris in the Dominican Republic or coffee farmers in Jamaica have easier access to credit than farmers trying to grow vegetables for the local market. Certainly, these nations need foreign exchange to develop their economies and to repay their foreign debt. Although export agriculture does create foreign exchange, Caribbean nations must pay for the necessary infrastructure, farm machinery, fertilizer, and pesticides to support it. The emphasis on export agriculture also results in increasing food import bills.

The national savings of the Caribbean people wind up for the most part in the hands of the transnational banks, but these banks are reluctant to authorize loans for the basic needs of Caribbean residents. Quick to open branches in the areas of major employment and foreign investment like the bauxite mines and oil refineries in order to collect the deposits of the workers' paychecks, the banks do not allow more than a small percentage of those savings to flow back into productive local projects. The personal loans authorized by the banks go most often for the purchase of luxury goods by the middle and upper classes. This often unregulated use of scarce foreign exchange to pay for nonessential goods means that dollars and pounds are not available to cover the bills for essential imports like fuel and medicine. A study of bank lending in Trinidad found that while the banks would finance consumer durables like cars, they would fail to find funds for real estate purchase and for the development of local industries.[4] Resentment against the lending priorities of the transnational banks has been building for a long time. In 1925, the Canada-West Indies Conference published this complaint about transnational finance: "When a country like Canada or the United States wants to build a big hotel, companies are formed and the money is supplied by either the banks or the insurance companies. In Jamaica, we can neither get the banks nor the insurance companies to loan us any money to put up hotels."[5]

Locally owned banks are hard pressed to compete with the TNCs because they lack the connections with the foreign importers and exporters. Because the local banks do not have easy access to hard currency, they often have to ask the larger transnational banks for transfers of foreign exchange. The foreign banks can also maintain a leading position through their control of new banking technology, like the computer accounting systems that are currently transforming the banking industry. Their more powerful marketing structure and international resources also allow the foreign banks to convey to the public an image of stability and security that local banks cannot rival.

Attempting to Control Foreign Banks

In the last several years, several Caribbean governments have tried to control or reduce the power of the transnational banks, using one of the following three strategies: miniaturization, nationalization, or localization. None of the three plans has succeeded in bringing banking under any significant degree of Caribbean control. Miniaturization is the attempt to channel public and private savings into government banks, thereby shrinking or "miniaturizing" the funds available to the TNCs. Guyana has had a degree of success with this strategy because its large public sector patronizes the National Cooperative Bank rather than the foreign banks. Private businesses in Guyana, however, invariably still use either Chase or Royal Bank of Canada as their main bankers. In Jamaica, despite the government's campaign to attract public support, the Workers Bank of Jamaica controls only about 10 percent of deposits. Because of their fear of being denied access to foreign capital, none of the Caribbean nations, with the exception of Cuba, has dared to nationalize the entire transnational banking sector. Cuba compensated the Canadian banks to their satisfaction, but it expropriated the U.S. banks, and Citibank is still demanding compensation for its claimed losses.[6]

Localization, the third and most common strategy, refers to the partial sale of stock in the Caribbean branches of transnational banks to local investors.[7] Jamaica and Trinidad required the foreign banks to offer at least 51 percent of their shares to the public. But 51 percent ownership does not necessarily bring about local control, because the shares are dispersed among a large number of local holders, and the foreign headquarters still determines all major bank policies. Even when the local owners can assume a modicum of control over bank policies, localization frequently is just a change in identity from expatriate capitalists to local capitalists. Local ownership may mean, as one Caribbean observer noted, "a bunch of local wealthy men who may be in a position to strangle the small entrepreneurs even more."

In his book *Multinational Banks and Underdevelopment*, Maurice Odle identified the main shortcomings of the localization strategy: (1) no effective control because of the dispersion of share holdings, (2) no enforced safeguards to prevent other nonnationals from acquiring available shares, and (3) the authorization of high share prices to placate the foreign bank owners.[8] Before becoming prime minister, Michael Manley attacked localization as a public-relations gimmick but later supported the localization strategy. The Jamaican and Trinidadian governments gave the foreign banks five years to localize, but most failed to meet the deadline. The most recalcitrant have been the U.S. banks and the Canadian Imperial Bank of Commerce.

The experience in Jamaica and Trinidad has indicated that localization has not altered the conservative pattern of bank lending established by the TNCs. The populace, more concerned about credit availability than who owns the banks, has not seen any substantial change in lending policies. What it has seen is only a change in appearances: the Bank of Nova Scotia is now Scotiabank; the Canadian Imperial Bank of Commerce simply changed its name to Bank of Commerce; and, in Trinidad, the Royal Bank of Canada is now the Royal Bank of Trinidad & Tobago. Some of the transnational banks even welcome localization, since it allows continued high earnings and continued overall control while diminishing the risks and responsibilities of direct ownership.

New Source of Profits

When their direct ownership diminishes, the foreign banks tap a new source of profits in the licenses and fees they charge affiliate banks. They even charge for the use of trademarks and trade names. The Royal Bank of Canada, for instance, bills Royal Bank Jamaica for the traditional symbols of the globe and the lion and for the use of banking terms like Fasteller and Termplan. The TNCs have comfortably accommodated themselves to the Caribbean nationalism of the 1970s and have managed to maintain a tight hold on regional banking. Sometimes the banks themselves initiate the change away from total ownership because they see local participation as a way to ensure continued access to that financial market. The non-U.S. banks usually do not regard total equity control as critical in their profit-making strategies, since the bank's first source of funds is its clients, not its shareholders. In contrast to the tolerance by British and Canadian banks of local control plans, U.S. banks have on occasion left the country rather than abide by local participation regulations.

Sometimes the transnational banks see localization strategies as a way to unload unprofitable operations onto a Caribbean government. For example, the Royal Bank of Canada in Grenada and the Bank of London and Montreal in Trinidad both introduced the idea of complete disinvestment to the island governments. No matter how unprofitable their banks, the TNCs have consistently demanded high compensations for selling out their interests. Anxious to promote good relations with the developed economies and to maintain their reputations for having good investment climates, the Caribbean nations have acceded to the demands of the banks for excessive compensation. Even with reduced control, the transnational banks often still set the standards for the country's financial sector. Local banks generally follow in lockstep the standards for credit and financial management established by the foreign banks. One reason for this is that native bank managers generally receive their training from the TNCs and have assumed all the foreign-based attitudes about risk aversion.

Power of Global Banking

While some Caribbean governmens have proceeded to nationalize other leading sectors of their economies, they have shied away from moving on the banking sector even though it represents a crucial area of national economic control. The banks have transmitted an all-powerful image and a mystique of inviolability that leaves the islands feeling powerless and dependent. It is the common belief that without the foreign banks a nation will be cut off from the flow of international capital. In recent years, the Caribbean nations, like most third world countries, have relaxed rather than tightened their efforts to control the transnational banks. In direct contrast to the nationalism of the last two decades, the region, now beset by serious economic crisis, is taking pains to do whatever is necessary to create a favorable investment climate for the foreign corporations.

The transnationalization of the banking business has created an all-embracing international credit system beyond the regulation of sovereign states. The efficiency and ease of global computer communication coupled with the expansion of international offshore financing has produced a new transnational reality that subverts notions of sovereignty. Despite localization and nationalization strategies, the transnational banks have actually increased their ability to influence the economic activity, prices, and capital flow in the region. The banks, together with their fellow foreign corporations, have created the context within which the Caribbean nations carry out their management functions.

The distorted form of economic development in the Caribbean reflects with alarming clarity the policies of the transnational banks. Their lending strategies have aided the construction of an unbalanced economic structure based on imports from the industrial world and the export of unprocessed agricultural produce and minerals. Efforts by the Caribbean nations to manage exchange rates and control capital are often thwarted by the transnationally controlled banks, which, owing to their international character, can easily evade national monetary controls. Another negative effect of the foreign control of banking in the Caribbean is that it obstructs the financial integration of the region.

In the Caribbean, the banks have always been the biggest buildings on the block. The Canadian Imperial, the Royal Bank, and Barclays remain as living symbols of colonial presence on the islands. And the rise of Citibank and Chase Manhattan in the center of town is one sign that not much has really changed in the Caribbean—just the addition of a few more foreign names.

The Canadian Banks

Canadian banks have more foreign activity in the Caribbean than any other place in the third world. The maritime provinces of Canada have traded with the Commonwealth Caribbean since the days of slavery, when the plantation owners fed salted codfish from Newfoundland to their slaves and exported rum to quench a growing Canadian thirst. Canadian banking followed and abetted the active trading network between the West Indies, Halifax (Nova Scotia), and London. The Canadian manufacturers and distributors developed such a strong and profitable trading relationship with the English colonies that the Canadian Parliament once discussed the possibility of some type of political or economic union with the region. With the expansion of Canadian trade came the large chartered banks of Canada, which now have 313 branches in the Caribbean. The four largest Canadian banks, listed in Table 6B with their worldwide assets and regional branches, pervade the financial sector in the Caribbean.

TABLE 6B
CANADIAN BANKS IN THE CARIBBEAN
(July 1982)

Bank	World Assets ($ billions Canadian)	No. of Carib. Branches	Internatl. Earnings as % of Total Earnings
Royal Bank of Canada	$89.6	109	37%
Canadian Imperial Bank of Commerce	69.4	58	36%
Bank of Montreal	63.5	3	32%
Bank of Nova Scotia	54.7	143	49%

Sources: Bank Annual Reports; *Polk's Banking Directory*

"We've always been a hard-core international operation," said an official of the Bank of Nova Scotia, the Canadian bank with the highest percentage of its assets invested internationally. One of the reasons for the Canadian banks' interest in operations in the Caribbean is that the region has traditionally been a surplus-generating area for the banks, meaning that operations in the Caribbean take more in from deposits than they lend out locally. In 1919, the *Monetary Times* commented: "As is well known in Canadian banking circles, no Canadian capital has been required for the extension in foreign countries by the Royal Bank, as the foreign deposits have always greatly exceeded the foreign commercial loans." Like other international banks, the Canadian banks channel a good deal of this surplus from local depositors into international loan markets rather than meeting the credit needs of the Caribbean region. The banks are, however, attentive to the needs of other TNCs and foreign investors, particularly those from Canada. A former Canadian minister of finance estimated that at least 60 Canadian companies own or operate hotels and resorts in the Caribbean, and 200 Canadian firms supply goods and services to the industry. Also, the banks often provide the capital for Canadian firms, like the Falconbridge mining corporation, to invest in the Caribbean.*

GOING OFFSHORE TO THE ISLANDS

A newspaper comic strip shows two middle-aged white men, dressed in their swimming shorts, walking along a Caribbean beach lined with palm trees. Says one to the other: "The reason I like the Bahamas is the freedom and the lack of rules. I can do what I want to here." Asks the other: "What do you do? Snorkel?" "No," replies the first man. "I'm a banker."[9]

Tens of thousands of banks, insurance companies, and other finance corporations have gone to the Caribbean for a vacation and some solitude. They seek vacations from the array of government regulations and taxes that impede their pursuit of profit, and they like the isolation that the Caribbean offers them from the legal authorities of their home countries. These self-exiled companies conduct hundreds of billions of dollars' worth of offshore transactions—meaning business that has little or no effect on the residents or the economy of the place of business. The most active offshore banking centers are the Bahamas and the Cayman Islands, while most offshore insurance business occurs in Bermuda. The

*Sources: *The Banks of Canada in the Commonwealth Caribbean*, by Daniel Jay Baum (New York: Praeger Publishers, 1974); "International Dimensions of the Canadian Commercial with a focus on the Caribbean," Michael Kaufman (Canada Caribbean and Central America Policy Alternatives); Bank annual reports and statements

Netherlands Antilles have become a favorite place for corporations seeking a tax haven for in-house financing. Trying to attract a bigger piece of the offshore financial action are many of the smaller islands like Antigua, Montserrat, Turks and Caicos, and St. Vincent.

For the United States, the Caribbean has long served as a money laundry—a place where funds can be transferred in a way that prevents the IRS or the FBI from tracing the origin and the identity of ownership. Similar to the numbered accounts in Swiss banks, the Caribbean tax havens have provisions that prohibit revealing the names of account holders. One underworld money launderer told a federal agent in 1980: "You don't have to say your name. They don't know you; you don't know them. End of story."[10] A recent congressional study, "The Use of Offshore Banks and Companies," found that the use of Caribbean offshore facilities to evade the IRS has become so widespread that it can "literally involve the man next door throughout America." The money, circulating from offshore company to offshore bank, is always protected by a "tight wall of secrecy that surrounds their transactions."[11]

Briefcase-carrying businessmen board daily flights to Caribbean hideaways to store cash in the offshore banks and then return home in the evening. Tax havens have attracted everyone from middle-income families wanting to shelter a few hundred dollars to some of the largest banks and corporations in the world. But the dangers involved in doing business with Caribbean offshore companies were exposed in 1982 when the important Banco Ambrosiano of Milan collapsed after $1.4 billion of its deposits disappeared in the maze of Caribbean tax havens.

The offshore financial-center boom in the Caribbean is part of an international financial explosion in what is known as the Euromarket. For many years, London was the center of the circulation of Eurocurrency, which is a generic name for any of the major world currencies that remain outside their originating countries. The increasing flow of U.S. dollars into the world market in the 1960s, and the flood of petroleum profits in the 1970s, have been largely responsible for the boom in this international money market. The Euromarket has expanded to become an unregulated pool of $900 billion, 80 percent of which is denominated in dollars.[12] The money-center banks opened offices in offshore centers in the Caribbean like the Cayman Islands because of the ability of the banks to wheel and deal in billions of Eurocurrency without regulation or taxes. The money-center banks in New York, London, or Toronto use the Caribbean offshore banks as intermediaries between the major industrial countries in the movement of capital. The conditions of secrecy and nonregulation so necessary for the safe transfer of underground money from drugs and crime are the same operating conditions valued so highly by the world banking community.

The most rapid growth in the Euromarket in the last two decades has taken place in the Caribbean, where especially free conditions prevail. The Caribbean climate is right for money men. The United Nations estimated that 27 percent of the banks located in world financial centers (where banks gather to facilitate international finance) were in the Caribbean.[13] Although conditions vary from island to island, most offshore companies do not pay taxes on income, profits, capital gains, or dividend distribution. Nor are there any estate, legacy, gift, or succession duties. No tax treaties or country information exchanges threaten income in the home countries. No assets need be on deposit, and sometimes no distinction is made between companies and banks. Anybody can get into the offshore business in the Caribbean. Another attraction of the Caribbean is the use of the English language in the banking and legal systems. Parliamentary political systems reassure the financiers. To further allay concerns about the stability of the offshore centers, the Bahamas and other islands advertise a "built-in safety mechanism that allows foreign-managed assets to flee automatically to other unnamed destinations at any sign of war, violence, or secrecy laws."[14]

Offshore Banks: The Electric Bagmen

In the Bahamas and the Cayman Islands, the registry of banks looks like a *Fortune* magazine rating of the world's top banks, intermingled with scores of smaller banks trying to cash in on an expanding international money market. Twenty years ago, London and Switzerland were the major world financial centers. But with the growth of the transnational corporations, international lenders sought alternative locations that would give them the freedom to loan and transfer vast sums of money without any tax burden and without fear of exchange regulations. In the Caribbean Basin, tax-free, unregulated banking environments are offered by Panama, the Bahamas, and the Cayman Islands. Five ingredients make an attractive offshore banking center: absence of direct income taxation and reserve requirements, liberal exchange controls, modern communication systems, a stable political climate, and a time zone that corresponds with that of major U.S. bank headquarters.

The Bahamas evolved from a shady tax haven to an international offshore financial center managing over $150 billion.[15] With a population of only 235,000 people, the Bahamas now have 350 banks and are the world's second largest loan syndication center after London. The Bahamas have more than 25,000 registered trading companies, about 15,000 of which are active.[16] The islands serve as a major center for booked and actual interbank transactions, mostly for U.S. banks. The Bahamas are also a base for a $2 to $5 billion trust business, of which 95 percent is from the United States. The major Caribbean offshore banking competitor with the Bahamas are the Cayman Islands. Back in the 1960s, the Cayman

Islands had only two banks, but today this British protectorate of 15,000 people hosts 13,600 companies, including 360 banks. Canadian bankers reportedly were responsible for the skyrocketing progress of the islands as a world financial center. "It's a genuine Canadian Club," stated an article in *Canadian Business*, "which has transformed and now manages Cayman's economy."[17]

Shadow transactions are what bankers call most of the business that passes through the books of the offshore centers in the Caribbean. Tangible international capital rarely passes through Nassau or Grand Cayman. The banks register international loans in these offshore centers, but money stays in the bank vaults in New York and London. By transferring the funds on paper to the tax havens the banks can avoid income taxes. And by lending and borrowing money through their offshore facilities, the banks gain added liquidity because they do not have to abide by reserve requirements.

The expansion of the Euromarket has created a free-for-all in international finance that supersedes antiquated systems of national control of monetary and banking systems. In her 1975 book *Euro-dollars: The Money-Market Gypsies*, Jane Little described the Eurodollar market as "a truly international creature beyond the control of any single national authority. In trying to tame the market, central bankers have been in the untenable position of chasing an elephant with butterfly nets." This state of freedom from regulation has contributed, one financial expert said, "to the very grave crisis now enveloping the international banking systems." Symptoms of the cracks in the global financial system came with the collapse of two major U.S. banks: the Franklin National Bank in 1974, and the Penn Square Bank in 1982. Widespread fraud was suspected of Italian bank managers in the failure of the Banco Ambrosiano, which had channeled millions of dollars through Caribbean offshore centers.[18]

The 1982 investigation of Citibank's use of offshore banks to circumvent foreign bank currency laws revealed the shaky foundations of international banking. The Securities and Exchange Commission (SEC) found that Citibank had improperly shifted at least $46 million in currency-transaction profits from its branches in Europe to branches in the Bahamas to illegally escape the higher European taxes.[19] The House Subcommittee on Oversight and Investigations followed up the SEC investigation. The subcommittee's staff study concluded that monetary regulations of national governments are ill equipped to deal with evasions such as Citibank's. One Citibank vice-president called the bank's multimillion-dollar transactions in the Caribbean "rinky-dink deals," while another official called them "pure tax gimmicks." The recorded transfers to the Bahamas were just sham transactions, because the Nassau banks were really departments of the Citibank in Germany. As Representative Albert Gore said, Nassau was "just a device that recorded the transaction, just an electric bagman." Representative John Dingell, chairperson of the committee, said the Citibank dealings raise "the spectre of large multinational banks becoming a law unto themselves beyond the control of national governments. The present international finance crisis may simply be the most serious manifestation of this loss of control."[20]

The Dutch Antillean Loophole

The Netherlands Antilles have succeeded in capturing another type of offshore financial business that takes advantage of foreign tax treaties with the United States to escape U.S. taxes. Many of the U.S. TNCs have subsidiaries in the Netherlands Antilles through which they borrow long-term capital from the Euromarket. The Dutch isles lack natural resources, but they have an abundance of unnatural resources in the form of 15,000 registered corporations, most of which are U.S. corporations dealing in the huge unregulated pool of overseas dollars. A New York investment firm estimated that from 1978 to 1982, U.S. corporations borrowed over $22 billion in long-term Eurobonds—virtually all of which went through these obscure Dutch islands in the southern Caribbean.[21] U.S. corporations borrow capital through these islands to escape a 30 percent withholding tax that the United States imposes on interest payments to foreigners. European and Arab investors can also take advantage of the islands of Aruba and Curaçao to invest in a U.S. subsidiary based there, and thereby escape federal estate taxes. The IRS also suspects that these islands are being used by U.S. drug dealers and tax skimmers to recycle money into the United States.

The former tax commissioner of the islands, Harold Henríquez, said in 1983 that he had a list of 200 major U.S. corporations that had issued bonds through their subsidiaries in the Netherlands Antilles.[22] Among them are Atlantic Richfield Overseas Finance, American Telephone and Telegraph Overseas Finance, and Sears Overseas Finance. In Willemstad, the capital of Curaçao, corporations are on tap, ready to go with an already formed board of directors waiting for an owner to tell them what to do. Known as shelf companies, they can swing into action within one business day.*

Offshore Insurance: The Perils of Captivity

Like the transnational banks, the insurance industry has fled offshore to the Caribbean in search of a tax holiday. The Caribbean insurance industry, based in Bermuda, revolves around the reinsurance and the captive insurance business. A reinsurance company insures another in-

*Sources: *Wall Street Journal*, October 11, 1982; *Euromoney*, April 1983.

surance company. In this way, insurance companies broaden their exposure by spreading around their risks. Because some policies, like insuring oil tankers, are too risky for one insurance company, it transfers part of the risk to another larger company or group of companies. A captive insurance company insures the risks of its own parent company. Exxon, for example, has its own insurance company, called Ancon.

Captive insurance, a $7 billion industry in the Caribbean, permits the large industrial corporations to insure their own risks with coverage on favorable terms and conditions.[23] These in-house insurance companies set up offices in the tax shelters of the Caribbean. The premiums that Exxon pays to its captive company, Ancon, can then be reinvested by Ancon, and the profits from those investments are generally tax-free. Captive insurance, therefore, benefits the parent company, both by offering lower insurance rates than regular commercial companies and by earning profits on its own insurance payments through tax-free investments.

More than 200 of the top U.S. firms have captive insurers. Walton Insurance, for example, belongs to Phillips Petroleum; Bluefield Insurance to Mobil Oil; Bellefonte Insurance to Armco; and Transcon to Ford Motor Co. Thousands of smaller companies, groups, and trade associations have also found a haven in the Caribbean. Insurance companies, both captive and otherwise, operate offshore to avoid lengthy reports required by state insurance commissioners on their investment activity and to evade specific reserve requirements against potential losses. One Bermudian in the insurance business said that Bermuda looked good to company executives and risk managers because "they could go down to Bermuda, play golf, eat fresh fish, and set up a profit center."[24]

When Verbena Daniels, the island's registrar of companies, started working in the registrar's office in 1971, Bermuda had fewer than a hundred insurance companies. In 1983, there were 1,200, and Daniels said that she could only guess at how much business they do because her office was still processing the company reports for 1979.[25] Both the Cayman Islands and the Bahamas have amended their captive legislation to draw some of this business away from Bermuda. The U.S. Virgin Islands, too, have passed permissive legislation for insurance companies. But many U.S. corporations balk at settling their captive companies in the U.S. territory because of its vulnerability to the long arm of U.S. taxation.

Brass-Plate Development

Many of the other Caribbean islands also hope to become offshore financial centers. Turks and Caicos, in 1979, passed a banking ordinance that permits any company registering on the islands to be designated as a trust company with no questions asked. An authority on offshore centers calls the tiny, little-known island of Anguilla "the most liberal corporate domicile for offshore companies in the Eastern Caribbean."[26] Even the traditionally staid island of Barbados is promoting itself as an offshore center. Prime Minister Tom Adams told a group of London bankers that Barbados will not insist the banks hire a native staff: "I can assure you that we shall be liberal in the granting of work permits."[27]

No Physical Presence

Since they do not receive any substantial tax revenues, the islands count on fees and licenses to earn revenues for the government. Those governments in the race to become financial centers argue that additional income from fees and employment generated by the financial business will more than offset the loss of tax revenue and the costs of maintaining an adequate infrastructure for the offshore banks and corporations. In 1979, an IMF study challenged the assumption that offshore financial business really benefits smaller domains like Antigua and Montserrat.[28] These islands see only the paper trails from the transfer of international funds.

When most of the banks are nothing more than shells or brass plates, they generate little employment for the islanders. It is not uncommon for one lawyer-agent to operate 20 or more offshore businesses—all represented by a brass plate etched with the name of the offshore company hanging outside the door of the law office. The Caribbean islands usually do not view the offshore business as the best possible choice to build a stable, modern economy, but rather as one of the few available alternatives the tiny, resource-poor islands have to earn foreign currency. In St. Vincent, the licensing of offshore companies brings the government 5 percent of its annual income—replacing the subsidy received annually from the United Kingdom by this former British colony.[29]

A study of the industry found that 270 of the 300 banks licensed in the Bahamas in 1979 had no physical presence on the islands—they were just brass-plate banks.[30] The offshore banking business contributed only 10 percent of the gross national product and accounted for only 2 or 3 percent of the country's employment. These offshore banks are nothing more than "a plaque, a walk-in closet, a desk, a file cabinet, and a telephone."[31] Despite the billions flowing through the banks, the offshore industry is of no consequence in the local loan market. The absence of strong central banking institutions may mean the country is paying some of the unaccounted costs of hosting the offshore banks with its own unreported revenues.

Dirty Money

Fraud and corruption trail the offshore financial industry much as prostitution follows the tourism industry. The country's elites, its politicians, lawyers, and bankers, invariably develop ties with the fraudulent operators who are inexorably attracted by offshore dealing. Once integrity is lost, the very character of the people of the offshore centers becomes associated with fraud, secret deals, and dishonesty. A high official of the central bank in the Bahamas matter-of-factly stated that it is the duty of the bank to accept all proffered funds. "If you came into my office with one million dollars in your suitcase, I would take it," said the banker.[32] Notices such as one in a bank lobby in the Cayman Islands stating "We take no pictures" feed the image that many offshore banks do not care whether their customers are depositing hot cash. This undiscriminating attitude in accepting what is known as "suitcase currency" contributes to the regular use of offshore trust banks and registered companies by unsavory characters who have made the Caribbean their financial headquarters. Offshore centers are magnets for the drug trade. Drugs are a major, although unquantified, business in the Bahamas. The islands serve both as a physical transfer point for the underground drug business and as a safe place to launder drug profits through offshore corporations.

Offshore business is a step up and a shade lighter in Bermuda, which does not open its doors, as St. Vincent and other islands have, to fake banks, and has not extended a worldwide invitation for foreign companies to register there. The major offshore business in Bermuda is insurance, followed by personal investment trusts. Companies are subject to a bit more supervision, but the priority is to keep the companies on the island rather than scaring them off by any relaxation of the secrecy restrictions. The Bermudian police now abide by stricter regulations after an officer testified about the criminal activities of one registered firm. Reacting to their muzzling by the authorities, one police officer said, "We are serving the business/political interests who put business ahead of simple right and wrong."[33]

A congressional study team found that the attorneys in offshore centers regularly accept criminal business in connection with setting up and managing offshore corporations and trusts.[34] Residents say that the FBI regularly visits the island in what are usually futile attempts to track down a drug trafficker or fraudulent business operator. Returning from Antigua, the congressional team concluded, "Antigua needs assistance. It is impoverished, plagued with influence peddlers and foreign freebooters, with a local bar ungoverned by an ethical code and some local officials who are allegedly careless about favors or the foreign company they keep."

Of the three regions (Africa, Central America, and the Caribbean) studied by the Permanent Subcommittee on Investigations, the Caribbean islands were found to be the most vulnerable to involvement in corruption and criminal activities. The committee staff said this appraisal "conforms to our impression of gross inadequacies, improper influence, and reported criminal involvement in the Caribbean involving some banks, local officials, assorted traveling highwaymen, narcotics traffickers, and the like."

Financial Forecast

The workings of the financial sector, in all its onshore and offshore ramifications, reveal more than any other sector the exploited and fragile position of the Caribbean nations. The local commercial banks, those that deal with local savings deposits and loans, are almost completely dominated by the largest transnational banks in the world. As poor as this region is, the Citibanks, Royals, and Barclays continue to expand and to make higher profits than those earned back home in the United States, Canada, and Great Britain.

The consumer and commercial banking operations take the money off the top of the Caribbean economies—from trading, savings, and foreign-currency manipulations—thus depriving the economies of the required capital for internal investment and development projects. While most other economic sectors have suffered lately, the foreign banks have enjoyed increasing flows of funds. As long as the surplus generated by the Caribbean economies remains in the control of foreign banks, these economies will surely remain in their sorry state of dependency and underdevelopment.

These small and fragile Caribbean islands are an unlikely base for one of the world centers of international finance for offshore Eurocurrency financing. The world's leading banks and many smaller banks of the industrial world have taken advantage of the economic fragility of the Caribbean islands to demand privileges and exemptions. While offshore financing does provide some jobs and income, it cannot be considered as an integral part of the future economic development of the Caribbean.

Debt for Development

Who should be punished more: the addict or the money-pusher?
                                            —Luxembourg senior banker

Twenty years ago the Caribbean people began ridding their countries of their colonial masters. In the place of the crown agents and administrators from Buckingham Palace came Caribbean politicians who spoke of self-determination for their people. Not having the resources to develop their newly independent nations, the fledgling governments appealed to foreign lenders. Obligingly, the multilateral banks (like the World Bank) and bilateral lenders (like Canada and the United States) plied the new nations with loan after loan. Today, the Caribbean people are finding once again that they are not the masters of their own houses. The Caribbean countries have in a sense been mortgaged to foreign moneylenders, who are telling their governments how they should order their budgets and structure their economies. Unfortunately, the plans of the Caribbean people to build modern nations have not resulted in economic development, but rather in further dependence and debt. By 1980, the West Indies had turned into an archipelago of debtor colonies.

SINKING IN DEBT

If indebtedness were a sign of development, the Caribbean nations would have made great progress in the last 20 years. But for all their borrowing, the countries of the region have not shown any notable development. Instead, all they have are large trade deficits, falling international reserves, and massive debts. No longer are the Caribbean countries borrowing most of their money for productive development projects, but simply to pay the interest and servicing of their accumulated debt. The Caribbean nations have now come to their days of economic reckoning.

Unable to pay their bills and balance their budgets, governments have been ruthlessly cutting social-service programs. In Jamaica, government cutbacks have meant a severe shortage of nurses at the public hospitals

134

and a breakdown in the education system. In the Dominican Republic, the failure of the government to maintain disease immunization and eradication programs has contributed to an outbreak of malaria and other epidemics. Forty percent of all illnesses in the Dominican Republic can no longer be treated because the shortage of foreign exchange has obstructed the importation of critical medicines.[1] Also affected by the lack of foreign exchange are Caribbean companies, which cannot buy the materials and the equipment they need to run their businesses. An indirect result of third world indebtedness and the enforcement of austerity programs is that these countries can no longer buy as many goods from the industrial nations, and as a result become further mired in the international economic recession.

The extent of Caribbean indebtedness is alarming. The Dominican Republic, for example, had an external public debt of $6 million in 1960. By 1982, that public debt had increased 340 times to over $2 billion. In the Dominican Republic of 20 years ago, less than 1 percent of the income from its exports would have covered its annual debt service (total of interest and principal payments). Today, about 20 percent of export income goes just to pay off the country's debt service each year. Within the last ten years, the amount the Dominican Republic has to pay in interest on its debt has multiplied almost 25 times. This dizzy rise of interest on debt has resulted not only from the increase in the principal of the debt but also from the doubling and tripling of interest rates in the last 20 years.

Another way to show the magnitude of the debt in the Dominican Republic is to apportion the debt among the Dominican people. If the country's public debt in 1982 were shared by the entire population, every inhabitant would owe $328 to foreign creditors. The 1960s and 1970s are reputed to have been years of progress for the Dominican Republic. About all the Dominican people have to show for the last two decades of development, however, is a per capita debt that is over $300 higher than it was in 1960.[2]

This picture of indebtedness is not peculiar to the Dominican Republic but describes the plight of the entire region. From 1970 to 1982 the external public debt of Caribbean nations increased 700 percent, while the value of exports and the gross domestic product did not even double (Table 7A). Where does the money come from to pay for the loans? From multilateral lending institutions, donor governments, and, increasingly, private transnational banks—the very institutions that pushed the countries into debt in the first place. Most governments have been reluctant to halt the import of nonessential goods or to increase taxes on the wealthy as a way of improving their financial situation. Instead they have relied on debt financing to cover budget expenses. While almost all foreign lending was previously for development projects, an ever increasing pro-

TABLE 7A
REGIONAL ECONOMIC GROWTH
($ millions)

Country	External Debt		Exports		GDP	
	1970	1982	1970	1982	1970	1982
Bahamas	50	228*	na	1,182	na	1,353
Barbados	16	332	227	470	554	603
Dominican Republic	290	2,063	504	1,045	2,923	5,999
Guyana	123	933	298	247	529	560
Haiti	45	464*	111	219	904	1,380
Jamaica	192	2,060	1,123	903	3,371	3,181
Suriname	6	27	na	na	na	na
Trinidad	122	820	674	938	1,743	2,986
TOTAL	844	6,927	2,937	5,004	10,024	16,062
INCREASE	720%		70%		60%	

*figures for 1981

Source: IDB, Economic and Social Progress in Latin America, 1983

portion of international lending now goes just to pay annual debt-service bills.

All foreign lenders have increased their interest rates while shortening the period of time allowed to pay back the loans. As a consequence, annual service payments on the region's external public debt have increased more than twice as fast as the increase of total debt (Table 7B). Average interest rates paid by third world nations more than doubled in the last decade.[3] The funds for this debt servicing are coming directly out of reduced government budgets, which means that less money is available for education, health, housing, and other public services. In 1971, debt servicing consumed less than 5 percent of the budgets of the Caribbean governments. By 1981, public external debt charges had grown to an estimated 26 percent of Jamaica's revenues, 26 percent of the Dominican Republic's revenues, and 50 percent of Guyana's revenues.[4]

In 1982, the total external public debt in the Caribbean was over $18 billion (including Puerto Rico and Cuba). Even this hefty figure underestimates the true extent of Caribbean indebtedness, since it excludes debt that is not publicly guaranteed as well as public debt with maturities of less than one year. The Inter-American Development Bank (IDB) has estimated that 60 percent of the total external debt of Latin America and the Caribbean was external public debt, the rest being owed by the region's hard-pressed private sector.[5]

TABLE 7B
GROWTH OF PUBLIC DEBT
($ millions)

Country	External Debt		Service Payments on External debt	
	1970	1982	1970	1982
Bahamas	50	228*	7	19*
Barbados	16	332	1	29
Dominican Republic	290	2,063	12	305
Guyana	123	933	5	89
Haiti	45	464*	4	20*
Jamaica	192	2,060	14	380
Suriname	6	27	0	27
Trinidad	122	820	15	93
TOTAL	844	6,927	58	962
INCREASE	720%		1,560%	

*figures for 1981
Source: IDB, *Economic and Social Progress in Latin America,* 1983

Transnational Banks Increase Caribbean Lending

Besides the startling increases in debt, the most striking change in the "debt for development" system is the increase in private lending to third world governments. Figures for Latin America and the Caribbean show that in 1960 private sources accounted for about 50 percent of the region's debt. By 1982, private creditors (mainly banks) were responsible for nearly 70 percent of the area's external public debt.[6] The Caribbean debt picture reflects this increase in private bank debt. The percentage owed to private banks in the last decade has jumped almost 4 times in the Dominican Republic, 5 times in Trinidad, and 3 times in Jamaica.

Representatives from underdeveloped nations tell stories of being hounded by loan agents to borrow money from the major private banks. "I can hardly face going back to the hotel," said one country official attending a world banking conference. "There are six different banks waiting for me."[7] In the 1970s, the banks of the industrial nations, having more money than they could loan out to depressed local markets, sought out sovereign borrowers in the third world. Between 1970 and 1980, the debt of the third world to private sources increased 9 times.[8] The threat looms that these debtor nations will default on their loans. Especially threatened are the largest nine banks in the United States, whose loans to "developing" nations are equal to 220 percent of their total capital.[9]

Describing the recklessness of this private lending activity, Anthony Sampson writes in his book *The Money Lenders*, "Selling loans was like offering crates of whiskey to an alcoholic."

High Profits on Foreign Loans

In the Caribbean and other underdeveloped regions, the skyrocketing prices of oil and other imports have caused severe balance-of-trade problems and the consequent need to borrow foreign currency. Prices of imports rose by two-thirds for third world nations from 1970 to 1980.[10] Plummeting prices for agricultural and mineral exports have also deepened trade-balance deficits.

When the non-oil-exporting nations in the third world began hurting for foreign exchange to pay their bills, the transnational banks were being overloaded with deposits from oil-exporting nations. They began happily lending out their surplus funds to the underdeveloped world. Bankers felt safe in lending to sovereign nations because they believed the chances of default were slim. Even on loans to private borrowers in the third world, the loan losses are lower than on domestic loans.[11] The exorbitant interest rates and the short loan periods account for the profitability of foreign loans.

Providing additional security for private lenders are the International Money Fund (IMF), World Bank, and even bilateral lenders like the United States—all of which have increased lending for debt servicing and balance-of-payments support. The multilateral lenders and the United States, while cutting bank loans for development projects, have increased their emergency support for governments facing bankruptcy. Transnational banks now demand that Caribbean nations come to terms with the adjustment programs of the World Bank and the IMF before agreeing to lend more money.

Extent of Private Debt

Not only is private lending out of control, but it is not even properly recorded. A good part of the private lending is not included in the external public debt figures because those figures do not cover short-term (less than one year) public debt, or the substantial private foreign debt of the Caribbean nations. The home governments of the transnational banks do not even know how much money individual banks have lent to different foreign nations. One estimate of private bank lending in the Caribbean comes from the Bank for International Settlements in Switzerland. According to its figures, the private banks of the major capitalist nations have assets of over $160 billion in the Caribbean region.[12] Over $154 billion of those assets are in the offshore financial centers. Borrowers in the Caribbean states that are not offshore financial centers owed foreign banks over $6 billion as of March 1983.

The U.S. federal government keeps general records of the claims of U.S. banks on foreigners. Its figures, which cover only seven Caribbean nations, show that the debt to U.S. banks in the region (as of December 1982) was $18.6 billion.[13]* The nine largest U.S. banks control most of these loans. The nine largest U.S. banks control over 70 percent of U.S. private lending to the Dominican Republic, Jamaica, and Trinidad & Tobago.[14] Private bank lending has an exceedingly fast turnaround in the Caribbean. In the case of the Dominican Republic, 65 percent of the loans have a maturity of less than a year, while only 0.2 percent are for over five years.

THE INTERNATIONAL MONETARY FUND (IMF)

The main difference between the International Monetary Fund (IMF) and the other multilaterals is that the IMF does not lend to specific development projects. The IMF was founded to avoid the international financial instability that characterized the period before World War II. Its original purpose was to guarantee the stability of international exchange rates and to facilitate international trade.

With the advent of the Eurocurrency market, the IMF no longer even maintains the pretense that it regulates the international flow of exchange. The world's largest private banks shift billions of dollars around the world to manipulate the value of currencies. This huge Eurocurrency market has made the IMF obsolete as the central monetary institution of the capitalist world. The IMF has gained a new role, however, as guardian of the financial stability of the third world nations in the international capitalist order.

The IMF lends to third world nations when they experience temporary balance-of-trade problems or when they are burdened by more serious debt crises and current-accounts deficits. The IMF injects a sudden flow of foreign exchange into the debtor countries, which allows them to pay off their debt obligations and fulfill the demands by foreign investors and suppliers for foreign exchange.

In many ways, the IMF is like a fire truck that hurries around the world to douse financial crises with its loans. There is a large price to pay for IMF crisis relief, however, as many Caribbean nations have learned.

---

*Most of this debt is accounted for by claims on offshore financial centers in the Cayman Islands, Netherlands Antilles, Bermuda, and the Bahamas. Calculations of the non-offshore debt to banks in the United States are available only for Jamaica, Trinidad, and the Dominican Republic. U.S. banks and other private financial companies hold most of the over $8 billion public debt of Puerto Rico.

Not only do the loans have to be paid back, but the IMF attaches conditions to its lending that often require severe adjustments in the economic and political programs of the debtor nations.

When the IMF lends in cases of severe financial crisis, it requires the borrowing country to agree to an IMF-sponsored austerity or stabilization program. The debtor nation can receive the IMF's financial help only if it agrees to abide by the strict conditions imposed by these IMF programs. The purpose of the IMF stabilization programs is to restructure the economy and the budget of the debtor nations to allow them to pay off their debts and create an atmosphere conducive to international trade and investment. About 35 third world nations were participating in IMF stabilization programs by the end of 1983. Caribbean nations that have come under IMF programs are Jamaica, Antigua, Grenada, Guyana, Haiti, the Dominican Republic, Dominica, and Barbados.

The common trait of IMF stabilization programs is the assumption that the main causes of economic disorder are faulty internal policies rather than adverse world market conditions. Consequently, the solutions demanded by the IMF require substantial changes and sacrifices by the debt-ridden nation. The stabilization package demanded by the IMF for its loans generally includes the following conditions: (1) tight wage controls, (2) cutbacks in public spending, (3) incentives for foreign investment, (4) currency devaluation, (5) promotion of export, (6) elimination of price ceilings for basic commodities like food, and (7) divestiture of government-owned corporations. The country's workers and poor have to bear the burden of IMF's stabilization plans. In contrast, the local elite and foreign investors commonly remain unscathed by the IMF measures.

The first step of the IMF plan is to squeeze out money from the national budget and the workers' wages to repay a country's debts. That part of its plan is called its "austerity program." The second step concerns both the promotion of exports to increase foreign-exchange earnings and the implementation of policies to augment the supply of investment capital. According to the IMF, a country's balance of payments will improve if it increases its exports, and if its exports are made more competitive on the world market by lowering their prices through devaluation. Also, the IMF says that a country's economic equilibrium will improve if the government reduces the demand for imports by lowering wages and cutting government services.

The major problems of IMF stabilization programs are that they hurt the poorest sector of the society, undermine the long-run development process of the country, and do little to solve the long-term financial crisis. By tearing down protective shields against the intrusion of international capital and foreign goods, the IMF contributes to the breakdown of local capital formation. The IMF programs ignore external causes of third world debt and balance-of-payments crises such as high oil prices, declining terms of trade, rising interest rates, inflation in the industrial nations, and world recession. Instead, the IMF tries to force-feed debtor nations' adjustment programs that make the countries more vulnerable to and dependent on a world market that is prejudiced in favor of the industrial powers. IMF programs also work to undermine the position of those trying to follow alternative development strategies, like the Manley government in Jamaica. All this is concealed behind a veil of technical and scientific analysis, which, according to the IMF, carries no political or ideological bias. [15]

Because the amount of money that a nation allocates to the IMF determines its voting power, the large industrial nations, known as the Group of Ten, determine IMF policies and country programs. The IMF, more than the other multilaterals, has tried to maintain an appearance of objectivity, professionalism, and apolitical concern for the financial stability of member nations. In recent years, however, a series of flagrantly political lending programs has all but shattered that facade of objectivity.

Jamaica: "Between a Rock and a Hard Place"

In the 1976 elections, the people of Jamaica overwhelmingly endorsed a program of economic and social reforms that Prime Minister Michael Manley had initiated during his first term. Under Manley, the People's National Party (PNP) imposed price controls, enforced equal pay for women, legislated a land reform program, and mandated a minimum wage. These measures, combined with a program to increase government revenue from the bauxite industry, earned the PNP widespread support in Jamaica. But the social reforms and the economic nationalism of the Manley administration also had the result of frightening foreign investors and political leaders from leading industrial nations. They feared the arrival of socialism in Jamaica.

Shortly after the start of Manley's second term as prime minister, the country's economy started to slide backward. World recession and skyrocketing oil prices shook Jamaica's underdeveloped economy. Jamaica also faced a backlash from foreign investors. The bauxite industry felt especially threatened by the increased national control of the Manley government. To make matters worse, an anti-Jamaica press campaign in the United States sent the tourism industry reeling downward.

Looking over the country's shoulder was the IMF, which started pressuring Jamaica in 1974 to adopt one of its standard austerity programs. At first Jamaica resisted, but in 1977 the Manley government yielded to the demands of the IMF in an attempt to shore up its sinking economy. According to the IMF, the financial crisis in Jamaica was the direct result of mistaken government policies. The IMF negotiators said that high wages, a protected internal market, and an overvalued national currency all contributed to making the country's exports uncompetitive. Furthermore, the IMF told the Manley government that excessive spending on public welfare programs was causing a budget deficit and that government regulatory programs were causing the flight of capital. In short, the basic problem with Jamaica, according to the IMF, was that government policies favored labor over capital and the public sector over the private sector. The left wing of the PNP unsuccessfully opposed any acquiescence to the IMF and counterposed a plan of greater state intervention and broader economic reforms—a program that Manley vetoed.

To remedy Jamaica's economic crisis, the IMF imposed four major conditions for its loans: (1) a 15 percent currency devaluation, (2) a guaranteed 20 percent profit margin for private-sector investments, (3) a wage freeze, and (4) massive cutbacks in social services and public programs such as food subsidies. As a result of this IMF austerity program, prices for imported goods soared, unemployment reached 30 percent, and the general welfare of the Jamaican people sharply declined. By agreeing to the IMF plan, Manley cut into his own base of support; yet, at the same time, he felt he had no choice.

The IMF program brought the process of domestic reforms to a complete halt and undermined the living standard of the vast majority of Jamaicans. Manley thought the IMF reforms would ease the balance-of-payments crisis while appeasing the national bourgeoisie and foreign investors. The IMF plan did secure a higher level of debt payments to foreign creditors, but the economy remained in severe financial straits and capital continued to flee Jamaica. The government faithfully followed the IMF plan through 1978. Yet, when Jamaica failed by a slight margin to pass one of its performance tests in 1979, the IMF demanded harsher measures. It required a major reorganization of the structure of government administration, a paring down and rationalization of the public enterprises, and massive government cuts.

Defying the IMF

Feeling that it could bow no lower to the IMF and that there was nothing to gain by harsher austerity, the Manley government boldly broke off negotiations with the IMF in March 1980. In defiance of the IMF, the government turned back to its original program of democratic socialism. Jamaica's decision to buck the IMF won it the recognition and admiration of other third world nations, but left it dangling without any support from the multilateral banks and most foreign creditors. By that time Manley also found that he could no longer count on support from the poor and working people of Jamaica. As a consequence, the Manley administration suffered a clear defeat at the polls in 1980. His opponent, conservative Edward Seaga, offered the electorate "deliverance" from the economic disruption of the 1970s.

Seaga claimed that government mismanagement and Manley's program of democratic socialism had just about wrecked the country's econ-omy. To a question on the *McNeil/Lehrer Report* about how much of Jamaica's economic trouble was Manley's fault, Franklin Knight of Johns Hopkins University responded: "I would say not much. If you want to put it on a scale I would say it's about 10 percent mismanagement. I think the main problem is the high inflation rate, the downturn in the Western economy, and the enormous increase in the price of oil."[16] There was no question that the economy was in shambles, but the United States and Seaga placed all the blame on Prime Minister Manley, even though it was primarily the program of the IMF that had guided the course of the country's economy in the late 1970s.

Back to the IMF

Immediately after the 1980 elections, the IMF went back to Jamaica with an offer of over $650 million in loans at conditions considerably less stringent than it normally applies. The new government in Kingston hailed the 1981 IMF agreement as the linchpin in the country's economic re-covery. The program stressed supply-side economics, a theory that had gained popularity in Washington. The IMF program, along with USAID and World Bank loans, involved increased credit for investors, an em-phasis on the export of agricultural products, and a campaign to persuade foreign investors to set up offshore assembly plants. Even with the huge influx of grants and loans designed to build its industrial and agricultural export sectors, unfavorable market conditions prevented Jamaica from obtaining an increase in foreign-exchange earnings from the sale of its exports. The flood of capital into Jamaica caused its external public debt to shoot up to new heights. Although Seaga continued to profess his optimism about the progress of the economy, it became clear by 1983 that Jamaica had missed the economic targets set by the IMF by a wide margin. The gap widened between the government's rosy view of the economy and the reality experienced by both workers and the business community. A Kingston newspaper story in 1983 said Jamaica was caught between a rock and a hard place. "The rock is our desperate economic plight and the hard place is the IMF."[17] At first the IMF treated Jamaica tenderly, but with the Seaga government continually failing to reach IMF targets it has adopted an increasingly harder line.

By the end of 1983, Prime Minister Seaga yielded to a harsh IMF austerity program that many predicted would lead to widespread social unrest. A substantial devaluation of the Jamaican dollar meant windfall profits to the export sector and an increase in the cost of imports. The IMF also forced the government to increase prices for basic services, such as water, electricity, and transportation fuel, as well as eliminating price ceilings on basic food items. As with other IMF programs, the poor of the country were severely affected by the program while the export-sector industries (like the bauxite industry) greatly profited from the austerity measures and the devaluation.

Economists Richard Bernal and Norman Girvan concluded in a 1982 issue of *Monthly Review* that the IMF was "a major contributor to the downfall of the Manley government,"[18] and forced the government to endorse conservative economic policies that directly contradicted its stated political and social philosophies of democratic socialism. When Manley broke away from that contradiction, Jamaica and the rest of the third world learned the hard lesson that passive participation in the international capitalist system and acceptance of its rules of conduct are about the only way for a small, dependent country to survive within that system. Bernal and Girvan predicted that the price of the new agreements with the IMF "will be growing external indebtedness and a progressive loss of autonomy in economic decision making."[19]

Objections to IMF's Expanded Role

The upward debt spiral of third world countries and their increasing inability to meet debt payments have pushed the IMF into a vastly expanded role as watchdog for foreign lenders and creditors. Its increased work has also meant a need for more money from the developed capitalist countries to meet the epidemic of debt crises around the world. The IMF decided in 1983 to expand its lending capacity by almost 50 percent. Its request for a vastly increased financial commitment from the United States caused howls of protest from an unusual coalition of liberal and conservative politicians in Congress. The Reagan administration initially rejected the IMF petition, but then suddenly reversed itself and supported a more than $8 billion increase in the U.S. commitment to the IMF. President Reagan sent a letter to the U.S. Senate saying, "Passage of this legislation is of the utmost importance to the world economy, to the strength of the recovery, and to the U.S. position of leadership in world affairs."[20]

The U.S. Treasury has called the IMF "the backup of the system." That system, debt for development, is in crisis. The security of transnational banks is endangered by the inability of the third world debtors to meet their loan repayment schedules, even with the help of the IMF. Rather than providing the capital for development projects, the expanding indebtedness to foreign countries is crushing the development potential and draining the economic surplus of the region. The heavy indebtedness of the Caribbean nations to public and private lenders has come to be the most suffocating form of foreign control these small countries now endure.

The Multilateral Lenders:

STRUCTURING CARIBBEAN DEVELOPMENT

If we don't produce this expanded level of support, then comes the revolution. It's as simple as that. We have to do it, or else we'll be destroying ourselves.
— World Bank President A.W. Clausen, former president of BankAmerica

The job of readying the Caribbean nations for investments by TNCs and fitting the region into the patterns of international trade falls to the multilateral lenders. These are the international and regional banking institutions that provide the financing for such projects as hydroelectric dams, roads to mining sites, irrigation for coffee plantations, and assembly-industry zones. The multilateral lenders borrow their money mainly from the industrial nations and the large private banks and then relend it, primarily to third world nations. The foremost multilateral institution is the World Bank, which has its headquarters in Washington, D.C. Other multilateral institutions doing business in the Caribbean are the Inter-American Development Bank (IDB) and the Caribbean Development Bank (CDB).

WORLD BANK

The World Bank is the largest international financial institution in the world. Members of the bank include the governments of 145 nations. It is the large industrial nations, however, particularly the United States, that determine the policies and programs of the World Bank. The president of the United States appoints the president of the World Bank, currently A.W. Clausen, former BankAmerica president; his predecessor was Robert McNamara, former U.S. Secretary of Defense and former president of the Ford Motor Company. After leaving the World Bank, McNamara became a director of Royal Dutch Shell.

The World Bank has three divisions: the International Bank for Reconstruction and Development (IBRD), the International Development

Association (IDA), and the International Finance Corporation (IFC). The largest of the World Bank group is IBRD, which is responsible for over 90 percent of the bank's loans to the Caribbean. IBRD lends money at slightly below the commercial rate, while IDA lends only to the poorest third world countries at concessional, or soft, terms of interest and repayment. Jean Claude Duvalier's Haiti is the only Caribbean country that consistently receives IDA funds. Both IBRD and IDA require a government guarantee of repayment. The third member of the World Bank group, IFC, lends to nonguaranteed private projects.

Getting Your Money Back

Like any private bank, the World Bank is interested in the repayment of its loans. "Lending only to those [projects] with investment opportunities sufficient to produce a significant marketable surplus is perhaps the best way to reduce the level of default," concluded the World Bank in 1975 in its book *Assault on Poverty*.[1] Another common feature of its lending, and the lending of all multilateral banks, is that most of the funds are spent on things that cost a great deal of money and must be imported, like buildings, dams, expensive equipment, and foreign consultants. In that way, the donor nations get their money back by exporting to the countries with multilateral projects. According to one study, for every dollar it contributed to multilateral aid, the United States got back $1.08 in contracts and purchases.[2]

In Cheryl Payer's study of the World Bank, she concluded that the bank consciously uses its financial power to promote the interests of private international capital in its expansion to every corner of the underdeveloped world. According to Payer, the World Bank is "perhaps the most important instrument for prying state control of its third world member countries out of the hands of nationalists and socialists who would regulate international capital's inroads."[3]

New Directions in Banking

In the last 20 years, the World Bank has dramatically increased its commitment to agribusiness and rural development projects. The Institute for Food and Development Policy, while acknowledging the need for programs to improve third world agriculture, criticized the focus and nature of the World Bank's agricultural lending. In its book, *Food First*, the institute noted that the bank claimed to be allocating nearly half its rural credit to small farms, which means more than half its credit is going to medium- and large-sized farms. "The landless," the institute observed, "make up 40 to 60 percent of the population in many third world countries, even in the bank's conservative estimate."[4] Rural development, in World Bank terms, does not mean the development of the rural poor, but rather the development of the rural infrastructure. Rural development loans pay for electrification, roads, and large irrigation projects that reinforce the control of large landowners.

Another problem with World Bank agricultural lending is that it promotes export crops rather than production for the local market or for subsistence consumption. After all, small farmers who grow food to eat and to sell to their neighbors do not earn any foreign currency, unlike coffee or tobacco farmers. And it is foreign exchange that pays back the loans from the World Bank. The modernization of third world agriculture advocated by the World Bank fits nicely into agribusiness plans. Ready to benefit are bankers involved in rural credit services; agribusiness firms committed to the cultivation, processing, and marketing of crops and livestock; and the manufacturers of agricultural machinery, fertilizers, pesticides, seed, feed, and packaging.[5]

Another major change in the direction of World Bank financing occurred in 1980, when the World Bank began providing third world nations with loans that were not targeted for specific development projects. These nonproject loans are called "structural adjustment loans" because recipient nations have to agree to make certain structural adjustments in their economic policies. The loans are geared to improve an entire sector of a third world economy, such as assembly industries in Jamaica or public-sector management in Guyana. The changes required of recipient nations are detailed in an "action program" formulated by the World Bank. The structural adjustment loans are dispensed in stages so as to monitor the progress a borrowing country is making toward meeting the demands of its action program. The structural-adjustment loans and the attached conditions are very similar to the stabilization programs of the IMF.

Recently, World Bank operations have emphasized cofinancing and private-sector investment. World Bank President Clausen has frequently voiced his belief that transnational banks and industrial corporations should be in the forefront of the bank's development plans. "I see the transnational corporation," said Clausen, "as an important ally of creative and enterprising people who believe it's pragmatically possible to build a better and more productive global society that can enhance the living standards of everyone."[6] In keeping with that philosophy, the World Bank has structured its funding in the Caribbean to promote foreign investment and foreign trade rather than internal self-development.

Country Programs

In 1982, Jamaica received 69 percent of the World Bank's loans to the Caribbean.[7] The total of World Bank loans the Seaga government received that year amounted to $133 million—more than the island received from combined World Bank lending from the bank's birth, in 1946, to 1978. Over half the bank's 1982 lending to Jamaica went for a structural adjustment loan to reorient Jamaica's economy toward export industries and away from production for the internal market. The World Bank also lent Jamaica $13.5 million to expand its free-zone industrial park, and financed 30 separate programs of research and technical assistance designed to assist Prime Minister Seaga's campaign to make the island a "Caribbean showcase."

In the Dominican Republic, the bank is financing a tourist development project in Puerto Plata that includes condominiums, golf courses, and a Holiday Inn. In 1982 the World Bank announced $20 million in loans for two projects. One loan will finance the construction of a dock to unload coal vessels from the United States. Another smaller project was approved to provide technical assistance for coal and petroleum exploration. The World Bank's first loan to the Dominican Republic was used to create infrastructure for the foreign-owned nickel industry. A recent World Bank loan to Haiti went to the government's Industrial Development Foundation to improve its ability to attract and keep foreign industrial investment.

In Guyana, the World Bank has pressured the government, through a structural adjustment loan, to adopt measures that limit public-sector operations and encourage the expansion of the private sector, including foreign investment. In accordance with the wishes of the World Bank, the government in 1982 promised to invite foreign capital back into the bauxite industry, to establish an investment code, to curtail public involvement in the economy, and to initiate discussions with the IMF.

Its Articles of Agreement bind the World Bank to refrain from considering the politics of potential borrowers. The World Bank claims it has no political purposes behind its lending. By advocating increased foreign involvement in the Caribbean economy and reduced public control, however, the World Bank supports a brand of third world politics favored by the United States and other industrial nations. Since the thrust of its projects is to create favorable investment conditions, the bank often justifies its refusal to loan money to leftist governments on grounds that they do not offer proper conditions for investment and economic growth, while lending to unpopular right-wing governments that promote foreign investment and trade. In the cases of Brazil, Bolivia, and Chile, the World Bank authorized few or no loans for populist or democratic socialist governments, but approved large loans for military regimes that ousted the popular governments. In Central America, it has refused funding requests from Sandinista Nicaragua in the last few years and has favored the military-controlled governments in El Salvador, Guatemala, and Honduras.

Investing in the Caribbean

The third arm of the World Bank, the International Finance Corporation (IFC), is not a corporation, as its name suggests; it is a transnational lending and investment institution. Though its official name and goals suggest otherwise, it is not a private corporation. Not one provision of the IFC charter discusses helping the world's poor and hungry. The IFC is one of the few international financial institutions that can make both equity investments and loans without government guarantees. In other words, while most multilateral loans need the promise of the government to back the loan or investment in case of default, the IFC takes on the entire risk of financing in the third world. As well as directly helping companies, the IFC puts its money into local financial institutions with the goal of encouraging "the flow of capital." Over half IFC's $1.6 billion financial commitment, as of 1982, went to manufacturing companies.[8]

The IFC rechannels funds from World Bank members, bilateral agencies, other multilateral institutions, transnational banks, and private financial corporations. The United States, which holds almost 40 percent of IFC's shares, has successfully pushed the IFC to make the Caribbean Basin its priority. Among the IFC-financed corporations in the Caribbean in 1981 were Pegasus Hotels of Jamaica (the country's most exclusive hotels, owned by Trust House Forte of England), Cementos Nacionales (a Gulf + Western affiliate) in the Dominican Republic, West Indies Glass in Jamaica, Canning and Company from Trinidad, and a large poultry operation in Haiti called Promoteurs et Investisseurs Associés.

The IFC has placed special emphasis on the Caribbean region through its Caribbean Project Development Facility, which was founded in 1981 to organize financing for medium-sized corporations. The development facility operates on the premise that the potential exists for the development of private investment projects in the Caribbean ranging from a half-million dollars to $5 million. One of its $5 million financing ventures is with Jamaica Flour Mills (owned partially by Pillsbury), which will expand its milling capacity for imported wheat. This IFC facility, which receives most of its funding from USAID and the Inter-American Development Bank, also assisted the U.S.-owned Sealy Mattress Company in Antigua. In the Dominican Republic, the IFC arranged a cooperative financing program between the Agribusiness Council of New York and FIDE, the government's development bank. Representing the region on the Development Facility's board of directors are Carlton Alexander of Grace Kennedy Corporation and Sidney Knox of Neal & Massy Holdings.

INTER-AMERICAN DEVELOPMENT BANK

Alongside the World Bank there are regional multilateral banks. Each is like a mini-World Bank and takes its cue from the World Bank's policy initiatives. The regional multilateral financial institution for Latin America and the Caribbean is the Inter-American Development Bank (IDB). Possibly more than the other international financial institutions, the IDB uses its funding to support foreign investment and to back governments favored by the United States. The IDB stood behind the Somoza dictatorship in Nicaragua, and the biggest winners of its 1981 lending in Central America were war-torn El Salvador and Guatemala.[9] In line with the U.S. focus on the Caribbean, the IDB has started to flood the region with loans.

Only a very small percentage of IDB funding goes to projects that directly help people, like education, housing, and health care. Most loans support infrastructure projects that facilitate foreign investment. In 1981, a category it calls social infrastructure, which covers programs like managerial training for agribusinesses and industrial projects, received only 11 percent of IDB loans.

Private-Sector Support

The overriding objective of the IDB has been to promote private enterprise as a means of economic development. Even when the rhetoric of the World Bank contained phrases about helping the world's poor and establishing "new directions" in lending, the IDB was stressing direct and indirect private-sector support. Most of its loans indirectly assist private businesses, through development banks or through infrastructure projects like roads, industrial parks, and improved electricity services. IDB has worked closely with USAID to build a network of agricultural and industrial development banks throughout the region. It takes pride in its development banks in 11 Latin American and Caribbean countries and its support of 80 others.[10]

The IDB has helped establish industrial parks throughout the Caribbean that provide foreign investors with factory shells and necessary infrastructure. In Haiti, after financing one park in Port-au-Prince, it offered funding for another industrial zone in Cap-Haïtien. In 1981 and 1982, the IDB provided funds to publish guides for investors in the Dominican Republic and Haiti, conduct feasibility studies for prospective investors, build industrial parks and supply export financing in Barbados, and provide technical assistance to promote assembly industries. In 1982, it financed the expansion of a cement plant in Jamaica and a building-supplies company in Barbados.

CARIBBEAN DEVELOPMENT BANK

The Caribbean has its own regional multilateral institution called the

Caribbean Development Bank (CDB). The initiative to establish the CDB did not come from the countries of the region but from the industrial nations with economic interests in the area. After the West Indies Federation fell apart, a group of economic planners from the United States, Great Britain, and Canada, the Tripartite Mission, called for the founding of a regional development agency that would include a development bank.[11] Soon after, the Canada/Commonwealth Caribbean Conference in Ottawa formulated a proposal for the development bank, which was established in 1969. All the English-speaking Caribbean countries, including Belize and the British dependencies, are members of the bank, as well as four non-Caribbean nations—Colombia, Venezuela, Canada, and the United Kingdom, who are non-borrowing members. The three countries that formed the Tripartite Mission have provided 45 percent of CDB loan capital.

Most CDB financing flows to productive projects in agriculture, industry, and tourism. The regional bank considers as priorities infrastructure projects, like roads to banana-producing areas and electricity for industrial investments. Only 14 percent of the bank's funding since 1970 has gone to a category called Social and Personal Services, which includes technical consultations and training programs for industry.

Since its inception, over 25 percent of CDB financing has gone directly to the private sector in the Caribbean. Unlike other international financial institutions (except the IFC), CDB can make loans to private companies without government guarantees of loan repayment. In addition, the regional bank can invest directly in the equity of private enterprises. The CDB is the leading supporter of development finance corporations that act as intermediaries between the international financial institutions and the private sector. A CDB supervision program monitors the operations of 18 such development banks throughout the Caribbean. In 1982 over two-thirds of its private-sector lending went through these banks.[12]

Although the CDB has had a preference policy to fund firms with Caribbean ownership, most of CDB's private-sector lending has gone to TNCs. Indeed, the first CDB loan to the private sector went to a foreign-owned hotel. It is now CDB policy "to encourage more foreign investment at a time when there is great need for such investment." As a consequence, foreign investors can come to the Caribbean and borrow the capital they need from the CDB with easy terms, either directly through the bank or through the myriad of financial intermediaries in the region. As a further inducement to foreign investors, the CDB has financed the construction of factory shells and industrial zones in Antigua, Barbados, British Virgin Islands, Dominica, Montserrat, St. Kitts, St. Vincent, and St. Lucia. It also provides foreign investors with prefeasibility studies and project profiles of possible areas for investment.

The United States and the CDB

Although the United States has chosen not to become a voting member of the CDB, it exercises prevailing influence over the direction of CDB lending because of its large financial commitment to the institution. While it cannot vote at board meetings, the United States can vote with its money. To downplay its power in the region, the United States decided to rely on Canada, and to a lesser extent the United Kingdom, to uphold its policies in the region. The largest donor to CDB, the United States has lent $146 million in concessional funding to the bank since 1970.[13] It is responsible for about 50 percent of the bank's soft financial resources and about 30 percent of its total resources.

Most of the U.S. contributions promote foreign investment and are often coordinated with USAID. Major U.S. projects through the CDB include a restructuring of the development finance banks, creation of industrial estates for assembly factories, and programs to create more favorable foreign investment laws. The two nonregional voting members of the CDB are the United Kingdom and Canada, which together hold 32 percent of the total voting power (almost twice as much as any Caribbean nation).

In an openly political move, the United States stipulated that preinvasion Grenada could not share a 1981 grant to the Caribbean Development Bank for "human needs" in the region. The CDB rejected the U.S. grant, explaining that its charter prohibited decision-making influenced by the political character of any member country. Caricom, the regional trade organization, called the U.S. stipulation a case of "economic aggression." In 1983, Washington started negotiations with CDB officials over the possibility of becoming a voting member, in order to increase its power in determining regional lending priorities.[14]

U.S. CONTROL OF MULTILATERAL LENDING

Except for the Caribbean Development Bank, the Caribbean nations have little control over the policies and lending priorities of international financial institutions. Unlike voting power in the United Nations, where each nation has one vote, voting power in the multilateral banks correlates with the amount contributed by member nations. Consequently, the world's industrial nations, especially the United States, control multilateral lending. The top three donors control 34 percent of the voting power in the IBRD and 57 percent in the IDA. The top five donors to the IDB control 71 percent of its votes. In most "soft" loan decisions, under IDB regulations, if the United States votes no, the loan is automatically turned down. The United States is by far the largest donor to the World Bank group, the IMF, the CDB, and the IDB (Table 8A).

TABLE 8A
MULTILATERAL VOTING POWER, 1982
(%)

	United States	Caribbean Countries
World Bank		
IBRD	20.6	1.2
IDA	33.7	0.1
IFC	27.8	1.1
IDB	35.2	2.9
IMF	19.6	1.3
CDB*	29.6	13.4

*contribution, not voting power
Sources: Annual reports: World Bank, IFC, IDB, IMF, CDB, 1982

Charity has never been the reason for the large commitments by the United States to the multilateral banks. As Deputy Assistant Secretary of State Ernest Johnston explained to a congressional hearing in 1981, "The United States took the lead in creating and maintaining the multilateral development banks over the last 35 years not only because they are a cost effective means of providing development capital, but also because they play a vital role in the maintenance of the whole economic system."[15] As with its bilateral programs, Washington has used its financial and voting power in the multilateral institutions to obtain greater political and economic power in the Caribbean. Its lending policies are designed to extract short-term gains for U.S. interests rather than to create the conditions for long-term global stability.

In 1982, the U.S. Economic Policy Council (a high-powered group of academics and corporate executives) published a study entitled "U.S. Policies Toward the World Bank and the International Monetary Fund," which advocated continued strong U.S. financial support for the two multilateral agencies.[16] "With U.S. economy and national security so closely linked to events around the globe," the council said, "the U.S. stake in these institutions and in the entire multilateral system is even greater than it was when the Bank and the IMF began their work." Contrary to some criticism that the United States is wasting its money on these foreign-aid institutions, the council concluded that the "U.S. taxpayer benefits clearly from each dollar" the federal government commits to multilateral lending. The council's conclusion agreed with a 1978 State Department study that estimated for every dollar the government paid into the World Bank, two dollars would be spent in the U.S. economy through contracts and exports resulting from bank projects.[17]

Besides these direct benefits to the U.S. economy, multilateral projects benefit U.S. corporations as well by providing the infrastructure necessary for profitable investment. According to the Economic Policy Council, the international financial institutions, because of their ability to lend enormous sums with government guarantees, are "more capable and effective than the private sector" in creating the economic and financial conditions conducive to investment in the developing nations.

In support of continued U.S. contributions for multilateral lending, the U.S. Secretary of the Treasury said: "An economic environment which enhances the opportunity for private sector enterprise also enhances the prospects for sustained economic growth."[18] Washington, however, is reluctant to commit more funds to multilateral banks because it feels that direct U.S. assistance through USAID, combined with an improved defense posture, more directly enhances the development of private enterprise. As Deputy Secretary of the Treasury R. T. McNamara said in 1982, "Those who criticize the United States for our 'low' contribution to overseas development assistance should recognize the military security umbrella we provide for development."[19]

A QUESTIONABLE COMMITMENT

For the industrial nations, financial commitment to the multilateral institutions is a balancing act. While multilateral projects foster favorable investment conditions and increased trade, they are not subject to the large degree of donor control that bilateral aid projects are. Because of this lack of control and because the developed countries experience economic competition between one another, most have failed to commit even 1 percent of their gross product to official development lending. In 1981, the United States allocated 0.20 percent, Japan 0.23 percent, and Canada and Great Britain 0.43 percent of their national product to foreign development assistance. Of the developed continental nations, only Italy commits less proportionately than the United States, and only the Netherlands commits more than 1 percent.[20] The United States has sharply cut back its contribution of concessional loans to the international financial institutions, which has forced even the poorest nations to pay commercial rates for a growing proportion of their loans.

Almost four decades of multilateral lending to the third world have been instrumental in integrating the capitalist world into the third world and isolating the socialist countries. Multilateral loans have succeeded in increasing international trade and investment, but the billions of dollars in multilateral lending have bound the world's poor nations to a system developed by and for the industrial nations. While the loans have helped facilitate foreign investment and have opened the doors of the third world to the products of the industrial nations, the international financial institutions can make no valid claim that they have furthered the overall economic development of the underdeveloped countries. The rationale that development will trickle down to the underdeveloped societies is an unproven hypothesis.

Generally, multilateral lending has not alleviated the symptoms of underdevelopment: widespread malnutrition, poor or nonexistent housing, illiteracy, and lack of health care. Nor has it directly attacked the causes of underdevelopment, such as unequal terms of trade, highly skewed land distribution, and lack of national control over resources. In the last several decades, multilateral institutions have put over $3.3 billion into projects in the Caribbean, but few signs indicate that those projects have altered the widespread conditions of underdevelopment.

Million-Dollar Diplomacy:

U.S. GOVERNMENT IN THE CARIBBEAN

The Caribbean region is a vital strategic and commercial artery for the United States. Make no mistake: the well-being and security of our neighbors are in our vital interest.

—President Ronald Reagan

In the early part of the century, U.S. foreign policy in the Caribbean only came in the form of gunboat diplomacy. Marine invasions and the appearance of the U.S. Navy in the harbors of Cuba, Puerto Rico, Haiti, and the Dominican Republic kept the region in line with U.S. foreign policy interests. Lately, Washington has stepped up its military presence and involvement in the Caribbean, but it has also established a much stronger diplomatic presence in the region and tremendously expanded its foreign aid program.

In 1981, President Ronald Reagan announced a new regional policy—the Caribbean Basin Initiative (CBI)—that brought Central America and the Caribbean together into one arena. Reagan saw this as an arena where democratic capitalism would challenge the advancing threat of dictatorial socialism. The Second Cold War expanded to the Caribbean. But more than strictly ideological considerations were at play. Washington viewed the CBI as a way to enhance its already considerable economic stake in the region.

The world of death squads, counterrevolutionaries, and guerrilla warfare seemed far away from the tourist economies and parliamentary democracies of many Caribbean islands. While some Caribbean leaders expressed their uneasiness at being grouped with Central America, most of the area's conservative politicians readily adopted the rhetoric of anti-communism and private enterprise with the hope of getting a bigger portion of U.S. handouts.

In their scramble for the coins Washington tossed their way, the Caribbean countries started jostling each other for the bits of aid thrown to the region. By allocating aid to individual nations rather than establishing a regional, multilateral aid program, the United States has threatened the already fragile unity of the Caribbean. This bilateral approach, which arranges separate investment and trade treaties with each country, serves the interests of U.S. investors, who feel threatened when underdeveloped nations unite to protect their own interests. "One of the reasons why the Caribbean Basin Initiative is so favorable to U.S. multinationals," wrote Roger Burbach of PACCA (Policy Alternatives for the Caribbean and Central America), "is that the arrangements set up under CBI are bilateral. The United States goes to each country and works out a special trade agreement. There's nothing regional about it."[1]

While the United States has greatly expanded its economic and military involvement in the Caribbean in recent years, Washington hardly has its finger on the pulse of the Caribbean. There is little sensitivity to complex race and class issues at play in the region, or to the pressing need to build regional unity. Junior diplomats and USAID officials recently assigned to the region can often speak more knowledgeably about the diving and sailing spots in the Caribbean than they can about the intricacies of local affairs. Milan Bish, Reagan's ambassador to the Eastern Caribbean, remarked, "The trouble I'm having at the moment is remembering where some of these countries are."[2]

ECONOMIC CONSIDERATIONS

Historically, the Caribbean has been fertile ground for U.S. investments. In 1950 Cuba accounted for 5.4 percent of all U.S. foreign investment.[3] In the last three decades, U.S. investment in the Caribbean has been concentrated in the mineral industry in Jamaica and the Dominican Republic, in the oil industry in Trinidad and the Netherlands Antilles, and in the offshore financial industry. The U.S. government estimates that a fourth of all direct investment in developing countries is in offshore tax havens, mostly in the Caribbean islands of Bermuda, Netherlands Antilles, the Cayman Islands, and the Bahamas.

Figures provided by the Department of Commerce on U.S. direct investment give only the book value of the investments (what the company lists for tax and regulatory purposes), not the real or resale value of the investment. The U.S. Embassy estimated the real value of U.S. investment in the Dominican Republic at over 3 times the book or listed value.[4] In 1982, the book value of U.S. direct investment in the Caribbean was $29.1 billion, up 58 percent from 1977.[5] Most of this investment—about $22 million—was in finance-related investment, mostly in offshore finance centers. There was $6.2 billion in other forms of U.S. direct foreign investment: $2.1 billion in local banking and $4.1 billion in petroleum, mining, manufacturing, trade, and services. Almost half of

U.S. bauxite comes from Caribbean mines, and about 75 percent of U.S. oil imports flow through Caribbean sea lanes. Caribbean refineries supply U.S. customers with about 500,000 barrels of oil each day.

U.S. INTERESTS IN THE CARIBBEAN, 1982

Number of US firms	1,747
US direct investment (book value)	$29,096 million
Total trade	$9,229 million
Positive trade balance*	$1,880 million
Caribbean debt to US government	$1,852 million
Number of US military personnel**	10,580 troops

* dosen't include oil exports for the Bahamas, Netherlands Antilles, and Trinidad-Tobago
** includes Puerto Rico

Another measure of U.S. economic interests in the region concerns the quantity and direction of trade. Despite the large imports of sugar, bauxite, nickel, and oil, the United States still enjoys a positive trade balance with the Caribbean, meaning that it sells more goods to the Caribbean than it imports from the area. This favorable trade balance grew from $412 million in 1976 to $2.9 billion in 1982, an increase of 7 times.[6] The United States in 1982 had a total trade (imports and exports) of $27.5 billion with the Caribbean countries. Speaking in support of closer attention to regional affairs, Secretary of State George Schultz advised that a "stable, democratic, and prosperous Caribbean Basin means a much larger and growing market for our exports."[7]

THE POLITICS OF FOREIGN AID

The United States Agency for International Development (USAID) administers three main foreign assistance programs: Development Assistance, Food for Peace (PL 480), and Economic Support Funds. Most USAID projects fall into Development Assistance, including projects like road building, technical assistance, institution building, and credit institutions. During the 1960s and 1970s, a higher proportion of development assistance went to projects designed to help poor people—housing, education, and health. Development Assistance has recently been helping the private sector through infrastructure and industrial projects.

Economic Support Funds (ESF) are slush funds that Washington uses to inject cash into countries or regions that are of important strategic interest to the United States. All CBI appropriations came from ESF money. According to the State Department, the funds are "used to promote economic or political stability in regions which affect U.S. interests, national security, and achievement of foreign policy objectives." These funds, then, do not necessarily go to the world's neediest nations, but to those countries, like Jamaica, El Salvador, Israel, and Egypt, that Washington supports because of foreign policy considerations. The USAID economic officer in Jamaica remarked: "An ESF grant of $100 million allows a very flexible sort of arrangement in Jamaica. Unlike other program funding, we have more discretion with these funds and can respond to needs in a very timely manner."[8]

But Whose Needs?

Foreign aid does not represent the altruistic side of the United States. "The growth of the third world is critical to our own growth," explained USAID Administrator Peter McPherson. "About 90 percent of the world's population growth takes place in the third world, and we need the market."[9] Washington disperses its aid money to help, directly or indirectly, the economic or political position of the United States. The U.S. government gives aid for the following reasons: to promote U.S. exports of goods and services, to support U.S. foreign investment, to ensure the availability of natural resources in developing nations, and to tighten national security by rewarding friendly countries and penalizing unfriendly ones. Genuine charitable considerations play a small part in USAID programs. "Aid is not charity, it is business," observed Prime Minister Edward Seaga of Jamaica, a beneficiary of CBI assistance.[10]

Although foreign aid classifies as bilateral aid (involving two countries), USAID plans its projects with limited input from the assisted nation. But the recipient country must sign an agreement with USAID that commits it to come up with a certain amount (usually 25 percent) of counterpart funds for the project, and to abide by certain USAID policies. The most common condition attached to aid agreements is that project purchases be made from U.S. firms—a condition that has meant that three-fourths of U.S. foreign-assistance money remains in the United States. According to USAID's McPherson, "Two-thirds of what we give comes back in 18 months in the form of purchases."[11] Technical-assistance grants are a boon to U.S. universities, consulting firms, and research institutes, since all consultants hired under the program must come from the United States.

Not only does U.S. aid have strings attached, it usually comes in the form of loans rather than outright grants. Seventy-five percent of USAID assistance to the Caribbean in 1982 consisted of loans. Loans usually have a grace period of ten years before payment comes due, a factor that encourages current government officials to accept the loans without worrying about the repayment problems that later administrations will encounter. In 1982, Caribbean nations owed the U.S. government almost $2 billion for economic and military assistance received since 1946.[12] Most countries cannot repay all their debts, but that does not stop the United States from lending more money. It can use the debt to increase its political and economic leverage in the country. Cutting off aid would not make good sense either, since the aid money is largely spent in the United States.

In the early 1980s, Washington moved toward more bilateral financing, rather than increasing its multilateral lending in the Caribbean. USAID has not hidden its reasons for the bilateral approach. The agency explains that when dealing with projects that "require changes in public policy" it is more effective to deal directly with the government than to go through regional intermediaries like the Caribbean Development Bank.[13] In a pointed reference to preinvasion Grenada and Cuba, it added that bilateral aid programs also allow more flexibility to direct aid to countries that promote "equitable economic development" through private enterprise.[14]

Private-Sector Infatuation

Support for the private sector has become a common theme of all government aid programs. Population-control agencies are directed to sell contraceptives through retail outlets rather than public clinics, Peace Corps volunteers are working with chambers of commerce, and business associations have replaced social-service organizations as a USAID focus. By Washington's way of thinking, a project that does not aid the private sector wastes money.

USAID's Bureau of Private Enterprise, called PRE, was created in 1981 specifically to increase foreign investment and to build the private sector in the third world. PRE will put what President Reagan has called "the magic of the marketplace" to work in the Caribbean Basin. Directing the bureau are Robert Parra, a former Citibank executive, and Elise DuPont, wife of the Delaware governor and part of the blueblood family of chemical-company fame. "We plan to work with host governments to ensure they have the financial structure and investment environment needed for private enterprise to function effectively," affirmed DuPont, who calls PRE "the development banker."[15] USAID Director McPherson, outlining PRE's strategy, said it plans to launch joint ventures and to aid the private transfer of technology by linking investment partners in the United States and the third world. An important element of

TABLE 9A
AID FISCAL YEARS 1946–1984
($ millions)

Country	1946–80	1981	1982	1983	1984*	TOTAL
Bahamas	**0.3**	**0**	**0**	**0**	**0**	**0.3**
DA**	0	0	0	0	0	0
PL 480**	0.3	0	0	0	0	0.3
ESF**	0	0	0	0	0	0
Barbados	**1.3**	**0.1**	**†**	**‡**	**‡**	**1.4**
DA	0	0	0	‡	‡	0
PL 480	1.3	0.1	†	‡	‡	1.4
ESF	0	0	0	‡	‡	0
Cuba	**3.9**	**0**	**0**	**0**	**0**	**3.9**
DA	3.3	0	0	0	0	3.3
PL 480	0.6	0	0	0	0	0.6
ESF	0	0	0	0	0	0
Dominican Rep	**651.3**	**36.0**	**79.3**	**59.8**	**113.8**	**940.2**
DA	228.8	17.4	19.0	26.5	31.0	322.7
PL 480	212.2	18.6	19.3	25.3	42.8	318.2
ESF	210.3	0	41.0	8.0	40.0	299.3
Eastern Caribbean§	**167.3**	**27.0**	**66.7**	**53.2**	**55.0**	**369.2**
DA	157.0	27.0	30.1	18.2	30.0	262.3
PL 480	6.3	0	16.6	0	0	22.9
ESF	4.0	0	20.0	35.0	25.0	84.0
Grenada	**0**	**0**	**0**	**0**	**15.0**	**15.0**
DA	0	0	0	0	0	0
PL 480	0	0	0	0	0	0
ESF	0	0	0	0	15.0	15.0
Guyana	**131.4**	**1.2**	**1.8**	**0.2**	**1.0**	**135.6**
DA	109.0	1.2	1.7	0.2	1.0	113.1
PL 480	12.7	†	0.1	0	0	12.8
ESF	9.7	0	0	0	0	9.7
Haiti	**288.9**	**33.7**	**34.2**	**45.5**	**42.4**	**444.7**
DA	115.0	9.2	12.0	17.3	19.0	172.5
PL 480	115.4	24.5	22.2	18.2	18.4	198.7
ESF	58.5	0	0	10.0	5.0	73.5

Jamaica	178.7	71.0	136.9	101.6	108.5	596.7
DA	87.4	12.9	28.9	22.2	33.5	184.9
PL 480	80.3	17.1	17.5	20.0	20.0	154.9
ESF	11.0	41.0	90.5	59.4	55.0	256.9
Suriname	6.0	0	0.5	0	1.0	7.5
DA	3.3	0	0	0	0	3.3
PL 480	1.7	0	0	0	0	1.7
ESF	1.0	0	0.5	0	1.0	2.5
Trinidad	43.0	0	0	0	0	43.0
DA	9.7	0	0	0	0	9.7
PL 480	1.2	0	0	0	0	1.2
ESF	32.1	0	0	0	0	32.1
TOTAL CARIBBEAN	1,472.1	169.0	319.4	260.3	336.7	2,557.5
DA	713.5	67.7	91.7	84.4	114.5	1,071.8
PL 480	432.0	60.3	75.7	63.5	81.2	712.7
ESF	326.6	41.0	152.0	112.4	141.0	773.0

* all FY84 PL 480 figures were indefinite as of January 1984; the DA & ESF figures refer to allocations as of January 1984. All will probably increase during FY84
**DA—Development Assistance; PL 480—Food for Peace; ESF—Economic Security Funds
† less than 50,000
‡ Barbados joined the Eastern Caribbean category for US economic and military assistance in FY83
§ Eastern Caribbean includes St. Lucia, St. Vincent, Antigua and Barbados (since FY83); Dominica and St. Kitts (since FY84)
Sources: *U.S. Overseas Loans and Grants,* 1983 Annual Report of the Chairman of the Development Coordination Committee, Statistical Annex I; Joe Mussomeli and Chuck English, U.S. Department of State

the bureau is to "reform existing government policy regarding private investment."[16]

During its first two years, PRE hosted frequent tours by U.S. business owners to the Caribbean, and allotted tens of millions of dollars for feasibility studies, promotion, and financing for private investment in the Caribbean. But the magic has not taken hold. In Jamaica, PRE's four projects to increase credit for Jamaican businesses have gone down the drain. The U.S. government has spent vast sums to attract U.S. investors to the region, but for the most part the takers seem to be either small businesses that could not make a go of it in the United States or assembly industries that will have little effect on local economies.

THE CARIBBEAN BASIN INITIATIVE

The irony of the Caribbean Basin Initiative is that El Salvador, the country that really set the program in motion, does not touch the Caribbean Sea. Many of the island states in the Caribbean delighted in their inclusion in the regional aid program, although their problems have only an indirect relationship with the civil wars sweeping Central America.

Four elements made up the initiative that Congress passed in 1983: (1) $125 million in concessional lending to the Caribbean countries, (2) duty-free entry of specified Caribbean products for 12 years, (3) tax exemption for business conventions held in CBI-designated countries, and (4) the negotiation of bilateral investment and tax treaties. All these measures will primarily benefit U.S. corporations. Washington, in its foreign policy declarations, has neglected to consider the problems and the interests of the ordinary people in the Caribbean. The millions of Caribbean people who have been left outside the economic system have nothing to gain from tax investment credits, balance-of-payments support, and duty-free trade.

To the immediate support of Reagan's proposed initiative came the CBI Coalition, a lobbying group founded by David Rockefeller that included many of the top U.S. corporations active in the Caribbean: Alcoa, Control Data, Reynolds Metals, Eastern Airlines, and Tesoro Petroleum. Among the main opponents of the initiative was organized labor. The AFL-CIO's chief lobbyist told a congressional hearing that the CBI "is not designed for the benefit of the people of the region, but for the benefit of the multinationals."[17] One labor leader in San Diego asked, "Why should the American working class watch its jobs disappear as the multinational corporations decide to partake of the bonanza of cheap wages, non-existent health and safety conditions, and duty-free access to the United States?"[18] Labor unions contend that such programs contribute to the erosion of American jobs by encouraging U.S. factories to run away overseas.

The actual dollar component of the CBI was a drop in the bucket for the basin countries. High import costs and debt-service payments are draining the Caribbean Basin of its scarce foreign-exchange reserves—a loss that will not be compensated by relatively small CBI loans and grants. The $125 million in CBI concessional lending to the Caribbean nations constituted just 18 percent of the debt service on the external public debt of the Dominican Republic, Haiti, Jamaica, and the Eastern Caribbean. The duty-free trade access component of the CBI also falls far short of the kind of trade and investment program that is needed to reverse the slide of the region's economy. But then the CBI was only superficially concerned with the improvement of the conditions of the Caribbean people. The deeper concern was to deepen the region's economic connection and dependence on the U.S. government and its TNCs.

Before the authorization of CBI, 87 percent of the Caribbean Basin's exports already entered duty-free under existing trade preference agreements. Because of special-interest lobbying by U.S.-based manufacturers, Congress retained import duties on textiles, petroleum products, footwear, handbags, luggage, work gloves, leather apparel, and tuna, thereby narrowing the line of industries that can benefit from duty-free entry. Commenting on the limitations of the duty-free provisions of CBI, an article in *Inter-American Economic Affairs* observed that the products left to benefit were brassieres, shirts, pajamas, and men's underwear assembled in the offshore sweatshops common in the Dominican Republic and Haiti.[19] It has been estimated that there will be as little as a $100 million increase of trade from the entire Caribbean Basin, or just 1 percent of the region's current trade.[20] Corporations like Maidenform and Gulf + Western's Kayser Roth that already have plants in the region will experience windfall gains from these duty-free provisions.

Duty-free entrance to the United States requires that only 35 percent of the product's value be derived from the Caribbean. Labor and a small percentage of U.S.-produced materials can be counted to meet this 35 percent value-added criterion. A further exception to the 35 percent rule is that all material and labor from Puerto Rico and the U.S. Virgin Islands qualifies in determining local content. A TNC from the United States, therefore, can fulfill requirements for duty-free entry into the United States by manufacturing electronic components in Puerto Rico and using cheap Haitian labor for the labor-intensive part of the job.

Not a Giveaway

In the tradition of U.S. foreign aid programs, Uncle Sam was not about to give away something for nothing with the CBI. To qualify as CBI beneficiaries, the Caribbean nations had to sign loan contracts with Washington that required the countries to restructure their economies (and hence their politics) in ways pleasing to the U.S. government and U.S. corporations. Before they could receive any of the CBI benefits, the Caribbean nations had to promise to open their doors to foreign investors, revise laws on expropriation, and commit themselves to supplying the U.S. Treasury with requested tax and banking information when U.S. tax evasion is suspected. Officials from the State Department traveled to each of the CBI candidate nations to make certain that the

Caribbean countries rid their law books of statutes that obstructed the free flow of U.S. investment and trade.

In the loan agreements for CBI financial assistance, USAID attached the following conditions:

- Loans would be repaid with a low rate of interest.
- Assistance would be used to purchase U.S. goods and services.
- Countries would set aside sums equivalent to the loans in their own currencies to be used for programs determined by the beneficiary country and USAID.

The loan agreements also contain clauses that allow the United States to pry into the internal affairs of the recipient nations. Peter Johnson, executive director of Caribbean/Central America Action (CCAA), explained that the United States would favor these countries only if they "individually make the policy changes needed to contribute to their own growth."[21] This meddling in the internal affairs of the Caribbean nations is well worth the cost of the CBI for the United States. "With the CBI, we have a double whammy," one USAID official remarked.[22]

Barbados agreed "to provide such information relating to the economic and financial situation of Barbados as may be necessary." The CBI loan arrangement for Jamaica required "a comprehensive study of policies, practices, regulations and law constituting Jamaica's foreign trade and foreign payments regimes, a study of factors influencing investor attitudes, and a study of the feasibility of combining Jamaican agencies involved in investment, production, and export promotion activities." In the Dominican Republic, representatives of the president and the country's central bank must meet at regular intervals with USAID "to consult on the economic recovery of the Dominican Republic, including measures taken to assist and encourage" private enterprise development.[23]

Under the CBI, Washington also demanded that beneficiaries sign an agreement with the Treasury Department to pass on specific tax information about U.S. corporations in their countries. Countries like the Bahamas have expressed reluctance to sign such agreements because they would seriously threaten offshore financial business. Many countries feel that the associated conditions of the CBI hark back to the days when paternalism and colonialism characterized all foreign relations in the Caribbean.

At first, Puerto Rico and the U.S. Virgin Islands vociferously opposed most of the CBI provisions. The U.S. territorial possessions protested that the trade incentives extended to other Caribbean islands directly threatened their favored status with investors from the mainland. Lower production costs because of cheaper wages on the other islands have already clouded the investment climate of the U.S. territories. Recognizing their concerns, Congress yielded to several of the territories' demands. To improve the fortunes of the rum industry in the U.S. Virgin Islands, Congress exempted the Schenley liquor company from environmental standards, which means the company can continue to dump its wastes into the Caribbean. If the amount of taxes paid by rum companies in Puerto Rico and the U.S. Virgin Islands drops below acceptable levels, the president can immediately withdraw the duty-free treatment for Caribbean bulk rum. For the sake of Puerto Rico, which packs about half the tuna consumed on the mainland, Congress retained duties on tuna entering the United States. And, in line with Washington's strategy for using Puerto Rico as its regional surrogate, the island will be the center for USAID's training and technical assistance operations in the Caribbean. In addition, Washington is promoting Puerto Rico as the base location for twin plants with Haiti and Jamaica.

The Caribbean Basin Initiative must be viewed in the context of the increasingly competitive world trade market, which the United States no longer dominates. In one sense, the CBI is an attempt by the United States to gain a competitive edge on Europe and particularly on Japan, which has in the last ten years slowly begun to challenge the U.S. domination of the world market. Washington wants to direct the trade of the individual Caribbean nations to the United States rather than through Caricom. By advancing offshore assembly industries as a development strategy, the United States has provoked the islands to compete with one another in how cheaply they can offer their labor and how attractive their tax holidays are to corporations. A government official in Trinidad warned that the CBI has caused "the Caribbean nations to compete with one another above and under the table in a way that may weaken the regional integration movement."

AID AS FINANCE

USAID has become more like a bank than a social development agency. USAID Administrator McPherson explained this change in development thinking: "More and more of the donor community thinks of itself as a development banker who invests resources in programs where there is a real chance for growth and change as opposed to continued subsistence and dependence. This policy consciousness is substantially established among donors. It is clearly the wave of the future, especially given the scarcity of foreign assistance resources."[24] This coincides with the agency's philosophy that countries are underdeveloped because they lack capital, rather than because they lack control of capital and resources.

To put this policy into practice, USAID has created and maintained more than a dozen industrial development banks and several agricultural credit banks throughout the Caribbean. The agency, rather than directly serving as a bank to industries and agribusiness, establishes financial institutions to act as intermediaries between the private sector and foreign donors like USAID. The commercial banks, like development banks, have shied away from lending money to businesses and farms that produce only for the internal market. Development banks generally direct their loans to investments that produce exports and earn foreign exchange. As a consequence, the financial intermediaries have largely failed to promote local economic development. They function as a conduit to subsidize foreign investment in offshore assembly industries and agricultural export production.

Washington's new emphasis on assisting private-sector development in the Caribbean has resulted in a flood of money into the development banks. The agency uses the agricultural development banks to provide local capital for new export-production projects to grow bananas in Jamaica, flowers in the Dominican Republic, and coconuts in Dominica. Because they use U.S.-supplied credit, the local farm companies are obligated to buy U.S. farm products like fertilizers and tractors. The industrial development banks also frequently serve as low-cost sources of local capital for foreign investors. Rather than bringing their own money into the country, the foreign companies borrow money from the development banks at subsidized interest rates to cover their investment costs.

An extension of the development banking concept is USAID's entrance into the merchant-banking business. The USAID-backed merchant banks will oversee large industrial loans of $100,000 or more. Through the Caribbean Association of Industry and Commerce (CAIC), USAID created with a soft loan of $12 million a regional merchant bank, located in Barbados, that will provide long-term venture capital to ambitious industrial investments. Many Caribbean observers consider the regional merchant bank superfluous since the Caribbean Development Bank already makes generous loans to the private sector, but USAID could exercise more control over a bank it created.

USAID hopes that local investors will buy stock and provide a continuing source of capital to regional and local merchant banks that USAID organizes. Even representatives for the agency's Bureau of Private Enterprise (PRE) admit that the "whole area of venture capital hasn't worked out too well" because of the failure to generate local sources of capital once USAID has developed the company.[25] "There's no real market for stock in the Caribbean," one PRE official said candidly.[26] That fact, however, will not deter USAID from pouring still more private-sector development capital into the Caribbean. Until Congress asks to see the hard evidence of the magic of the marketplace, USAID will continue its disappearing tricks, using public funds as private giveaways.

Public Backing for Private Lobbying

Since 1980, one of Washington's chief strategies for the Caribbean Basin has been the creation and support of associations of business owners. The U.S. government then uses these business organizations to foster a good investment climate for U.S. corporations and to build a conservative lobbying force in local government. USAID, the overseer and financier of the strategy, provides the blueprint for the organizations, supplies the funds, formulates the goals, and assists with implementation. It calls this the "institution building" part of its development efforts.

Stateside, the business organization Caribbean/Central American Action (CCAA) provides most of the nongovernmental support for the strategy. The CCAA grew out of a similar group founded by Robert West, chairman of Tesoro Petroleum, called the Committee for the Caribbean. The committee viewed itself as "the timely instrument of enlightened U.S. business leadership."[27] In 1980, the State Department, with President Carter's approval, backed the formation of CCAA with Florida's governor Robert Graham as its chairperson and Tesoro's West as its president. Members of the "action" group included the chiefs of many of the top U.S. corporations doing business in the region, including Gulf + Western, United Brands, Coca-Cola, BankAmerica, Control Data, Reynolds Metals, and Exxon. Assuming the executive director's position was Peter Johnson, a career foreign service officer on leave from the State Department. From 1965 to 1967 he served as political officer in the Dominican Republic, and from 1972 to 1975 he held the same post in Costa Rica.[28]

In its first several years, CCAA was busy throughout the Caribbean hosting business conferences, advising governments, and introducing U.S. corporations to the profit potential of investments in the basin countries. Invariably, CCAA works in consort with U.S. government institutions like OPIC, USAID, and the State Department. In an interview in November 1980, CCAA's Johnson said, "We made very clear in our new bylaws that we were an apolitical organization, that we were unqualifiedly private sector with respect to funding." Johnson said that CCAA's work does have implications for national security, because "if the private sectors cannot perform . . . then you're not going to have the kind of productivity" that Caribbean countries need.[29]

Despite Johnson's claims that CCAA is completely private-sector and funded only by member dues, USAID gave the organization at least two grants as of September 1982. One of the grants increased coordination between the various chambers of commerce in the region. In 1983, USAID and the Small Business Administration funded CCAA to locate and attract at least 500 companies in the Caribbean that offer U.S. firms an opportunity for trade and investment. An Overseas Private Investment Corporation (OPIC) official said that OPIC works "fairly closely, on a day-to-day basis" with CCAA and that it "footed the bill" for CCAA's elaborate investment brochures.[30] CCAA deals with more than the business communities of the Caribbean islands. It sponsors conferences, such as the annual Miami Conference on the Caribbean. Willing partners in CCAA's plans for increased outside investment in the region are the largest Caribbean-owned businesses, such as Neal & Massy, Goddard Enterprises, Dominica Coconut Products, and Grace Kennedy, all of whom are represented on CCAA's board of directors. Also included among CCAA members are American Institute for Free Labor Development and its affiliate, the Caribbean Congress of Labor.

One sign of the growing importance of CCAA for the region was the election in 1983 of David Rockefeller as its chairperson. In 1983, CCAA became an affiliate of the Council of Americas, a Rockefeller-founded organization of corporations doing business in Latin America. A primary goal of the council is "to contribute to constructive change in business-government relations throughout the hemisphere."[31] Far be it from Rockefeller to call for the complete separation of business and government. He said private enterprise "has a vital role to play" in the region, but "the private sector could only fulfill this role with the help of government and public assistance."[32] Rockefeller saw the CBI as a perfect way to provide this government support, and headed another organization of TNCs, called the CBI Coalition, which lobbied for the initiative.

Two similar U.S. organizations that promote U.S. business in particular countries of the Caribbean are the Florida/Haiti Program and the U.S. Business Committee on Jamaica. Joe Thomas, the official liaison of the Florida/Haiti Program, works out of USAID's office in Haiti to encourage joint ventures between business interests in Haiti and Florida. The concept underlying the program is that Florida corporations export the more labor-intensive parts of their operations to Haiti. Also working closely with the U.S. government is the U.S. Business Committee on Jamaica, which David Rockefeller helped start shortly after Seaga assumed office. Neither program, despite USAID fanfare, can point to any notable achievements.

Reviving CAIC

In the forefront of USAID's Caribbean activities is the Caribbean Association of Industry and Commerce (CAIC). In 1981 and 1982, USAID authorized $1.1 million in grants to revive the almost dormant CAIC so that it could "create and promote an environment in which Caribbean economies can grow." Caribbean/Central American Action reports that it has been "closely involved in the CAIC revitalization effort." Not only does the U.S.-based CCAA largely set the policies of CAIC, but the two organizations share common directors. In 1981, John Stanley Goddard, chairperson of Goddard Enterprises of Barbados, served as president of CAIC and vice-president of CCAA. Serving as secretary of CCAA was Carlton Alexander, president of Grace Kennedy and also a vice-president of CAIC. Interestingly, both men are also directors of a USAID marketing project in the Caribbean called CATCO. Two other CAIC vice-presidents, Sidney Knox of Neal & Massy and Phillip Nassief of Dominica Coconut Products, are also directors of CCAA.

USAID and CCAA are using CAIC as their front organization for building chambers of commerce and manufacturers' associations throughout the Caribbean. As a USAID official in Jamaica explained, "The strategy of AID is to create a powerful private sector lobbying organization like we have in the United States that will be able to prevent the government from operating on its own without the input from the private sector."[33] He added that the "private sector needs to be taking positions on political issues in the society." Recognizing that the owners of business can be a powerful political force in the Caribbean, USAID is trying to build organizations in each of the countries and unite them as a regional force through CAIC—an organization almost totally funded by the U.S. government. In 1982, the treasurer of CAIC urged his colleagues in the business community "to stand up for their rights" and "to seek and obtain involvement in consultative forums" set up with the government of preinvasion Grenada "to ensure that Grenada's private sector is not deflated." He cautioned that "recent occurrences among Caribbean territories spelled the need for definite solidarity among regional businessmen."[34]

The U.S. government is also trying to bring the new Caribbean chambers close to chambers of commerce in the United States through a CAIC-sponsored Chamber Twinning program. USAID has provided funds that have permitted "Caribbean chamber leaders to visit their paired U.S. chamber in order to more fully comprehend the role, operations, and importance of a chamber to business development." The campaign brought Houston's and Jamaica's chambers together as twins, and Miami together with Trinidad & Tobago. Because USAID has educational requirements for its programs, CAIC initiated Junior Achievement courses modeled after U.S. Junior Achievement programs. The students, after dividing up into mock corporations, elect a board of directors, sell stock, and target markets for their products—all in the hope of becoming future promoters of private enterprise. Of direct benefit to U.S. investors is a training program initiated by CAIC with USAID money to train workers in St. Vincent to read garment patterns, assemble precut cloth, and meet company deadlines. Managing the training is Baylis Brothers (owned by U.S. Industries), a corporation with a garment factory on the island.[35]

Other training programs sponsored by CAIC are more attitudinal. At one seminar in St. Kitts, the association spoke of the need "to promote greater awareness among workers about their obligations and responsibilities to a productive and progressive occupational environment."[36] The chief reason the United States has promoted CAIC and other business associations has not been to improve local industrial development, but to lay out the red carpet for U.S. investment and trade. In its grant to CAIC, USAID instructed the association to complete the following tasks in the Caribbean: develop relations with the U.S. Chamber of Commerce, promote development by foreign entrepreneurs, produce an industrial strategy that will assist developed country companies to buy local companies, make personal calls on U.S. companies to induce them to invest in the Caribbean, and create local standing committees throughout the Caribbean of both local and foreign business people.

The Government's Private Voluntary Organizations

An essential ingredient in Washington's private-sector initiative for the Caribbean is what USAID calls private voluntary organizations, or PVOs. Technically, PVOs are private, nonprofit organizations that volunteer their services to aid development and improve the welfare of foreign nations. In fact, the most important PVOs working in the Caribbean, like CARE and the American Institute for Free Labor Development, receive most of their funding from the U.S. government—somewhat obscuring the USAID definition of "private" organizations.

Over the past decade, Washington has increased PVO funding by over 400 percent because it believes that PVOs are more efficient than government agencies in implementing U.S. foreign aid programs. Of the 63 PVOs active in the Caribbean, almost half (29) receive more than 50 percent of their funding from the U.S. government. PVOs that have refused USAID money say the government-supported PVOs have become tools of U.S. foreign policy in underdeveloped countries. Channeling USAID funds through PVOs is especially valuable in a nation like Haiti, where the Duvalier dictatorship has repeatedly used U.S. government funding for personal purposes, making it embarrassing for the U.S. to give directly to the regime.

The leading PVO promoting the expansion of private enterprise is the International Executive Service Corps, an organization of retired corporate executives created in 1964 by David Rockefeller. Throughout the Caribbean, elderly U.S. executives are busy building chambers of commerce, advising businesses, and fostering trade with the United States. USAID likes to funnel money through PVOs to provide credit for small businesses and farmers, but limits the credit to purchases of U.S. goods and agricultural inputs. USAID funds the International Executive Service Corps to the tune of $23 million a year, of which $600,000 supports

65 U.S. "executive volunteers" to "develop private enterprise" in the Eastern Caribbean.

The USAID-funded Pan American Development Foundation, which also receives support from many of the largest TNCs, has channeled USAID funds to two private-sector promotion foundations. Similarly, the U.S. government gives money to the Credit Union National Association, which in turn finances a network of credit unions across the Caribbean. Another PVO, Partners of the Americas, aids the development of small businesses in three countries in the West Indies; another, the National Office of Social Responsibility, trains the youth of St. Lucia in skills necessary to work in foreign assembly plants. The Caribbeana Council, which receives almost half its funding from USAID, develops projects to promote exports and to open opportunities for foreign investment in the region. The council's other supporters include the U.S. Information Agency, WR Grace, Barclays Development Fund, and British American Insurance.[37]

TRAINING CARIBBEAN UNION ORGANIZERS

An affiliate of the AFL-CIO, the American Institute for Free Labor Development (AIFLD), was founded in 1962 to train labor leaders and to foster the formation of conservative unions that would combat the spread of socialism and communism in Latin America and the Caribbean. Although AIFLD promotes itself as a labor organization, the U.S. government, through USAID, pays 96 percent of its bills. U.S. corporations doing business in the region also support AIFLD. J. Peter Grace of the WR Grace Company, a firm with extensive operations in the Caribbean, served as AIFLD's first chairperson. An early executive director, who was not at all hesitant to admit the true character of this labor-corporate alliance, said: "We are collaborating with the Council of Latin America [now the Council of Americas] which is made up primarily of U.S. business institutions that have activities in the area. Our collaboration takes the form of trying to make the investment climate more attractive and inviting to them."

Director of AIFLD's Eastern Caribbean Office Mike Donovan remarked in a recent interview that AIFLD has been virtually alone among U.S. institutions in demonstrating a consistent commitment to the Caribbean over the past 20 years. AIFLD, in fact, has been instrumental in shaping politics in the Caribbean, particularly in Guyana and the Dominican Republic. Caribbean scholar Frank McDonald, in a 1971 essay on U.S. relations with the West Indies, wrote:

American corporations and AID programs represent only two sides of a triangular penetration of the Commonwealth Caribbean economy. The third side, without which the ease of this process would be severely threatened, is the organized "Americanization" of the Caribbean trade union movement's role in Caribbean politics. With the sole exception of Trinidad, most major political parties are rooted in a labor union and the vast majority of premiers, prime ministers, and even leaders of the opposition are themselves trade unionists. Thus, the axiom holds that the politics or ideology of the trade union movement will affect the policies of the regional governments and that the more receptive Caribbean labor is to the presence of American investment and management patterns, the more so will be the regional politicians.[38]

Through the Caribbean Basin Initiative, President Reagan has set aside $2 million above its normal operating budget for AIFLD to enable it to increase its activities in the region. USAID's Peter McPherson, in a 1982 address to AIFLD graduates, stressed the "important role which trade unions in the Caribbean must play if the initiative is to succeed." He said, "Free trade unions are crucial to the development of free societies." McPherson recalled that as a Peace Corps volunteer in the 1960s he had worked in the AIFLD training center in Peru and had seen first-hand the result of AIFLD programs: "well-trained, committed labor leaders." In its CBI Implementation Plan, USAID stated that it "will encourage AIFLD to work with the labor unions to gain their cooperation and support for the CBI."[39]

Guyana

Chief among U.S.-sponsored labor operatives in Latin America was Serafíno Romualdi, an early regional representative of the AFL and later director of AIFLD. Romualdi moved back and forth between Caribbean countries trying to break progressive labor organizing. He began trouble-shooting in Guyana as early as 1951, when the United States started worrying about the growing popular power of a Marxist politician named Cheddi Jagan. Romualdi interacted with the union of sugar workers (an organization formed by the sugar company), which had strong ties with the AFL-affiliated Inter-American Regional Labor Organization (ORIT), which in turn was a member of the International Confederation of Free Trade Unions. This organization was established by the CIA to oppose and subvert progressive and communist unions throughout the world.

In 1953, Cheddi Jagan, an intellectual of East Indian descent with strong support among Guyanese canecutters, became the prime minister of what was then called British Guiana after his party won the election. That party, the People's Progressive Party (PPP), immediately passed a labor relations bill that facilitated the recognition of new unions. Directly threatened by the bill was the ORIT-affiliated sugar-workers union, a conservative labor union that existed with the approval of the Booker

McConnell sugar company. Most Guyanese workers favored the more progressive Guyana Industrial Workers Union. But the labor relations bill never took effect, since British gunboats arrived in Georgetown and suspended the constitution "to prevent communist subversion of the government."[40] The AFL and Romualdi publicly supported the landing of the British troops even though the government was democratically elected.

Neither Jagan nor Romualdi left the political or labor scene. Despite obstacles presented by the British, Jagan again achieved political power in 1962. Romualdi then led a campaign of strikes and subversion to undermine Jagan's government. AIFLD exploited racial tensions between blacks and East Indians through a series of political strikes that eventually did topple the elected government. Jagan said: "Local trade unionists known to be hostile to the government—and none others—have been trained by the AIFLD to overthrow my government. Serafino Romualdi, head of the institute [AIFLD], has declared his opposition to my government."[41] Forbes Burnham, the Guyanese political leader backed by the anti-Jagan unions, came to power as the head of the People's National Party (PNP), which relied on black urban workers and the middle-class community for its support.

The London *Times* reported that the collapse of the Jagan government "was engineered largely by the CIA," using the "Guyanese trade union movement."[42] The *New York Times* also affirmed Jagan's charges that the CIA, "operating under cover of the American union, helped the pro-Burnham public employees unions organize strikes" in 1962 and 1963.[43] The London *Sunday Times* commented that Jagan's ouster was "relatively inexpensive for the CIA, accomplished with around $250,000."[44] Guyana lost a popular government and received generous amounts of U.S. aid and police training for the new government of Forbes Burnham.

Dominican Republic

In his 1969 book, *American Labor and United States Foreign Policy*, Ronald Radosh reported: "The activities of the American-backed unions in the Dominican Republic serve as the clearest evidence of how American unions have been used by the State Department, the CIA, and American corporations for their own chosen purposes."[45] The same combination of characters active in Guyana—AIFLD, Romualdi, ORIT, and the CIA—played a similar role in breaking trade union solidarity and undermining progressive politics in the Dominican Republic. The AFL-CIO's representative to ORIT, Andrew McLellan, said the purpose of American labor in the Dominican Republic and elsewhere in Latin America was "to teach the principles of democratic trade unionism. . . . We also teach defense tactics—how to recognize Communist penetration and defeat it."[46] Through CONATRAL, the federation of unions associated with AIFLD in the Dominican Republic, the State Department and the leadership of the AFL-CIO blocked progressive political change in the country and supported military solutions.

After the asassination of the country's dictator of thirty years, Rafael Trujillo, most people of the Dominican Republic wanted a reformist government. CONATRAL, however, led a campaign of criticism against the elected government of Juan Bosch, and offered crucial support to the military regime of Donald Reid Cabral. After Dominican armed forces overthrew Bosch and installed Cabral, CONATRAL stated that it "hailed unconditionally the heroic gesture which our armed forces have made in the name of liberty, democracy, and justice [by removing] the pro-Communist government."[47]

In 1965, Serafíno Romualdi received the Cabral government's highest decoration, the Order of Duarte, Sánchez, and Mella, which made Romualdi a Knight Commander in the eyes of the Dominican military. At the ceremony President Cabral told him, "The government of the Dominican Republic wishes to reward, with the highest decoration at its command, your lifetime services on behalf of the free trade union movement." He praised the AIFLD official for helping to "transform into free democratic unions what had been a slave labor movement." Romualdi graciously accepted the reward "as recognition of what the labor movement of the United States has done in defense of freedom in the Dominican Republic."[48]

Just as the AFL-CIO backed British military intervention in what was then British Guiana, the U.S. labor hierarchy and its foreign associates supported the U.S. invasion of the Dominican Republic in 1965. CONATRAL alone among the country's labor organizations backed the intervention, saying, "For the sake of democracy, we will accept anything—even intervention."[49] Andrew McLennan of the AFL-CIO called General Elias Wessin y Wessin, the reactionary military officer who led the repression of the popular rebellion, "one of the few incorruptible top elements in the Dominican army."[50] The U.S.-sponsored trade unions were influential not only in molding Dominican politics but also in shaping the country's investment climate. In her important study of the AIFLD's role in the Dominican Republic, Susanne Bodenheimer wrote that AIFLD has "served American interests at the expense of Dominican workers. For one thing, American labor, which is dedicated to the preservation of the capitalist system, has furthered U.S. business interests in Latin America by weakening the principal obstacle to U.S. corporations, namely a labor movement sufficiently united and militant enough to exert pressure for fulfillment of its demands."[51]

AIFLD, which spent $1.6 million in the country between 1962 and 1969, broke the unity of the Dominican labor movement, setting the stage for U.S. investment in cheap-labor assembly plants in the country. From its founding in 1962 through 1981, AIFLD trained 28,778 Dominicans in the principles of free labor organizing.[52] Julio de Peña Valdéz, the director of the Confederación General de Trabajadores, says that the competitive Confederación Nacional de Trabajadores (CNTD) is associated with AIFLD. "The CNTD," said Peña Valdéz, "is the reappearance of CONATRAL which lost support among workers because of its very counterrevolutionary activities. They try to penetrate other unions, and they pay off the workers through stipends for labor courses and travel to the United States. They present things that attract and compromise the workers."[53] In the Dominican Republic, AIFLD has broadened its organizing scope to include small farmers. It helped organize a national agrarian organization called Federación Nacional Agraria Campesina to expand agricultural export marketing and processing. In addition to the AIFLD support, USAID backs the small-farmers' federation through programs in farm marketing and administration.

Programs to Improve Labor Relations

Mike Donovan directs AIFLD's operations in the Eastern Caribbean from a small office in Bridgetown, Barbados. Donovan dismissed charges that AIFLD is a front for the CIA, but readily admitted that the labor organization is anticommunist. As in Latin America, most AIFLD activity in the Eastern Caribbean is educational. It sponsors training sessions for union members in organizing and political philosophy and recommends union leaders for further training in the United States. Courses sponsored by AIFLD at its George Meany Labor Studies Center outside Washington include: "Role of Organized Labor in Developing Democracy," "Political Theories and the Labor Movement," and "Trade Unions and Productivity." Between 1962 and 1981 AIFLD gave in-country courses to more than 49,778 Caribbean unionists.[54]

In conjunction with AIFLD, the International Communications Agency (ICA) (the U.S. information and propaganda agency) has financed several "Solidarity Trips" that arrange meetings between regional union leaders and union leaderships in the United States. Members of the Amalgamated Clothing and Textile Workers and the International Ladies' Garment Workers Union have met with their counterparts in the unions that represent workers in the many garment assembly plants in Barbados, St. Lucia, Antigua, Curaçao, Trinidad, and Jamaica. The International Communications Agency has also arranged meetings between U.S. and Caribbean unions in the petroleum industry in Curaçao and Trinidad.

Tim Hector, leader of the Antigua/Caribbean Liberation Movement, says that Antigua "is an excellent case study of how AIFLD breaks up the solidarity of labor by isolating the leftists in the unions and buying off workers through trips and payments."[55] In Antigua, AIFLD has managed to gain a firm hold on one of the two important unions in the country and, according to Hector, has prevented the development of a united and progressive labor movement. In the past, AIFLD-associated unions in Jamaica and Grenada adopted reactionary policies. In Jamaica, the U.S.-trained unionists joined the conservative opposition against the progressive Manley government. The Grenadian Seamen and Waterfront Workers' Union, whose leaders received training by AIFLD, helped break a popular strike against the Gairy dictatorship in 1976, and then in 1979 tried to organize a political strike against the new progressive New Jewel government.[56]

AIFLD has gained influence in Caribbean unions through its recently established Eastern Caribbean Development Fund, which AIFLD says is "for strengthening unions in the English-speaking Caribbean by helping them finance buildings, housing, community centers, and union offices."[57] AIFLD works with unions that are members of the Caribbean Congress of Labor, which is affiliated with ORIT. The Eastern Caribbean Development Fund projects include construction of combined union and community centers in St. Lucia, St. Vincent, Barbados, and Dominica. In Jamaica, AIFLD provided financing for the Joint Trade Union Center, established a women's component of the trade union center, and has sent five Jamaican women to the George Meany Center for political education courses. USAID, which funds AIFLD, has been working in Jamaica "to improve the industrial relations climate in Jamaica by facilitating understanding between labor, management, and the Ministry of Labor."[58] The agency funded a study to improve labor relations in Jamaica by strengthening the government's labor-management conciliation service. The U.S. Embassy's commercial officer said that striking unions are a major deterrent to foreign investment in Jamaica, and that the United States is making funds available to "train union leaders" and "to teach management and labor how to negotiate."[59]

In 1981, AIFLD, with Force Ouvrière (a French labor federation), initiated new educational programs for unions in the French Caribbean. Union representatives from the French territories attended the George Meany Labor Studies Center's new Afro-American Labor College, which brought the Caribbean unionists together with French-speaking union leaders from Africa. A representative from Guadeloupe echoed the AIFLD message when he told the gathering, "It is our duty to safeguard democracy and to contribute to its expansion," and "Whoever wants to be free must also establish free organizations."[60]

PEACE CORPS

While eating pizza on a Friday evening in Santo Domingo, a disgruntled Peace Corps volunteer complained that his job was to set up an accounting system for farmers—none of whom were particularly poor when compared with most of the people of the Dominican village where he worked. In the Dominican Republic, as in the other Caribbean countries, the Peace Corps is increasingly helping to build private enterprise rather than building schools and health centers or helping the poor. Following the Reagan administration mandate, the Peace Corps now has its own Office of Private Sector Development.

An example of this new trend toward business promotion is in Montserrat, where a volunteer serves as business manager to the island's Development Finance and Marketing Corporation, whose purpose is to promote industrial development. In St. Lucia, Peace Corps volunteers are providing businesses with assistance in pricing, bookkeeping, and inventory control. The major task of a volunteer assigned to Antigua is to negotiate with potential investors, explain business possibilities, and arrange financing for new investments.

Even the American Chamber of Commerce in the Dominican Republic asked the Peace Corps for assistance in its promotional work. The director of the Peace Corps explained to a congressional budgetary committee that the U.S. Chamber of Commerce has directed its foreign chambers to try to establish joint projects with the Peace Corps. Explaining the change, the Corps director for inter-American operations said, "Our image has changed like a flower that is blooming. Now we are seen as a serious development agency around the world."[61]

FOOD FOR PEACE AND PROFIT

Proponents of the U.S. food-aid program usually justify the $1.5 billion yearly expense because it supports U.S. agriculture, not because it feeds malnourished people. Supporting a congressional authorization for the PL 480, or Food for Peace program, the president of CARE, a major food-aid distributor, put the foreign aid program in its proper context. He said: "PL 480 has opened new markets for American agricultural products. Many countries have 'graduated' from PL 480 and are now customers of American agriculture. Of the ten countries that are billion-dollar customers for U.S. farm products, seven are former recipients of Food for Peace aid." In testifying before the congressional committee, the CARE president added that all the major customers for U.S. nonfat dry milk and grain sorghum are graduates of the Food for Peace program, as are eight of the ten largest customers for wheat, cotton, and rice, and seven of the largest buyers of soybeans, corn, and feed grain.[62]

Feeding Friends

From its beginning in 1954, the PL 480 program has been primarily a food-marketing and agricultural subsidy program. Humanitarian concerns have always been only a secondary purpose of Food for Peace. The priorities of the PL 480 program fall in this order: to help the U.S. farmer, to develop U.S. trade, to provide support for governments friendly to the United States, to aid foreign investment projects, and, finally, to feed the hungry. The Department of Agriculture calls Food for Peace "one of the United States' most successful market development tools." The amount and direction of the food aid varies according to grain surplus conditions in the United States and political conditions abroad. When U.S. farmers have too much sorghum, the government buys it. Then when a friendly foreign government needs an extra boost, Washington increases its food-aid allotment.

The program has shipped tobacco worth hundreds of thousands of dollars to the third world under the guise of helping needy nations. From 1955 to 1981, $0.7 million worth of tobacco went to Guyana and $5.2 million to the tobacco-producing Dominican Republic. The government tobacco shipments help alleviate market surpluses in the United States and develop markets for U.S. products in underdeveloped nations.[63]

In the last 30 years, the United States has shipped over $500 million in food aid to the Caribbean nations.[64] The Dominican Republic has been the largest recipient, followed by Haiti and then Jamaica. With the Reagan administration, there has been a marked increase in food aid to the region. The value of food aid from 1980 to 1982 increased from $10 million to $17.5 million for Jamaica, from $15.8 million to $22.2 million for Haiti, and from $0.6 million to $16.6 million for the Eastern Caribbean. The $16 million increase in food aid to the Eastern Caribbean, excluding Grenada, was part of the Reagan administration's plan to ensure support from the region for its foreign policy and foreign-investment initiatives. Keeping citizens of friendly governments fed is merely a side effect of increased PL 480 shipments, which provide balance-of-payment support for those governments having a hard time digging up the dollars to pay for food imports.

Over half the PL 480 food is not given to hungry people but is sold on the commercial market. Earnings from such sales are then used for budgetary support of the recipient government. The U.S. aid agreements often require Caribbean governments to spend the income from these food sales on projects that directly or indirectly benefit foreign investment and trade. In 1982, for example, USAID required that in exchange for increased food aid, Jamaica would make "policy commitments and provide project support for a substantial restructuring of its agricultural sector."[65] The resulting plan furthered export crop production in Jamaica. As Secretary of Agriculture John Block once explained, food aid can "tie countries to us," and in that way "they will be reluctant to upset us."[66]

Food for Factories

Haiti—the hungriest nation in the hemisphere—provides a vivid and shocking example of how the United States uses its food aid. According to the United Nations, people in Haiti are getting hungrier every year despite increasing quantities of food aid. Why? Corruption among government officials is one reason. Free food destined for the poor often ends up in the hands of army officers or in the stores of merchants. Consultants hired by USAID found that ranking officers from Volunteers for National Security (VSN) seized food from distribution programs. In one case, a VSN commander withheld food from his underlings so he could lend them money at exorbitant interest rates. Fake community groups, known as "zombie" organizations, are set up to receive food aid. An official for a private voluntary agency said, "They go in, grab the food and scram. As far as social development goes, it's baloney."[67] A *Miami Herald* reporter found that Haitian smugglers sell PL 480 food to merchants in Florida for resale in grocery stores in the local Haitian community.[68] Another reason for the increasing hunger is that food aid is tied neither to agricultural reforms nor to the promotion of local food production. The PL 480 assistance often actually discourages local farming by saturating the market with foreign food products.

The three main beneficiaries of the food program in Haiti are the Haitian government and the two foreign-owned mills that process the PL 480 shipments: Canadian Pacific's subsidiary Maple Leaf, and a new vegetable-oil mill called Sodexol owned by Universal Seeds and Oil Products. A USAID proposal noted that if Haiti sold its PL 480 soybeans to Sodexol, the Haitian government would generate $26.8 million.[69] As much as 75 percent of the mill's soybeans will come from PL 480 shipments under the plan. Furthermore, if the entire milled product were exported out of the country, Haiti would also benefit from the foreign exchange that would enter the country upon the export of the vegetable oil. The World Bank and the IMF criticized the new Sodexol plant because of its need for imported inputs and expensive machinery, which will reduce the country's foreign-exchange reserves.

In addition, the factory has little need for Haitian workers and will force domestic food-oil refiners out of business. USAID did not join in the protests against the proposed mill, and now feels it "provides opportunity for a set of objectives fully consistent with USAID objectives."[70] The United States will export soybeans for use by Sodexol, which will then provide not food products, but "ample supplies of high quality oilseed meal for livestock and poultry feeds for Haiti and other developing nations in the Caribbean." The animal-feed grain shipments, therefore, will directly serve the interests of the poultry and cattle farms, like U.S.-

owned Haitian American Meat, and not the millions of hungry Haitians who rarely eat meat. The USAID agency feels that it may be able to effect several market and agricultural policy changes in Haiti by using the soybean shipments to Sodexol (which is partially owned by the Haitian government) as leverage. Given the failure of past negotiations with Duvalier about reforms, however, even indirect benefits to the people from the new mill seem remote.

The Haiti USAID Mission, upon examining the PL 480 program, noted that U.S. wheat and flour shipments to Haiti resulted in "rapidly growing commercial demand for bakery products."[71] The 15 percent annual increase in demand for refined bakery products will require Maple Leaf to build another mill by 1985. Because of the flood of wheat flour on the market, due largely to PL 480 shipments, USAID reports that "masses of urban poor and rural peasants are buying bakery products, which are high priced even by U.S. standards."[72] In Haiti, as in other third world nations, U.S. shipments of wheat have altered domestic consumption patterns from locally grown rice to wheat products (which, owing to the climate, cannot be grown locally). The U.S. government will be supplying Haiti and the Maple Leaf mill not only with more wheat to meet increasing demand but also with the grain needs of the Maple Leaf feed-mill as inputs for poultry and livestock production. As the ultimate justification for increased PL 480 food to Haiti, USAID explained that the country "must depend upon increasing volumes of . . . agricultural raw materials in the years immediately ahead if it is to avoid a major foreign exchange crisis or devaluation."[73]

The PL 480 programs are much the same throughout the Caribbean. Washington has given instructions to USAID missions that the food program in Caribbean nations be renegotiated to increase its benefits to private enterprise.[74] New U.S. investments in poultry breeding in Jamaica and the Dominican Republic will directly gain from stepped-up shipments of feed grain. From 1955 to 1981, the United States shipped $35 million worth of feed grain to Jamaica and $18 million worth to the Dominican Republic.

Investors from the United States receive benefits from the funds created by the governments' sale of PL 480 food. Washington requires that Caribbean recipient governments use this income as counterpart funds for USAID projects, most of which directly aid U.S. investment projects. A study by the Presbyterian Church found that while food aid has done some good, "it has also helped unpopular governments to remain in power, discouraged local food production, and increased the dependence of some developing nations on imported foodstuffs."[75] That conclusion, in addition to the program's role in supporting foreign investors and U.S. farmers, is a good summary of the benefits of U.S. food aid in the Caribbean.

OPIC: INSURING AMERICA'S INVESTMENTS

The U.S Congress established the Overseas Private Investment Corporation (OPIC) to insure U.S. private corporations against foreign investment risks due to war, expropriation, currency inconvertibility, revolution, insurrection, and civil strife. Since its founding in 1969, OPIC has expanded its services to include loans for direct investment, feasibility studies, business education and training, and sponsorship of investment tours to foreign nations. Instead of simply insuring foreign investments, OPIC plays the role of the Pied Piper to entice U.S. corporations to invest overseas. OPIC stands in the forefront of Washington's efforts to promote U.S. investment in the Caribbean. The government corporation calls its mission to expand investment in the region the Caribbean Challenge. Typical of OPIC's view of the Caribbean, a promotional advertisement featuring an OPIC-backed enterprise in St. Lucia said: "Some people only see an island paradise. World's Finest Chocolate saw an island of opportunity. With OPIC's unique political investment insurance, they saw a promising place to start a cocoa plantation."[76]

Joining forces with AID's Bureau for Private Enterprise, OPIC has mounted a campaign to attract investors to the Caribbean that includes newspaper advertising, direct mail promotion, satellite-linked business conferences, and frequent tours of the Caribbean for U.S. business people. In October 1982, OPIC financed a lavish electronic spectacle called the Caribbean Telemission, which brought Caribbean business leaders together with 500 U.S. business executives in a "live-by-satellite" television broadcast.

Best-Insured Region

Caribbean nations now lead the list of countries where U.S. investors have benefited from OPIC programs. Encouraged by the Reagan administration, Congress broadened the scope of OPIC in 1981 to allow it to provide insurance and financing to all but the wealthiest of third world nations, including projects in the more developed of the Caribbean nations, like Barbados. In 1981, the Dominican Republic received more insurance than any other country in the world; and in the two categories of expropriation coverage and insurance claims, Jamaica and the Dominican Republic held the number-one and number-two spots, respectively. That same year, the Caribbean Basin accounted for 54 percent of OPIC insurance coverage and financing.

Reflecting President Reagan's emphasis on the region, OPIC lending from 1980 to 1981 increased from zero to $51 million in Jamaica, from zero to $1.2 million in Haiti, and from zero to $2.6 million in the Dominican Republic. The three nations of Antigua, Dominica, and St. Lucia received OPIC insurance and loan assistance for the first time. Of the 20 projects assisted by OPIC in 1981, nine were in Caribbean islands. The total Caribbean OPIC expenditures, counting both insurance and loans, increased 32 times from 1980 to 1981.[77]

Chief commercial officer for the U.S. Embassy in Jamaica, Debbie Coates, said in a 1983 interview: "The United States has a real interest in making Jamaica successful since we are pouring a phenomenal amount of money into this country. OPIC, for example, has a higher visibility here than in any other country of the world. In other words, OPIC is gambling more on Jamaica than any other place in the entire world." In Jamaica, OPIC has taken to guaranteeing large loans through commercial banks instead of issuing direct OPIC loans. The mechanism of guaranteed loans presumably allows OPIC to facilitate lending more money than is available directly in its reserves.

In 1981, Alumina Partners of Jamaica—a joint venture of Anaconda, Kaiser, and Reynolds Metals—received a generous $50 million loan guarantee to open a new bauxite mine in Jamaica. The second-largest loan that year went to a joint venture involving Pillsbury for a flour mill. OPIC agreed to pay for a project involving Control Data, Reynolds Metals, and Grace Kennedy that will study training needs of Jamaican businesses. Rural Ventures, a project designed by Control Data to set up an agricultural marketing information system, also received OPIC assistance.

The director of OPIC's investment mission to Haiti, in December 1981, told a gathering of Haitian and American business people that OPIC's commitment to Haiti "has no end."[78] The brochure printed for the mission said that for the American investor Haiti offered both "an industrious people, dependable, friendly, and eager to respond to productive challenges" and "a tradition of respect for private property and foreign ownership." Although OPIC is now stepping up its promotion of loans and insurance for investment in Haiti, it had already insured 24 investments by such companies as Citibank, Haitian American Meat, Beloved Toys, Tennessee Handbags, International Electronics, and Sylvania.

OPIC has also backed several tourist resorts in Haiti, including the U.S.-owned Habitation Leclerc, which *Travel and Leisure* magazine called "a Haitian hideaway playground to satisfy bored internationals." The travel magazine described the resort in this way: "The Leclerc estate is separated from the raffish area surrounding it by a high wall, and, once within that compound, a different world exists." Three of the ten 1982 OPIC projects in Haiti were tourist hotels, and two other insured projects will be manufacturing dentures for the U.S. market. One 1982 OPIC project provided start-up funds for a leather-dog chew manufacturing plant in Haiti. OPIC hailed the U.S. investment as a project that would increase the foreign-exchange flow to Haiti. Further benefits of the venture are doubtful, however, since it is likely that the dog chews will be going to the more affluent dogs in the United States.

Seizing what they saw as a good opportunity to cash in on President Reagan's focus on the region, several south Florida entrepreneurs formed the Caribbean Basin Investment Corporation to identify promising agri-business opportunities for U.S. investors in the region. In the next four years, the fledgling corporation hopes to invest in 40 projects worth up to $100 million. In May 1982, OPIC signed a letter of intent to finance up to 50 percent of the cost of a CBI Corporation feasibility study for a project to process vegetable oil in Barbados. OPIC President Craig Nalen highly praised what he called a "pioneer effort." He said the Miami corporation "is a positive indication of what the business community can do in implementing the President's Caribbean Basin Initiative call for broader private sector participation in the development process."[79] Officials of OPIC have pleaded ignorance of the fact that the directors of the corporation are also directors of the Cuban American National Foundation, an anti-Castro lobbying organization. Three CBI Corporation directors serve on the board of the Cuban-American Public Affairs Council and the corporation president, Francisco Hernández, participated in the Bay of Pigs invasion of Cuba in 1962. Hernández is also president of Agro Tech International, a poultry-breeding farm insured by OPIC in the Dominican Republic. Through its Direct Investment Fund, OPIC has bought equity in the Dominican venture, which is designed to purchase animal feed from another Hernández company in south Florida.

EXIMBANK

The U.S. Export-Import Bank (Eximbank) works like an insurance company for U.S. exporters by using U.S. government funds to guarantee the payment for goods shipped overseas. It also encourages the foreign purchase of U.S. goods by offering financing below the market rate. A company in the Dominican Republic with access to Eximbank financing is more likely to buy U.S. materials than the same materials from another country, because the financing costs less. Similarly, U.S. corporations are more likely to trade with a country where Eximbank credits are available.

The U.S. government uses Eximbank funds to promote U.S. policy objectives by refusing insurance and loans to countries it wants to chastise and increasing funds available to countries it wants to reward. During the Manley government in Jamaica, Eximbank dropped its funding to zero. In contrast, it provided $6 million in loans in 1981 after the conservative Seaga government gained power. In an unusual move, Eximbank approved a $15 million line of credit to the Bank of Jamaica to finance the purchase of U.S. goods. Because of its nationalist policies, Guyana, like Manley's Jamaica, has fallen victim to the politics of Eximbank lending. Since the 1965 U.S. Marine intervention in the Dominican Republic, Eximbank has regularly issued the country trade credits, even though the bank recently had to reschedule payments for over $7 million in export credits because of failure to pay.

The Reagan administration has directed Eximbank to increase financing to the Caribbean region as part of its Caribbean Basin Initiative. Eximbank lending to the Eastern Caribbean went from zero in 1980 to $10 million in 1981 to $19 million in 1982. For the first two years of the Reagan administration, Eximbank followed a conservative lending policy in line with Reagan's conservative fiscal policy. But this changed in 1983 when the president reversed his policy and encouraged the bank to increase its use of subsidized credit for target countries. Washington embarked on a campaign to subsidize U.S. exports directly through below-market interest rates, an arrangement that particularly favors the Caribbean Basin nations. In addition, a $1 billion "war chest" was being planned to support the growth of U.S. exports through credit and promotion programs. A congressional representative from Virginia complained about the new direction in Eximbank lending: "This appears to turn Eximbank into a foreign aid agency." According to a study by the Congressional Budget Office, even before the advent of the new liberal lending and insurance program, the U.S. public was providing an annual subsidy to Eximbank as high as $900 million.[80]

JAMAICA: CARIBBEAN SHOWCASE

Cynicism pervades the offices of the USAID Mission in Kingston. In one office, a manager of agricultural programs said, "Nobody wants to say anything negative about all these marketing projects. The tendency is to close your ears and push them through." Down the hall, another program director expressed his skepticism about the official infatuation with Jamaica. "One has to wonder," he said, "why Washington is pouring so much money into this place. It is phenomenal, truly phenomenal. We have consultants from the United States knocking on our doors for money and then handing in reports we never have time to read." USAID officials agreed that they have more assistance funds than they can responsibly manage. "Frankly," admitted one official, "we can't keep track of all the projects we have going down here."[81]

In 1982, the United States pumped enough money into Jamaica to make it the world's third-highest per capita recipient of U.S. aid, after Israel and El Salvador. Soon after their inaugurations in 1980, Prime

Minister Seaga and President Reagan established a close mutual-admiration relationship. The admiration society extends to the wives of the heads of state. Seaga named a new library in Jamaica the Nancy Reagan Library in honor of the first lady, and USAID presented its first Humanitarian Service Award to Mrs. Seaga for her work at a children's hospital. The two conservative politicians continually espouse their belief in the "magic of the marketplace."

"Cannot Afford to Fail"

"The overall U.S. foreign objective," according to USAID's 1984 budget presentation, "is to help make the Jamaican approach to economic development a successful one to serve as an example to other developing nations in the region." Washington blames the failure of the previous government on its "communist" policies—not taking into account the U.S. campaign to destabilize the Manley government by cutting off almost all foreign assistance. During the Manley administration the United States reduced food aid and development assistance, eliminated OPIC and Eximbank investment and insurance programs, and obstructed multilateral lending.

With the election of Seaga, Jamaica left the doghouse for the parlor, becoming a priority country for all foreign aid agencies. Table 9B shows the sudden increase in U.S. support for Jamaica from 1980 to 1981. In the first three years of the Seaga government, Jamaica received an amount equal to 65 percent of all U.S. assistance to the country for the last 30 years.[82] Asked in an interview if the Jamaica experiment was really working, the U.S. Embassy's commercial officer replied: "It has to work because Reagan has boasted so much about Jamaica and poured so much money in here. Neither Reagan nor Seaga can afford to have this experiment fail. Both of them have gambled everything they have to prove that private enterprise will cause Jamaica's economy to take off and jump through the hoop again. They just cannot afford to have it fail."[83]

Advice Easy to Come By

Not only is Jamaica flooded with USAID money, but it has also been overrun by U.S. consultants. In the first half of 1982, USAID authorized 49 different consulting contracts with the Jamaica National Investment Promotion (JNIP), costing $2.5 million and designed "to assist the private sector" with technical and training assistance.[84] Other training grants have taken Jamaican officials to visit a free export zone in Panama, a flower packaging farm in Hawaii, and a banana chip factory in the Philippines. In all the Jamaican government ministries, USAID consultants have been busy devising, revising, training, planning, and directing. A

TABLE 9B
U.S. ECONOMIC ASSISTANCE TO JAMAICA, 1980 AND 1981
($ millions)

	1980	1981
AID	2.7	12.9
PL 480	10.0	17.1
ESF	0	41.0
OPIC	0	51.0
Eximbank	0	21.4
Housing Guaranty	0	15.0
TOTAL	12.7	158.4

Source: *U.S. Overseas Loans and Grants and Assistance from International Organizations,* 1983 Annual Report of the Chairman of the Development Coordination Committee, Statistical Annex I

common complaint in government circles in Kingston, even among strong Seaga supporters, concerns the large number of foreigners paid by USAID to tell Jamaicans how to manage their country. The following are representative clauses in these consultancy contracts:

• A one-year salary incentive program for the chief coordinator of the prime minister's staff
• Assistance to JNIP to develop joint-venture agribusiness projects with foreign investors
• Visits by representatives of the National Urban League and United Negro College Fund to Jamaica to promote private-sector management training
• U.S. Department of Labor assistance to revise Jamaica's system of labor-management relations
• Technical assistance to the Port Authority, Bureau of Revenue, Sugar Research Institute, Ministry of Agriculture, National Development Bank, Ministry of Youth, Agricultural Marketing Corporation, National Planning Agency, National Water Commission, Bureau of Standards, Jamaica Public Service Company, and others

The thrust of USAID's agricultural programs is to attract U.S. investors and to encourage increased export-crop production. USAID sponsored a study entitled "Agribusiness Investment Opportunities in Jamaica," which outlined companies that might be open to U.S. investment. One large project called Agriculture Sector Structural Adjustment aims to reform the country's rural economic life by restructuring land policy and tenure systems, shifting production to the private sector, and expanding agricultural credit. In the view of U.S. consultants, agriculture in Jamaica would be substantially better off if the Jamaican government turned over its landholdings to U.S. investors like United Brands, small farmers stopped growing yams and breadfruit and started picking bananas and pruning flowers for export, the sugar cooperatives were turned over to Gulf+Western and Tate & Lyle, and the U.S. provided agricultural credit obligating Jamaican farmers to purchase U.S. fertilizers, pesticides, and farm machinery.

USAID has manufactured an elaborate marketing system, designed primarily to ship produce to the United States. The produce marketing plan involves a sophisticated computer data-base system set up by Control Data and its Jamaican affiliate, Rural Ventures. What is lacking, noted a USAID agricultural expert, is something that money cannot buy, namely, the farmer organizations that will produce for this agricultural marketing project. "We have to call them organizations rather than cooperatives," he remarked, "because cooperatives is a bad word with the Seaga administration."[85]

HAITI: A HOLE IN THE BUCKET

In 1971, Haiti got a new president-for-life when François "Papa Doc" Duvalier died and his son Jean-Claude "Baby Doc" assumed control of the National Palace. Although Baby Doc has promised the United States to improve the human rights situation in Haiti, he has gambled on Haiti's proximity to Cuba to continue to milk the United States for a steady flow of economic aid. Without that aid, conditions in Haiti would deteriorate further and possibly set off a popular rebellion that Duvalier could not control. In the last decade, the Duvalier dictatorship has kept its stranglehold on the country, repression continues, and poverty worsens. Nonetheless, Washington has steadily escalated its aid to Haiti. From 1962 to 1982 Haiti received $268 million in food and development aid from the United States.[86] The sharpest increases have come from 1980 through 1983. Foreign assistance sustains the Duvalier dictatorship. Foreign donors, led by the United States, account for two-thirds of Haiti's budget for public works and 40 percent of its total budget.[87]

Since 1979, as many as 40,000 emigrants have left their country to go to the United States.[88] The U.S. government in 1980 spent over $250 million maintaining refugees on its own shores.[89] In the early 1980s, the United States conditioned its aid program to Haiti on the agreement that the Haitian military and coast guard would crack down on their illegal emigrants. Washington also stepped up military and police aid to the dictatorship's notorious armed forces.

President Reagan sent Duvalier an enthusiastic letter in 1981 that praised the regime both for its "determined opposition" to "Cuban adventurism" and for its support of "private enterprise and economic reforms."[90] Reagan was referring to Haiti's new incentives to foreign investment as evidence of Duvalier's support for economic reforms. But a broader look at Haiti's economy reveals the lack of substantial economic reform and a steady decline in the quality of Haitian life. From 1973 to 1983, the external debt increased 10 times and the trade deficit increased 5 times.[91] During the same period, Haiti's food production per capita decreased as its economy became more wage-oriented, so that people in both the city and countryside became decidedly worse off.

Washington has only to look at a 1982 study of its own aid program to discover the extent of corruption and exploitation in Haiti.[92] Among the study's findings were the following:

- Overhead expenses ate up one of every two aid dollars.
- The U.S.-sponsored Haitian Development Foundation was spending $165 to administer every $100 in loans to small businesses. Haitian officials used USAID money for overseas trips, to buy cars and hire chauffeurs, and to organize fund-raisers where costs exceeded donations.
- USAID spent over $100,000 to train Haitians to operate coffee-processing centers that closed down by the time the training was complete. The agency spent $5 million for fertilizer that Haitian farmers refused to use because it burned their crops.
- At a cost of thousands of AID dollars, Haitian road department employees were flown to Louisiana for welding courses.
- Haitian officials regularly used foreign aid to buy fancy jeeps, increase their salaries, and hire cronies.
- When USAID funded the construction of 180 miles of rough roads on the island of La Gonâve through its food-for-work program, there were only nine motor vehicles on the entire island.

Although USAID has had to terminate at least five development programs in the last five years, the United States is intent on increasing U.S. aid to Haiti, but with a different tack. To explain additional aid in 1982, USAID told Congress: "The U.S. foreign assistance program plays an important and growing role in stimulating and facilitating the interest of U.S. business in investment in Haiti, particularly in agro-industry."[93] No longer does Washington feel the need to justify aid in terms of human development. Instead, support for private enterprise has become the criterion for foreign assistance. The USAID mission in Port-au-Prince has visions of a bright new future for Haiti: "The country's proximity to the U.S. market and the one-way free trade proposal of the CBI make the prospects for Haiti as the 'Taiwan of the Caribbean' real indeed."[94]

The Development Finance Corporation (DFC), which USAID founded in 1982, leads the growing list of private-sector organizations supported by USAID in Haiti. To start the DFC, Washington dropped over $5 million into the laps of Haiti's business leaders, who constitute DFC's board of directors. Two U.S. consulting corporations, Arthur D. Little and Capital Consultants, helped USAID prepare the proposal for the DFC, which is described as "the link between the investor community and international financial institutions." Like the string of similar USAID-founded financing corporations, the DFC in Haiti is designed to promote industrial development through the input of concessional (or easy) capital. But the money will primarily be going, not to develop the industrial potential of Haiti, but to provide capital for U.S.-owned assembly industries producing for the U.S. market.

In 1982, with its new private-sector orientation, USAID opened the Office for Private Enterprise Development in Haiti. USAID provides most of the funds for the Haitian-American Chamber of Commerce, the Private Sector Committee for Development, and the Haitian Development Foundation (which assists small business). The agency also plans to fund several Florida banks and U.S. insurance companies to provide guaranteed credit for housing construction by a U.S. company in Haiti. Other private-sector support programs include the publication of the slick *Investor's Guide to Haiti* and the hiring of a representative of the Florida Advisory Board on Haiti to help promote investment from Florida.

Addressing an assembly sponsored by the Haitian-American Chamber of Commerce, former U.S. Ambassador to Haiti Ernest Preeg said the progress of the private sector in Haiti reminded him of a song he sang as a Boy Scout called "The Upward Trail." The ambassador assured the business community in Haiti of the "close cooperation" of the U.S. government. The United States is satisfied with the "strengthened ties that have developed," he said, promising to work "toward even closer collaboration in the period ahead."[95] The tens of millions of dollars the United States has poured into Haiti's private sector has gratified this elite community. The flood of U.S. bucks has set the chosen private sector on the upward trail. In the words of Preeg's old favorite: "Singing, singing, everybody singing as we go. We're on the upward trail."

Washington's approach to agriculture in Haiti in the last 20 years has resulted in neither increased food production nor better food distribution. As a result, over 500,000 rural Haitians have escaped the misery of the countryside for the destitution of the urban shantytowns.[96] USAID agricultural credit and marketing programs strongly encourage small farmers to switch from subsistence food production to cash crops like coffee. The sad result of this type of "agricultural reform" is that the small farmers have become victims of dropping coffee prices, rising fertilizer costs, and an exploitative coffee export tax. Meanwhile, the supply of yams, corn, and beans for the rural market is dwindling. In its 1984 strategy statement for Haiti, USAID called for "a long-term effort to stimulate coffee" and other cash crops. It noted that this effort to build agricultural exports was "well-suited to the involvement of U.S. agribusiness."

One of the few agricultural endeavors on which Haitian peasants relied was pig raising. Pigs constituted the only source of cash for many peasants; in Haitian slang, pig and bank are the same word. In reaction to the rapid spread of the African swine flu among Haiti's pig population, USAID sponsored a $14.5 million program that eliminated all pigs in the country. To replenish the stock the United States is sponsoring the dissemination of more than 5,000 disease-free pigs, but through the Haitian government, rather than directly to former swine owners. Observers predict that pig raising among Haitian peasants is now a thing of the past.

While USAID frequently demands that governments liberalize their policies concerning foreign investment and trade, it rarely challenges government policies that contribute to inequitable land and income distribution. Programs that USAID calls "agricultural reform" deal at best only with the symptoms of the agricultural crisis in Haiti. The agency complains that small farmers growing grain, corn, and root crops on steep hillsides are contributing to severe erosion problems. Its solution is to begin taking out of production "much of the marginal land now under annual crops and turning this land to tree crops [like coffee] and forest."[97]

The U.S. reform program will require the "systematic removal from annual crop production of almost 30 percent of the land now tilled." Its "tree crop strategy" will replace the subsistence crops with "coffee, cacao, and other high value tropical produce." These planned alterations in agricultural patterns will require increased imports of fertilizers and pesticides, leading to what the agency calls "great market interdependence with the United States." USAID says the "displacement of farmers from marginal land" will provide an excellent pool of labor for public-works brigades to reforest the hills and work on infrastructure projects like rural roads. Handouts of PL 480 food will be used to pay these public-work brigades. USAID calculates that the food aid, together with proposed Haitian government nutritional programs, will temporarily have to cover the loss of food production. In the end, export earnings from the coffee trees and other tropical produce will provide a "sustained national capacity to meet food security requirements." The planners at the USAID mission do not say why they are so certain that Baby Doc Duvalier will see fit to dish out these export earnings to the masses of landless Haitian peasants. Meanwhile, the agency is promoting U.S. agribusiness projects to grow cattle, vegetables, and flowers for the U.S. market.

EASTERN CARIBBEAN: CAUGHT UP IN THE USAID STRATEGY

The Eastern Caribbean islands have revolutionary Grenada to thank for Washington's sudden interest in them. At the U.S. embassies in Antigua and Barbados, talk about the U.S. role in the Eastern Caribbean invariably turned to the impact of Grenada's young revolution. Officials at the USAID headquarters in Barbados readily admitted that Maurice Bishop had more to do with the U.S. government's newfound concern for the economic plight of the region than did any requests for aid made by other Eastern Caribbean politicians. Washington wanted to make certain that the fever for revolutionary change did not sweep from island to island. Rather than direct U.S. economic aid to improve the lot of the poor or to help set the region on its own path to economic development, Washington chose to use its aid to encourage foreign investment in the region and to support the already established local private sector. After the U.S. invasion, Washington immediately authorized $15 million for the island. Along with the aid came the predictable USAID effort to increase foreign investment. Also involved in this campaign was the White House's Office of Private Sector Initiatives, which together with OPIC and CCAA sponsored a visit to the island by interested U.S. investors.

Favored Nations

During the Reagan administration, the island states of the Eastern Caribbean became the subregion of Latin America and the Caribbean with the highest per capita economic aid from the United States. In 1982, for example, the countries of the Eastern Caribbean (including Barbados) received more per capita economic aid than did the poorer countries like Honduras and Haiti. The tremendous increase in economic aid to this region had nothing to do with poverty and everything to do with the new strategic importance given to the Eastern Caribbean by Washington.

USAID guidelines for economic aid priorities state that funds go to the poorest of the underdeveloped nations. In contrast to desperate conditions in other areas of Latin America, the health and education conditions in the Eastern Caribbean are good, infant mortality is relatively low, and literacy is high. The average per capita gross national product (GNP) almost reaches $2,000—well above the international poverty line of $796 set by the World Bank.

In its CBI Implementation Plan for the Eastern Caribbean, USAID noted that the islands suffer from their small domestic markets and limited import-substitution opportunities. Consequently, the USAID planners reasoned that "any growth strategy must concentrate on export promotion."[98] What was needed, according to USAID planners, was to turn the islands into more productive export platforms for tropical produce and assembled goods to be sold on the U.S. market. This U.S. economic development strategy runs directly opposite to the hope of Caricom planners to build up regional industries and markets, rather than increasing dependence on foreign investment and foreign markets.

Not willing to choose a socialist path of development, the Eastern Caribbean islands felt they had no alternative but to rely on U.S. development strategy, which gives a central role to foreign investment. Referring to this new push to attract foreign investors, President Kennedy Simmonds of St. Kitts-Nevis said that underdeveloped countries have to offer "10 to 15 year tax holidays for investors in industry, agribusiness, and tourism" as well as having "to provide adequate electrical power and telecommunications" in order to have any chance of attracting foreign investment. "The money for all these things," he said pointedly, "can only come from USAID."[99]

Change in Programming

Not only does the Eastern Caribbean get more U.S. economic aid than ever before, but it also gets it through new channels. In the 1970s, USAID delivered its economic aid to the region through the Caribbean Development Bank (CDB). USAID started to decrease its use of CDB as an intermediary, however, when the CDB refused to honor its demand that preinvasion Grenada be excluded from development programs that aided other Eastern Caribbean nations. The bank directors said that to accept the stipulation "would result in the bank appearing to be operating as an instrument of U.S. foreign policy."[100] Although the United States in the past had expressed its confidence that CDB was doing a fine job administering USAID funds, donations to the CDB were cut drastically after the bank's refusal to bow to U.S. pressure.

Starting in 1981, aid that had previously gone through the CDB was rechanneled into bilateral programs between USAID and the individual islands. Although the change vastly increased administrative work for USAID, the agency said the bilateral programs "can achieve foreign policy objectives better than assistance channeled through intermediaries." The almost exclusive focus of USAID's new bilateral programs in the region has been to encourage private-sector growth. In its 1983 study of USAID in the Eastern Caribbean, the General Accounting Office (GAO) found that USAID is "aggressively promoting private business investment" in the region. It noted, however, that the amount of money being spent seemed excessive given the possible results.[101] From 1981 through 1984, USAID authorized $85 million to promote private-sector investment in the region. These figures do not include the substantial sums being spent by OPIC, Eximbank, and the Department of Commerce for the same purpose.

The GAO summarized USAID's private-sector program goals in the region as follows: (1) to identify investment opportunities and package them for financing; (2) to provide financing; and (3) to support private-sector organizations, create infrastucture, identify markets, and provide training. Ongoing efforts of USAID in the region to encourage investment include the negotiation of bilateral investment treaties with the United States, structural adjustment programs that persuade the countries of the region to revise their investment laws to make foreign investment more attractive, and regular forums to initiate dialogue among foreign investors, local business owners, labor leaders, and government officials. Specific programs in what USAID calls its "broad strategy" to promote the private sector and foreign investment are the following:

- A $5 million grant to Coopers & Lybrand to place private consultants in policy-level positions of the National Planning Offices of six islands to develop potential investment projects between the U.S. and local investors
- A $4 million loan to the Latin American Agribusiness Development Corporation (LAAD) to develop agribusiness opportunities in the region
- A $9 million loan and a $3.3 million grant to establish a regional merchant bank to finance investment
- A $1.1 million grant to revitalize the Caribbean Association of Industry and Commerce (CAIC)
- $5.5 million in loans and grants to finance construction of factory shells for foreign investors
- $4.4 million in loans and grants to establish a regional trading company called CATCO (managed mainly by Carlton Alexander, principal owner of Grace Kennedy and a director of CCAA)

Limited Results

In its study, the GAO found that the USAID Mission in the Eastern Caribbean had more money than it could properly administer. On the last day that the money could be allocated in fiscal year 1982, the mission was hurriedly dishing out all the funds. One GAO investigator reported that the USAID officials were adding amendments to aid agreements only minutes before the signing ceremonies. The GAO report pointed out that by rushing to dispense its funds, USAID in the Eastern Caribbean was probably violating the provisions of the Foreign Assistance Act, which requires that projects be thoroughly planned.

After more than two years of the private-sector campaign, the GAO found limited documented results. Although officials at the USAID headquarters in Barbados expressed optimism to GAO investigators about the potential of the campaign, they could only cite one U.S. company that had made even a tentative commitment to invest as a result of USAID initiatives. When interviewed privately, USAID and embassy officials were not optimistic about increases in foreign investment and employment. No one at the USAID Mission in Barbados was willing to say how many, if any, jobs had been created by their programs, although some staff members remarked about all the money being handed over to U.S. consultants, particularly Coopers & Lybrand.

While the GAO report did not suggest termination of USAID's expensive campaign to increase private-sector investment, it did suggest that the effort may be a very large waste of taxpayers' money. It noted that even using the most generous estimate of the number of jobs that could be created by USAID private-sector programs, "the cost per job created could be very high." If 10,000 jobs were created as a result of the $58 million spent by USAID from 1981 to 1983 for private-sector development, the cost per job would amount to $5,800, or almost 3 times the annual average per capita income of the Eastern Caribbean. The General Accounting Office also noted the "immediate beneficiaries of USAID's projects appear to be well-established business concerns in the region, such as national chambers of commerce and affluent private businessmen." At the end of its report the GAO asked, "Can AID target its private-sector projects so as to benefit the poor majority?" But, given the U.S. government's preoccupation with investment telethons, business committees, and factory shells, that question no longer seems to concern U.S. foreign aid agencies.

Caribbean Alert:

THE MILITARIZATION OF THE REGION

Government boots, government boots, why we need so many, many government boots?
—Popular 1983 Barbadian calypso protesting that country's militarization

The U.S. Department of Defense considers the Caribbean Sea its backyard pool. From 1898 to 1965, the U.S. military intervened a total of 15 times in Puerto Rico, Cuba, Haiti, and the Dominican Republic. A lull in U.S. interventionism followed the 1965 Marine invasion of the Dominican Republic, but since 1979 Washington has treated the Caribbean waters as a U.S. territorial sea. The escalation of U.S. military presence in the region resulted, as many Caribbean observers predicted, in the October 1983 U.S. Marine invasion of Grenada. Like the 1965 Marine adventure, the primary justification given for the Grenada operation was to "save American lives."

"Our presence, when we can make it felt," said the commander of U.S. forces in the Caribbean in May 1983, "gives confidence to the existing democratic countries in the Caribbean."[1] Since 1979, beginning with a mock invasion by 1,800 Marines on the shores of the Guantánamo base in Cuba, the U.S. military has mounted elaborate shows of sea, air, and land force to demonstrate that it means business in the Caribbean (Table 10A).

In 1981, the Pentagon upgraded the Caribbean Contingency Task Force in Key West, Florida, to one of three full-grade Atlantic NATO commands. It then staged Ocean Venture '81, a war game that let it be known that the United States was willing to use force against Grenada. During these maneuvers, code-named Amber and the Amberdines, a not-too-veiled reference to Grenada and its two smaller islands, U.S. troops simulated an invasion of an island off Puerto Rico. The next year witnessed Ocean Venture '82, which gathered 45,000 U.S. troops in the largest peacetime maneuver ever staged by the Pentagon. In October 1983, Operation Urgent Fury was the real thing: 6,000 U.S. troops invaded Grenada after internal political turmoil on the island.

196 ·

TABLE 10A
U.S. MILITARY EXERCISES
IN THE CARIBBEAN, 1979–1983

1979		Mock invasion by 1,800 Marines at Guantanamo
1980	Solid Shield '80	Exercise involving 20,000 personnel, 42 ships, and 350 aircraft at Guantanamo and Puerto Rico
1980	Readex '80	Landing of Marines at Guantanamo and naval drills off Puerto Rico
1981	Ocean Venture '81	Exercise involving 16,870 personnel, 12 ships, and 100 aircraft
1982	Readex '82	War games involving 39 ships, 200 aircraft, and one British ship
1982	Ocean Venture '82	Month-long $12 million military game involving 45,000 troops from all branches of the armed forces, 60 ships, and 350 aircraft, with cooperation from the Royal Netherlands Marines—largest peacetime maneuver ever by the U.S.
1982	Falcon Vista	Naval maneuver with Honduras
1982	Safepass '82	War games north of Cuba involving 30 warships from six Western nations
1983	Readex '83	War games involving 77 warships, including British and Dutch
1983	Universal Trek	Sea and land exercise involving 5,000 U.S. troops and the National Guards of Puerto Rico and the U.S. Virgin Islands

Sources: "Implicaciones de la Participacion de la Guardia Nacional de Puerto Rico en las Maniobras Militares," Proyecto Caribeno de Justica y Paz, *Puerto Rico Libre*, June/July 1982

U.S. MILITARY PRESENCE

After its victory in the Spanish-American War of 1898, the U.S. military secured a dominant position in the Caribbean. During and after World War I, U.S. military authorities exercised almost absolute authority in Puerto Rico, Cuba, the Dominican Republic, and Haiti. The military presence of the United States further expanded during World War II. In exchange for 50 aging destroyers, Great Britain granted 99-year leases for U.S. military bases in Antigua, St. Lucia, Jamaica, British Guiana, and Trinidad & Tobago. The U.S. territories of Puerto Rico and the Virgin Islands also experienced a rapid military buildup during the war.

The 1959 revolution in Cuba upset U.S. total military control of the region, and two years later the United States responded with the unsuccessful Bay of Pigs invasion of the country. In the 1962 "Cuban Missile Crisis," a standoff between the United States and the Soviet Union brought the world to the brink of nuclear war and forced the Soviets to reduce their military role in Cuba.

The success of Grenada's nationalist New Jewel Movement in 1979 represented yet another threat to U.S. control in the Caribbean. Since then the Department of Defense (DOD) has embarked on a program to arm and train the military and police of the Eastern Caribbean islands. Direct U.S. military presence in the region includes 10,000 military personnel stationed on bases and in communications and tracking facilities throughout the region (Table 10B).

Military Training for Better Understanding

Before Congress terminated the training program for foreign police in 1973, more than 4,000 Caribbean police from the Dominican Republic, Guyana, and Jamaica were trained.[2] In Guyana, immediately following the CIA-engineered expulsion of Prime Minister Cheddi Jagan, USAID started an extensive training program of Guyanese police, which graduated more than 900 in four years. Another program to train foreign military personnel has put more than 6,000 Caribbean soldiers and officers through U.S. military schooling (Table 10C). This training, which takes place in the United States, Panama, and within the countries themselves, offers courses in Counterinsurgency Operations, Urban Counterinsurgency, Military Intelligence Interrogation, and Military Explosives and Detonations. Justifying the program to Congress, the Department of Defense said: "The International Military Education and Training (IMET) provides soldiers with a better understanding of U.S. society, institutions, and goals. Never before in history have so many governments voluntarily and continually entrusted so many personnel in such sensitive positions to training by another government."[3]

Since 1980, the United States has expanded its military training program for Haiti and the Dominican Republic to now include Antigua, Barbados, Dominica, Jamaica, St. Lucia, St. Vincent, Guyana, and Suriname. The training of Haitian soldiers has increased dramatically since 1980. The total number of Caribbean defense forces receiving U.S. training increased from 75 in 1980 to 334 in 1983. These Caribbean defense forces are now regularly included in international training sessions such as the "jungle warfare" get-together sponsored by the U.S. Army in the Panama Canal Zone in 1982.[4]

TABLE 10B
U.S. MILITARY INSTALLATIONS

Location		Function	Personnel
Antigua	Naval facility	Ocean research, tracking	191
	Air Force	Tracking site, tracking	na
Bahamas	Atlantic Underwater Test and Evaluation Center	Naval test site	na
	Eastern Test Range	Air Force missile-tracking station	na
Bermuda	Tudor Hill Lab	Naval test site	na
	Naval Air Station	Patrol aircraft	1,904
	Naval facility	Ocean research	175
Cuba	Guantanamo Naval Station	Operating base	2,673
Puerto Rico	Camp Santiago	US Army & National Guard training	122
	Fort Buchanan	Army Reserve training	1,053
	Roosevelt Roads	Naval base	3,009
	Sabana Seca	Naval communication	459
	Vieques	Naval fleet training	na
	Puerto Rico IAP	Air National Guard activities	994
TOTAL			10,580

Source: "List of All Military Installations including FY1982, Authorized Full Time Assigned Personnel, Territories and Foreign Areas," Department of Defense, 1983

The Caribbean Military Buildup

Direct military assistance through the sales and financing of arms, boats, vehicles, and planes is also on the upswing in the Caribbean. Asked by the chairperson of the Senate Appropriations Committee to explain the need for military aid programs in the Caribbean, a Pentagon spokesperson replied: "The security forces of all [the countries] have insuffi-

TABLE 10C
CARIBBEAN MILITARY TRAINED UNDER
IMET, 1950–1983*
(number of students)

Country	1950–79	1980	1981	1982	1983	TOTAL
Antigua	0	0	0	0	10	10
Barbados	1	13	12	19	26	71
Cuba	523	0	0	0	0	523
Dominica	0	0	7	8	9	24
Dominican Rep	4,218	47	163	129	157	4,714
Guyana	0	0	11	29	10	50
Haiti	623	10	27	26	32	718
Jamaica	11	0	8	20	73	112
St. Lucia	0	0	2	4	9	15
St. Vincent	0	0	1	0	8	9
Suriname	0	5	7	2	0	14
TOTAL	5,376	75	238	237	334	6,260

* Does not include number trained by Puerto Rican National Guard
Sources: "Foreign Military Sales, Foreign Military Instruction Sales, and Military Assistance Facts, as of September 1984," Department of Defense; Letter from the DOD, December 7, 1983

cient or antiquated equipment which is inadequate for their defense roles. With particular regard to the Eastern Caribbean, the assistance will be used to strengthen the defense force of Barbados and the Coast Guard units of Antigua, Dominica, St. Lucia, and St. Vincent." He added that these islands now "must be on alert to possible efforts of even very small bands of foreign-supported invaders to take over their governments by force."[5] Military assistance to the Caribbean (including IMET) from the United States has increased almost 7 times between 1979 and 1983. Many countries have never before been beneficiaries of U.S. military aid, and others that have previously had American military training are receiving increasingly higher authorizations (Table 10D, p. 209).

Besides granting military aid to Caribbean nations, the United States also authorizes commercial sales of military equipment and weapons. If a nation is found to be violating human rights, it can be denied these commercial purchases. The DOD's eligibility list, however, still regularly includes a country as repressive as Haiti. From 1980 to 1982, commercial purchases increased from zero to $200,000 for Haiti, $300,000 to $1 million for the Dominican Republic, and $50,000 to $200,000 for Jamaica.

PUERTO RICO: A U.S. SURROGATE

In the last few years Puerto Rico has assumed new importance for U.S. military strategists. The headquarters of U.S. Naval Forces in the Caribbean, the U.S. possession has played a leading role in recent military maneuvers in the region and in the 1983 invasion of Grenada. The U.S. Atlantic Fleet has markedly increased its use of the Naval Weapons Training Facility, an installation for training and artillery range practice. The training facility coordinates many joint U.S. maneuvers both with NATO countries and with South American allies. In 1983, the U.S. Navy sponsored two major military maneuvers that took place off Puerto Rico's coasts. Also, the U.S. Infantry Brigade conducted joint exercises on the island with the local National Guard to insure optimum military preparedness by the island's security forces.

Puerto Rico has seven U.S. military installations: three operated by the Navy, three by the Army, and one by the Air Force. The Roosevelt Roads Naval Station in Puerto Rico is the center of naval control for the entire Caribbean and South Atlantic. One of the largest naval facilities in the world, the base handles 45,000 aircraft and 1,200 ships each year.[6] At another base, Fort Buchanan, the U.S. Army trains the Army Reserve and the National Guard. The Puerto Rican press reported in 1983 that the Ramsey Air Force Base, which the Pentagon had closed for ten years, is now reopening and being converted into a military communications center as part of the U.S. military buildup in the region.

The increase in military operations runs contrary to a 1983 resolution of the UN Special Committee on Decolonization, which demanded that the United States reduce its military activities in Puerto Rico, particularly on the island of Vieques. Many Puerto Rican political, religious, and youth groups also oppose the military buildup, as well as the use of the island for U.S. intervention in Central America and other Caribbean islands. Peter Berkowitz, a member of the Puerto Rican Institute for Civil Rights, said, "The U.S. military buildup and occupation of Puerto Rican territory constitutes another denial of the right to self-determination of the Puerto Rican people." According to Berkowitz, the buildup "poses an extremely serious threat to peace in the Caribbean and Latin America."[7] Radical opposition groups in Puerto Rico have targeted the U.S. military presence by carrying out assaults on air bases. After a 1981 terrorist attack destroyed nine jet fighters on the Air Force base, the Air Force stated, "Concern for subversive terrorist elements in Puerto Rico is a major issue that will play heavily into the decision as to what the Air Force does in Puerto Rico in the future."[8]

The Pentagon has given the Puerto Rican National Guard (PRNG) a central role in its military strategies in the Caribbean. It covers most of the expenses and personnel costs of the 12,000-member PRNG, which is regarded as the best trained and equipped National Guard unit of the United States. In 1982, DOD spent over $72 million on reserve and guard pay. The PRNG has not only served to control local social unrest, but since the early 1980s has also assumed a surrogate role for the United States in regional military matters. The first sign of the guard's regional role came in 1980 when 50 soldiers of the Barbados Defense Force went to summer training camp in Puerto Rico.[9] In 1982, security forces from Barbados and Dominica received training from the PRNG. The Jamaican Defense Force regularly attends training sessions in Puerto Rico.

The PRNG is strategically important not only because of its location, but also because its troops are bilingual. About 200 PRNG members participated in the 1983 maneuvers in Honduras. The PRNG can be used as an intermediary in the flow of military aid and training to its Caribbean neighbors, particularly those that belong to the Regional Defense Force. A congressional mandate prohibits the use of foreign aid, either economic or military, in the training of foreign police.

An Occupied Island

The Puerto Rican residents of the island of Vieques have continually opposed the U.S. Navy, which owns two-thirds of the 33,000-acre island.[10] The expropriation of most of the island has meant an end to the cattle and sugar industries. Carlos Zenon, a fisherman from Vieques, said, "Before the Navy came to Vieques, we had a sugar mill and small cattle farms, but unemployment is now between 45 and 50 percent." The practice shelling is common from 7:00 A.M. to 11:00 P.M. five days a week, and as a result of delayed detonation of bombs and missiles, over a dozen Vieques residents have been either mutilated or killed.

In 1978, the people of Vieques joined to oppose directly the military occupation of their island, and forty fishing boats successfully blocked a U.S.-sponsored multination war game. The group, called Pescadores Unidos, stopped another naval maneuver in 1981.[11] In an attempt to "improve community relations," the U.S. Navy began a Sea Cadets program in Vieques that recruits local children as young as 11 years old. The program trains Puerto Rican youngsters in wilderness survival and the use of hand arms as well as encouraging the proper patriotic spirit.

In 1983, the Department of Defense initiated a campaign to generate more private-sector jobs in Vieques in an effort to improve its image on the strategic island. The new Private Sector Initiatives Program, which DOD calls a "mini-Fomento," was designed to attract more industry to Puerto Rico with special emphasis on Vieques. Under this program the Puerto Rican government will exempt new corporate investors from local taxes for 25 years. As part of this effort, in October 1983 Commodore Diego Hernández, commander of U.S. Naval Forces in the Caribbean, invited the chief executive officers of the top ten U.S. defense contractors to Vieques to examine the prospects of opening defense-related manufacturing. One of the top ten, General Electric already has a manufacturing plant on the island. Pointing out the importance of these firms, Commodore Hernández said the combined sales of the firms constitute an estimated one-third of the U.S. gross national product. Hernández also noted that there was "high-level backing" for the campaign, including the personal involvement of Vice-President George Bush.[12]

The corporate visit came shortly following the signing of an agreement between Puerto Rico and Washington to terminate "without prejudice" all litigation brought against the Navy for the shelling on Vieques. The Navy agreed to limit, but not to terminate, its shelling exercises. The director of the Private Sector Initiatives Program, Roger Sattler, said that DOD is giving Puerto Rico "a lot of special attention" because it "plays a particularly important role in the Caribbean, both from an economic and defense standpoint."

Defense Contracting Boosts Economy

In 1982, DOD had procurement contracts with 219 mostly U.S.-owned firms doing business in Puerto Rico. While other sectors of the economy have been slowing down, the value of DOD contracts increased 28 percent in 1982. The largest single contract went to Propper International to manufacture camouflage combat caps. Gibralter Industries of New York, the second-largest contractor, is manufacturing fatigues for the Air Force. RCA was listed as the third-largest DOD contractor in Puerto Rico.[13]

The DOD spends about $423 million a year in Puerto Rico. This includes about $200 million in contract expenditures for weapons, military construction, and maintenance of military installations. Another $223 million goes for personnel expenditures. The DOD said that these figures do not take into account the "undoubtedly large amounts of defense subcontracting activity with firms on the mainland."[14] Neither do the figures include the costs of the practice bombings or the frequent military maneuvers coordinated in Puerto Rico.

DOMINICAN REPUBLIC: A HISTORY OF INTERVENTION

In May 1916, U.S. Marines landed in the Dominican Republic on the pretext of establishing public order and ending a civil war. They declared martial law and established a U.S. military government that lasted until 1924. This early history of U.S. military intervention set the stage for the institution of one of the hemisphere's most brutal dictatorships, and a subsequent U.S. Marine invasion in 1965.

The 1916 intervention met opposition from the country's ruling elite, who refused to lend governmental or military support to the U.S. military. As a consequence, the Marines started training the new Dominican National Constabulary, which replaced the country's other military units. In 1921, the U.S.-backed military government founded the Haina Military Academy. Among its first graduates was Rafael Trujillo Molina, who later became chief of the National Guard. With U.S. support, Trujillo had turned the guard into a national army by 1928, which he used to establish himself as president through a military coup in 1930. Trujillo ruled the Dominican Republic with an iron hand for the next three decades, with the help of military training and equipment from the United States.

In 1936, the general changed the name of Santo Domingo, the oldest city in the Americas, to Ciudad Trujillo. He honored himself with 40 or more grandiloquent titles, including Great Benefactor, Father of the New Fatherland, and Genius of Peace. Grateful for U.S. assistance, General Trujillo in 1953 made the Dominican Republic the first Latin American state to sign a bilateral mutual defense assistance agreement with the United States. By 1959, half of all Dominican government expenditures were military related. The Cuban revolution shook the complacency of the U.S. State Department, which came to fear that a popular revolution in the Dominican Republic would follow the Cuban example. To forestall that possibility, the Central Intelligence Agency engineered the assassination of Trujillo and backed the new military government with over $10 million in arms.[15]

A widespread popular revolt, including progressive factions of the military, threatened the military junta in 1965. The U.S.-imposed military leader, Colonel Pedro Benoit, sent Washington a cable requesting U.S. troops "because a Communist takeover threatens." Washington responded that no troops could be sent unless U.S. lives were threatened. Another cablegram quickly followed from Colonel Benoit that read: "Regarding my earlier request, I wish to add that American lives are in danger." That same day 400 U.S. Marines arrived in Santo Domingo, and eventually 23,000 U.S. troops occupied the country to crush the popular revolt, while yet another 10,000 waited aboard naval vessels offshore. During the ensuing rebellion, 2,500 Dominican civilians died at the hands of U.S. and Dominican soldiers.[16]

In 1980, the *Washington Post* reported that the Dominican military was "very preoccupied with what's happening around them in El Salvador, Nicaragua, Jamaica, and Grenada." Commander-in-Chief of the U.S. Atlantic Command Harry S. Train, on a trip to the Dominican Republic in 1980, offered the government "all types of military aid to combat communism."[17] U.S. Ambassador to the Dominican Republic Robert Anderson, in a speech entitled "The Dominican Republic: Cornerstone for Caribbean Stability," stated, "The very location of the country in one of the most important strategic and commercial arteries for the United States speaks for itself."[18] The memories of intervention remain strong in the Dominican Republic. The visit by two U.S. warships to the country in

1983 sparked off several days of demonstrations that resulted in three deaths.[19]

HAITI: FOSTERING CONSTRUCTIVE RELATIONS

The U.S. Marines occupied Haiti from 1914 to 1934. As their legacy, they built a few roads and sewers, founded a pro-U.S. militia, and established the Marines Club. Today, tour guides encourage visitors to keep abreast of cultural events sponsored by the club, which is a "center of culture" in Port-au-Prince. In 1957, "Papa Doc" Duvalier came to power with the support of the U.S.-trained militia. Fearing a Cuban-style revolution, President Dwight D. Eisenhower poured generous amounts of military assistance into Haiti.

Despite continued human rights violations under "Baby Doc," Washington has persisted in providing military aid to the repressive regime. The Department of Defense says its military aid program "is intended to foster constructive relations with the Haitian military." It says, "By encouraging development of a corps of professionally trained and competent officers, the program can contribute to the development of a more modern and progressive Haitian state."[20] Washington claims that its program to provide the Haitian military with ammunition, small arms, and light machine guns will "ensure continued exposure of the Haitian military to U.S. values and practices."[21]

The Reagan administration also initiated preliminary negotiations with Duvalier about a plan to lease territory for a military base near a harbor known as Mole Saint-Nicolas, which is directly across the Windward Passage from Cuba. In 1983, Washington admitted the presence of U.S. Army engineers near Mole Saint-Nicolas, who supposedly were checking a malfunctioning hydroelectric dam—except that no dams exist in the area. It has been reported that Duvalier turned down an initial offer of $500 million for the rights to build a base and that Washington later upped the offer to $780 million. Also in 1983, Washington arranged an accord with the Dominican army to cooperate with the Haitian military in the event of an exile landing in Haiti.[22]

COMMONWEALTH CARIBBEAN: NEW ARENA FOR U.S. DEFENSE

The English-speaking Caribbean islands, most of which do not even have regular military units, have become militarized almost overnight. The Pentagon, which previously had paid little attention to this part of the Caribbean, began to place high strategic value on the islands after the Reagan administration entered the White House. Before 1980, Jamaica was the only English-speaking Caribbean island ever to have received significant quantities of U.S. military aid. But from 1981 through 1983, the Pentagon saw fit to pour large quantities of military equipment and weapons into the region. Approximately 85 percent of all U.S. military aid ever received by the region (Antigua, Barbados, Dominica, Jamaica, St. Lucia, and St. Vincent) was given in these three years. Continuing this trend of escalating military expenditures, the U.S. Congress allocated these six countries a 145 percent increase for 1984 over 1983.

Eastern Caribbean

The U.S. security interests and priorities in the Eastern Caribbean, as defined by the Pentagon, are fourfold: (1) to promote the continuing development of stable democracies that share U.S. regional interests and concerns, (2) to prevent the Eastern Caribbean states from moving into an anti-U.S. orbit, (3) to encourage and support the region's security initiatives, and (4) to protect U.S. security interests in the Caribbean sea lanes.

The militarization of the region was reflected in the formation of a Regional Defense Force in 1982, when Barbados, Dominica, St. Lucia, Antigua, and St. Vincent signed a joint security and military cooperation pact. The Grenadian revolution and pressure from Washington spurred the region to prepare itself militarily. In the forefront of the Regional Defense Force was Barbados, the only country that had a standing militia unit.

Although the rationale for the Regional Defense Force was to defend the Eastern Caribbean islands against external threats and to deal better with problems of drug running and poaching, critics charged that the regional unit was formed to protect the island governments from internal, not external, threats. The use of the Barbados Defense Force, the coordinating member of the regional group, to quash a 1979 Rastafarian rebellion in St. Vincent established a precedent of using the security forces of other islands to handle internal disturbances and revolts. In 1982, Prime Minister Vere Bird of Antigua praised the formation of the Regional Defense Force, saying, "In this region, we cannot afford to have another Cuba or Grenada."[23]

Another regional organization formed recently is the Organization of Eastern Caribbean States (OECS). Its members are the small English-speaking islands in the Eastern Caribbean, excluding Barbados. This was the organization that requested (at the invitation of the U.S. State Department) U.S. intervention in Grenada in October 1983. The charter of the OECS provides for the handling of cases of external aggression in the region but notes that decisions about these cases must be unanimous. Three OECS member islands, Montserrat (a British colony), St. Kitts-Nevis (which gained its independence only a month before the invasion), and Grenada did not vote for the invasion. Three other nations, however—Jamaica, Barbados, and the United States, none OECS members—participated in the OECS meetings that authorized the invasion. Following the invasion of Grenada by U.S. Marines, St. Kitts-Nevis joined the new ad hoc regional security force, called the Caribbean Peace Force.

Barbados and Jamaica: The Vital Cogs

Barbados, which had received a mere $6,000 in military aid before 1980, became the center of U.S. militarization of the Eastern Caribbean by 1982. Although Barbados is not a member of the Organization of Eastern Caribbean States, the U.S.-trained Barbados Defense Force is the crucial element in the Regional Defense Force for the Eastern Caribbean. By the time of the invasion of Grenada, hundreds of members of the Barbados Defense Force had been trained by United States military and the Puerto Rican National Guard. The country had also received several hundred thousand dollars in military aid.

In an attempt to explain the sudden military importance of Barbados, USAID in 1982 stated: "Barbados is a vital cog in the regional security posture. The country has important physical assets whose use by a hostile power would be detrimental to U.S. interests." Barbados, which has little to offer in natural resources except beautiful beaches and fields of sugarcane, proved to be an important physical asset not to some hostile power but to the United States, which used Barbados as the staging ground for its invasion of nearby Grenada.

Jamaica is the other "vital cog" in the U.S. security posture in the Caribbean. Military aid to the island increased from zero under the Manley government in 1980 to an initial allocation of over $4 million in 1984. In December 1982 Jamaica signed a memorandum of understanding with the Puerto Rican government to allow for training of the Jamaica Defense Force (JDF) by the Puerto Rican National Guard.

Upon proposing increased military assistance to Jamaica, the Department of Defense said the security aid will promote four U.S. objectives in Jamaica: (1) economic recovery based on revitalization of the private sector, (2) increased professionalism and effectiveness of the JDF, (3) cooperative relations between U.S. and Jamaican authorities, and (4) improved JDF capability to meet possible threats from externally supported subversion. The security assistance proposal notes that the failure of Washington's program for Jamaica "would confirm the view of those in the Caribbean and elsewhere in the third world who argue that cooperation with the IMF and stimulation of the private sector is a fruitless endeavor."[24]

Training the "Police"

Although Congress has expressly forbidden U.S. training of foreign police, the U.S. military has been doing just that in the Commonwealth

Caribbean. Both the Department of Defense and the Department of State have had a difficult time defining what are police and what are military in the region. "We're not training police forces, they're security forces," said Chris Webster of the Department of State's Grenada Task Force.[25] When questioned further, Webster admitted, "Yes, they are police forces, but they are the only security forces on the island so they have more than police responsibilities. They are quote, unquote police." To clear up this case of mistaken identity, Harvey Lampert of the Department of State's Office of Political-Military Affairs said, "We don't train police— they're militia units."[26]

Needing regional military representation from the OECS, the Department of Defense decided to take the local constabulary along for the ride into Grenada during the October 1983 invasion. Since the invasion, the United States has stepped up the training of these "quote, unquote police" both in Grenada, where they are stationed as a "peacekeeping force," and at home in their respective islands.

The Department of Defense in late 1983 allocated $15 million to pay for the maintenance and training of what it calls the Caribbean Peace Force. In the months following the invasion, there were about 200 members of the Caribbean Peace Force from the islands of Jamaica, Barbados, St. Lucia, St. Vincent, Dominica, Antigua-Barbuda, and St. Kitts-Nevis stationed in Grenada. The Department of State said that the $15 million was not being used to pay for their salaries but was only used for "logistics, training, food, and equipment."[27] These funds come from a special "peacekeeping" account, which in the past has only been used to pay for multinational observers at trouble spots such as in Sinai, Cyprus, and Lebanon.

The regular IMET program handles the ongoing training for the "defense forces" of the Eastern Caribbean. Justifying the need to give military training to these small islands, the DOD, in its 1983 budget presentation to Congress, said that its training programs "are designed to assist these countries in developing the expertise needed for their own self-defense while simultaneously discouraging excessive dependence upon the United States." A staff study mission of the Senate Committee on Foreign Affairs in 1982 recommended that USAID funds be used to train police in the small Caribbean islands despite a former congressional prohibition of foreign police training. The study said, "Such an exception should not undermine the legislative intent to prevent U.S. complicity in internal suppression." The study went on to state, however, that the "islands should be encouraged to maintain a well-trained police, similar to SWAT (Special Weapons Assault Team), capable of handling terrorist or organized group violence. Such training is best done in the United States."[28]

From being a region characterized by its lack of military institutions, the Commonwealth Caribbean has rapidly become a militarized zone.

Opposing this trend, the Barbados Peace Committee protested that the Barbadian people "have no wish to be part of a regional police force for the Ronald Reagan government."[29] Other Caribbean groups have called for the establishment of a Caribbean Zone of Peace that would prohibit foreign military aid or intervention in the region.

"The emphasis on security is ultimately destructive of the society," wrote Caribbean expert A. Vaughn Lewis. "It further draws the United States into the local political system, establishing [it] and its representatives as the ultimate mediators of the local political system. . . . The process of modernization of the security forces has strong ideological content, in addition to its technological content. Already . . . the modernization process suggests to the military a sense of their political status as the only virtuous sector—as the guardians of the system." Lewis warned that this process is all too similar to the process of militarization of politics in Central America. "It is therefore important," he concluded, "that the Caribbean leadership not succumb to this model."[30]

TABLE 10D
U.S. MILITARY AID TO THE CARIBBEAN, 1950–1983*
($ thousands)

Country	1950–1980	1981	1982	1983	1984**	TOTAL
Eastern Caribbean	0	17	925	2,196	7,300	10,438
Antigua	0	0	0	†	†	
Dominica	0	12	317	†	†	
St. Lucia	0	5	308	†	†	
St. Vincent	0	0	300	†	†	
Barbados	64	61	170	77	‡	372
Bahamas	0	0	0	0	5	5
Cuba	15,085	0	0	0	0	15,085
Dominican Rep.	34,622	565	4,375	5,597	5,070	50,229
Grenada	0	0	0	0	15,000§	15,000
Guyana	0	28	40	25	5	98
Haiti	5,117	122	241	687	75	6,242
Jamaica	1,226	96	1,075	2,426	4,200	9,023
Suriname	27	30	23	0	0	80
Trinidad	85	15	0	0	0	100
TOTAL	56,226	934	6,849	11,008	31,655	106,672

* includes Foreign Military Sales (FMS), Military Assistance Program (MAP), and International Military Education Training (IMET)
** 1984 funds are allocated; the figures may increase by the end of the fiscal year
† at date of publication figures were not available for individual countries, but are reflected in the Eastern Caribbean figure
‡ during FY1983 Barbados was added to list of Eastern Caribbean countries, so no separate figures for Barbados were available for 1984
§ this $15 million ws given out of Peacekeeping Funds, not as DOD military aid
Sources: Foreign Military Sales, Foreign Military Construction Sales and Military Assistance Facts as of September 1982, DOD, 1983; DOD and Department of State phone interviews, December 1983

Great Britain and the Caribbean

The power and glory of the British empire have faded away in the Caribbean, but colonial vestiges remain. The crown still rules six small territories, and several nations have chosen to remain part of the British Commonwealth. For three hundred years before World War II, Great Britain wielded the major influence in the region, from the Bahamas on the north, Belize (then British Honduras) on the west, and Guyana on the south. The English-speaking states shared plantation economies and a brutal history of slavery. England abolished slavery in the 1830s, but the territories remained tied to one-crop economies that produced bananas or sugar to ship to London. Because abolition of slavery created a severe loss of laborers, England later passed laws to make owning land difficult for former slaves in order to keep them working on the plantations. The colonial government in Jamaica enacted Ejectment and Trespass laws to harass freed slaves who would not accept labor-market conditions as dictated by the planters.

The decline of the British empire in the West Indies began with World War II, when Great Britain accepted 50 old destroyers from the United States in exchange for 99-year leases on seven commonwealth islands to build military bases. The occupation by American soldiers of the British colonies marked the ascent of American culture, politics, and economics in the Commonwealth Caribbean. The slogan "America in Britain's Place," which originated during World War II, carried both positive and negative connotations. In the last four decades, the United States filled the vacuum created by England's departure from the Caribbean. Even on the islands that remain British colonies, the dollar reigns supreme.

Soon after the war, Great Britain formed the Anglo-American Caribbean Commission with the United States to chart the region's future. Subsequently, Holland and France, the other major colonial powers in the Caribbean, joined the commission. The European powers wanted to maintain their trade advantages but recognized that their own state of indebtedness after the war prevented them from keeping their monopoly trade and investment position. The superior economic status of the United States allowed it to exercise a growing influence in the Caribbean, to the chagrin of old colonial powers. Out of the Caribbean Commission came the idea for the creation of the West Indies Federation, which was to be a political and economic organization of the Commonwealth territories. Rivalries and separate ambitions of the British colonies tore apart the externally imposed union. After the breakup of the federation in 1961, the Caribbean colonies started gaining their independence from Great Britain.

The independent states have remained members of the Commonwealth of Nations, a loose affiliation of countries that recognize the crown as a symbol of the Commonwealth. No nation in the Commonwealth is pledged to go to the defense of the others, and no formal policy exists among them as a whole. The relationship between the Commonwealth Nations and Great Britain varies with each nation and changes with international trends. Most of the independent Caribbean members of the British Commonwealth have a governor-general who is a figurehead representing only the crown and not the British government.

The Caribbean members of the Commonwealth of Nations and their dates of independence are as follows:

Barbados	1961
Jamaica	1962
Trinidad & Tobago	1962
Guyana	1966
Bahamas	1973
Grenada	1974
Dominica	1978
St. Lucia	1979
St. Vincent	1979
Antigua-Barbuda	1981
St. Kitts-Nevis	1983

Although attitudes toward the British crown vary greatly among the Caribbean people, loyalty to the monarchy still exists. Queen Elizabeth filled the Kingston stadium on her February 1983 trip to Jamaica, where she was given a royal reception by the Seaga government. Many have found the pomp and circumstance of British royalty more appealing than the nitty-gritty of self-rule. In the Cayman Islands, banners in the downtown area celebrated 1983: "Cayman Islands—150 years of parliamentary rule." The colony's shops sell Prince Charles and Princess Diana memorabilia, from coffee mugs to sterling napkin rings. Most Caribbean people, however, are glad to be rid of colonial trappings despite the security they represent.

The aftermath of the 1983 U.S. invasion of Grenada illustrated the Caribbean's ongoing political shift away from Great Britain and toward the United States. Prime Minister Margaret Thatcher's initial condemnation reflected Great Britain's indignation at the arrogance of Washington. The British considered the unilateral action by the United States in its former territory a slap in the face. The later posture of support by Thatcher indicated the country's resignation to U.S. strength in the Caribbean. The United States was able to rally many Caribbean leaders to support the military action in Grenada. Government officials like St. Lucia's John Compton and Barbados's Tom Adams, by showing their loyalty to the superpower, demonstrated their lack of respect for or subservience to Great Britain. As U.S. trade, financial assistance, and investment increase in the region, the Caribbean countries turn less frequently to Great Britain for political leadership or guidance.

Colonies or not, many Caribbean islands remain tied to Great Britain through the migrant stream. From 1964 to 1972, more than 14,000 physicians, scientists, and other professionals migrated to England.[1] The European Economic Community Information Service reported that the United Kingdom's health services and the postal and public transport services would cease to function without their staffs of Caribbean origin. But West Indians in Britain regularly suffer racial discrimination and police harassment, and Parliament often discusses new legislation that would further limit the migration of West Indians to England.

FOREIGN POLICY AND AID

Division in the British Parliament over relations with the West Indies surfaced after the Foreign Affairs Committee of the House of Commons, in a December 1982 report, recommended a new Caribbean foreign policy. Conservative members of Parliament criticized the report as anti-American and pro-Cuban. The committee contended that the root causes of political turbulence in the Caribbean area are poverty and injustice. It lambasted the Reagan administration for its "paranoid antagonism" to leftist governments and for its view of the Caribbean as a "theater of East-West confrontation." The report strongly recommended that Great Britain "seek to open the door to an amelioration of U.S.-Cuba relations and to Cuban participation in Caribbean economic development agencies" while seeking to dissuade Cuba from supplying arms and military training in the region. Other recommendations included improved aid programs through regional multilateral institutions, assurance that aid programs like the CBI would meet real needs, and support for the concept of a "Caribbean Zone of Peace." The report, which did not set well with Prime Minister Thatcher, demonstrated a widespread sentiment in what was once the foremost imperial power in the Caribbean for a less self-centered and more reasonable attitude about the problems of Caribbean development.

In 1981, Great Britain gave the Caribbean $45 million in aid, with Jamaica being the largest recipient. As part of its aid to Jamaica, Great Britain gave the island a $9 million loan to finance the purchase of British goods and services. From 1976 to 1980 England was the major donor to Dominica, Grenada, St. Lucia, and St. Vincent. The British government's police-training program in the Commonwealth Caribbean costs over £750,000.

The British Development Administration has recently tried to increase the interconnections between aid and private-sector development. Operating under the Overseas Development Agency, which coordinates foreign aid, is the quasi-governmental Commonwealth Development Corporation (CDC), founded in 1948 to provide development capital to infrastructure and basic industries. Rather than divesting its interest in the companies it helped start, the CDC in the last 35 years has deepened and widened its control in important Caribbean investments. Most CDC firms in the Caribbean are utilities, finance companies, and tourism businesses. The development corporation has investments in most of the Commonwealth Caribbean, with Jamaica and St. Lucia leading the list in the number of CDC corporations. Two new CDC

TABLE II A
MAJOR BRITISH TNCs IN THE CARIBBEAN

Banks	Barclays Bank
	Lloyds Bank
Tourism	Trust House Forte
	Grand Metropolitan
	British Airways
Agriculture	Great Industries
	Tate & Lyle
	Booker McConnell
	BAT Industries
Other	Taylor & Woodrow
	Commonworth Development Corporation
	Cable — Wireless (operations in 13 islands)

Source: The Resource Center, Compilation of Corporations, 1984

investments in 1981 included a coffee project and a flour-milling firm, both in Jamaica.

TRADE

Great Britain has enjoyed increasingly favorable balances of trade with the Caribbean. In 1982, Britain exported to the entire Caribbean over £100 million more than it imported from the region. England's favorable balance of trade with its Caribbean colonies is even more pronounced. The colonial states imported from England more than 3.5 times what they exported in 1982.[2] In terms of corporate dominance, British agricultural companies have divested their Caribbean holdings in the last 20 years but maintain a majority interest in the trade of rum, sugar, and bananas. It is difficult to state the exact extent of British investment in the West Indies both because Great Britain does not publish country-specific figures on foreign investment and because it is often hard to categorize companies as being local or British. As the commercial officer for the British Embassy in Barbados commented, "It is difficult to determine what is British and what is Barbadian after over a hundred years. Investment and investors are now woven into the island's society and economy."[3]

BRITISH POSSESSIONS

Great Britain still appoints the governors and is responsible for the defense and foreign relations of its colonies in the Caribbean: Anguilla, the British Virgin Islands, Bermuda, Montserrat, Turks and Caicos, and the Cayman Islands. The governor represents the queen and retains responsibility for external affairs, defense, and internal security. Each colonial legislature is made up of Her Majesty, the Senate, and the House of Assembly.

In the 1600s, Irish settlers nicknamed Montserrat the Emerald Isle and left generations of redheads and English-speakers with a hint of brogue. The British tried to transform Montserrat into a plantation economy, with large acreage and imported slaves, but the terrain proved too rugged. The Virgin Islands, the Cayman Islands, and the Turks and Caicos all provided hideaways for buccaneers and pirates. The first settlers of the Cayman Islands were deserters from the British army who left Jamaica when England took power there. Early settlers in the Turks and Caicos included loyalists unhappy with the rebel victory in North America.

Bermuda, settled by the English in 1612, requested crown colony status in the 1600s, but has always had strong ties to the United States.

During the American Revolution, Bermudians smuggled gunpowder to General George Washington. In the Civil War, Bermuda residents sent supply ships to run the North's blockade of the Confederacy. Bermudians themselves had a bit of the colonialist in them, establishing colonies in a Bahamian island and in the Turks in the mid-1600s. The Turks settlement provided Bermudians with salt, which later became the base of Bermuda's economy. The Turks and Caicos were considered part of the chain of Bahamas islands until 1874, when they became part of Jamaica. Since 1962, when Jamaica declared independence from Britain, the islands have been a crown colony. The Caymans also belonged to Jamaica until its independence, when the Caymans became a separate crown colony.

In the game of musical colonies, the United Kingdom made a mistake when it came to Anguilla. The colonists grouped Anguilla with St. Kitts-Nevis and made them a single crown colony in 1825. In 1966, disgruntled Anguillans put up a fight when the British declared the three islands one associated state, which would have prevented Anguillans from governmental decision-making. After the tiny island angrily seceded from St. Kitts-Nevis in 1969, the British literally dropped a "peacekeeping force" of paratroopers into Anguilla, but no fighting took place. In 1971, England took Anguilla back under its wing, and five years later the colony happily agreed on a new constitution providing a ministerial system as a dependent state with elected representatives.

ECONOMY

Most crown colonies depend on aid from the United Kingdom for their relatively high standards of living. Tourism, offshore financial activity, and agriculture are the main economic sectors. Montserrat produces enough fruit and vegetables for its own needs, but relies on the United Kingdom for almost everything else it consumes. The government is encouraging the production of sea-island cotton and the construction of a tannery and leatherworks. After Texas farmers started growing the famous Bermuda onions, the only important agricultural export left for Bermuda was the Easter lily. Bermuda imports 80 percent of its food. In the Turks and Caicos, crayfish and conch fishing, along with salt mining, are the only important economic activities. On the Cayman Islands, turtle fishing has ceased since Nicaragua stopped allowing the islanders to fish for turtles in its waters, but island residents have now started turtle farming to maintain the traditional industry.

Two of the key tax havens in the world, Bermuda and the Cayman Islands, depend on offshore finance for their economic stability. The Cayman Islands, which levy no direct tax except an annual $10 head tax on residents, have a strict secrecy law and have abolished all exchange controls. Cayman government revenue for 1982 came mainly from customs duties, stamp duties, and bank and trust licenses. More than 360 banks were registered in the Cayman Islands in 1982,[4] and the islands boast more telex lines per capita than any other country in the world. Bermuda, which is the number-one spot in the Western Hemisphere for insurance and reinsurance, has over 5,400 such companies registered.[5] Most of these companies are owned or controlled by U.S. parents, which are responsible for 75 percent of foreign investment in Bermuda. The British Virgin Islands also host offshore banking facilities. Turks and Caicos are trying to attract offshore financial business from the nearby Cayman Islands, which are becoming crowded and expensive. Even the tiny colony of Anguilla has entered the offshore financial competition, and now has more than 50 offshore "brass-plate" banks. The future of the offshore businesses is shaky owing to the recent U.S. moves to control Caribbean tax havens.

The proximity of the English colonies to the United States has helped create successful tourist industries. The Tourist Board of the Turks and Caicos boasts that the islands are "As Close to Paradise as This World Offers!" The islands are opening up to extensive tourism developments like condominiums and large land sales. In 1965 a wealthy American, with his friends the DuPonts and Roosevelts, negotiated a large tract of land in exchange for constructing roads and an airstrip on the Turks and Caicos, and built the Third Turtle Inn. Princess International owns the two largest hotels on the islands, and Canada's Condor Ltd. is constructing the Mariners Inn, while several U.S. entrepreneurs have also recently invested in the Turks and Caicos's growing tourist sector. The Club Méditerranée arranged for a 600-bed "holiday village" to be built by Britain's Johnston Construction. Critics of the plan in Great Britain's House of Commons have charged that British aid is subsidizing a private development project that will bring few benefits to the colony. The British have belatedly realized that the French corporation prefers to bring in most of its own employees (insisting that they be bilingual), and to import virtually all its food and beverages.

Bermuda, a popular tourist spot since World War I, has the highest incidence of return visitors of any Caribbean nation. The local government enforces building codes so that no high-rises interrupt the views. Foreign investment dominates Bermuda's hotel industry, which is exempt from a law requiring 60 percent Bermudian ownership in all other businesses. A source of pride for Bermudians are the black clubs, which promote their own culture. Tourism also contributes major revenue to the British Virgin Islands and holds promise for expansion. On Montserrat, villas for investment or retirement to serve Canadians, Americans, and the British, typify the tourist scene, which has overtaken agriculture as the leading industry.

Tourism on the Cayman Islands did not begin until after the mid-

GREAT BRITAIN AND THE CARIBBEAN · 217

1960s, before which time the government sent letters to inquiring tourists warning that the islands had a poor electric supply, bad roads, and a lot of insects. The tourist board changed its approach and introduced Pirates Week, a festival complete with treasure hunts, a float parade, and even a pirate invasion. The Caymans also offer timesharing, a plan in which purchasers buy one, two, or more weeks in a villa for the time of year that suits them. Anguilla passed a law barring foreign investment in hotel development on the grounds that the large proportion of foreign ownership in the tourist industries on other islands has resulted in few local benefits.

On Little Cayman, an oil transshipment terminal has been increasing its throughput, and the local government is considering allowing the construction of an oil refinery. The construction industry on the Caymans is booming: British American Company is building a $10-million complex, and the Office Developments Company will construct an office building. Other industry in the crown colonies include plastics and electronic appliance manufacturing in Bermuda, and a radio station on South Caicos that airs religious programs for the entire Caribbean. Quality Media Corporation of Columbus, Georgia, plans religious broadcasts in the appropriate language to Cuba, the Dominican Republic, and the English-speaking islands. Montserrat hosts Radio Antilles, the largest and most powerful commercial station in the Caribbean.

ISLAND SKETCHES

Anguilla

After the display of patriotism for Britain in the mid-1960s, the 6,700 Anguillans indicate no desire for independence. Remarkable for its dry climate, beaches, and reefs, Anguilla is trying to develop a "controlled tourist industry" that will generate income but leave the island's beauty intact.

Bermuda

Less than 600 miles off the coast of South Carolina, Bermuda is located in the Atlantic Ocean, not the Caribbean. Almost half the population of 72,000 is of European descent, the rest being African. Although some call Bermuda "the little Switzerland of the Atlantic," the facade of peace hides deep racial resentment. Murders, assassinations with consequent executions, and riots marred the 1970s, culminating in the declaration of a state of emergency and the occupation of the island by British troops to restore order. Segregation of black lower-class Bermudians from the wealthy white minority was not officially abolished until the 1960s.

Despite the racial problems, Bermudians enjoy almost full employment. A self-governing colony, Bermuda is preparing a report on independence, which it considers a possibility in the distant future. Enthusiasm for independence comes from the black middle and upper-middle classes, while the white Bermudians oppose independence because of financial risk and sentimental ties to Britain.

British Virgin Islands

A group of more than 40 islands, the British Virgin Islands are among the most prosperous in the Eastern Caribbean. Almost 90 percent of the 13,000 inhabitants live on the largest island of Tortola. The colony depends on British assistance, a stable fishing industry, and a healthy tourist sector, particularly yacht chartering. A portrait of the Queen hangs in most hotels and shops, but the U.S. dollar is the currency of the colony, which has close economic ties with the U.S. Virgin Islands.

Cayman Islands

The three Cayman Islands—Grand Cayman, Cayman Brac, and Little Cayman—are situated between Jamaica and southwest Cuba. About 90 percent of the 20,000 Caymanians live on Grand Cayman, which is gaining the reputation of the "condominium and investment capital" of the Caribbean. The islands boast free water wells, an unusual phenomenon in the region. Caymanians are free from taxation and wartime conscription and passed a law that prohibits the entry of Rastafarians and hippies.

Montserrat

Retiree tourism is the backbone of the Montserrat economy, which operates at near full employment. With only 12,000 people, Montserrat offers quiet and undisturbed living. George Martin, producer for the Beatles, built a modern recording studio in Montserrat, where artists like Paul McCartney and Duran Duran come to record. Heading the only dependent territory in Caricom, Montserrat's government is considering independence as a possibility in two to three years. Although the loss of aid is a factor against independent status, the territorial government believes the change would enhance the island's position in Caricom. Montserrat's independence would probably set off a chain reaction among the other British dependencies in the region.

Turks and Caicos

The Turks and Caicos offer 230 miles of beautiful beaches, most of them unmarked by human footprints for days at a time. The government, which wants to fill these beaches with tourists, has succeeded in attracting foreign investors to develop the industry. New projects provide hope for the sector, particularly the proposed Club Med resort development, for which the British government had constructed an airport and roads. In the mid-1970s a now defunct bill in the Canadian Parliament proposed that the Turks and Caicos become part of Canada, which would then enhance its trade in the Caribbean and be in a position to build a free-trade zone in the islands. An American company is converting the former U.S. Navy base on Grand Turk into the Medical University of the Caribbean. About 340 offshore companies have registered on the islands, and the government's hope of becoming a popular tax-haven location is turning into a reality.

Canada and the Caribbean

The Caribbean offers an unparalleled opportunity to Canadian exporters and investors.
—Canadian Association of Latin America (CALA)

Saltfish and rum brought Canada and the Caribbean together in the 1770s. West Indian plantation owners found that salted cod from Newfoundland served as a cheap, easy source of protein for their slaves, while the maritime provinces acquired a taste for Caribbean rum. Saltfish cooked with the ackee fruit became the national dish of Jamaica, while a rum concoction called "screech" became a potent Canadian drink. Through trade rather than direct colonial ties, Canada gained major economic influence in the West Indies. The Caribbean has been Canada's primary imperial frontier: its source for tropical produce, outlet for manufactured goods, and region of leading growth for its mining companies and banks. "The British West Indies," observed one historian, "became to Canada what China was to the United States: a source for constant visions of unrivaled trade opportunities."[1]

TRADE

The West Indies remain among Canada's most profitable outlets for foreign trade, although the United States has long since outdistanced Canada as the region's major trading partner. In 1981, Canada experienced a positive $368 million trade balance with the Caribbean.[2] Canada exports over 18 times the amount it imports from the Leeward and Windward Islands, 3 times as much from Haiti, and 4 times as much from Barbados. Canada enjoys an especially lucrative market in Cuba, which ranks as Canada's fourth-largest export market in Latin America. In 1981, balance of trade with Cuba favored Canada by $256 million.[3] One factor affecting the balance of trade is Canada's significant presence in the tourist industry in the Caribbean through hotels, airlines, and tour operators. Suntours alone took 400,000 Canadian tourists on 3,000 flights to the West Indies in 1979.[4]

INVESTMENT

The book value of Canadian direct investment in the Caribbean islands (excluding the mainland Caribbean) amounted to $851 million in 1977.[5] Offshore financial investment accounts for about 65 percent of listed Canadian investment in the region.[6] Most of Canada's direct investment in the region is in banking, bauxite, or transportation. The Latin American Working Group of Toronto contends that the book value reported by Canadian corporations represents only the "tip of the iceberg" and that the "asset value of Canadian-owned subsidiaries" in Latin America "might be three, five, or even in some cases ten times greater than the equity value."[7] Together, the Caribbean and Latin America account for almost 30 percent of Canada's investment in underdeveloped countries.

TABLE II B
MAJOR CANADIAN TNCs IN THE CARIBBEAN

Banks	Royal Bank of Canada
	Bank of Nova Scotia
	Canadian Imperial Bank of Commerce
Tourism	Scott's Hospitality (Holiday Inn)
	Canadian Pacific
	Air Canada
Manufacturers	Bata
Insurance	Sun Life Assurance
	Imperial Life Assurance
	Dominion Life Assurance
Agriculture	Maple Leaf Mills
	Quaker Oats of Canada
	Global Food Processors
	Seagram
Minerals	Alcan Aluminum
	Falconbridge

Source: The Resource Center, Compilation of Corporations, 1984

Three of Canada's leading banks belong to the "Big Four" in banking in the Caribbean. Along with Barclays of England, the Canadian banks— Royal Bank of Canada, Bank of Nova Scotia, and Canadian Imperial Bank of Commerce—have dominated Caribbean banking since the turn of the century. The large Canadian banks are an exception to the pattern of

U.S. corporations outnumbering other foreign TNCs. Canada's banks in the Caribbean frequently have special departments that serve Canadian investors, exporters, and importers. With the exception of the banks and insurance firms of Canada, the most pervasive Canadian firm in the West Indies is Bata Shoes, which sells shoes throughout the Caribbean and has manufacturing plants in Guyana, Trinidad, and Suriname. Some corporations that identify themselves as Canadian or have their headquarters in Canada, however, are not truly Canadian. Falconbridge, for instance, which has mining interests in the Dominican Republic and Suriname, is beholden not to Canadian shareholders but to Superior Oil of Texas, which owns the controlling stock in the mining company.

FOREIGN RELATIONS

Perhaps because Canada itself has experienced economic dependency on the U.S. and Britain the country has maintained unusually good relations with the underdeveloped world. It undoubtedly has a better image than any other industrialized country doing business with third-world nations. One reason Canada has been able to maintain its good reputation is that it has relied on the might of England and the United States to enforce favorable investment climates and trade conditions in countries with which it does business.

In the Caribbean, Canadian investors know their interests will be protected, along with those of U.S. investors, by Canada's powerful neighbor to the south. This unstated but continuing relationship with Washington has affected Canada's foreign policy and its foreign aid program. Ever since World War II, Canada has regularly acted as a surrogate for the United States in its Cold War politics. According to a study by the Latin American Working Group, this inferior position has often meant that the United States has dictated the direction of Canada's foreign aid.[8] In the 1980s the United States, Great Britain, and Canada decided jointly how they would divide their foreign aid programs in the Caribbean, with Canada receiving responsibility for air transport, water resources, agriculture, and education programs. Canada expressed its willingness to take over the task of "looking after" the interests of the United States and the United Kingdom in the Caribbean.[9] However, in the cases of Cuba and Grenada, Canada kept its business and diplomatic relations with the two socialist nations despite U.S. pressure. For Canadian business, money that comes from trade relations and foreign investment often supersedes ideology.

The degree of influence exercised by the U.S. government over Canada became all too evident in 1981, when Canada suddenly reversed its position on the Central American crisis after direct pressure by then

Secretary of State Alexander Haig. Instead of opposing U.S. intervention, the external affairs minister announced: "I would certainly not condemn any decision the United States takes to send offensive arms to El Salvador." He added that the United States "can at least count on our quiet acquiescence."[10] The U.S. invasion of Grenada highlighted the lack of real power that Canada has in the region despite its pervasive economic presence. Canada was not even informed in advance of the invasion, despite the fact that many of its citizens were living in Grenada.

FOREIGN AID

In the late 1970s Washington failed to persuade Canada to limit its foreign aid to Jamaica and Grenada. Several years later, however, the Reagan administration did succeed in inducing Canada to increase its aid to Washington's two target countries in the Caribbean, Haiti and the newly conservative Jamaica. Canada increased its aid to Jamaica from $7.7 million in 1979 under the Manley government to $17 million in 1981 under Seaga.[11] Initially, Canada dramatically increased its aid to the Duvalier regime but then made a sudden reversal in 1981 after Haiti failed to meet its obligation to the International Monetary Fund.

The Canadian government directly supports the expansion of Canadian investment and trade in the Caribbean through its foreign aid agency, the Canadian International Development Agency (CIDA). The Canadian Association of Latin America (CALA) represents the interests of Caribbean businesses in the region. The organization receives its main funding from what CALA calls a "generous contractual arrangement" with the Industrial Cooperation Division of CIDA. "It is my belief," stated CALA's chairperson in 1980, "that continued cooperation between the government and private sector in Canada is essential if we are to obtain maximum benefit from the tremendous opportunities offered to us by the booming economies of Latin America and the Caribbean."[12]

CIDA also indirectly supports the interests of Canadian investors by granting loans to foreign governments to build infrastructure that facilitates foreign investment and by promoting a pro-foreign investment attitude among Caribbean governments and private organizations. Canada has an aid program called Canadian Executive Service Overseas that supports consulting by retired Canadian business executives. Canada also backs foreign trade through its Export Development Corporation.

At a meeting of Canadian business people, an official of the government's International Trade and Commerce Department said that the "do-gooders and the bleeding hearts" of CIDA have to take a harder look at foreign aid as a way to promote Canadian business: "Aid money is often a device, a tool, to get into a market. It's a toehold."[13] The Canadian official gave a hypothetical example of aid to a place he called Bongo Bongo. According to his scheme not only could a project in Bongo Bongo foster Canadian trade, but it could also benefit Canada by including a technical assistance and management contract that would specify use of Canadian consultants and technology. In the early 1980s, Canada acceded to the demands of the private sector by giving increased emphasis to the economic development potential of its aid programs. "Much greater weight," declared Prime Minister Pierre Trudeau in 1982, "will be attached to economic factors in the design of foreign policy and the conduct of our foreign relations."[14]

Following the lead of the United States, CIDA in 1982 funded CALA to help build and strengthen local private-sector organizations in the Caribbean. The Canadian government also finances the annual conventions between CALA and Caribbean business owners. Soon after the United States established the U.S. Business Committee on Jamaica, headed by David Rockefeller, Canadian businesses brought together by CALA formed the Canada-Jamaica Business Committee. Included on this committee are the following corporations: Bank of Nova Scotia, Bata, Seagram, Alcan, Maple Leaf Mills, Imperial Optical, Petro Canada, Manufacturers' Life Insurance, Northern Telecom, IBM Canada, Hudson's Bay Company, Holiday House, Four Seasons Hotels, Air Canada, and Wardair International.[15]

During the 1970s, the Commonwealth Caribbean, the region with the highest per capita bilateral aid from Canada, received over $225 million from CIDA.[16] In 1980, Canada sponsored 143 projects in the Commonwealth Caribbean, with over half the aid concentrated in Jamaica and Guyana. In 1981, the external affairs minister promised to triple aid to the region by 1986.[17] The three major components of Canada's strategy to bolster Canadian exports and to reassert the country's commercial status in the Caribbean are increased aid, a 1979 Trade and Economic Agreement with Caricom, and support for business organizations.

By increasing aid, Canada directly bolsters trade because no less than 80 percent of the country's bilateral aid must be spent on Canadian goods and services.[18] This represents one of the highest levels of tied aid among the major donor nations. Canada has also committed higher levels of military and police training in the Caribbean, especially in Jamaica and Trinidad & Tobago. The government justifies the training as being consistent with its foreign policy interests in maintaining the "internal security and stability" of the region.

Although Canada has had no colonies in the Caribbean, it has succeeded in building a considerable foreign presence in the region. Canada has never resorted to military strength to protect its foreign interest in the Caribbean. Instead it has relied on the military power of Great Britain and the United States to keep the area safe for foreign investors.

While Canada has certainly espoused a foreign policy that is much broader and more accommodating than that of the United States or Great Britain, it has been content, for the most part, to fill the role of junior partner in maintaining the pattern of foreign control in the Caribbean.

France and the Caribbean

The islands of Martinique and Guadeloupe float in a crystal sea thousands of miles away from Paris. But so tight are the ties between these French departments and their parent nation that they might as well be a part of the mainland. French Guiana, located on the northern coast of South America, is also a French department but sports less of a French flair than do the islands. Traveling through Martinique and Guadeloupe makes one feel more like on a trip to France than to the Caribbean. The French gendarmes, the wine and cheese, the pastry shops, the well-tended pastures, the continental dress, and the prevalence of the French language all make these French dependencies seem like another province in France. Yet important differences set continental France apart from its departments. Ninety percent of department citizens are black; most people prefer the Creole language to French; the territories are not industrialized; unemployment is about 3 times as high as in France; and the economies of the departments rely on French aid and trade to sustain relatively high standards of living.

By the turn of the century the French had thriving sugar plantations worked by slaves in all three colonies, making France a major world sugar producer. In the 1800s, Guadeloupe's aristocracy, dissatisfied with French rule after slavery was abolished, declared the island's independence and invited England to take over the island. For more than 20 years, Guadeloupe seesawed between the two imperial powers. Settling the question, Frenchman Victor Hughes arrived in Guadeloupe and set up guillotines that disposed of 4,000 rebellious Guadeloupeans, establishing the French once and for all as the colonial power in the island. Martinique and French Guiana shared a similar, although less bloody, history. Martinique's claim to European history is that it was the birthplace of Napoleon's wife/consort Josephine.

In 1946, the French government, after a popular referendum, categorized the three colonies as French overseas departments, which made them almost as much a part of France as Versailles. Paris recognizes the *Antillais* and *Guyanais* as French citizens who can vote in national elections, can receive French social benefits, and must comply with French compulsory educational regulations.

Martinique bills itself as "a bit of France in the Caribbean" and Guadeloupe's principal city calls itself the "Paris of the Antilles." Although a Caribbean flavor lingers, the high-rise buildings and elegant hotels do not appear tropical. "The French don't build island hotels," says one tourist guidebook, "they build French hotels on an island." The descendants of neither the black slaves nor the white slave owners feel completely French. A common joke in the departments is that a French Caribbean person visiting France is *Antillais*, but upon arriving in New York becomes French.

The departments politically are integral parts of France. They have eight elected representatives in the French Assembly and Senate out of a total membership of 480. Appointed by Paris is a prefect who administers each overseas department. A constant reminder of French imperial control is the 3,000-strong French military garrison stationed among the old colonial forts in the departments. During emergencies, France sends the riot police from Paris across the Atlantic. Explaining the need for the military, a colonial minister said the soldiers "inspire good behavior." Each department has a locally elected government responsible for domestic affairs. In an attempt to reduce the strong central control exercised by the general councils, the Mitterand government authorized the creation of regional councils that give the department citizens easier access to government. Right-wing politicians opposed the reform, fearing that the regional councils would come under the control of leftists and would be a forum for separatist agitation. During the first regional elections in 1983, their fears proved well grounded, as left-leaning parties fared well in all three departments.

ECONOMY

Exports of bananas, sugar, rum, and tropical fruit constitute the main sources of nongovernmental income for the French Caribbean. Guadeloupe is the major supplier of molasses to Bacardi of Puerto Rico. Guaranteed markets in France for bananas, fruit, and sugar products provide an artificial support for the agricultural sectors in the departments. Higher costs and a minimum wage make the produce of the French colonies uncompetitive on the world market. Even in 1980, when world sugar prices were high, the French government was subsidizing the costs of sugar producers in the French departments.

In contrast with the rest of the Caribbean, U.S. investors do not control most foreign investment. "French companies have the inside track here," noted an official of the U.S. Embassy in Martinique.[2] French authorities have instituted special tax advantages to encourage French corporations to invest in the overseas departments. Authorities in the departments refuse to distinguish between companies from France and those based in the departments and do not consider companies from France to be foreign investors. Department officials do admit, however, that companies headquartered in Paris dominate the leading sectors of the economy. French corporations own the gas and electric utilities, the banking and insurance industry, the trade and transportation sector, and the tourism industry. Club Méditerranée, Hotels Meridien (owned by Air France), and the PLM Corporation control the executive and tourist hotel business in the French Antilles. Elf-Aquitaine, the French oil giant, is responsible for making refined petroleum products the leading export of Martinique. Portions of the economy not under Paris-based control are dominated by a small group of white families.

During the last decade, TNCs from the United States have pushed their way into the French Caribbean. United Brands, through a French subsidiary, has a firm hold on the banana industry in the French Antilles, and Chase Manhattan is becoming an important bank on the islands. Other U.S. corporations with investments in the French departments include Continental Grain, International Paper, Bacardi, Holiday Inn, Texaco, PepsiCo, and Honeywell. Non-U.S. TNCs with foreign investment in the French Caribbean are Canada's Bata Shoes, Royal Bank of Canada, Booker McConnell (UK), and Cable & Wireless (UK).

The departments, grossly dependent on French trade, suffered a trade deficit in 1982 of nearly $900 million with France. French Guiana imports from metropolitan France 45 times as much as it exports.[3] Even with their large sugar and banana exports, the French Antilles import 5 times the amount they export to the continent. Bolstering the dependent economies are French assistance, remittances from relatives in France, and the high salaries paid to government employees (who receive a wage 40 percent higher than that paid in France as compensation for their work in an overseas department). Migration to France has provided a convenient escape valve for the dependencies. While about 800,000 people live in the island departments, an estimated 600,000 French Antilleans live in France.[4]

Flows of government funds from France amount to several times the national budgets of the departments.[5] French critics of the subsidy of French Guiana and the Antilles have likened the three departments to the dancing girls of Paris—meaning that France is paying the departments' bills because it likes to keep them for its pleasure and amusement. The writer Aimé Césaire, a respected progressive politician of Martinique, said, "We live now on French aid. If that aid were removed and we continued to live as we do now, we would face a crisis. But there is the crucial part. We would not, we could not, live in our present fashion. We must change our standards of living, emphasize our own culture, our own traditions." Césaire has called for "association with, rather than domination," by France.[6]

POLITICAL STATUS

The debate over independence often concerns the advantages and disadvantages of living in what many call a "borrowed paradise." In some ways, the French Antilles constitute an oasis in the Caribbean. The per capita income of over $3,500 in Martinique sounds like the bells of paradise to the people in neighboring Dominica, who have a per capita income of only $620. Guadeloupe has the reputation of being the world's third-largest per capita consumer of champagne—a drink many Guadeloupeans prefer to locally produced rum. But world recession and the decline of traditional agricultural industries have undermined the department economies. High unemployment and the high cost of living have heightened the sentiment for some type of independence from France. Many French and department residents alike want autonomy for the French Caribbean rather than assimilation or independence. Opposed, often violently, to notions of independence are groups of what are known as assimilationists, who are tied to right-wing parties in France. The Civic Action Service and Guadeloupean Armed Defense Group, both right-wing organizations, vow to "protect Frenchwomen and children from blind terrorism."[7]

Although opinion polls do not show a broad-based desire for independence, the independence movements are visible and vocal. In French Guiana, proindependence groups won 9 percent of the seats in the 1983 local elections and now hold a balance of power. In 1982, eight proindependence groups in Guadeloupe formed a unified organization of liberation forces. Several groups are committed to independence through means outside electoral politics. In the summer of 1983, the *Alliance Révolutionnaire Caribienne* claimed responsibility for the first simultaneous bombings in all three departments, damaging property in 18 governmental and corporate targets. The independence movement has wide support in Paris, where there is a militantly proindependence radio station that broadcasts around the clock in Creole to the large French Caribbean community.

Even those in the Caribbean who support the department status often express their understanding of the independence movements. A local executive in Guadeloupe observed: "The French are different from other colonialists. They want to be loved for their own sake. The French are trying to erase the differences by making you like themselves. But if you are trying to raise somebody up to your own level without recognizing his identity, one day he is going to say 'Hey, but I'm not you.' Having this psychological attitude plus the volcanic state of the economy, you have the fuse and the bomb."[8]

Some proindependence leaders have quieted their pleas since the socialist government of François Mitterand took office in Paris. But an island newspaper complained: "The government of Mitterand employs a very anticolonial and antiimperialist language in the third world. But in the Antilles, France maintains the same repression that the government of the right has also maintained against independence movements."[9] While Mitterand's government did open an official inquiry into the cultural problems of the overseas departments and established a new decentralized administration to tone down French authoritarian attitudes, the French government does not support independence of the departments. Expressing what has become an increasingly popular opinion, Aimé Césaire once said, "What we have now are camouflaged colonies. We have no voice, no say. There are real advantages in our departmental status. But we must have a greater degree of control over our own destiny."[10]

ISLAND SKETCHES

Guadeloupe

The northernmost island of the Windwards and the largest of the territories, Guadeloupe is formed by two large islands, Grande-Terre and Basse-Terre, separated by a narrow sea channel, with a smaller island, Marie Galante, to the southeast. Under Guadeloupe's wing are two dependencies: St. Martin (the French half of the smallest island in the world shared by two sovereignties) and quiet St. Barthélemy. Americans, like the Rockefellers, and several French families, like the Rothschilds, have private resorts on what is known as St. Barts.

Political terrorists from Guadeloupe have been responsible for several bombings in recent years, including an attempted bombing of Air France jets. In 1983, unknown assailants killed the right-wing owner of the country's largest banana plantation for what police believed to be political reasons. As in the case of the other French departments, less than 2 percent of the island's trade is with the non-French Caribbean and only 5 percent with the United States. Export receipts from the colony cover the costs of less than 15 percent of its imports.

French Guiana

Located only a few degrees north of the equator on the northeastern shoulder of South America, French Guiana is a land of fertile coastal plains and dense tropical rain forests. Only travelers in small river-going boats can reach the vast forested interior. The movie *Papillon* depicted the horrors of the infamous French overseas penal colony. Less developed than the French Antilles, French Guiana has a substantially higher infant mortality rate and a per capita income a full $1,000 less than that of the other two departments. Its principal exports are sugar, timber, and shrimp. A couple of small companies from Florida have gained a hold on the colony's shrimp industry. Although it is one of the most sparsely populated nations in the world, French Guiana does not produce nearly enough food for its 66,000 residents. Guianese people complain that the vast timber, gold, and bauxite reserves remain undeveloped because of French economic control. The department's representative in the French Senate called for political-prisoner status to be granted to six proindependence militants in jail in France. He told the French press that France was "incapable of developing Guiana." The proindependence politician warned, "We are the last generation willing to reason and debate here in Paris."[11]

Martinique

The Indians called Martinique "Madinina," or "land of flowers." The birthplace of revolutionary writer Frantz Fanon, Martinique is a beautiful mountainous island whose economy is on the skids. Unemployment, stagnation, and a severe balance-of-payments crisis threatens the atmosphere of easy living that distinguishes Martinique from other islands in the Windward chain. Plans by the French government to scale down the sugar industry have met local opposition that wants to further develop the industry by finding new markets and producing sugarcane byproducts. The island is still suffering the aftereffects of Hurricane Allen in 1980, which destroyed the department's banana industry. Martinique's white "beke" merchant class has a strong hold on the local commercial sector and the sugar industry.

Plans by the French government to diversify agricultural production through such French companies as Compagnie Fruitière have enraged the vested interests of the "bekes." Another change in Martinique has been the arrival of thousands of white French immigrants who want to settle in the Caribbean. They are threatening native residents by taking over local housing and competing for even the most menial jobs. The poet-mayor of Fort-de-France called the influx of French "genocide by substitution."[12] Continental France has supported the continuing destruction of the sugarcane industry in the interest of protecting European beet growers.

Netherlands Antilles

Two groups of Caribbean islands form the Netherlands Antilles. Near Venezuela's coast are the "ABC" islands of Aruba, Bonaire, and Curaçao. The second group, forming part of the Leeward chain, are Saba, St. Eustatius, and St. Maarten. More than half the total population of 250,000 of the Netherlands Antilles lives on the island of Curaçao. Although the official language of the islands is Dutch, most people in the ABC islands speak Papiamento, an interesting mixture of Romance, African, and Arawak languages, while the residents of the Leeward Islands speak English. Many Dutch Antilleans speak Spanish in addition to Dutch and Papiamento. The Netherlands Antilles together form an autonomous part of the Kingdom of Netherlands. The Dutch crown appoints a governor, and the island residents elect their own legislature.

After coming to the islands in the 1590s, the Spanish cleared the tropical jungles for crops and exported the peaceful Arawak Indians to South American gold and silver mines. Although the Spanish did ship 2,000 Indians from Aruba to the mines of Hispaniola, they also left undisturbed some of the native population, so that Aruba now is the only island in the Netherlands Antilles with an indigenous Indian population. In search of a salt supply, the Dutch sailed to the Caribbean in the mid-1600s. The Dutch colonized the rugged island of Saba, but never settled there, and later allowed English mariners to establish a small colony. The Dutch gravitated toward Curaçao for its deep harbor. Curaçao's first industry resulted from the need of the merchants to repair their ships after the long voyage from Holland. The island's ship-repair dock, currently owned by Royal Dutch Shell, is the largest dry dock and bunkering facility in the Western Hemisphere.

OIL

In the early 1900s, Shell Oil and what is now called Exxon determined the course of history for the Netherlands Antilles when they established oil refineries and transshipment complexes in Curaçao and Aruba. Refined oil from the Netherlands Antilles supplies a large amount of the oil consumed by the eastern United States. This industry currently supports the economy of the islands. Aruba named one of its main streets after an early general manager of Exxon's Lago refinery. Crude oil is their major export, and refined oil accounts for 95 percent of the value of their exports. Petroleum refining produces over a fifth of the GDP, but only a 20th of the employment of the two islands. Shell's Curaçao refinery, the third largest in the Shell group, specializes in refining Venezuelan crude oil to make lubricants. In the last several years it has operated at half capacity and plans to further reduce the refinery's personnel. Although it showed an operating profit in 1982, Exxon's refinery is also operating at below capacity. Shell's ship repair yard and oil transshipment terminal, the biggest in the Shell group, employ only a small number of workers and have little crossover into the local economy.

The companies have resisted government attempts to increase taxation of the industry, including the proposed imposition of an "environmental levy" and the revocation of a ten-year tax holiday enjoyed by the terminals. As it stands, the only revenue for the government from the terminals is a modest annual payment. The third transshipment terminal in the Netherlands Antilles, located in Bonaire, transfers Middle Eastern oil from supertankers to smaller vessels delivering oil to Northville Industries, a U.S. corporation, and dominates the oil industry in Bonaire.

The refining and transshipment industries have suffered economically for several reasons. Development of oil fields in the North Sea and Alaska present new competition for Venezuelan oil, which constitutes 60 percent of input into the Dutch Antilles' petroleum sector. Government officials, however, say the principal crippling factor is U.S. energy policy and legislation. The U.S. Crude Oil Equalization Program, introduced in 1974, made refined products from the islands more expensive than those from U.S. domestic refineries. The refineries, having lost the traditional U.S. market, have tried without success to diversify into other markets.

Laundered oil has become a source of embarrassment for the Netherlands Antilles' government and The Hague. In 1982, the Amsterdam-based Shipping Research Bureau revealed that both the Netherlands and its Caribbean colonies were major transshipment ports for the laundering of oil supplies for embargoed South Africa. The Dutch government does have an oil embargo against South Africa, but the embargo does not extend to the Netherlands Antilles, even though The Hague controls foreign relations of the islands. The local government of the Netherlands Antilles has been reluctant to interfere with the business of the three big oil terminals on the islands for fear they may leave. Most oil supplied from the three transshipment terminals in Curaçao, Aruba, and Bonaire originates from countries that officially embargo South Africa. Shell Curaçao told the Shipping Research Bureau that it did not sell its own oil to embargoed South Africa, but refused to say whether any of the other companies that use its terminal send their oil to South Africa.[1]

ECONOMY

Only a very small percentage of the economic product of the Netherlands Antilles comes from agricultural production. The government is promoting cattle raising and horticulture, which are export-oriented. The islands import almost all their food and other goods, including all clothing, household items, and raw materials for manufacturing. Venezuela, which supplies crude oil to the refineries, and the United States are the Dutch colony's major trading partners. The few manufacturers on the islands, such as Amstel Brewery and Curaçao Liqueur, import most of their basic materials. The U.S. Department of State reported, "American goods are generally popular among most sectors of the society and are sought by South American tourists who consider the Netherlands Antilles a shopper's paradise."[2]

Another important contribution to government revenues is offshore financing and banking. The islands attracted $1.4 billion in U.S. deposits in 1981.[3] About 40 percent of the 25,000 registered companies are "brass plates," not active in the Dutch territories but merely mailbox offices.[4] A tax treaty between the United States and the Netherlands Antilles has made the islands a multimillion-dollar tax haven. The "Antillean window," as it is called by the U.S. Treasury Department, brings in $50 million each year and employs 5,000 people, who maintain the financial and banking activity in the islands.[5] The United States is reviewing and expecting to change the tax treaty that created the Antillean window, which expires in 1984. The Netherlands Antilles view tinkering with the tax treaty as a threat to the welfare of the colony. If the United States breaks the trade agreements, the financial community in the Dutch West Indies may crumble in a matter of months. Officials of the Netherlands Antilles worry that corporations are already beginning to avoid the usual Antillean window and incorporate instead in Bermuda.

The Netherlands Antilles continue to encourage U.S. and other foreign corporations to invest in the islands. Aruba and Curaçao both maintain free zones, where all goods are imported and exported duty-free. The government imposes virtually no restrictions on foreign ownership of enterprises permitted to operate in the Netherlands Antilles. Duties are levied on items competing with the few locally produced items, but generally the government offers programs to attract industry and investment. The islands advertise a right-to-work law. Nevertheless, the U.S. Department of Commerce rated the business climate in the colony as "lousy, poor to abysmal," and listed, as deterrents to corporate activity in the Netherlands Antilles, the strong labor unions and the poor government attitude in the implementation of laws relatively favorable to foreign interests. Foreign manufacturers in the colony include Continental Milling, Advance Biofactures, Data Systems, Jervis International, Thomassen & Driver, Volkswagen, and Schlumberger.

Because of its income from the oil industry, the Antillean window for corporate financing, and the financial aid from the Netherlands, the Dutch Antilles enjoy a per capita income level similar to that of the lesser developed European countries like Portugal, Greece, and Ireland. Wages range from $70.92 to $117.50 per week, but the cost of living is higher than in the United States, and unemployment is the major social and economic problem.

POLITICAL STATUS

The main Caribbean policy goals of the Netherlands are to lead its colonies to independence, to maintain commercial relations, and to continue to aid them through bilateral and multilateral programs. The Netherlands have had the distinction worldwide of giving a higher percentage of its gross national product in foreign aid than any other donor nation. Dutch corporate investment in the Caribbean is limited, although two Dutch corporations, Royal Dutch Shell and Heineken, have extensive regional operations.

In 1969, when the Netherlands Antilles government called in Dutch troops to suppress a protest of oil workers, The Hague started to press seriously for the independence of its Caribbean colonies. The Charter of the Kingdom obligated the Dutch government to respond to the request for troops to quell the disturbances in Curaçao. After receiving bad press for this colonial fire fighting, the government was determined to release its Caribbean colonies. But most of the colonial islands look warily upon independence because the three bulwarks of their economies—tourism, oil refineries, and the offshore financial industry—are threatened by world economic recession and changes in U.S. government regulations. The Netherlands Antilles government is demanding continued financial assistance from the Dutch. It feels that when it becomes independent its economic development will depend on positive commercial relations with the United States.

Independence from the Netherlands and the desire of the Arubans for their separate independence are longtime controversies that have recently been at least partially resolved. Arubans resent the domination of the central colonial government, which operates from the larger island of Curaçao. The origins of Aruban separatism lie deep in historical and racial differences, but also in the Arubans' belief that their island's shores possess oil reserves. Aruba, already financially stronger than the other islands, has demanded power to grant oil concessions and has begun negotiations with Exxon over control of the huge Lago refinery on the island.

A 1983 agreement with the Dutch government grants Aruba "separate status" within the six-island colony in 1986 and complete independence in 1996, with the option that Aruba can extend its separate status beyond that date if desired.[6] Aruba pledged "close and enduring cooperation" to the other five Antilles. With the government assuming the promised cooperation to be financial and Aruba not willing to subsidize the smaller and poorer islands, details in the agreement still need to be refined. While Arubans have pushed for independence, Curaçao and the other islands consider the Dutch to be more anxious for their independence than they are. Curaçao does not want independence without strong Dutch commitments for additional financial aid.

ISLAND SKETCHES

Aruba

Comprising the most linguistically versatile island in the Caribbean, Aruba's inhabitants speak Spanish, English, Portuguese, and Papiamento. Famous for golden beaches and black gold, Aruba is financially more secure than the other Antilles owing to its healthy tourism sector and refining industry. Aruban political leader Betico Croes expressed "mixed feelings" about concessions that have been made to achieve a peaceful route to independence.

Bonaire

The scuba capital of the Caribbean, this relatively new tourist spot is a major oil transshipment terminal. Salt recovery also contributes to the island's economy. The population of 9,000, which is 100 percent literate, has so far kept its island one of the most unspoiled in the Caribbean.

Curaçao

Curaçao is the home of the colony's central government and the largest of the six islands. Its capital, Willemstad, is the Antilles' industrial, commercial, banking, and convention center. The drydock, ship bunkering, and oil transshipment operations in Curaçao are the largest in the Western Hemisphere. Spanning the harbor is the tallest bridge in the Caribbean, called the Queen Juliana Bridge. Because the industry has attracted many workers from outside the islands, Curaçao's inhabitants are reputed to come from as many as 79 countries.

Saba

The dry tip of an otherwise ocean-covered volcano, Saba offers eight distinct levels of tropical foliage. Because neither the industrial nor the tourist sectors are very lively, the inhabitants make their living as seafarers.

St. Eustatius

St. Eustatius, or Statia as it is commonly called, was once known as the Golden Rock because of its importance as a trade center. The island has returned to a sleepy life-style, but may be reawakened by the construction of an oil transshipment terminal.

St. Maarten

Sharing a small island with the French, St. Maarten depends on tourism, a tuna fishery, and rum distilling for its livelihood. The Dutch side of the island is more developed than the French side, with bigger hotels and more commercial activity.

Puerto Rico

There can be no question of the wisdom of taking and holding Puerto Rico without any reference to a policy of expansion. We need it as a station in the great American archipelago misnamed the West Indies, and Providence has decreed that it shall be ours as a recompense for smiting the last withering clutch of Spain from the domain which Columbus brought to light and the fairest part of which has long been our heritage.
—1898 *New York Times* editorial

If you want to take a Caribbean vacation but do not want to leave the United States, then Puerto Rico is a perfect choice. Not only is it a possession of the United States, but it also has many of the features that distinguish the United States: Miami-style high-rise hotels, Las Vegas-style nightlife, and Bronx-style slums. It is a little America with crowded freeways, fast-food restaurants, and an American flag just about everywhere you look. Puerto Ricans have determinedly kept their Spanish language, but it is fading fast. Just as Puerto Ricans have a mixed national identity, so they are forming a mixed language. Signs around San Juan, for example, proclaim "Casa for Sale." At the Isla Verde Airport, the signs are bilingual, but the English precedes the Spanish, a symbol of the entire situation in Puerto Rico.

HISTORY

For one brief year in its history, Puerto Rico enjoyed hard-earned autonomy while under Spanish rule, which it had endured for four hundred years. But in 1898, the Spanish flag was hauled down from the El Morro fortress in San Juan and the U.S. flag was unfurled. The United States defeated Spain in the Spanish-American War; and, in complete disregard of the island's constitution, its autonomous institutions, and the wishes of the population, it took Puerto Rico as its colony. From 1898 to 1900, the U.S. military directly ruled the island, after which a U.S. civil government administered the affairs of the colony. In 1917, Puerto Ricans became U.S. citizens, not by their own choice, but by a decree from Washington.

In 1946, the United States permitted Puerto Rico partial self-government, whereby the island residents could elect their own governor and formulate their own constitution. The U.S. government retained the right to veto any changes in the island's constitution, and Puerto Ricans were not permitted to vote in presidential elections or send representatives to Congress. In 1950, the United States conferred upon Puerto Rico the status of Commonwealth or Free Associated State. Adolf A. Berle, assistant secretary of state for Inter-American Affairs, declared at the time, "Puerto Rico has independence in everything except economics, defense, and foreign relations."[1] The new status allowed Puerto Rico a slightly longer leash, but Puerto Ricans remained without representation in Washington.

Puerto Rico in 1948 began its famous Operation Bootstrap program to attract investment from the mainland. It was a program of industrial incentives that exempted new investors from Puerto Rican taxes. Corporations investing in Puerto Rico could also take advantage of a federal law (now known as the "936 program") that effectively exempted U.S. investors in Puerto Rico from paying taxes on income earned in Puerto Rico. The combined exemption made the island very attractive to U.S. firms. Puerto Rico's first elected governor, Luis Muñoz Marín, described the island's agricultural economy in the late 1940s (which specialized in sugar, coffee, and tobacco) as "providing all the after-dinner benefits without the dinner." Muñoz planned to move the island away from dependence on traditional agricultural exports by attracting mainland industries that could take advantage of the bountiful supply of cheap labor in Puerto Rico. Besides the tax incentives, Puerto Rico's industrialization program provided the infrastructure, factory buildings, and trained workers for new investors. Largely successful, Operation Bootstrap and the expanded industrialization incentive programs that followed turned the island's economy around in two decades. Only 13 U.S. factories operated on the island in 1947, but by 1980 over 2,000 U.S.-owned plants were manufacturing goods for the mainland market.[2] From being regarded in the 1940s as the "poorhouse of the Caribbean," Puerto Rico grew to become the region's most well-to-do state. Operation Bootstrap became the model of dependent industrialization for the rest of the Caribbean, but the other islands have never been as successful as the U.S. colony in building an export-based industrialized sector.

The U.S. territory's ascent to a degree of prosperity was not solely the result of the investment of mainland corporations. It depended on federal aid programs, generous tax exemptions, and a steady migration to the mainland of jobless Puerto Ricans. Migration served as the safety valve that released the overflow of unemployed workers. Never in the last three decades of Puerto Rico's "economic miracle" has the increase in new jobs kept up with the population growth.

ECONOMY

As the U.S. economy slips, the Puerto Rican economy is falling headlong into unemployment, bankruptcy, and poverty. Unemployment in Puerto Rico has steadily grown since the territory embarked on its industrialization plan. The official unemployment rate, which stood at 11 percent in 1940, rose to 25 percent in 1983. If Puerto Rico were a state, it would be by far the poorest in the United States. In 1983, the United States showed a 4 percent increase in the rate of bankruptcy, while Puerto Rico suffered a 73 percent increase, about a third of which were cases of local business failures.[3] The island's per capita income of $3,900, high by Caribbean standards, is about one-third the national average and one-half that of the poorest state, Mississippi. Yet Puerto Rico's cost of living is much higher, over 8 percent higher in San Juan than in Washington, D.C. Over 60 percent of Puerto Ricans live below the poverty level, and one of every nine adults is illiterate. Cutbacks by the Reagan administration in job training, food stamps, and social services have sharpened the economic crisis for tens of thousands of Puerto Ricans.

Another indicator of the weak state of the economy is the island's growing public debt, $8.2 billion by the beginning of 1983, which represents 65 percent of the island's gross national product. Puerto Rico's public corporations account for about 75 percent of the island's public debt, most of which is held by the large New York banks and investment firms.[4] Were it not for Puerto Rico's connections with the United States, its debt problem would be ranked among the worst of the underdeveloped world.

With the decline of the sugar industry in the 1950s, migration to the United States became a common alternative for Puerto Ricans who could not find jobs on the island. During the 1950s, when the industrialization program actually did provide new jobs, over 50,000 Puerto Ricans were leaving their homeland each year because of island unemployment. Manufacturing did not grow fast enough to offset the decline in agriculture during the 1950s and 1960s. As hard times continue, the number of Puerto Ricans packing their bags for life on the mainland is increasing. The migration to the United States for the first two years of the 1980s was over half the total migration for the 1970s. The number of Puerto Ricans living in the United States is estimated to be at least 2 million, compared with the island's population of 3.2 million. University graduates and professional workers now form a high proportion of those emigrating. At least 20 percent of the doctors who graduate from the island's four medical schools are currently leaving the island to practice in the

United States.[5] Without this escape valve, Puerto Rico would be burdened by an unemployment problem much larger than the 25 percent unemployment rate it now endures.

Public spending shores up Puerto Rico's economy. The government employs 40 percent of the active workforce, and about two-thirds of the population depend on federal government aid.[6] By constructing 70 percent of the industrial and commercial sites on the island, the Puerto Rican government provides the base for business profits. The island government owns over $346 million in buildings and land used by the 936 corporations.[7]

The government of Puerto Rico praises private enterprise and foreign investment, but does not like competition. It opposed most provisions of the Caribbean Basin Initiative (CBI) because the program would attract prospective investors to the other Caribbean islands and take business away from Puerto Rico. The territorial government warned that if the CBI were passed, "the island's ability to maintain an acceptable development rate would be seriously impaired." Island politicians pointed out Puerto Rico's disadvantages compared with other Caribbean states: its relatively high minimum wage, its burden of environmental regulations that other islands do not have, and its inability to lure tourists with duty-free shops.

Welfare State

Total federal disbursement to Puerto Rico in 1982 was $4.4 billion—more than the combined annual budgets of the Dominican Republic, Haiti, Jamaica, and Trinidad & Tobago. Of that sum, federal transfers to individuals amounted to $2.8 billion, a third of which was in the form of food stamps.[8] Federal funds represent about 35 percent of the island's gross product, and federal transfer payments to individuals constitute about 25 percent of the disposable personal income on the island, probably the highest benefits of any colony in history.[9] In the last 20 years, as the island has become more industrialized, federal funding as a percent of the GNP has increased almost 2.5 times. The aid serves to keep the colony afloat economically and to provide the infrastructure and cheap labor for the benefit of the thousands of U.S. investors on the island.

The largest chunk of federal aid, the food stamp program, benefits over 450,000 households or about 50 percent of the population. Many workers in the 936 plants receive food stamps to supplement their low wages earned on the assembly line. Since the beginning of the food stamp program in 1975, there have been fewer strikes and a lower level of militancy in Puerto Rico, apparently because of the security offered by the food coupons. "Through food stamps, and other social programs, American taxpayers are subsidizing the presence of U.S. companies on the island and allowing them to reap greater profits," said Dr. Neftali

García, a chemist and a prominent social activist. "Food stamps enable the corporations to keep wages low, by defusing the pressures for better wages."[10]

AGRICULTURE

Investors from the United States first became interested in Puerto Rico because of its agricultural rather than its industrial potential. In the 30 years that followed the U.S. occupation in 1898, sugar production grew by over 900 percent. By 1930, the sugar crop absorbed over 40 percent of the island's cultivated area, employed almost half of all agricultural laborers, and accounted for a third of the island's economic activity.[11] In those same three decades, the production of tobacco for the U.S. market increased over 5 times. The drive to expand agricultural exports forced many small farmers, called *jíbaros*, from their land and into the rural labor pool for the sugar, tobacco, and coffee estates.

The push to industrialize Puerto Rico that started with Operation Bootstrap undermined both the agricultural export sector and local farming by the remaining small growers. From ranking as the island's largest economic sector, agriculture has shrunk to the smallest part of the island's economy, constituting only 4 percent of the GNP. Puerto Rico has become a net *importer* of sugar, and imports over 90 percent of its food needs. Louisiana, California, and Colorado now produce most of the rice and beans that Puerto Ricans eat. Since 1970, the amount of land used to grow crops has dropped 36 percent. The number of farm workers has sharply decreased, falling from 21 percent of the workforce in 1960 to 5 percent today. Because agriculture's multiplier effect on incomes and employment is greater than that of tourism, trade, or the government sector, the drop in agricultural employment has severely affected the island's economy.

Dr. Larry Simon of Oxfam/America, in a statement before the Subcommittee on Inter-American Affairs, warned, "In examining models of development on which to base foreign economic assistance, the Puerto Rican lesson must not be overlooked." He noted that the development plan for other Caribbean islands currently promoted by the United States emphasizes light industry and export agriculture and neglects the importance of small farms that produce food for the local market.

THE 936 PROGRAM

The major attraction for mainland investors is a provision of the U.S. Internal Revenue Code called Section 936, which effectively exempts investment income in Puerto Rico from federal income tax. According to the U.S. Treasury: "No alternative to Puerto Rico exists for receiving tax-free, high-yield returns on financial investments."[12] The U.S. Treasury estimates that because of these tax breaks, the overall rate of return to the operating assets of 936 corporations is 4.1 times greater than that of mainland firms. Corporations like Pfizer enjoy substantially reduced federal income taxes because they do not have to pay taxes on income from their Puerto Rican subsidiaries. In 1982, the pharmaceutical giant reported that (because of its tax-exempt operations in Puerto Rico and Ireland) it paid income taxes at the rate of 38 percent rather than at the statutory rate of 46 percent.[13]

The tax revenue loss to the U.S. Treasury is estimated to be about $1.2 billion a year, which means theoretically that U.S. corporations are saving at least that much by doing business in Puerto Rico.[14] In the case of some manufacturing companies, the Treasury found that it is losing more than three dollars in taxes for each one dollar in wages paid to workers in Puerto Rico. Overall, the corporations save an average of $17,000 in taxes per employee, while the average wage paid these workers is $12,000 a year. In several companies, the revenue loss per job exceeded $100,000. Critics maintain that the federal government could create far more jobs by direct federal outlays, such as those under the CETA program. Another concern is that corporations maintain only a token presence on the island to avoid taxes. For all the hoopla about the success of the 936 program, the manufacturing corporations taking advantage of Section 936 employ only 72,000 workers, or 9 percent of the island's workforce.

Because of Puerto Rico's special relationship with the United States, U.S. corporations have made a practice of consigning what are known as intangibles—patents, management techniques, and trademarks—to their subsidiaries in Puerto Rico. In this way, income that the companies make on selling and licensing the use of these intangibles is accredited to their Puerto Rican subsidiaries under Section 936 and allows the parent corporations to increase the pool of tax-exempt Puerto Rican income. The IRS has charged that this practice "distorts" or artificially lowers the income reported by the corporations on the mainland.

Fomento, the Puerto Rican agency that promotes investment, has countered the criticisms of the 936 program by arguing that the costs of the program are overestimated and that the program keeps U.S. corporations that would otherwise locate in an underdeveloped nation outside the U.S. territorial area. To Puerto Rico, Section 936 of the Internal Revenue Code is not a loophole but the base of the island's economy. Some 2,200 companies, which depend on the provisions of Section 936, account for over 50 percent of the island's GNP.[15]

For U.S. corporations, Puerto Rico constitutes a sanctuary from federal taxes and the higher wage rates of the mainland. The average hourly manufacturing wage rate in Puerto Rico is about 55 percent of the average U.S. mainland rate; only 11 percent of all Puerto Ricans belong to unions, compared with 19 percent on the mainland.[16] The low wages and tax exemptions have made Puerto Rico what Fomento calls a "profit island" for U.S. investors. In Puerto Rico, the profit/sales ratio and the profit/equity ratio are 35 and 36 percent, respectively, while the corresponding rates for the United States are 8 and 16 percent.[17]

A sanctuary for the holding of financial assets, Puerto Rico charges no tax on bank deposits, bonds, and other securities. Total Puerto Rican financial assets held by qualifying corporations total about $8 billion. Mainland banks with branches on the island, particularly Chase Manhattan and Citibank, manage the assets. European, Canadian, and U.S. banks hold about 70 percent of the bank deposits of 936 funds and over 85 percent of other bank deposits in Puerto Rico.[18] The government has made futile attempts to channel this investment income into productive investments on the island. But rather than being put to work to develop the economy of Puerto Rico, the funds have either flowed out of the economy through the international banking system or have been used to finance the island's enormous public debt. Instead of having Citibank in New York buy Puerto Rican bonds, for example, Citibank in San Juan buys the bonds, and the income is tax free. "The 936 financial investments in the Puerto Rican capital market have made only a small contribution to the financing of physical investment in Puerto Rico," concluded the U.S. Treasury in its study of the 936 program.

LOCAL INVESTMENT INCENTIVES

Besides the federal tax exemptions, Puerto Rico offers its own series of tax breaks and incentives to investors. Since 1948, Puerto Rico has complemented the 936 tax program by exempting firms from local tax for 5 to 30 years. A number of public corporations, especially Fomento, furnish a whole gamut of services for manufacturers, such as worker training, factory shells, free zones, transportation, and financing. Director of Fomento José Madera explained that it is the "role of the government to stimulate and assist the private sector to put its diverse resources and creative energies" to work.[19] In its promotional brochure, titled "Profit Picture: Puerto Rico, USA," Fomento advertises a "unique training program" that provides a salary reimbursement of up to $20 a week for trainees for up to three months. The state corporations that offer services to U.S. companies are supported by taxes and are heavily indebted. Mainland investors hold several billion dollars of public bonds that pay for these state corporations, which operate at a loss to serve U.S. private investors. The obligation to pay back the debt falls mainly on the Puerto Rican taxpayer.

Operation Bootstrap was initiated with the intention to gradually reduce and then eliminate the tax exemption offered corporations as they became settled on the island. Instead, the Puerto Rican government has extended and expanded its tax exemptions, in addition to providing plants at low rent, cash grants to cover start-up costs, and low-interest loans to finance the investment. Originally, Puerto Rico was going to terminate all local exemptions by 1962, saying that the continuation of the exemption from local taxes would deprive the government of needed revenue. The government in the 1950s warned that the incentive program would cause an imbalance in the island economy by opening Puerto Rico to domination by U.S. corporations—a concern that proved prophetic.

Once accustomed to the exemption from local as well as federal taxes, the 936 corporation threatened to leave the island when the local exemption terms ran out. The Puerto Rican government caved in to the corporate pressure, and in 1954, 1959, 1963, and 1978 it passed extensions of the original exemption periods and lengthened the original term of 10 years to a current period of 30 years. If and when a corporation's term runs out, the governor has the power to and often does waive the regulations to continue the firm's tax-free status. Each year the Puerto Rican government receives in tax revenues only about 3.5 percent of the net income of the 936 corporations, hardly enough to pay for all its expenses in infrastructure, promotion, and administration.[20]

Local tax exemptions no longer attract corporations to the island but merely keep them there. Thirty-five years after the start of Operation Bootstrap, Puerto Rico has hardly progressed beyond its initial position of giving mainland corporations special treatment that it cannot offer its own residents or its own business. It has given up trying to pull itself up by its own bootstraps, but is still trying to make a living bending over to shine someone else's shoes.

INDUSTRY

Puerto Rico promotes itself as the "second home of American business." The *Wall Street Journal* called the island the "most profitable address" of U.S. corporations. It is the location for more than 350 manufacturing subsidiaries belonging to 112 of the 500 largest U.S. corporations. Each year, the more than 2,000 U.S. firms that have "second homes" on the island bring about $3 billion in profits back to the United States.[21] In 1980, U.S. investment in Puerto Rico of $16.2 billion represented about 8 percent of all (nonfinance) U.S. foreign investment throughout the world; about 3 times more than the combined U.S. (nonfinance) foreign investment in the rest of the Caribbean.[22] Profits from the island account for 22 percent of all (nonfinance) profits from U.S. foreign investment throughout the world.[23] Puerto Rico is also the largest per capita consumer of U.S. goods in the world, constituting a market with an annual value of over $5.5 billion. An ever-increasing transfer of funds from the U.S. government, however, has been required to keep this profit paradise functioning.

U.S. corporations dominate the island, controlling 81 percent of manufacturing assets, 85 percent of retail sales, 81 percent of the labor force, 65 percent of housing construction, 60 percent of banking and finance, virtually 100 percent of marine and air transport, and most of the means of communication.[24] The U.S. Department of Commerce reports that mainland firms finance 90 percent of the new industrial investment in Puerto Rico. The locally owned business sector is confined to professional services and small retail and service operations, with the exception of several elite Puerto Rican families that have important interests in finance and construction. The flood of foreign investment has driven small local investors out of business. The early garment plants can no longer compete with the transnational apparel companies, and small Puerto Rican stores and restaurants have lost out to the likes of McDonald's and Penney's. The U.S. corporations have pushed out the smaller Puerto Rican industries and those at a lower level of technological development. Commenting on this displacement, a former Puerto Rican governor remarked: "It's a David and Goliath situation."

The corporations that invested in Puerto Rico between 1950 and the mid-1960s were mostly light industries attracted to the island by the low wages. As wages increased, however, these labor-intensive plants started to pull out of the island or to automate their production. They could find cheaper and less organized workers in Haiti, the Dominican Republic, or Taiwan. Since 1965 investment has taken place primarily in the areas of pharmaceuticals, instrument manufacture, petrochemicals, and refineries—highly mechanized industries that use a great deal of land, water, or electricity. In industry, as in agriculture, corporations in Puerto Rico have tended to increase the amount of capital and reduce the amount of labor in their investments. Consequently, while there has been an increasing quantity of U.S. investment, there are fewer jobs available. Referring to the domination of the island, Dr. Neftali García said: "Most Puerto Ricans are taught how much we receive from the United States, but few learn about the capital the corporations take out."[25]

The largest U.S. investor in Puerto Rico is Union Carbide. Other major investors are Westinghouse, which has 31 plants on the island, and General Electric, which has 17. Large-scale projects by investors from foreign countries include codfish processing by Vetril Químico (Portugal), the manufacture of medical filters by Sartoris (West Germany), and tuna canning by Mitsubishi (Japan).

TABLE II C
MAJOR INDUSTRIES OF PUERTO RICO

Industry	No. of Plants	U.S.	Other Foreign	Selected Corporations
Metal products	161	54	10	Borden, Century Brass, DuPont, GTE, Crown Cork & Seal, National Can, Sam Wallace
Electrical & electronics	159	129	4	Westinghouse, Matsushita, (Japan), General Electric, GTE, Motorola, Intel, North American Philips
Apparel	345	185	6	Blue Bell, Chesebrough Ponds, Consolidated Foods, Gulf+Western, Esmark, General Mills, Warnaco, Manhattan
Food processing	379	28	8	Beatrice, Borden, Castle & Cooke, Central Soya, Coca-Cola, Conagra, CPC International, General Foods, HJ Heinz, IC Industries, Nabisco Brands, PepsiCo, Philip Morris, Ralston Purina, Warner Lambert
Instruments	101	81	11	General Electric, Allen Group, Medtronics, United Technologies, Abbott Laboratories, Westinghouse
Jewelry	44	32	5	Avon, General Mills, Lenox
Computers	30	30	0	ITT, Digital, Westinghouse, Wang, Honeywell, Hewlett Packard, McDonnell Douglas
Nonelectrical equipment	83	56	2	Ford, ITT, Rexnord, Storage Technology, General Electric
Petrochemical & refining	29	21	4	Phillips Petroleum, Hercules, Exxon, Gulf Oil, Allied Chemicals, Sun Company
Plastics	48	24	0	Union Carbide, Polymer, Pharmaseal, Seagram, Travenol, GTE Sylvania, Culbro, Firestone, Revlon

| Pharmaceutical | 92 | 81 | 9 | Eli Lilly, SmithKline, Beckman, Bristol-Myers,Johnson & Johnson, Schering-Plough, DuPont, Abbott Laboratories,Pfizer, American Cyanamid |
| Personal care | 17 | 10 | 4 | Alberto Culver, Carter Wallace, Johnson & Johnson, Chesebrough Ponds, General Cosmetics |

Source: Economic Development Administration of Puerto Rico

The Pharmaceutical Capital

Pharmaceutical plants seem to be as common as resort hotels in Puerto Rico. Seventeen percent of the capitalist world's pharmaceuticals come from Puerto Rico, which has attracted all the top pharmaceutical corporations in the United States with federal and local tax incentives.[26] Each year firms like Eli Lilly, American Hospital Supply, and Bristol-Myers ship over $1 billion in pharmaceutical and medical products to the mainland.[27]

Not one of the 92 pharmaceutical plants on the island is unionized. As one pharmaceutical executive put it: "We fight unions in any way we can. We think we can do a better job for our workers than any 'third party.' We've never had a union, and we intend to keep it that way."[28] Besides the strong antiunion stance of the corporations, the relatively higher wages received by workers in the drug factories explain the total lack of union representation in this important sector in Puerto Rico. Workers in the pharmaceutical sector form part of a labor aristocracy on the island. Although they only receive about half the wages paid on the mainland, these workers earn much more than the employees of the garment plants. The companies have been successful in making many of the pharmaceutical workers feel a part of the corporate family by sponsoring company sports and cultural activities and even making company psychologists available to the families of their workers.

The unorganized workforce is not the main attraction for the pharmaceutical firms, however; it is the 100 percent exemption from federal and local taxes. The pharmaceutical companies are capital-intensive and generally more profitable than labor-intensive industries. As such, exemption from income taxes assumes great importance for the pharmaceutical industry. The U.S. Treasury, in its report on the 936 program in Puerto Rico, concluded that the high-tech industries like pharmaceutical manufacturing do not generally merit their tax exemptions because they create relatively few jobs. It found that the 1980 tax exemption per employee in the pharmaceutical industry averaged $59,000 for the 936 corporations in Puerto Rico.

The U.S. Treasury has become particularly concerned about the pharmaceutical industry's use of Section 936 because it has discovered that many pharmaceutical corporations have been guilty of wrongfully allocating income to their Puerto Rican subsidiaries to gain additional tax benefits. It has been difficult to determine the extent of this tax evasion, however, because the companies can easily switch the bulk of their profits to their Puerto Rican subsidiaries through a TNC practice called transfer pricing. The corporate parents can sell their Puerto Rican subsidiaries raw materials cheaply but pay an inflated price for the final product, thus boosting tax-free subsidiary earnings while minimizing the profits earned by the parents, which are subject to federal tax.

Environment

When the pharmaceutical firms started coming to Puerto Rico, the government promised them that they had no need to be concerned with the impact of their activities on the environment. Either the enforcement of environmental regulations would be lax, or the Puerto Rican government itself would take care of any waste problems. The 15 years of disposing poisonous liquids from the pharmaceutical plants into rivers, aquifers, and the ocean now presents a serious problem for the people and the government of Puerto Rico, but it is still a problem that the island government has refused to approach openly for fear of scaring off industry. Yet the government's own Environmental Quality Board has repeatedly warned that the "pathway from the point of contamination to the population is very short."[29]

Although Puerto Rico is a "profit paradise" for U.S. corporations, it is also a polluted paradise, the most polluted island in the Caribbean. "If people really knew what the quality of their drinking water is, there would be a revolution in Puerto Rico," commented the director of planning for the Corps of Engineers in San Juan.[30] Taken together, the facts of environmental destruction seem to describe the conditions of a northeastern U.S. industrial center, not a tropical island.

- Analyses of 19 underground wells used primarily for drinking water in 1983 revealed that all but one of them were contaminated with toxic and potentially carcinogenic chemicals.
- Industrial production of solid waste on the island amounts to 1,600 pounds per year for every person, which is 300 pounds more than per capita production on the U.S. mainland.
- If the trend in solid waste production continues, the annual production by the year 2000 could cover the whole island with six inches of compacted solid waste.

- Most water in Puerto Rico is in violation of existing water-quality standards.
- Ninety waste dumps in Puerto Rico have been labeled "potentially hazardous" by the island's Environmental Quality Board.
- In the last 20 years, about 50,000 tons of oil have been accidentally spilled off the coasts of Puerto Rico.
- Warm water discharges from oil complexes and thermoelectric plants is equivalent to 50 percent of all water discharged by all the rivers flowing on the island.
- Repeated spills from a polyvinyl chloride plant led to the hospitalization of more than 500 island residents during the 1970s.
- The Rincon Nuclear Plant, closed down by the Nuclear Regulatory Commission because of radioactive leaks, has to stay closed for 140 years to allow the radiation to subside to "acceptable" levels.

Puerto Rico may be the New Jersey of the Caribbean, but it is unlikely that any serious governmental action will confront the island's environmental problems until some disaster affects the industrial plants. The principal polluters in Puerto Rico are the pharmaceutical plants, the refineries, the petrochemical industry, and the rum industry. The major force lobbying against better environmental regulations on the island is the Puerto Rican Manufacturers Association, which represents primarily U.S. corporations. Most notorious for its pollution of nearby communities is Union Carbide. The Industrial Mission, a church-sponsored environmental organization, has charged that the "incidence of pulmonary and skin diseases near the Union Carbide plant in the Humacao district has reached catastrophic levels."[31] It says that despite protests from the community, Union Carbide has continued releasing thousands of tons of poisons into the air each year. The chairperson of the environmental committee of the Manufacturers Association is also the government-affairs director for Union Carbide in Puerto Rico.

POLITICS

Politics in Puerto Rico is divided more by positions on the status of the island than by traditional political philosophies. The three major status positions in Puerto Rico are: (1) the *independistas*, who want full autonomy with full-fledged nationhood; (2) the supporters of commonwealth status, who want more autonomy and a new accord with the United States; and (3) the advocates of statehood, who want to legitimize the lack of autonomy with increased participation and full representation. Rafael Hernández Colón, leader of the Popular Democratic Party (PDP), which supports the present commonwealth status with certain modifications, contends the island should loosen its ties with the United States, but does not believe that complete independence is the answer to the island's problems. The Partido Nuevo Progresista (PNP), which holds the governor's seat through 1984, supports statehood status for Puerto Rico. In 1983, San Juan Mayor Hernán Padilla broke off from the ruling PNP to form another statehood party called the Puerto Rican Renewal Party. The leading independence parties are the Marxist Puerto Rican Socialist Party (PSP), led by Juan Mari Bras, and the Puerto Rican Independence Party (PIP), led by Rubén Berrios.

Independence parties can no longer count on the widespread popular support for Puerto Rican independence that was common on the island from 1898 through the 1950s. The members of the independence parties come mostly from the professional and educated classes, and can only count on about 5 percent of the vote in an island-wide election. "During the eight decades of U.S. intervention, the people of Puerto Rico have been subjected to a most systematic ideological indoctrination against independence," wrote one Puerto Rican *independista*.[32] Independence activists charge that since 1960 there has been a U.S. government campaign to crush the island's independence movement, using such methods as illegal phone tapping, infiltrating agents into independence organizations to create conflicts, planting anti-*independista* stories in the media, circulating fabricated letters and documents to discredit leadership, and training right-wing terrorist bands to harass the movement. The U.S. government has used federal grand juries to intimidate and repress the Puerto Rican solidarity and independence movement. Several members of this movement were arrested in 1983 and 1984 for refusing to collaborate with grand juries investigating the activities of armed liberation groups.

A number of small groups of radical terrorists have chosen the path of armed resistance to win the national liberation of Puerto Rico. Operating underground in the United States is the FALN (Fuerzas Armadas de Liberación Nacional), which has gained notoriety because of a long series of widely publicized bombings since 1974. With a few notable exceptions, such as the lunchtime explosion in a downtown Manhattan tavern, all the FALN bombings have seemed planned for times when human presence was sparse. The latest bombings have struck the stock exchanges, Chase Manhattan Bank, the headquarters of Merrill Lynch, and military installations in Puerto Rico. Another leftist terrorist group called the Macheteros has confined its attacks to targets within Puerto Rico, such as Fort Buchanan and the San Juan power station. They sign their actions with a red flag and a machete. Other armed groups are the Comandos Revolucionarios del Pueblo and the Organización de Voluntarios para la Revolución.

The United Nations Special Committee on Decolonization has voted for the past ten years for resolutions stating that Puerto Rico is a colony which should be independent from the United States. The committee has repeatedly affirmed the "inalienable right of the people of Puerto Rico to self-determination and independence." In 1983, the committee passed a resolution deploring both the U.S. government's decision to enlarge its military installations in Puerto Rico and the participation by the National Guard of Puerto Rico in U.S.-sponsored military maneuvers in Central America.

Independence would hardly guarantee a brighter economic future for Puerto Rico, because separation from the United States would surely jeopardize the billions of dollars of U.S. corporate investments on the island and would close the door to emigration to the United States. As in the French and Dutch Caribbean, the independence movement in Puerto Rico, while based in a long history of popular struggle against the "mother country," can no longer promise that the result of independence would be an improvement of the economic conditions of the colony.

Three flags are raised over the McDonald's in downtown San Juan: the Puerto Rican flag, the U.S. flag, and the flag of McDonald's golden arches. The Puerto Rican government is little more than a managing committee for the interests of the United States and its corporations. Any meaningful change in the international status of Puerto Rico will have to take into consideration its subservient relationship not only with the U.S. government but also with the TNCs that rule the economic life of this Caribbean colony.

U.S. Virgin Islands

After David and Laurance Rockefeller donated the land for the U.S. Virgin Islands National Park, which covers two-thirds of the island of St. John, they promptly built a luxury resort called the Caneel Bay Plantation to capture the boom in the tourist business resulting from the attractions of the underwater coral park. There is little in the U.S. Virgin Islands that can be considered locally owned. Its shopping centers, banks, restaurants, parks, factories, even its government are appendages of the mainland. License plates in this U.S. territory read "American Paradise," and to sun-starved U.S. visitors the islands may seem a paradise. But the combination of unemployment, crime, dull and low-paying assembly-line jobs, and the lack of political self-determination has convinced many residents that the Virgin Islands are not their kind of paradise.

The Virgin Islands are unique in having had Denmark as their main colonial ruler. But since all colonial powers administered basically the same type of sugar economy that exploited slave labor, there was not much difference between French, British, Dutch, or Danish colonial rule. Realizing then that the sugar industry would never revive, the Danes began looking for buyers for the islands. The U.S. government, concerned as early as 1917 that unfriendly bases in the Caribbean might threaten the Panama Canal or even the United States itself, offered $25 million to the willing Danes for the islands. The U.S. Virgin Islands, administered until 1931 by the U.S. Navy, later became a territory, taking on U.S. culture and language. The territory's government says that its residents "substantially enjoy the same rights as those enjoyed by mainlanders." Although the residents do elect their own local government, they cannot vote in presidential elections and have only a nonvoting representative in the U.S. Congress. The federal government determines the territory's foreign policy and maintains veto power over any constitutional changes approved by the Virgin Islands. In effect, the U.S. Virgin Islands are a colony of the United States.

FREEDOM FROM TAXES

"Where else," asks the U.S. Virgin Islands Industrial Development Corporation, "can you cut your corporate tax 90 percent and earn a 39 percent to 80 percent profit?" Like Puerto Rico, the U.S. Virgin Islands are a tax haven for U.S. corporations. The Naval Appropriations Act of 1922 provided that residents or businesses incorporated in the islands could satisfy their federal income tax obligations by paying their taxes to the territorial government of the islands. To attract investors, however, the government of the islands exempts them from 90 percent of their corporate tax obligations and offers an array of other incentives including rebates of 90 percent on customs duties and 100 percent exemptions from real property tax, gross receipts tax, and excise tax. Together these exemptions make the U.S. Virgin Islands one of the best spots in the Caribbean for U.S. investors.

In 1980, the U.S. Treasury reported there were 48 corporations taking advantage of these exemptions from income tax. Four corporations in the petroleum refining, alumina processing, and concrete products industries accounted for 78 percent of the total assets ($1.9 billion) of exempted corporations. These same four corporations accounted for 93 percent of the combined income of exempted corporations and received $36 million, or 88 percent of the total tax rebates from income tax. The total income tax subsidy in the U.S. Virgin Islands in 1980 was $40.5 million.

U.S. CORPORATE ACTIVITY

U.S. corporations control every sector of the economy of the islands. The Hess Oil Virgin Islands Corporation, which has invested $850 million in plant and equipment (as of 1983) on St. Croix, is the largest private employer in the islands. The second largest is Amca's Litwin Pan American Corporation, the construction firm that subcontracts for the oil refinery. The company with the third-largest workforce is Martin Marietta Aluminum, followed by the Virgin Islands Telephone Corporation, a subsidiary of ITT. The Caneel Bay Plantation, owned and operated by Rockresorts (a Rockefeller family company), is the fifth-largest private employer on the islands.

The dominant part of the manufacturing sector involves the assembly of watches and small instruments by U.S. corporations like Becton Dickinson, Timex, Bulova, Hamilton, and Waltham. A complete exemption from excise taxes and reduced income taxes have attracted fourteen watch manufacturers to St. Croix. Together, the watch-assembly plants enjoyed close to a million dollars in income tax rebates in 1980. Such pharmaceutical producers as Coopers Laboratories and Schering-Plough have also located on the territorial islands. Amerada Hess, the largest private investor in the islands, operates the world's largest oil refinery in St. Croix. Hess, in taking advantage of the islands' exemption from a U.S.

law prohibiting foreign-flag vessels from engaging in domestic commerce, saves $2.15 per barrel of oil shipped.[1] After a long dispute between Amerada Hess and the territory's government, the two parties signed a contract in 1981 that committed Hess to paying 2 cents per barrel on oil produced plus financing a technical training school for young and unemployed islanders. Besides expanding its refinery, Hess is also considering construction of a containerport. Another key company in St. Croix is Martin Marietta, a processor of alumina. The new coal-conversion project at the Martin Marietta power plant and the expansion of the Hess refinery will bring the total of new investment for U.S. corporations to $1 billion.[2]

"Discover the benefits," proclaim the government's industrial development brochures. Undoubtedly, there are benefits for U.S. corporations in the Virgin Islands, such as exemptions from corporate income tax and from the requirement to use expensive U.S.-flag ships for transportation. Nowhere in the brochures, however, is there any mention that the islands suffer from a severe shortage of water. There is hardly enough water to satisfy the territorial residents, let alone the more than one million tourists each year and an array of U.S. manufacturing plants. Despite all the financial attractions of investing in the islands, industrial promotion has not been looking up recently. The government boasts of an inventory of more than one hundred companies that have expressed serious interest in locating in the territory, but writing letters of interest and putting down the money are two different things. The islands' preoccupation with attracting investment became so intense in 1983 that the government fired the industrial promotion director for not succeeding at his job.

About one-quarter of the residents of the U.S. Virgin Islands are immigrants who came to work in the tourist industry and later at the oil refinery. In the 1950s, the Immigration and Naturalization Service (INS) started issuing work permits to the natives of other Caribbean islands, mainly Puerto Rico. This immigration and the boom in the tourist industry caused the territory's population to jump from only 30,000 in 1960 to about 100,000 in 1982. The early migrant workers, called in to build hotels and docks, lived in ramshackle slum housing. Despite having to pay 30 percent of their wages in taxes, they could not receive any government services.[3] With the tourist business slowing down and unemployment steadily rising, federal authorities and the local government have stopped allowing work certificates and are deporting "alien" residents.

Another important part of the territorial economy is the rum industry, which contributes one-sixth of the government's revenues. A special advantage for the territory is a U.S. law that gives back to the U.S. Virgin Islands all the excise taxes collected on the rum imported into the United

States from the islands. More anxious to protect its industry than to protect its paradisiacal setting, the territorial government, together with Puerto Rico, successfully lobbied the U.S. Congress to exempt the rum industry from the discharge regulations of the Clean Water Act. The exemption means that the two distilleries owned by Rapid American's Schenley Corporation are allowed to discharge their millions of gallons of waste directly into the Caribbean Sea.

Antigua-Barbuda

From 1674 through the early 1970s, sugar dominated the economy of Antigua-Barbuda. Antigua's slaves were among the first in the British West Indies to benefit from the abolition of slavery in the early 1800s. Sugar gradually declined but remained the number-one crop until 1972, when the government shut down the industry, having nationalized it several years before. The government owns 60 percent of the agricultural land, but half that land is underused or completely abandoned.[1] Currently the government is attempting to reestablish the sugar crop to meet local demand.

With the decline of sugar came the rise of tourism, which now represents the largest source of government revenues. Although vital to the economy, tourism employs less than 10 percent of the total labor force, and the vast majority of the luxury hotels on the islands have foreign ownership. An Antiguan government official complained that because 95 percent of the hotel reservations and payments are made overseas, only a small percentage of the revenue actually enters Antigua. "The [hotels] bring in only enough money to pay local salaries and wages [and the potential of] greater inflows of deposits to Antigua's banking system are not realized."[2] The Mellon family owns the island's Mill Reef Lodge, an exclusive club that has its own guards and imports all its needs from outside the island. "It is totally self-contained," observed one Antiguan. "It's as if it weren't in Antigua." More than in most Caribbean islands, tourism in Antigua is characterized by gambling, drugs, and prostitution.

Antigua exports clothing, rum, and mineral fuel lubricants. According to an Antiguan labor leader, most foreign investors are small capitalists who cannot make it in the United States. Maidenform's Rachel Needlecraft, the largest manufacturer in Antigua, has more than 300 employees in its plant and imports material from the U.S. to assemble brassieres. Antigua boasts the newest Coca-Cola bottling plant operating in the Caribbean. Salada, a subsidiary of Kellogg, distributes a variety of processed foods in the two islands. The largest shareholder of Antigua and Barbuda Meats Development Corporation is a British citizen.[3] Other large foreign-owned businesses in Antigua include Holiday Inns and Sealy Mattress of the U.S., and Scott's Hospitality of Canada. An estimated 33 offshore banks do business in Antigua, which has just passed a new law to attract more offshore banking activity. Opponents of the new law claim that offshore banking has connections with organized crime and that the law will increase underworld activity on the islands.[4]

POLITICS AND FOREIGN POLICY

Antigua's international relations differ from those of many of its neighbors. Although decidedly pro-United States, Antigua is negotiating with the People's Republic of China toward establishing an embassy on the island. Several years ago the Space Research Corporation used Antigua as a transshipment point for South African-bound military weapons that were manufactured in the United States. The military operates tracking stations in the country, from which Antigua receives $1.4 million a year in rent. A Voice of America station that broadcasts to the entire Caribbean and an increasing number of Texan evangelists add to the U.S. influence in Antigua. The U.S. Embassy's political officer in Antigua claims the native population holds no resentment toward the U.S. presence. "In fact," commented officer Bruce Thomas, "when we celebrate the Fourth of July it's like a national holiday here, too. Everyone comes to the base for the festivities."[5]

Despite the firm support of Antigua for the United States, Washington delayed approval of its eligibility for Caribbean Basin Initiative (CBI) benefits because of a dispute over satellite reception. Antigua had been receiving signals for Home Box Office (HBO) and other programs and rebroadcasting them throughout the country, free. The Motion Picture Association and other program producers objected and pressured Washington to deny CBI benefits to the culpable Caribbean nations. Minister of Economic Development Hugh Marshall said that he found it inexplicable that the United States would hold up the CBI program over such a minor matter. Marshall also noted, "Some people in the United States evidently don't appreciate what a valuable vehicle television is in communicating what the American principles of democracy, free enterprise, and personal liberty are all about. . . . Television," Marshall said, "is a very effective instrument of foreign policy."[6]

In late 1983, the government of Antigua-Barbuda reluctantly succumbed to IMF demands to cut back government spending by cutting back civil-service employment and the salaries of government workers. The Antiguan government is not above using repressive measures to crack its opposition. It closed the offices of *Outlet*, the voice of the leftist party, the Antiguan Caribbean Liberation Movement (ACLM). In addition to the closing, the government initiated a court action against the publication. An established organization with ties that go beyond political party connections, ACLM is helping to create an alliance of scattered political parties and unions that will challenge the administration of Prime Minister Vere Bird.

The Bahamas

Located only 50 miles from the Florida coast, the Bahamas do not physically qualify as Caribbean islands, but this chain of 700 mostly uninhabited islands in the Atlantic definitely resembles other Caribbean nations. Beautiful beaches, a lively nightlife, an import-dependent economy busy with offshore financial activity, and a history of slavery and colonization combine to make the Bahamas very much like some of its neighbors to the south. But so Americanized are the culture and commerce of the islands that they seem like extensions of the Florida keys.

During the American Revolution, the British created an important supply base in the Bahamas, which the Yankee navy attacked and occupied for a day. When the war ended, 6,000 loyalists sought refuge in the Bahamas and introduced slavery on a large scale to the islands. Bahamians lent a hand to their Confederate neighbors during the Civil War by helping ships run the North's blockade. Later, the U.S. Volstead Act made the Bahamas a bootlegger's paradise until the early 1930s. Just as the end of the Civil War damaged the Bahamian economy, the repeal of Prohibition brought it to a virtual standstill. In the World War II years, the Bahamas provided a strategic point for Allied flight training and antisubmarine operations. The U.S. construction company that built the military installations paid white workers twice what it paid blacks.[1]

ALWAYS SOME SORT OF RACKET

The days of blockade-running and bootlegging set the stage for the modern-day Bahamas. As one Bahamian civil servant put it, "There has always been some sort of racket."[2] The U.S.-Bahamian connection was further deepened when U.S. citizen Walter Groves casually decided in the 1950s to buy his wife a lumber company on the pine island of Abaco. The company became enormously successful, and Groves obtained 50,000 acres on the island of Grand Bahama, on which he developed the town of Freeport and established several casinos. This kicked off the tourism industry, which now provides more than two-thirds of the country's gross national product and employs a quarter of the islands' workers. In comparison with other Caribbean islands, the country's tourist trade ranks first in size (in terms of rooms available) and second in number of staying visitors.[3] In May 1983, the French Club Med's Paradise Island Hotel joined with the U.S.-owned Resort International's Britannia Beach Hotel to create one of the largest resort/casino complexes in the world. The Bahamian tourist industry, which began by attracting only the most elite tourists, changed in the 1950s to mass tourism, which brought thousands of visitors to the islands.

Three-quarters of all hotel rooms in the Bahamas are owned, indirectly or outright, by American interests.[4] Robsutt, a Bahamian corporation owned entirely by U.S. interests, owns the Xanadu Princess Hotel in Freeport. Other companies owning hotels in the Bahamas include Playboy, ITT's Sheraton, Scotts Hospitality (Canada), and England's Trust House Forte. The government-owned Hotel Corporation is completing a controversial 730-room hotel with a casino and convention facilities. Critics point out that the timing of such a project is unfortunate, since tourism is declining. In addition, the Reagan administration has refused to grant the Bahamas tax-exempt status for U.S. business conventions. This exemption would have substantially increased convention cruises, which account for a third of the Bahamas' cruise-line business.

Also hurting the tourist trade in the Bahamas is their reputation for bad service, rundown conditions, and high hotel prices, as well as complaints that Bahamians make tourists feel unwelcome. Major crime, which jumped 10 percent in 1981, and drug traffic also keep prospective tourists away. Little of tourism's potential earning power goes to the Bahamas; 81 cents of every tourist dollar spent in the Bahamas finds its way back to the United States.[5]

OFFSHORE INDUSTRIES

Most profits from the key sectors in the economy leave the country for the United States. Establishing this pattern in 1955 was the Hawksbill Creek Act, masterminded by Walter Groves, which exempted companies from all direct taxation and eliminated most regulations governing offshore financial business. Reputed to be the largest international finance or Eurodollar center outside London, the Bahamas host about 350 financial institutions, including a hundred Eurocurrency branches of mostly U.S. banks. The second-largest revenue earner after tourism, banking generates about $100 million a year for the Bahamas, but offshore financial activity has never been smooth sailing for the islands.

The U.S. government, concerned about tax fraud and criminal matters, is trying to negotiate with the Bahamas to allow an open exchange of information about the country's offshore financial activity, but the Bahamas, like other Caribbean tax havens, rely too heavily on offshore banking to lift their secrecy agreements. Because the U.S. Federal Reserve Board has facilitated the return of some Euromarket business to the United States, Bahamians predict a gloomy future for the financial sector. Officials fear that other banks will follow Citibank's decision to shift a portion of its Eurodollar business from Nassau to New York.

The Hawksbill Creek Act, in addition to creating a tax haven, granted 50,000 acres for a price of one British pound an acre to Wallace Grove's Grand Bahama Port Authority, which built a deepwater harbor and an airport in return for the land and other concessions. The Freeport industrial complex houses most of the Bahamas' manufacturing activity, most of which was introduced in the mid-1960s. Smith Kline Beckman, the only major corporation to enter the Bahamas in the 1980s, opened its Franklin Chemicals plant not far from Syntex and Cooper Labs, two other U.S.-owned drug manufacturers in the complex. Two other U.S. corporations, Diamond Crystal Salt and U.S. Steel's Bahamas Cement, have both closed owing to financial difficulties. U.S.-owned Charter Oil acquired controlling interest in the Bahamas Oil Refinery, which is operating at a quarter of its capacity. Other U.S. companies in the Bahamas include Continental Telephone, Westinghouse Electric, Texaco, Northwest Industries, GAC, and United Technologies. The U.S.-owned Bacardi has produced bulk rum from its Bahamian plant since the mid-1950s.

Adding to the American presence in the Bahamas are the U.S. military installations: missile tracking stations, U.S. Navy and Coast Guard facilities, and an underwater test and evaluation center. The United States ranks as the Bahamas' leading trading partner, accounting for 75 percent of its nonpetroleum exports and imports. Many parts of the Bahamas resemble the United States—the town of Governor's Harbor looks like New Hampshire in the summer, and the U.S.-created Freeport resembles a non-neon Las Vegas. One Bahamian police official remarked that the United States should "learn that the Bahamas are not part of greater Dade County." But many Bahamians accept the identification with the United States, prefer U.S. goods to locally produced items, and admire American culture. The Bahamas boast of 14 championship golf courses, and prominent eateries include Kentucky Fried Chicken and Howard Johnson's.

Drug trafficking provides employment for many people living in the remote, more sparsely populated islands of the Bahamas. Because these "Out Islands" straddle key shipping lanes, they also constitute a major smuggling route. Not only an export item, drugs rank alongside alcoholism as the main problem of Bahamian society, which has the third-highest rate of alcoholism in the world.

Most Bahamian islands have a limestone formation and superficial topsoil unsuited for agriculture, but two fertile islands produce a wide range of crops and bear many acres of timber. These operations, which are all U.S.-owned, supply local demand and capitalize on the occasional crop failures in southern Florida when frost damage occurs. Parker Groves and Kendall Limes, the world's largest grower of limes, cultivate 1,000 acres at Lucaya Estates and on Andros Island. Dominating the dairy industry in the Bahamas is General Milk of IC Industries' subsidiary, Pet. General Seafoods, a General Foods subsidiary, has operations in the Bahamian fish industry, which supplies crayfish, the country's top agricultural export. Analysts who have conducted studies on the water surrounding the islands report that DDT and DDE were present in low but widely distributed levels in plankton, shrimp, and fish.[6] The Bahamas have virtually no laws protecting their land, water, or air.

Of the hundreds of islands in the Bahamas chain, only 14 are populated; two islands, New Providence and Grand Bahama, account for more than two-thirds of the country's population. The birth rate is rising at a staggering rate; half the births are to teenagers; and people under 20 years of age represent half the population. Unemployment, hovering around 20 percent, is complicated by the fact that many Bahamians refuse to take menial jobs that they call "Haitian work." The large number of mostly undocumented Haitians in the Bahamas work for minimal wages as farmhands, maids, gardeners, and construction workers. The white minority of the Bahamas controls most of the wealth in the islands, where 15 percent of the population earns 40 percent of the country's total disposable personal income.

POLITICS

Many Bahamians have become disgruntled with Prime Minister Lynden Pindling, who guided the nation to its independence with the Progressive Labor Party (PLP). A party of mostly black membership, the PLP successfully challenged the political control of a clique of wealthy white businessmen commonly known as the Bay Street Boys. The PLP's base of support among the trade unions and the Baptist churches, however, has eroded as the country's economic crisis has intensified. Opposing the PLP is the Free National Movement (FNM), which has called for even closer relations with the United States. The FNM wants to negotiate a defense treaty with Washington to protect the islands from "Cuban aggression." Youth groups, which have become increasingly large and vocal, include the Student National Action Party, which in 1983 led 300 high-school students in a demonstration to protest the lack of jobs. Also growing in the Bahamas is the Rastafarian movement, which has experienced several clashes between its members and Bahamian police. The Vanguard Socialist Party sends Bahamians on scholarships to Cuba and proposes a society along the lines of that country.

A more dangerous threat to the Pindling administration than any opposition political party was a television broadcast by NBC-TV in late 1983 that alleged drug-related corruption among Pindling's senior ministers. Pindling commented to a Royal Commission of Enquiry that "the only fellow I am sure of is myself, tell you the truth, I ain't sure about nobody else." In denying a claim that 70 percent of illicit drugs entering the United States pass through the Bahamas, Pindling estimated the figure at 20 or 30 percent. According to the February 1984 issue of *Caribbean Insight,* the commission's investigation has uncovered bribery of officials and illicit drug deals with organized crime figures and with American financier Robert Vesco. The hearings may lead to several resignations and possibly early elections.

For the time being, however, Pindling and the PLP grope for solutions to critical unemployment and growing unrest. In a case study of the Bahamas, author Ramesh Ramsaran warned, "These solutions, almost without exception, always revolve around one or a combination of the following: a) more tourists, b) more foreign investors, c) more land development . . . , d) more Freeport type development, and e) more casinos."[7]

Barbados

In Barbados, the hotels serve afternoon tea, and the magistrates sport white wigs. Although far from Great Britain, surrounded by the Caribbean on one side and the Atlantic on the other, with 260,000 people mostly of African descent, Barbados nevertheless resembles Britain so strongly that some call it "Little England." The only Caribbean nation to have been subjected by only one colonizing country, Barbados was under British rule for over 350 years until 1966, when it gained independence. The island takes pride in having the third-oldest parliamentary system in the British Commonwealth of Nations.

AGRICULTURE

The production of sugar, the country's top agricultural export, has come upon hard times. On Barbados (unlike other islands, where the industry has been nationalized), private owners have retained large interests in the sugar industry. In an unprecedented move, the government stepped in with financial assistance in 1982 to ease the industry's worst crisis in history. Nine sugar estates were put up for sale, and in 1982 production slumped to its lowest level since 1948.[1] Sugar is also losing its workers: almost 30 percent of the sugar workers will retire by 1987 and will not be replaced by other Barbadians.[2] Young people prefer working in the manufacturing and tourism sectors to working in an industry that is haunted by memories of slavery. Because of the sugar crisis, farmers have begun to diversify into onions, peanuts, sea island cotton, and other products. Barbados cultivates a higher percentage of its land (60 percent) than other Caribbean nations,[3] and it also consumes the greatest quantity of pesticides per capita and per unit of land in the region.

Good news in agriculture comes from the milk and poultry producers, who are rapidly expanding and modernizing their operations. The government, the British-owned Northern Dairies, and the New Zealand Dairy Board have a large and flourishing venture called Pine Hill Dairies. Other foreign corporations active in the country's food-processing industry include Foremost-McKesson's Mount Gay Distilleries and World's Finest Chocolates, both U.S.-owned; Tate & Lyle's Caribbean Antilles

Molasses, George Borwick's Caribbean Confectionery, and BAT Industries, all based in Great Britain; and Canadian Pacific's Purity Bakery. During the 1960s, the fishing industry was a major export earner, particularly in shrimp, but rising fuel costs and the establishment of international fishing zones brought the industry to a complete halt by the mid-1970s. Manufacturing, mainly of clothing and electronics components for the U.S. market, leads the export sector in Barbados.

INDUSTRY

Accepting the model of industrialization that was the basis of Puerto Rico's Operation Bootstrap, Barbados in 1958 passed a major law providing various fiscal incentives to manufacturers. The Barbados Industrial Development Corporation, which has a branch office in Manhattan, boasts that companies which normally pay their American workers about $6 an hour can find willing workers in Barbados for only $1.50 an hour. The government's industrial development corporation distributes a film to promote the country's virtues called "Barbados, the Profitable Paradise." Plant expenses rival those of Southeast Asia, and in fact some locations in Singapore and Hong Kong actually cost manufacturers more.

Barbados has attracted both regular assembly operations and some subassembly plants, like Microdata and Clairex, which send goods worked on in Barbados to Puerto Rico for further processing and for export to the U.S. and Europe. Subcontractors that produce for larger U.S. firms constitute about a third of all the island's manufacturing plants.[4] Some U.S. corporations have expressed concern that Barbadian union activity may hamper the island's industrial growth. The manager of Corcom, a U.S.-owned company that employs more than 400 Barbadians (Bajans) in its electronics plant, said: "There's a lot of union activity now. Many people, including ourselves, are concerned."[5] The Barbadian government has not challenged the antiunion stance, but rather has indirectly encouraged it through its industrial promotion. The country's development corporation proudly boasts, "You can judge an island by the companies it keeps." Those companies include U.S. Industries, Becton Dickinson, TRW, Caribbean Data Services, Esmark's Playtex, Intel, Bristol-Myers, and Berger Paints (UK).

ECONOMY

With the third-highest per capita income in the region, Barbados was once a star performer in the Caribbean economic picture, but now it faces a dismal financial future. The balance-of-payments deficit is eating up scarce reserves, and Barbados has recently deviated from its history of avoiding large debts. The government and the Barbados Central Bank, at nonconcessional rates, borrowed almost $50 million from the Orion Bank Group, a syndicated lending consortium led by Royal Bank of Canada. Under the CBI, the United States has loaned Barbados $7 million for an economic adjustment program to buy U.S. products and to promote export production. The Barbadian government reluctantly agreed to strict IMF measures that immediately increased unemployment and limited government spending. The opposition party disapproved of the IMF measures because of the job losses and higher local interest rates, saying the arrangement places the island in the hands of "doctrinaire IMF bureaucrats." The government has cut all major capital expenditures except for the construction of the new, prestigious Central Bank Building, which the United Kingdom Export Credit Guarantee Department agreed to finance.

The decline of tourism, which contributes more than half the country's foreign-exchange receipts, has shaken the entire country. Barbados, one of the most densely populated countries in the world, sees more tourists annually than it has residents. Even with the strain tourism puts on the lives of Bajans, the government promotes it widely, and most citizens support it as a reasonable source of income. Observers cite the following reasons for the decrease in the number of tourists to Barbados: the collapse of leading Canadian tour operators that brought Barbados 25 percent of its tourists, the world recession, and the fact that hotel rates are 10 to 15 percent higher than at resorts in other Caribbean islands. Trust House Forte's Sandy Lane Hotel has the reputation of being one of the higher-priced establishments in the entire region. An old slave estate called Sam Lord's Castle, owned by Marriott, also attracts a flush clientele. Over 70 percent of the country's Class A and luxury hotels belong to foreign corporations.

Although famous for its British atmosphere, Barbados does its major trading with the United States. Its tourists come mainly from Canada and the United States, and U.S. corporations are the major foreign investors on the island. Prime Minister J. M. G. (Tom) Adams and the ruling Barbados Labour Party have long supported U.S. hegemony in the Caribbean, but in 1982 Adams did criticize several stipulations of the CBI. Although interested in promoting more private investment in Barbados, Adams claimed that the bilateral agreements sought by the United States might compromise the sovereignty of the Caribbean countries. When it came to the sovereignty of Grenada, however, Adams took a slightly different stance and fully supported the U.S. invasion of the neighboring island. Along with other conservative Caribbean prime ministers, Adams rationalized the invasion as necessary to protect regional security. Riding on a wave of popularity since then, Adams has considered an early call for elections, with hopes he would be easily reelected, as was Jamaica's Edward Seaga.

During the invasion of Grenada, Barbados's tourist industry experienced a new twist, serving the hundreds of reporters clamoring to enter wartorn Grenada. To keep the hotels filled for an even longer period, the Barbadian government has invited the now homeless St. George School of Medicine, whose American students were "rescued" by U.S. Marines during the U.S. invasion of Grenada, to establish temporary operations in Barbadian hotels. The government has also initiated a quarter-million-dollar advertising campaign to assure prospective tourists, scared off by the Grenada headlines, that Barbados is a safe place to visit.

The self-content and somewhat superior attitudes that have characterized Bajan life are starting to crack under economic pressure. The drop in the tourist trade has taxicab drivers waiting idly beside their polished American cars and begging business from any tourist passing by. Lining up in the morning for work in the industrial zones, the employees, mostly female, grumble that their low wages cannot possibly cover the inflationary cost of living.

Politics has lately taken a more acrimonious tone in Barbados. Prime Minister Tom Adams, the target of a biting calypso song, "Mr. T," warned calypsonians against using their music to "spread hatred" in the society. The state-owned Caribbean Broadcasting Commission (CBC) banned that song and another one by Mighty Gabby called "Boots," which CBC said "denigrates the Barbados Defense Force." The Barbadian government has little sense of humor during these critical times. So ashamed was the government of its pact with the IMF that it tried to keep secret the details of the austerity agreement. The country's subservience to the IMF and to the United States has sadly diluted the nation's pride in its independence.

Cuba

Before its revolution, Cuba was, more than any other Caribbean or Central American state, the tropical patio of the United States. U.S. corporations controlled the sugar industry, owned the utilities, and had invested more in Cuba than in any other Latin American or Caribbean nation. Over 11 percent of all U.S. foreign investment in Latin America and the Caribbean was in Cuba.[1] When Fidel Castro and his rebel army came to power in January 1959, U.S. firms controlled 40 percent of raw sugar production; 90 percent of telephone, light, and power services; half the public railways; and a quarter of all bank deposits.[2] They also dominated the refining and distribution of petroleum, the exploitation of mineral resources, most of the tourist sector, and a substantial part of the manufacturing. Since the 1920s Cuba had been the glamour and sin spot of the Caribbean, luring tourists with its casinos, its nightclubs, and its reputation for iniquity. The island also served as a hangout for mobsters like Meyer Lansky, who kept dictator Fulgencio Batista rich while managing their underworld empires unhindered.

The Cuba of Batista, Lansky, and United Fruit came crashing down when the rebel bands from the Sierra Maestra entered Havana on New Year's Day, 1959. The mob fled to Florida and the Bahamas, Batista found haven with fellow dictator Trujillo in the Dominican Republic—and the U.S. corporations became public property. But the United States was not prepared to let Cuba slip out of its control. President Dwight D. Eisenhower and later President John F. Kennedy authorized CIA plans to invade Cuba, but the Cuban militia easily defeated the invasion at the Bay of Pigs in April 1961. CIA strategy then switched to elaborate assassination attempts against Castro, including plans to poison his famous cigars. In attempts to destabilize the economy, the United States spread viral diseases among the pigs and poultry in Cuba.[3]

The Cuban revolution and anti-imperialist movement did not arise full-blown out of the Sierra Maestra, but had been growing since the 1880s. José Martí, who died fighting for Cuba's independence from Spain, warned about the dangers of U.S. hegemony. His prediction proved true when, after three U.S. presidents tried to buy and annex the island during the 1840s and 1850s, the United States finally won the island from Spain in the Spanish-American War. In 1902, the United States granted the island independence but retained its Cuban naval bases. The infamous Platt Amendment of 1902 gave the United States the right to intervene to ensure "the maintenance of a government adequate for the protection of life, property, and individual liberty." Making good use of the amendment, Washington sent in U.S. troops from 1906 to 1909, in 1912, and again from 1917 to 1923 to quell rebellions against the U.S.-imposed government.⁴ The U.S. Congress in 1934 passed the Reciprocal Trade Agreement, which assured continued access to the Cuban market to U.S. business by keeping Cuban duties low on U.S. products and reducing quantitative restrictions on imported goods. The tight U.S. control of the economy prevented Cuba from participating in the wave of industrialization that swept through other less dependent Latin American nations in the 1930s and 1940s.

Under U.S. military supervision, U.S. corporations had come to control 40 percent of the land area of Cuba by 1927. Between 1925 and 1933, the United States backed Gerardo "The Butcher" Machado to look after U.S. interests in Cuba. When popular resistance began building up against Machado, Washington turned to Fulgencio Batista. In the 1950s, students and workers joined in active opposition to the bloodthirsty Batista. Because U.S. aid and military assistance propped up the Batista dictatorship, the struggle included a strong element of anti-imperialism. Fidel Castro, a young attorney who led the protests against Batista in the 1950s, described the conditions that eventually led to the 1959 revolution.

> Eighty-five percent of the small farmers in Cuba pay rent and live under constant threat of being evicted from the land they till. More than half our most productive land is in the hands of foreigners. In Oriente, the largest province, the lands of the United Fruit Company and the West Indies Company link the northern and southern coasts. There are two hundred thousand peasant families who do not have a single acre of land to till to provide food for their starving children. Ninety percent of the children of the countryside are consumed by parasites which filter through their bare feet from the ground they walk on.⁵

Fidel Castro marched into Havana in 1959 with a loyal army but without an organized party or clear platform for the future. At first the new revolutionary government rejected the label of communist or socialist. Within a year of Batista's departure, Cuba's land reform and new economic self-determination brought it into direct conflict with U.S. corporate interests of United Fruit, Citibank, and Texaco. The United States insisted on immediate cash payments for nationalized land of U.S. companies instead of the 20-year bond payment program suggested by Castro. In 1960, the die was cast for the future of Cuba when the government nationalized three U.S. oil companies after they refused to refine oil from the

Soviet Union. Washington immediately cut off Cuba's sugar quota and later imposed a complete trade embargo on the island, hoping to force it into submission. Instead, the U.S. pressure pushed the revolution further to the left and to an alliance with the socialist world.

Washington's efforts to destabilize and topple the new government had the opposite effect: Castro successfully appealed to the Cuban people to protect their country and their revolution against Yankee imperialism. During the first three years of the revolutionary government, however, more than half a million people—business owners, professionals, and landowners—decided to leave their homeland because they saw the revolution moving directly against their interests. Supporters of Castro called those who left Cuba *gusanos,* or worms. Twenty-five years after the 1959 revolution, Cuba remains subject to a U.S. embargo and to constant threats from Washington.

But Cuba has gained strength and stature because its ambitious goals to equalize and improve the country's standard of living have largely been realized. Over the years, Cuba has shown a steadfast commitment to the continuation of the class revolution. To meet its promise to bring equality to the Cuban people, the government has taken firm stands when dealing with both the international capitalist class and the remnants of the ruling class within Cuba.

REVOLUTION TAKES HOLD

The government headed by Fidel Castro has institutionalized socialist revolution in what is the largest Caribbean country in both land mass and population. A quarter century after the Cuban people chased the dictator Fulgencio Batista out of the National Palace, the more than 9 million Cubans born since 1959 visit the palace, now the National Museum, to learn about their colonized and brutal past. Much has changed since 1959: women constitute 40 percent of the militia, black Cubans can now enter the Havana Yacht Club, infant mortality has dropped to the lowest in Latin America, and prostitution no longer exists. Other things have not changed: the economy, for example, still depends on King Sugar. Part of the population looks longingly at the consumer culture of the United States, complaining about the existence of political prisoners and a lack of freedom of press and speech. Critics charge that Cuba simply switched dictators, but reportedly the vast number of Cubans, when they complain about some government program, say that it would be better "if only Fidel knew about this."

In the early stages of socialism in Cuba, the government tried to steer the economy away from dependence on sugarcane and toward diversified agriculture and industrialization. Because the soil was poorly suited to other crops and because the young nation lacked technical skills and a financial base to support large-scale industrialization, Cuba returned in the 1970s to a sugar economy. Cuba also faced a time of political reckoning after concluding that popular support was dwindling because the government failed to increase material wealth substantially and because too few participated in the political process.

To encourage active popular participation in determining policy and programs, the government broadened the role of mass organizations. Local and regional elections were instituted, and the Communist Party leadership created methods for popular feedback and checks on the bureaucratic management of the economy. Municipal councils, the base of the new but limited system of representative democracy, began to manage local services and elect members to provincial and national assemblies. Determined to reduce the paternalism of the state, the government mandated that all major legislation be subjected to mass discussion and criticism before actual enforcement.

Although Cuba has no independent unions, the party leadership created councils whereby the workers in a company elect a committee of five representatives in secret balloting. Workers bring their grievances against management and management brings its complaints about worker performance to the work councils for judgment. In his book *Revolution and Economic Development in Cuba*, Arthur MacEwan applauded the decentralization of decision-making. "From a narrowly economic point of view," he said, "political participation is an essential element in the effective functioning of a system based on general equality."[6]

Certain freedoms, though, are absent in Cuba. Although they are free to practice the religion of their choice, Cubans cannot propagate that religious faith. Political criticism is not the national game that it has become in the English-speaking Caribbean; it is a serious matter that can result in one's being labeled a counterrevolutionary, or perhaps being put in jail. Cuba contrasts sharply with other Caribbean nations in this and other ways. Havana does not have the sprawling urban slums that characterize Kingston and other Caribbean cities. No growing influx from the countryside to the cities burdens Cuba as it does other Caribbean nations.

Unemployment, while increasing in Cuba, is still under 5 percent at a time when most Caribbean nations are suffering from unemployment rates higher than 20 percent. The streets of Havana and Santiago see little crime and have no beggars. Another marked difference is the promotion and enjoyment of local culture in Cuba, while the other Caribbean nations have become markets for U.S. culture. Although Cuba is strikingly different from the rest of the Caribbean, it exercises considerable influence in the region. While some Caribbean people see Cuba as the nemesis of Westminster-style democracy in the region, many see it as an example of what the entire Caribbean could be if it could get out from under the colonial or neocolonial yoke.

Although it has made tremendous strides forward, Cuba has not been able to escape completely the conditions of underdevelopment. But its accomplishments impress even hardened skeptics.

- Cuba is regarded as one of the few Latin American countries where gastrointestinal inflammation and respiratory infection are no longer leading causes of infant mortality.
- In 1982, infant mortality was 19 per 1,000 live births, the lowest in Cuba's history. This compares with more than 60 per 1,000 before the revolution and with 14 per 1,000 in the United States.
- The number of medical practitioners has doubled since 1959.
- Malaria, diphtheria, and polio have been eliminated.
- Before 1959, there were 18 refrigerators, 49 radios, and six TV sets for each 100 houses with access to electricity; the figures now are 63 refrigerators, 135 radios, and 79 TV sets.
- There were 1.3 million housing units before 1959, of which only half had access to electricity; now, of the 2.4 million housing units, 79 percent of them have access to electric supply.[7]

The Cuban revolution put particular emphasis on educational programs, which make up the government's second-largest budget item. The country's literacy rate has risen to 96 percent from 32 percent before 1959, and a third of the Cuban population is participating in some sort of schooling, whether it be primary education, technical training, or adult night classes.

ECONOMY

Much separates Cuba from the other Caribbean nations, but one common feature remains: the dependence on exports to the world's industrialized nations. Cuba, in fact, is more dependent on a single export than any other Caribbean state. About 80 percent of the country's export earnings come from sugar, two-thirds of which goes to the Soviet Union and other socialist nations of the Council for Mutual Economic Assistance (COMECON) market.[8] The Soviet Union pays in kind, not in cash, for Cuba's sugar, and the value of goods supplied in 1982 was 3 to 4 times the free-market price.[9] Cuba also supplies the nonsocialist world with an International Sugar Organization quota of 3.1 million tons, the third largest on the free market. As before the revolution, Cuba is the world's largest exporter of sugar. This dependence on sugar caused a severe downturn in Cuba's economic situation in 1982, when sugar prices dropped from 40 cents to only 8 cents a pound. The plummeting sugar prices would have been disastrous if all Cuba's sugar had been sold on the world market, but the guaranteed market and prices offered by the Soviet Union tempered the crisis.

Nickel is Cuba's second-largest export, while tobacco is its third. Cuban nickel reserves constitute approximately 10 percent of the world's known supply, and the island has recently embarked on a major campaign to expand its mining and processing capabilities in this high-revenue-producing industry.[10] Cuba claims that U.S. pressure has caused a steel company in England to withdraw from signing a major nickel purchase contract. Although Cuba has backed away from its ambitious industrialization plans of the 1960s, the country has created the region's best industrial capability for supplying local needs. It produces its own cement, fertilizers, textiles, domestic consumer goods, processed food, and agricultural machinery. The government has also stepped up investment in the fishing industry.

The Cuban revolution had to face the enormous effects of the U.S. economic blockade, which severely damaged Cuba's efforts to develop its economy. All Cuba's equipment and machinery had come from the United States, so it could no longer buy parts to keep cars, tractors, and sugar mills functioning. The embargo drove the country into the socialist market half a world away. The Cuban government is not at all satisfied that only 20 percent of its trade is with Western nations, since it relies on Western trade for foreign exchange. "We use hard currency," said Castro, "to import medicines, food, raw materials for industry and in construction, and spare parts."[11] The leading capitalist trading partners with Cuba are Canada, Japan, and Spain.

A 1982 study by Cuba's central bank estimated that the embargo had cost Cuba over $9 billion in lost trade, over and above the uncalculated hardships caused by its inability to import products from the United States.[12] A report by the U.S. Department of Commerce found that the U.S. embargo "has been and continues to be not only a major, but a crucial impediment to Cuba's efforts at diversifying and expanding its hard currency trade."[13] Another debilitating factor is the country's large military bill, which amounts to about 10 percent of the annual budget. Finance Board President Francisco García Valls described military expenses as being "relatively high because of the threats from North American imperialism."[14]

AGRICULTURE

It was in the rural areas that the revolution first took hold and had the most far-reaching effect. In the 1940s and 1950s, because of the high degree of absentee and foreign land ownership, only about 20 percent of land was cultivated, although 60 percent was tillable.[15] The intensity of land use increased tremendously after the revolution, and the income of peasants similarly improved. By 1963, the government had completed its basic land-reform program, created over 100,000 additional independent landowners, and placed 60 percent of the country's agricultural land in public hands. Despite the dependence on the sugar sector, production of food for local consumption showed a marked improvement: by 1971 rice production had risen 4 times and fruit 3.5 times, and egg production had quadrupled.[16] In prerevolutionary times, all milk was imported, and only 5 percent of Cuban children had milk each day. Cuba now produces two-thirds of its milk consumption and provides each child with a liter of milk a day.

Although Cuba allowed peasant farmers to retain private land, it relied on state farms for most sugarcane production. One immediate benefit was the substantially higher wages received by canecutters and sugar mill employees. The Cuban government had also expected the level of production to increase based on the uniformly higher wages and the array of moral incentives (public commendations and nonmaterial rewards given by coworkers and the government for good spirit at work) offered workers. It found, however, that despite the improved conditions and the input of substantial quantities of volunteer labor from city residents, production remained relatively stagnant. By the early 1970s, the Cuban government concluded that moral incentives alone would not move workers to greater participation and productivity. Rather, without unemployment and the threat of hunger, workers had become complacent and tended toward absenteeism. Workers who were putting in full days and working hard felt cheated because the loafers in the workforce took home the same paycheck and could always count on a job.

Cuba took steps to introduce material incentives in agricultural and industrial production. The government now offers workers prizes of consumer goods or the first choice to acquire cars, vacations, and appliances as rewards for productivity and for other qualities such as leadership and commitment to the "collective good." Some critics have called the introduction of material incentives the "Sovietization" of Cuba's economy, because of the Soviet Union's reliance on material incentives and its wide discrepancies in pay scales. Other observers say that, unlike the Soviet Union, Cuba has effectively integrated its material incentives programs without losing sight of the revolution's objectives. "It is quite likely," noted Cuban authority Arthur MacEwan, "that an unskilled worker on the production line who puts in extra volunteer hours and who is an example and leader for other workers will have an opportunity to purchase the refrigerator before a highly paid but less hard-working technician."[17] Another observer of this process noted, "The Cubans have reorganized their material incentive system, guarded against its inequality-generating tendencies, and continued their heavy reliance on moral incentives."[18]

Another successful change in the pattern of concentrated state ownership has been government encouragement to form private cooperatives. The state owns about 80 percent of the arable land but has been distributing an increasing amount to private cooperatives. Cooperatives in Cuba own over 40 percent and private small farmers close to 60 percent of nonstate agricultural land.[19] "Our revolution should have promoted cooperatives earlier," admitted Castro.[20] The number of farm cooperatives has jumped from 44, covering 6,100 hectares (a hectare is 2.5 acres) in 1977, to more than 1,400 cooperatives owning almost 700,000 hectares in 1982.[21] The government considers the rapid rise of the cooperative movement a triumph in its agricultural reform. Young people, who had shown an inclination to leave private family farms, are moving to the cooperatives in large numbers.

Small farmers and cooperatives play an important role in agriculture, and the government has encouraged production from this sector, which produces 18 percent of the sugarcane, over 80 percent of the tobacco, 60 percent of the noncitrus fruit, and about two-thirds of the spring vegetables.[22] As members of the National Association of Independent Farmers, small farmers work in friendly competition with state-owned farms. They generally support the revolution and benefit from it through their inclusion in free health services, free educational opportunities, and other social security programs.

A widely appreciated sign of the government's expansion of economic freedoms was the appearance, in 1979, of a monthly tabloid called *Opina*, which has a popular classified section that offers services ranging from sauna baths to the repair of venetian blinds. It also features film-star confessions and articles concerning consumer problems. One article about state distribution systems asked, "Why do they keep us waiting? Don't they know that in socialism, too, time means money?" Also evident in Cuba is the surfacing of a small private sector of plumbers, hairdressers, and carpenters, who once worked clandestinely. New supermarkets and department stores now offer a wide variety of food and consumer items. While Cuba has been on an upswing of private consumption, the country faces rough times in the years ahead as its debt crisis worsens and threats from the United States increase. In a 1981 speech to the National People's Government Assembly, Fidel Castro said that Cuba was "sailing in a sea of difficulties."[23]

CUBA AND THE CAPITALISTS

Like other third-world nations, Cuba has fallen into a debt trap. In 1983, Cuba announced that it was not able to meet the interest payments on its accumulated external debt of over $3.2 billion. Unlike other debtor nations, Cuba is not a member of the International Monetary Fund (IMF) or other multilateral organizations. However, Cuba has had to negotiate separate loan-rescheduling pacts with governments and private banks that have made loans to Cuba. Neither the U.S. government nor U.S. banks participated in the rescheduling talks because they have not loaned Cuba money since the imposition of the trade embargo in 1962.

Besides agreeing to a number of austerity measures, Cuba promised its creditors that it would publish regular economic statistics, the lack of which has been a constant sore point between Cuba and foreign banks. Cuba's creditors have generally been pleased by the government's attitude toward its debt and its attempts to improve the country's economic performance, despite the difficulties caused by the falling price of sugar. "We have our foreign debt and we are going to service it," said Castro in October 1983, "because it is a matter of honor and basic consideration towards the banks and financial institutions which had faith in us."[24]

Desperate for foreign exchange, Cuba in 1982 opened its doors to foreign investment with a new law on "economic associations between Cuban and foreign entities." The new investment code allows foreign corporations to establish joint ventures with the Cuban government in selected sectors of the economy like tourism and export manufacturing. Cuba's campaign to attract foreign investment could not have come at a worse time, given the country's external debt position and the hostile attitude of the Reagan administration. At the same time that Cuba announced the investment law, Reagan declared a ban on travel by U.S. citizens to Cuba and on transfers of any U.S. funds to Cuba.

Cuba now allows up to 49 percent foreign ownership of joint ventures, autonomy in hiring, and supplies from overseas sources. Like other Caribbean islands, Cuba advertises its "stable climate." "There's no risk of revolution because that's already been done," said a Cuban government official. "There's no danger of strikes. If the workers are the owners of the factories, it's not likely they will strike themselves."[25] Cuba's low wage rates, which are on the same level as those of Taiwan, Hong Kong, and the Philippines, are also part of the attraction. "The incentives are, by any measure, attractive and are similar in many respects to those offered by developing countries keen on luring foreign investors," commented the conservative U.S. *Journal of Commerce*.[26] Cuba has been hoping to attract foreign capital in such existing operations as an under-utilized pharmaceutical plant outside Havana, an automobile battery factory in Manzanillo, and a factory to make construction materials from sugarcane waste. As of 1982, some 24 foreign companies were registered in Cuba, primarily trading firms but also a few companies with government contracts for last-stage processing of imported materials like textiles.[27]

A year after the investment code took effect not a single foreign investor had taken advantage of the legislation. A survey found, however, that most foreign diplomats thought that the investment scheme held promise. "If Cuba gets its debt problems sorted out and the world economy makes an upturn, then foreign interest in the new law will undoubtedly increase," said one diplomat.[28] Because vacationing in Cuba has become popular among Europeans and Canadians, two transnational corporations, Club Méditerranée and Tower International, have expressed strong interest in investment in Cuba's tourism industry. Partly to handle the increased tourist trade, the government is building a new airport, 3 times larger than the present one. Cuba offers the cheapest Caribbean vacation, featuring some of the region's best beaches and most spectacular nightlife. "Next winter, Cuba will be the country to watch," remarked David Gorman, president of the St. Lucia Hotel Association.[29]

REGIONAL POLITICS

"Revolution cannot be exported," says Castro. "Revolution pertains to an ideology, a way of life, which cannot be exported."[30] While it may not be exporting revolution, Cuba has been quick to aid left-leaning governments in the region and to encourage leftist parties. Its main influence in the Caribbean, however, has not been financial but exemplary. The Cuban revolution in 1959 was a cataclysmic event in the Caribbean, demonstrating the possibility of an alternative path to development for other Caribbean nations.

Caribbean politics have been determined largely by the reaction to the revolution from both the United States and the Caribbean nations themselves. The United States justified its two invasions—in the Dominican Republic in 1965 and Grenada in 1983—on the grounds of forestalling a Cuban-style revolution and removing Cuban influence. Caribbean politicians have often defined themselves by their support or opposition to Castro, and Reagan's Caribbean Basin Initiative program has served to build ties to the United States and keep the Caribbean nations away from the magnetism of the Cuban revolution. Cuba is widely respected throughout the Caribbean for its support of Angola and its solidarity with black Africa. In this region, where race issues are often downplayed, Cuba has taken care to promote Afro-Caribbean cultural and political relations.

Cuba lost an important ally in the Caribbean when Jamaican Prime Minister Michael Manley was replaced by Edward Seaga in 1981. Although Michael Manley was careful to distance the democratic socialism of Jamaica from the revolutionary politics of Cuba, Manley and Castro were friends. During the Manley government, Cuba promoted extensive academic, cultural, and political exchange programs in Jamaica, opened an embassy in Kingston, and began regular airline flights between the two nations. In the view of the U.S. State Department, "Jamaica became a special target for Cuba. . . . Cuba was instrumental in smuggling arms and ammunition into Jamaica."[31] The State Department claimed that "considerable amounts of Jamaican youth received military training in Cuba" during the Manley years, when 1,400 *brigadista* youth were trained in political indoctrination. No proof of the charges was offered, and Cuba denied providing arms or military training to Jamaica. In October 1981, Edward Seaga, Manley's successor, expelled all Cuban diplomats on the excuse that Cuba had failed to return three fugitive Jamaican criminals. The two islands—only 150 miles apart—could not be further apart politically. Seaga's Jamaica allies itself with the United States while Cuba maintains that, being a Latin American and Caribbean nation, its trade and alliances should be mainly with its neighbors. "We are Latin Americans," declared the government in 1973, "and in the future we should integrate ourselves with Latin America."[32]

Two prominent means of Cuban influence in the region are scholarships to study in Cuba and the distribution of Cuban papers and magazines throughout the Caribbean. The pro-U.S. government of Eugenia Charles in Dominica, which claimed that scholarship students are forced to study Marxism-Leninism and to undergo militia training in Cuba, refused to allow Dominican students to accept Cuban scholarships. Cuba denies the allegations, as do scholarship students from other islands. "We offer scholarships," said the Ministry of Foreign Affairs, "in spite of our social and economic problems, to demonstrate our solidarity with other poor third-world countries."[33] In the offices of leftist parties and movements throughout the Caribbean there are usually stacks of the Cuban newspaper *Granma*, which is distributed widely in both English and Spanish. Cuba also helps these opposition groups print their own newsletters and pamphlets by offering mimeograph machines and training.

Cuba has become a leading voice in support of the self-determination of third world nations throughout the world. During the years of chairing the Non-Aligned Movement (from 1979 to 1983), Cuba and Fidel Castro gained increased international stature and respect for principled positions against U.S. imperialism and for solidarity with underdeveloped nations.

Cuban-U.S. Relations

U.S. policy has come full circle from the days of the Bay of Pigs. For a while during the administration of Gerald Ford and in the early days of Jimmy Carter's presidency, Washington softened on Cuba by easing restrictions on U.S. corporations trading with Cuba, by establishing an interest section in Havana, and by dropping the demand that Cuba sever its relations with the Soviet Union as a precondition for normalization.

Succumbing to his more conservative advisers, President Carter slowly toughened his position on Cuba and set the stage for the hard-line attitudes of the Reagan administration. Reagan has made the Caribbean country's commitment of troops to the government of Angola a linchpin in U.S.-Cuban relations. Washington, which supported Angola's antigovernment, right-wing guerrillas, calls Cuba a Soviet puppet and has threatened a military response to any further Cuban military commitment overseas.

The former chief of the U.S. interest section in Havana, Wayne Smith, in 1982 called the Reagan administration's Cuba policy "hackneyed" and "unrealistic," saying the president seemed "determined to make past mistakes all over again."[34] He said that the administration's approach to Cuba "evokes a painful sense of déjà vu." Indeed, the officially propagated belief that Cuba has caused all the ills of the hemisphere has little to do with the reality of Latin American politics and economics. The policy goals of the United States and the stability of the region are certainly not furthered by threatening statements from the administration or politicians like Senator Barry Goldwater, who said that Cuba should become the 51st state.

"Principal U.S. objectives in Cuba," said Smith, "should be to reduce Soviet influence, to moderate Cuban actions abroad, and to encourage a liberalization process in Cuba itself. Clearly, confrontation works against the first and third goals. Castro can neither loosen his relationship with the Soviet Union nor relax discipline at home as long as he fears the appearance of Marine divisions on his beaches." Smith concluded, "It is unrealistic to expect that Cuba could or would sever ties with Moscow. A reduction in Soviet dominance, however, is no less in Cuba's interest than in America's."[35]

In response to U.S. threats and destabilization efforts, Cuba has created a military force that Washington fears. The U.S. State Department reports that Cuba has by far the most formidable and largest military force in the Caribbean Basin with the exception of the United States itself. More than 2 percent of the Cuban population belongs to the active military or to the reserves, compared with an average of less the 0.4 percent in other countries.[36] In 1983, when the United States began a noticeable increase in its military presence in the Caribbean, the Cuban government mobilized the entire country to repel a possible U.S. invasion. Cuba said it would be able to put 6 million of its 10 million inhabitants under arms if the United States attacked the island. According to an article published by the journal *Foreign Policy*, the United States could occupy the island only if the U.S. military stripped every other theater of operations of conventional forces, including Western Europe and the Persian Gulf.[37] The State Department and Pentagon regard highly the discipline and determination of Cuba's military forces and do not underestimate the popular support for the socialist government. "This country may be wiped off the face of the earth," declared Castro, "but it will never be intimidated or forced to surrender."

Washington has continually rejected Cuba's offers to negotiate issues of contention between the two countries. Days before the U.S. invasion of Grenada in October 1983, the Cuban government expressed its anxiety over the tense situation and its willingness to talk with the United States to ensure that no Cuban or American lives would be lost. Washington ignored those pleas as it has ignored other suggestions to negotiate such matters as immigration and the Central American conflict. President Reagan turned down these gestures of negotiation, saying that talking with Cuba would "offer nothing new." In 1983, Castro told reporters that Cuba would stop shipping arms to Nicaragua and sending advisers to Central America if other countries agreed to do the same. "We are perfectly willing to agree to rules of the game, but they must apply to you as well as to us," a senior official told a U.S. representative.[38] "Clearly negotiations with Castro are not part of the administration game plan," said Wayne Smith. "This is unfortunate."[39] The United States has preferred to engage in long-distance debate with Cuba, but the U.S. public gets to hear only Washington's arguments.

Rather than trying to find ways to live peaceably with Cuba, the United States has constantly tried to provoke Cuba and its ally, the Soviet Union. The frequent violation of Cuban airspace cannot be justified by information-gathering, since this is abundantly provided by satellites. A more likely purpose is to test Cuban air defense systems and the state of readiness of its air force. The downing of a U.S. plane by the island's Soviet-supplied antiaircraft missile system would be a bonus for President Reagan's strategy, but Cuban gunners have shown restraint. In 1982, the Reagan administration began to discuss publicly the possibility of a U.S. attack against Cuba, supposedly to prevent Cuban support for Nicaragua and Central American guerrillas. Secretary of State George Schultz referred to the possibility of a "surgical intervention" that would involve punitive air strikes on Cuban airports and oil installations.

The proposed attack was discussed in relation to Cuban threats to jam U.S. radio broadcasts if the United States started beaming propaganda from the planned Radio Martí station in Florida. Cubans found it irritating but also somewhat amusing that the United States planned to name the propaganda station after the Cuban patriot and early anti-imperialist, José Martí. It is not as if Cubans do not have access to U.S. news: moving across the radio dial in Havana, about half the stations are American. The Voice of America, which comes to the island on medium wave, has a wide audience. Of more concern to the Cubans than another radio station are the military training camps in Florida, from which groups such as Alpha 66 claim to be preparing for an invasion of Cuba. Richard

R. Fagen, in an article in *Caribbean Review*, commented on the stability of the Cuban revolution despite all efforts to undermine it.

> Even the most optimistic of Castro's Washington enemies by now must have abandoned the fantasy that the revolutionary government is about to crumble, that there is some diplomatic or economic straw that will break Fidel's back. Despite invasion, subversion, exodus, isolation, mismanagement, adventurism, and a catalog of other misfortunes (some external, some self-inflicted) of Jobian proportions, the Cuban Revolution continues. Additional threats from the imperialists, as U.S. policy-makers should have learned years ago, only strengthen Cuban resolve, only rally support for the government.[40]

The Soviet Union in Cuba

The 1962 Cuban missile crisis brought the world to the brink of nuclear war when the United States imposed a blockade against Cuba until the Soviet Union agreed to remove nuclear warheads and other offensive weapons systems from the island. Premier Nikita Khrushchev originally demanded that the United States remove its nuclear weapons along the Soviet border in Turkey but later rescinded that requirement. In the end, Soviet missiles were removed when the United States agreed not to invade Cuba. The Soviets also promised never to reintroduce the missiles and agreed to United Nations monitoring of Cuba to see that the accords were honored.

Since 1962, there has been no evidence that the Cuban-Soviet military alliance has constituted a direct threat to U.S. national security. The 1962 agreements have been extended twice at the request of the United States to prohibit the construction of Soviet nuclear submarine bases and to prevent a buildup of Soviet ground troops. Foreign policy analysts generally agree that as long as this arrangement remains in force—and the United States constantly checks to see that it is not violated—Cuba presents practically no real military danger to the United States. But the powerful right wing of U.S. politics wants the United States to disavow the agreement under the pretense that the Soviet Union or Cuba has been violating it.

Cuba depends on Soviet trade and economic and military assistance, but in recent years the Soviet's lack of hard currency and its own economic problems have resulted in substantial cutbacks in aid. It is difficult to calculate the extent of Soviet aid, since much of Cuban trade with the Soviet Union is in barter. A NATO (North Atlantic Treaty Organization) report estimated that Cuba received a total of $3 billion from the Soviet Union in 1981, or 60 percent of all Soviet aid to the third world. Most of the Soviet aid to Cuba is economic, not military.[41] NATO estimated a

1981 military aid figure of $54 million for Cuba—less than that received by Ethiopia, Vietnam, North Yemen, Afghanistan, Mozambique, or Angola.

In addition to its military aid, the USSR purchases 72 percent of Cuba's exports and accounts for 60 percent of its imports.[42] In Washington's view, Cuba is a Soviet colony. "A new imperialism has expanded in the East," said the U.S. Defense Department, "and is expanding still, stretching from the center of Europe . . . and the crown colony is the Caribbean, the island of Cuba."[43] The Pentagon claims that the Soviet Union's presence in Cuba includes a 2,600-member military brigade, a major intelligence-collection facility that monitors U.S. communications, and 2,000 advisers that provide technical expertise for sophisticated weapons. Grenada and Jamaica have been the only other Caribbean nations to become Soviet trading partners.

Although the Soviet Union has backed the Cuban revolution from the earliest days, relations between the two nations have not been entirely friendly. Cuba has always adopted more of a nationalist approach to politics than the Soviet Union appreciates. During the first ten years of the revolution, Cuba openly criticized the Soviet Union for, as one commentator put it, "sacrificing proletarian internationalism on the altar of peaceful co-existence." Cuba cited the Soviets' willingness to do business with right-wing regimes in Latin America, their capitalist-type trade relations with the third world, and their inadequate defense of North Vietnam. Along with foreign-policy differences, Cuba adopted an approach to socialism that contrasted strongly with that of the Soviet Union.

While the Soviet Union has used the dependent relationship to pressure Cuba to conform to its policies, its aid has given the Cuban government a great deal more freedom to determine the direction of its economy than most underdeveloped nations. In a 1983 essay entitled "Cuba and the Contemporary World Order," Nita Rous Manitzas noted that the government-to-government nature of Soviet aid has given Cuba's central authorities "considerably more control over national economic development and more effective autonomy than most developing countries now enjoy. Whatever may be the intrinsic motives of the Soviet Union," she wrote, "the structure and the style of their assistance in the Cuban case helped rather than hindered the national trajectory of the revolution."[44]

While Cuba's foreign policy has certainly followed the outlines of Soviet policy, its military involvement in Angola and its support of leftists in Central America cannot be dismissed as surrogate missions of the Soviet Union. Its involvement in Africa dates back to the early days of the revolution and Che Guevara's guerrilla ventures. Likewise, its support of Nicaragua arises from Cuba's own identification with revolution in underdeveloped Latin American nations. Unfortunately, however, many of the principal stands that formerly characterized Cuban foreign policy have been submerged in obeisance to the Soviet Union, notably its approval of Soviet positions regarding Czechoslovakia, Ethiopia, and Afghanistan. Summarizing the foreign policy of Cuba, Rous Manitzas said:

> The essence of Cuba's international behavior over time has been a mixture of ideology and opportunity, of values and realpolitik, of convergence and disjunction with the pulls and pressures of a great-power alliance. The catalytic agent in this complex mix has been rational choice, the ability of Cuba's leadership to perceive the finite perimeters of their space and maneuverability vis-à-vis the international order, and their ability to act accordingly. While the options and consequences may never be optimal, they have not up to now proved fatal.[45]

Dominica

It is important, in Dominica, to know which way the wind blows. Three recent hurricanes have swept through the lush island, pulling off the tops of the coconut trees and flattening the newest crops of bananas. Depending on the way the wind is blowing, pilots will refuse to land at the oceanside Roseau Airport for fear of being blown away from the narrow runway. In Dominica, politics too are a fickle and stormy affair. Candidates are swept in and out of office, opponents of the government languish in jail, and the police are trigger-happy. At first glance, Dominica seems the sleepiest, most peaceful of the Caribbean islands, but it is a country where there is always a controversy stirring, some new storm brewing.

Although the largest in area of the British Windward Islands, Dominica has the smallest population. Its 80,000 citizens are mostly of African descent with a small settlement of Caribs living on the island's Carib Indian Reservation. The virtually undisturbed rain forests are a dreamland for botanists, and the island is a haven for birds and wildlife unknown in any other part of the world. For two centuries, Dominica alternated between French and British control. The troops of both countries faced fierce opposition from the Carib Indians, who attacked guerrilla-style from hidden bases in the thick mountain jungles. Tired of fighting for the small piece of colonial real estate, Great Britain in 1805 paid France for the island. The British pushed the Caribs onto a reservation where they live an isolated life as basket weavers and canoe builders. In 1930, a brief disturbance broke out, now called the Carib War, over the smuggling of tobacco and rum. A British warship, the HMS *Delhi*, landed a troop of Marines, who quelled the rebellion.

REPRESSION BY THE FREEDOM PARTY

Shortly before independence in 1978, the parliament passed the Prohibited and Unlawful Societies Act, commonly known as the anti-Dread law because it banned the Dreads, a Rastafarian-associated group. Six months after the independence celebrations, the island's defense force killed two participants in a demonstration protesting the government's attempts to

284 ·

pass legislation that would further restrict union and press freedoms. The killings fueled popular opposition to the Patrick John administration and eventually led to his ignominious resignation. Moving into the position of chief of state was a Roseau attorney and politician, Eugenia Charles.

Although Charles, the Caribbean's first woman prime minister, refuses political labels, she is an outspoken supporter of private enterprise and the foreign policies of the Reagan administration. "There isn't any capital to be capitalist with," Charles once remarked, "and we're certainly not communist."[1] Before Grenada's revolutionary government collapsed, Dominica's Charles had called for sanctions against the island and had given wholehearted approval of Washington's efforts to create a regional security force excluding Grenada.

When President Reagan announced the invasion of Grenada on international broadcast, Eugenia Charles stood by the podium to demonstrate her complete agreement with his decision. Shortly after her television appearance, the U.S. government granted $10 million in assistance to the Charles administration. Within Dominica, Charles keeps a tight rein on democracy. Her party, the Dominica Freedom Party, sponsored a law called the Anti-Terrorist Act, which gave the country's security forces carte blanche in their exercise of power. Prime Minister Charles attempted to push through a draconian treason law, imposing death by hanging for anyone convicted of "forming an intention to overthrow the government by force of arms" or anyone "who adheres to enemies of the state."[2] In 1982, Amnesty International reported that since Charles assumed office, soldiers had killed 13 persons, more than in the previous 20 years.[3]

As in most Caribbean countries, politics in Dominica is extremely factionalized. Four political parties compete for the small vote, including one nontraditional party called the Dominica Liberation Movement Alliance. A coalition of four leftist groupings, the alliance takes a nationalist, anti-imperialist view of the economy, sympathizes with the Cuban revolution, and opposed the invasion of Grenada. Despite Dominica's small workforce, it has five major unions. Actively involved in the divided trade union sector is the American Institute for Free Labor Development (AIFLD), which has ties with three of the unions.

A BANANA ISLAND

About one-third of all Dominicans live abroad, reflecting what many consider to be a dead-end life in the Caribbean's least developed island nation. The 1981 census recorded the population at a full 6,000 less than had been expected.[4] A major cause of the recent emigration of Dominicans was the visitation since 1979 by several hurricanes, which devastated the island's economy. For two years, neither the treasury nor the Banana Growers Association (BGA) received any income from the banana industry. When international relief money came, it all slipped into the hands of the government managers rather than those of the hard-hit farmers. Demonstrating their persistence and endurance, Dominica's farmers succeeded in producing another crop of bananas shortly after the hurricanes.

One of the first foreign corporations to set up operations in Dominica was United Fruit's Canadian Banana Company. The notorious American banana giant arrived in 1933 but left when the European banana market dried up during World War II. In 1952, Geest Industries acquired a 15-year contract for the island's entire banana crop and today remains the sole purchaser and exporter of Dominica's bananas. The banana industry in 1982 became the center of a raging controversy involving the prime minister, USAID, the country's private sector, Geest Industries, and the Dominica Farmers Union (DFU). USAID offered to assist the ailing industry, but required that loan money be used to pay for U.S. consultants and U.S.-made farm implements, and that the banana industry be turned over to private investors. Washington has concluded that Dominica's problems with the industry stem from the fact that it is in the hands of banana-grower cooperatives and government employees. Therefore, the U.S. government devised a solution that would "privatize" the industry. Without consulting the small farmers, Prime Minister Charles signed the loan agreement with the United States.

"There is no quick fix to a country's development problems," reasons the Dominica Farmers Union, "and more particularly there is no imported quick fix. Failure to learn this lesson has led Prime Minister Charles to sign an agreement with USAID which repackages the old answer of free enterprise and private sector control over the labor of farmers and workers."[5] The DFU agrees with USAID that the management of the growers' association has been inefficient and corrupt but disagrees that the answer lies in turning the industry over to large private investors like the Royal Bank of Canada, Barclays, or Gulf+Western. The union predicts that the USAID project in the banana industry will mean "two years of sun and sand" for U.S. agribusiness technicians while U.S. accountants remedy the industry's cash flow by limiting credit to farmers, controlling loan repayments, cutting prices paid to farmers, and paying farmers in kind with U.S. chemicals.[6]

A large part of the problem, says the DFU, has nothing to do with hurricanes, corrupt officials, or the lack of fertilizers, but involves Geest Industries, which has made millions from the bananas grown by low-paid farmers. Popular opposition has forced USAID to back down at least temporarily from its overall plan to restructure the industry. But there is fear that because the United States has allied itself with the prime minister's office, leaders of the local business community, and foreign banks on the island, the long-term interests of the workers and small banana farmers will be ignored.

Land ownership is skewed in Dominica, with less than 2 percent of the farms occupying over half the land.[7] Beside bananas, coconuts and limes are important products of Dominica's agricultural sector. In 1983, L. Rose, a subsidiary of the British corporation Cadbury Schweppes, sold its century-old business in Dominica to a government joint venture. Because the company allowed the industry to run down, the country's lime workers and farmers constitute one of the most destitute rural sectors in the entire Commonwealth Caribbean. Another major agroindustry in Dominica is the processing of coconuts into oil and soap. Dominica Coconut Products, which produces soap on contract for Lever Brothers and Colgate Palmolive, controls most of the industry. Its millionaire owner, Phillip Nassief, is a member of a Syrian clique of business people who dominate the country's private sector. Nassief, a board member of Caribbean/Central America Action (CCAA) and the Caribbean Association of Industry and Commerce (CAIC), has close connections with U.S. corporate interests and U.S. regional politics.

Dominica exports most of the world's supply of bay oil as well as producing timber and vanilla for export. The U.S. firm International Flavors and Fragrances exports tropical scents and flavors from Dominica. The USAID-financed LAAD corporation has plans to finance a large forestry project and is also considering a coffee processing and packaging facility. Asked to come to the island by USAID and CCAA, Gulf + Western did feasibility studies for investment in the timber industry to manufacture railroad ties and for investment in Dominica's reactivated lime industry.

FOREIGN INVESTMENT

An enthusiastic supporter of President Reagan's push for foreign investment in the Caribbean, Prime Minister Charles has been trotting around the globe in search of investors interested in setting up shop in Dominica. She claims that six assembly plants would change the entire economic and social makeup of the island. Dominica has two industrial parks waiting next to its two airports but has had little luck locating new investors. Several regional corporations, like Neal & Massy, use Dominica as a base to produce clothing for the Caribbean market, and Bata of Canada has a shoe-assembly plant on the island. The advent of factory production of clothing and shoes has meant the ruin of the few tailors, seamstresses, and shoemakers in Dominica. Major British corporations in Dominica are Barclays, Lloyds Bank, Commonwealth Development Corporation, and Cable & Wireless. Other U.S. companies in Dominica are Coca-Cola

288 THE OTHER SIDE OF PARADISE

and Misener Marine Construction, which has a $3 million contract to expand the deep-water harbor outside Roseau. Two Dominican firms produce retread tires under contract for the U.S. and Caribbean markets.

One of the island's leading foreign investors is Ross University, an offshore medical school for U.S. students who were not accepted by mainland universities. Following the invasion of Grenada, Dr. Robert Ross, who heads the medical school that bears his name, wrote a letter congratulating President Reagan and criticizing the administration of St. George's medical school in Grenada for initially claiming that the invasion was not necessary. In a letter to Reagan, Dr. Ross said, "Had the situation happened in Dominica, I certainly would have called on you for assistance." Ross praised Prime Minister Charles, telling Reagan that Dominica enjoys "extremely close ties with the United States and Ross University because of her." Dr. Robert Ross, a millionaire businessman, is not a medical doctor. He holds an honorary degree in humane letters from the Southern College of Optometry in Memphis.[8]

A small and poor country, Dominica is extremely vulnerable to foreign control. The influence of U.S. organizations like the American Bible Society, Carnegie Corporation, Inter-American Foundation, AIFLD, Technoserve, and the Southern Baptist Convention filters through the social and economic life of Dominica. The island has been the target of bizarre plots of mercenaries from the United States and a center of outlandish international deals. While presiding over an interim government, one politician signed a secret deal with a California firm to sell Dominican citizenship and passports to supporters of the Shah who were fleeing Iran.

A previous Dominican government also secretly authorized a Free Port Agreement with a fly-by-night Texas firm that was trying to evade the oil embargo on South Africa by shipping oil from Dominica. Without even consulting the parliament, another Texas firm nearly acquired 12 percent of the island's best land on a 99-year lease to build an industrial zone and airport for an annual rent of $100.[9] Popular protests prevented the implementation of any of the spurious deals. Referring to Dominica, a vice-president of Gulf + Western said that it is a country where private investors can "construct a political system that will maintain a favorable climate for U.S. business."[10]

Dominican Republic

An extremely diverse country, the Dominican Republic, which shares the island of Hispaniola with Haiti, has 20 distinct geographical zones ranging from deserts to rain forests. For centuries a colonial outpost of Spain, the Dominican Republic has a population that is mostly of mixed blood and Spanish-speaking. A state of hostility has existed between the Dominican Republic and its neighbor Haiti since the early part of the 19th century, when the newly independent nation of Haiti took control of the Dominican Republic for 22 years through 1844. Spain once again assumed control of the Dominican Republic in 1861, but withdrew four years later.

The United States became the next foreign power to dominate the Dominican Republic. In the late 1860s, Washington gave serious consideration to annexing the country. In 1904, the United States placed the Dominican Republic under a receivership, whereby the United States would manage the government's revenues until publicly incurred debts to U.S. private companies were repaid. The U.S. Navy occupied the country in 1916, supposedly to forestall a possible invasion by a European power. A U.S. military government ruled the Dominicans for the next eight years and created a Dominican security force to take its place when U.S. soldiers left in 1924. Washington arranged another receivership agreement with the country in 1932 that allowed the United States to administer 55 percent of the country's customs revenues to pay back loans from U.S. companies.

THREE DECADES OF DICTATORSHIP

During the Marine occupation, a former guard at a sugar plantation, Rafael Leónidas Trujillo, became a member of the U.S.-established Dominican Constabulary. After the Marines left, he rose to commander of the constabulary and in 1930 installed himself as president. Trujillo built a totalitarian state complete with torture chambers, population checkpoints, wiretaps, and concentration camps. For 31 years, Trujillo ruled the Dominican Republic as if it were his own estate and killed hundreds of thousands of opponents to the dictatorship. In 1937, his security forces murdered at least 12,000 people, mostly Haitians, in just one night. The terror protected his economic empire, worth as much as $1 billion. Trujillo and his family and friends controlled 60 percent of the nation's economic assets, owned the best lands, most of the sugar industry, cement works, tobacco farms, and shipping concessions. Trujillo, as opposition leader Juan Bosch wrote, had "substituted himself for the entire capitalist class."

Along with his personal advancement, Trujillo granted the United States vast concessions in the country's economy. U.S. presidents embraced Trujillo as a reliable anticommunist and strong supporter of the United States until 1961, when Washington concluded that Trujillo's brutality made him more a liability than a valuable ally. In 1961, a team of assassins, with the alleged backing of the CIA, liquidated Generalissimo Trujillo.

In the country's first free elections in 40 years, the Dominican people elected Juan Bosch in December 1962, but the military removed the populist president only ten months later. In April 1965, a civilian and military coalition in Santo Domingo mounted a popular revolt to restore the constitution and the Bosch government. The Constitutionalists, as they called themselves, were close to victory over the antidemocratic right-wing forces when President Lyndon Johnson ordered the U.S. Marines to the Dominican Republic on the pretext of saving U.S. lives and countering "communist subversion." The U.S. military stayed for over a year until Joaquín Balaguer, a long time associate of Trujillo, was installed as the country's new president. Backed by a flood of U.S. aid, the Balaguer government restored economic and political stability and opened the country to foreign investment. Balaguer retained the presidency until 1978, when power passed to Antonio Guzmán, the leader of the Partido Revolucionario Dominicano (PRD). Salvador Jorge Blanco became president in the elections that followed Guzmán's suicide in 1981.

POLITICS

A civilian government led by one of the two major parties administers the Dominican Republic, although there are frequent rumors of a military coup. The PRD's Jorge Blanco is a firm supporter of business and foreign investment, but has also managed to keep a certain degree of social liberalism in his government. Joaquín Balaguer, who leads the principal opposing party, Partido Reformista, is further to the political right than Jorge Blanco, although both support the United States. Juan Bosch heads the Partido de la Liberación, but he no longer enjoys a strong mass base. Showing potential for the eventual winning over of many Dominicans is the Front of the Dominican Left, a coalition of leftist organizations that advocates a socialist approach to the country's economic woes.

Dominican union leaders complain they live in a fraudulent democracy, pointing out that security forces regularly crush labor confrontations, especially those with foreign-owned firms. Union advocates describe the ruling party's labor policies with the saying, "Civil liberties stop at the door of the factories." In the summer of 1983, the repression spread to include the country's leftists, one hundred of whom were rounded up in a two-week-long haul by the military. Forces also arrested leaders of the Independent Peasant Movement and 30 people from a remote provincial village that had declared a "strike" to demand the building of a local school. The wave of repression resulted from an unsubstantiated report of a guerrilla training school circulated by the Dirección Nacional de Investigaciones, the government's main agency of political intelligence, which has often been accused of being under CIA control.[1]

While the Dominican government has kept up friendly relations with the United States, nowhere in the Caribbean, with the exception of Cuba, does popular resentment against "Yankee imperialism" run so high. Several U.S. invasions, the presence of the CIA, longtime U.S. support for the bloody Trujillo dictatorship, and the economic power of Gulf+Western are all reasons for the anti-American tenor of left-of-center politics in the Dominican Republic. However, the presence of an estimated 800,000 Dominicans in the United States, the Dominicans' affection for baseball and U.S. culture, plus the economic dependence on the United States, all mitigate any overall condemnation of U.S. imperialism.

ECONOMY

One of the most economically diversified Caribbean nations, the Dominican Republic has a large natural-resource base that offers the possibility of progress. Foreign control of all the major sectors, however, has siphoned off the surplus wealth of the country and prevented true economic development. Sugar dominates the country's exports, with other leading exports of coffee, tobacco, nickel, gold, garments, and leather products—all headed for the U.S. market. Predominantly an agricultural economy, half of all Dominicans still live off the land, and agricultural products make up 75 percent of the exports.[2]

From 1969 to 1976, the country experienced significant economic progress that resulted from massive amounts of U.S. aid, large increases in foreign investment, and a boom in sugar prices. Since 1981, however, severe drops in sugar and nickel prices have badly impaired the Domin-

ican economy. The crisis took its toll on the three most important autonomous state agencies—the State Sugar Council, the Dominican Electricity Corporation, and the Dominican State Enterprises—all of which were
close to bankruptcy by 1983. Petroleum imports cost the country about
half its total export income each year.

Like the other Caribbean nations, the Dominican Republic has instituted an austerity program to deal with the flagging economy at the in-
sistence of the International Monetary Fund (IMF). The country began
a three-year IMF program in 1982 that has meant tax increases, wage
cuts, longer working hours, and less foreign exchange available to pay
for imported goods. The IMF and the United States have tried to restructure the economy to concentrate more on export production, but it
was this very reliance on exports that put the Dominican Republic in
such a shaky position when the world market slumped for the nation's
leading exports. In a speech delivered to the American Chamber of
Commerce, however, Bernardo Vega, governor of the Central Bank, said
the aim of the new economic policies was to eliminate what he saw as
the antiexport bias of previous policies. "An 'outward looking' policy instead of an 'inward looking policy' is being promoted," he said. Rather
than encouraging import substitution, Vega said that the government, in
accordance with the desires of the IMF and USAID, will increase its aid
to the "outward looking" sectors of tourism, industrial free zones, mining, and agroindustry.[3]

In January 1984, President Jorge Blanco wrote a letter to President
Reagan in which he warned that if his country was forced to abide by the
IMF's terms for continued aid, "it could undoubtedly provoke social tensions so strong that it could alter the peace and the most important functioning democratic process in the Caribbean." In his response three months
later, Reagan dismissed the warning. Four months after President Blanco's letter, the most serious civil disturbance since 1965 erupted throughout the country. The protests occurred as the government began to im-
plement its second round of IMF-ordered adjustments.

Reacting to the demonstrations, the police and the military killed at
least 55 protesters and arrested over 4,000. Only two weeks earlier, President Reagan had said the Dominican Republic shines like a beacon for
freedom-loving people everywhere. In response to the popular opposition to its policies, the Dominican government closed down two radio
stations and a television station and ordered national police to occupy
union headquarters to prevent meetings that could organize further
demonstrations. The killings and the mass arrests shattered the democratic and peaceful image of the country, and demonstrated how easily
the government would turn again to repression to control popular unrest.

AGRICULTURE

In the Dominican Republic, the world's fourth-largest sugar producer, sugarcane is cut mainly by Haitians. Of the 20,000 canecutters, fewer than 3,000 are Dominicans. During the peak season, they work ten hours a day, six and a half days a week. Many work camps for the canecutters have no sanitary facilities, and the workers live in small, dark rooms furnished only with iron bedframes without mattresses. "In the entire continent, there are no human beings who receive more cruel treatment than the Haitian *braceros* in the Dominican Republic," said Haitian migrant specialist Antonio Veras. Haitian labor also predominates in the coffee industry. Even though the Dominican Republic counts on the hard labor of the Haitian workers to produce two main agricultural exports, Dominicans generally treat the Haitians as less than human beings and call the work they do "slave work."

Sugarcane production provides 40 to 60 percent of the country's export income and employs one out of every ten Dominicans. The Cuban revolution gave the Dominican Republic a big boost because the United States stopped importing sugar from Cuba, which had been its largest supplier. In the last 15 years, the Dominican Republic has provided the United States with most of its imported sugar. Over 85 percent of Dominican sugar goes to the United States. In 1982, Dominican dependence on the U.S. market was shaken when the Reagan administration instituted a system of duties and quotas to reduce the quantities of imported sugar entering the United States. The new sugar policy was designed to take pressure off both U.S. sugar growers and the U.S. government, which has been keeping U.S. sugar prices artificially high. Without the protection of Washington, U.S. sugar prices would drop to the depressed world-market level, and many U.S. sugar producers would likely get out of the business.

The sugar quota and import duties have been disastrous for the Dominican economy. But while the state sugar operations have faced substantial losses, the largest private producer in the country, Gulf+Western, has not fared too badly. Over the last four years it has been quietly boosting its other sugar operations in Florida. The company, in fact, did not even lobby against the imposition of quotas, evidently confident that the Dominican government would not allow its operations there to suffer from restricted access to the U.S. market. In the past, the Dominican government has given Gulf+Western preferential access to the best-paying and guaranteed sugar markets, even at the expense of state-owned operations.[4]

The government manages just over half the Dominican Republic's sugar land, and Gulf+Western and the Vicini family own the bulk of the other half.[5] Gulf + Western operates the country's largest sugar mill at La Romana and produces about a third of the island's sugar. A few months after the landing of U.S. troops in 1965, Charles Bluhdorn of Gulf + Western began purchasing shares of the South Puerto Rico Sugar Company, which was the largest U.S. investment in the Dominican Republic. The company wanted to sell out for a low price because of the chaotic political climate that followed the assassination of Trujillo in 1961. Counting on the ability of the United States to pacify the popular rebellion, Gulf + Western made a large investment in the country's sugar industry. Since 1967, when it bought out the remaining shares of South Puerto Rico Sugar, Gulf + Western has invested over $100 million in a variety of industries and has expanded to become the island's largest landowner, employer, and exporter. In addition to sugar, the company exports meat, citrus, and tobacco. Besides its huge sugar operations in the Dominican Republic, the company produces sugar in Florida, where it depends on temporary workers from Jamaica.

Representatives of the U.S. National Council of Churches learned through fact-finding missions that the company violates decent wage standards for its sugar workers. Most canecutters receive less than $3 a day for cutting one to two tons of cane during the six-month cutting season. Undocumented Haitian cutters receive only about $2 a day. Gulf + Western responds that workers also receive supplementary benefits like housing, which the company builds with its own cement and construction firms. Despite the company's claims to the contrary, the Interfaith Center on Corporate Responsibility (ICCR) concluded in its report on Gulf + Western's operations in the Dominican Republic that it "has not made a significant contribution to the human development of the canecutters."[6] A company spokesperson said, "Give them more money and they'll spend it on a bottle of rum or cock fights. These people are in a state of hopelessness."[7] From the start, the company has tried to suppress all worker organizing in the sugar industry, a campaign that has resulted in the firing of many union organizers and the arrest or death of others.[8] Commenting on this repressive situation, Bishop Juan Felix Pepén of La Romana said in a 1979 ICCR Report entitled "Gulf + Western in the Dominican Republic: An Evaluation," "There is no possibility of free unionization or association, not even for unions of a Christian orientation. The company will not tolerate them. The local authorities seem to submit to company decisions."

Even with Gulf + Western's dominance in the Dominican Republic, other TNCs operate extensively within the country. The tobacco industry is controlled by TNCs, including Philip Morris, BAT Industries (UK), RJ Reynolds, Culbro, and Gulf + Western's former subsidiary Consolidated Cigar. International Paper and Georgia Pacific have interests in the lumber and paper industry, and United Brands produces pineapples and bananas. The Dominican Republic is the center of operations for the Latin American Agribusiness Development (LAAD) corporation, which finances eight projects in the country, including a farm owned by Southland that grows okra for the U.S. market.

MINERALS

Every day the company bus picks up miners from the center of a town called Bonao to take them to the nickel mine owned by Falconbridge of Canada. Farmers in the valley where Bonao is located say that crop productivity has dropped drastically because of pollution from the nearby nickel mine. Only the steady smoke, which rises from the Falcondo mine and fills the valley, can be seen from Bonao.

Opened in 1972, the huge complex is unusual in Latin America: not only is the nickel mined there, but it is also processed and formed into bars of ferronickel ready for use by industry in the United States and Canada. Other mining companies have kept the mining and processing separate to reduce the potential of nationalization. But nationalization is not something that Falcondo worries about, because the company has already established strong bonds with both the U.S. and the Dominican governments. The company structured its financing to lessen the chances of nationalization by funding the operation with loans rather than providing its own capital. Large U.S. insurance and investment firms put up the money for the project, and the U.S. Overseas Private Investment Corporation (OPIC) insured the loans. USAID financed a preinvestment study to determine the feasibility of the project and to gauge the local political climate. Falcondo, a subsidiary of Canadian-based Falconbridge, is also tied to the World Bank, which provided part of the original financing for the mine.

Capital from the United States, rather than Canada, is behind Falconbridge and Falcondo: Superior Oil of Texas owns controlling interest in Falconbridge, and U.S.-owned Armco is the second-largest shareholder of Falcondo after Falconbridge. Although Falcondo has cultivated close relations with the national government, there have been a number of confrontations resulting from the company's failure to pay taxes. In 1975, the government claimed the company was not declaring its profits in order to avoid taxes. Falcondo took three years to answer the government's charges, and the government took three more years to ratify the validity of the tax claim. Responding to the government's repeated complaints that it was not paying enough taxes, Falconbridge insinuated that it might leave the country. But after a couple of very bad years, Falcondo operations picked up in 1983 when oil costs, which account for about 60 percent of its expenses, started dropping, and Falconbridge has toned down its threats to leave.

In Bonao, Falcondo is not well liked. One of the main irritants is a section of Bonao designed by a U.S. firm for the management of the mine. Called Barrio Gringo by the townspeople, it presents a striking contrast to the rest of Bonao. As in a typical U.S. suburb, all the homes have front lawns, carports, and all the "essential" amenities of American life. Social life in Barrio Gringo revolves around a private club with tennis courts, billiards, a movie theater, and an Olympic-size swimming pool. Technically, only salaried employees can enter the club, but it is a regular hangout for many North Americans living in the Dominican Republic. Members of the Peace Corps, for example, often take privileged weekend breaks at the club. Guards patrol the entrance to the exclusive neighborhood and demand that "outsiders" go back to their part of town.

One of the centers of life for Dominicans in Bonao is the miners' union, which, unlike the company, has established a good rapport and identity in the town. A representative of the union, Francisco Canela, complained about the low salaries of the workers and the alliance between the government and the company. "The politics here are in the interest of the foreign investors," said Canela, "making it hard for unions like ours to stand up for the interests of the workers. So 'blando' [pliable] is the government that it will give in to whatever the foreign companies want, and it will call out the military to protect the corporations." A common complaint of the Falcondo miners is that older workers are often fired for fear they may develop obvious cases of silicosis (a lung disease caused by inhalation of silica dust) while still on the job. Concerning this problem of workers' health, Canela said, "The medical clinics here are controlled by the company and they always tell the workers they don't have silicosis, but when they can afford to go to a private doctor it is a different story."[9]

The other major mining venture in the Dominican Republic is a gold mine, which until 1979 was owned and managed by Rosario Mining, a U.S. firm. In an amiable deal, the government, which already owned 46 percent of the mine, bought the balance of the shares for $70 million, considerably above the book value of the mine. The government is still paying American Express back for loans that financed the purchase. Rosario Mining, owned by Amax, continues to provide management and technical services, giving the TNC a great deal of control at the nationalized mine. Near the Haitian border is Alcoa's bauxite mine, the oldest mining venture in the country, temporarily closed because of unprofitable market conditions.

FOREIGN INVESTMENT

Corporations from the United States hold about two-thirds and Canadian corporations about a fourth of the total registered foreign investment. The United Kingdom is the only other foreign nation with a large amount of investment in the Dominican Republic. A study by the Central Bank found that from 1969 to 1978 just 15 foreign corporations accounted for 80 percent of the profits that were repatriated by all 107 registered foreign investors.[10] These corporations, of which ten are U.S. firms, were the following:

United States	Other Foreign
Gulf + Western	Falconbridge
Exxon	Royal Bank of Canada
Texaco	Nestle/Carnation (CODAL)
Citibank	Shell
Rosario	Bank of Nova Scotia
GTE	
Atlantic Richfield	
Colgate-Palmolive	
Wometco	
Philip Morris	

The study found that during this period Rosario had repatriated 179 percent of its registered capital. In 1978, it had repatriated $15 million in profits, without reinvesting any of its profits in the Dominican Republic. The next year when Rosario sold out to the government for $70 million, its registered capital was only $8 million. In the case of Texaco, its subsidiary Texaco Caribbean was able either to reinvest or to repatriate over 8 times the capital that it had initially registered from 1969 to 1978.[11]

In 1978, the government passed Law 861 to reduce the flow of capital out of the country. A study by the Central Bank, however, found that in 1981 foreign corporations took out 31 percent of their registered capital even though the law permitted only 18 percent to leave the country each year. If this rate of 31 percent outflow of profits is maintained, the foreign corporations will have recouped their original investment in little more than four years.

Food processing is one of the most concentrated areas of foreign investment in the Dominican Republic, although local business owners did resist the intrusion of foreign capital. Some of the largest food processors in the world do business in the Dominican Republic, including Beatrice

Foods, Borden, Campbell Soup, Colgate-Palmolive, Nabisco Brands, Dart & Kraft, Gerber Products, HJ Heinz, Stokely-Van Camp, General Mills, United Biscuit's Keebler (UK), Seaboard (Canada), Carnation, and Nestlé (Switzerland). Two TNCs control 100 percent of the flour production; four TNCs hold 95 percent of the bread, pastry, and cookie business; four TNCs control 80 percent of the production of cooking oils and margarine; and four hold 100 percent control of the animal-feed business.[12]

An editorial in *El Nuevo Diario*, a daily newspaper in Santo Domingo, noted: "We import detergents in order to put them in boxes that are also imported and then mark them: 'Manufactured in the Dominican Republic.' The best raw material for the manufacture of detergents is sugarcane. We import all the ingredients to feed animals, to such an extreme that the farm chickens raised in the Dominican Republic may be called 'imported chickens,' since the corn, all the protein, and even the original chickens were imported. The animal feed we use is mixed in the Dominican Republic but the basic grains are imported."[13] To add fuel to the author's fire, the largest poultry farmer in the Dominican Republic is a U.S. business called Agrotech, which has received over $1 million in easy financing from OPIC to expand its business.

Although it does not represent a significant percentage of the actual foreign investment in the Dominican Republic, the activity of U.S. corporations in the country's four industrial free zones is a major aspect of foreign corporate presence. In the free zones, corporations assemble products, mostly garments, for export to U.S. markets. The country's Law 299 grants a 100 percent exemption from Dominican income taxes and duties to foreign companies that set up business in the free zones, which receive a 70 percent subsidy from the government.[14] A study by the U.S. Embassy reported that while the law authorizes tax incentives for only 8 to 15 years, in practice the terms have been routinely extended, and "it is thought that the benefits will continue indefinitely."[15]

More than 25 U.S. firms have garment or shoe assembly plants in the free zones of the Dominican Republic. They include Bestform, Esmark, Gulf + Western, Manhattan Industries, Consolidated Foods, and Interco. At least three U.S. electronics corporations have assembly plants in the country: North American Philips, Becton Dickinson, and Integrated Electronics. Four U.S. companies that manufacture toys—Ideal Toy, Mattel Toys, Milton Bradley, and Quaker Oats (Fisher Price)—use cheap Dominican labor to assemble their dolls and games. Over 80 percent of the approximately 22,000 workers employed in these zones are women who are paid about 65 cents per hour. About a hundred firms (many of which are subcontractors for U.S. companies) located in these free zones produce almost entirely for the U.S. market, and labor organizing is made impossible by joint government-corporate security and repression.

Describing the benefits of the free zones, a government-sponsored report remarked, "Technical training of the workforce and the transmission of an 'industrial discipline' are among the large contributions of the free zones."[16] The government lists the creation of employment as the major reason it is promoting free-zone assembly plants. But the jobs have failed to keep up with the rate of growth of the urban population. In 1970, there were seven jobs in industry for each hundred urban inhabitants, but there were only five jobs per hundred by 1977.[17]

THE IMPERIAL FRONTIER

Dominicans recognize the United States as a kind of shadow government. The three main institutions of this shadow government are the U.S. Embassy, USAID, and the American Chamber of Commerce, which is located in Gulf + Western's Hotel Domingo. Two other powers that the Dominican government must reckon with are the largest private corporations in the country, Falconbridge and Gulf + Western.

The United States has about two-thirds of the registered foreign investment in the Dominican Republic, while the second-largest country in foreign investment is Canada.[18] USAID stated that U.S. investment in the Dominican Republic is as much as 3 times the U.S. foreign investment registered with the country's Central Bank because many of the investments are not registered, and those that are registered include only the book value.[19]

As a result of the extensive U.S. diplomatic and corporate presence, U.S. citizens in the country number more than 20,000. Former president Balaguer said that one of the objectives of his foreign policy was to avoid any confrontation with the United States, a policy that his successors have also carefully followed. "We should not lose sight of the fact," said Balaguer, "that the United States will always have a decisive influence on our economic destiny."[20] Former president Juan Bosch wrote that for the United States, the Dominican Republic and the Caribbean are the "imperial frontier." While the Dominican people acknowledge the preeminent role of the United States in the economy and politics, many object to it. When two U.S. warships stopped in Santo Domingo in 1981, they were greeted with several days of demonstrations during which the police killed a protester. Widespread demonstrations also occurred when Vice-President Bush visited the country the following year. Again in 1983, several protesters were killed by police during protests against visits by U.S. warships.

The American Chamber of Commerce in the Dominican Republic, one of the largest and most powerful chambers in Latin America, represents the interests of the more than 500 firms. The longtime director of the chamber, Wilson Rood, says that even more U.S. investors in the country are involved in small businesses.[21] The chamber successfully lobbied for a more relaxed law on foreign investment by giving notice to the government that U.S. business would start withdrawing from the country if the law was not passed.

Besides being its largest foreign investor, the United States also ranks as the Dominican Republic's largest source of imports and largest purchaser of its exports. More than in any other Caribbean state with the exception of Puerto Rico, U.S.-imported products pervade the local market. While U.S. foreign investment in the country may be as high as $500 million, U.S. corporations count on the Dominican market for about $800 million in annual sales. A U.S.-sponsored survey found that 1,598 U.S. companies export from the United States more than 10,000 products that are sold in the Dominican Republic.[22]

Rather than decreasing its influence as the democratic institutions of the country have developed, the U.S. government has increased its role in the internal affairs of the Dominican Republic. Through USAID, Washington has pressured the Dominican government to adopt policies that benefit U.S. trade and investment in the country. In 1982, the United States loaned the country $41 million to cover the balance of payments on U.S. goods and services imported by the Dominican private sector. The USAID mission required that the Central Bank match the U.S. loan with $41 million in Dominican pesos to finance programs jointly monitored by the U.S. and Dominican governments. This $41 million in counterpart funding will go to three areas: (1) four financing facilities within the Central Bank to provide credit and technical assistance to aid private-sector development, (2) private voluntary organizations that increase private-sector participation in development, and (3) infrastructure projects that are necessary for the expansion of private-sector activities. Always included within USAID's definition of private sector are the operations of U.S. corporations, which will be the main beneficiaries of both the balance-of-payments support program and the counterpart funding provided by the Dominican government.

Not only does the United States determine how its loan money is spent, but it also uses the loans as leverage to change government policies. The Dominican Republic USAID Mission specified in its balance-of-payments support agreement in 1983 that members of the mission would meet regularly with top government officials to discuss national economic issues, and that USAID would have access to government financial information. Furthermore, the mission noted that the loan agreement and continuing support of the Dominican government were dependent on the favorable outcome of the government's negotiations with the IMF over the institution of an austerity program. USAID has pressured the government to cut back the few government social-service programs and to drop tariffs that protect local industries from competition from foreign goods.

GULF + WESTERN'S EMPIRE

La Romana, an area in the southeastern part of the island, is the domain of the U.S. conglomerate Gulf + Western. All good comes from Gulf + Western in La Romana: the baseball stadium, new roads, schools, health programs, the tax revenue, the fire station, and most paychecks. That is the side the company likes to portray, but there is another side that does not come out in company press releases and annual reports. It is the story of broken unions, starving peasants, and economic power. "Gulf + Western Americas Corporation has become a model for American companies in Latin America," says Gulf + Western about its giant subsidiary in the Dominican Republic. Certainly no example better illustrates a U.S. corporation taking advantage of cheap labor and resources and the pliable government of a Caribbean country. "Our experience has shown," said a company spokesperson, "that free enterprise can work for the benefit of the developing world."23

Ranking as the 61st-largest corporation in the United States, Gulf + Western is the prototype of a modern conglomerate. Corporate wizard Charles Bluhdorn founded the company in 1958 through a merger of two other corporations with the money he made playing the commodities market. Bluhdorn pushed Gulf + Western to become a major corporation by high-powered trading techniques. The eccentric executive died in a plane crash in 1983 while returning to New York from the Dominican Republic.

In 1983 the *Mergers and Acquisitions* Journal rated Gulf + Western as the second most active acquirer among TNCs. Making a lavish show of the corporation's good fortunes, Bluhdorn paid *Time* magazine $3.5 million to reproduce the company's entire 20th anniversary annual report. When comedian Mel Brooks made the film *Silent Movie*, he depicted a company called Engulf Devour, whose greedy, power-mad executives bought anything and everything just for the sheer pleasure of ownership. His model was Gulf + Western, a company that bought more than 100 other firms in its first 20 years.24 Bluhdorn's death has brought changes to the conglomerate; his successor, Martin Davis, said he is not inclined to wheel and deal in the famous Bluhdorn style. Most assets in the Dominican Republic, however, will stay firmly in the hands of Gulf + Western.

Among its subsidiary corporations are Simon & Schuster, Madison Square Gardens, Paramount Pictures, New York Knickerbockers, Simmons, Kayser Roth, New Jersey Zinc, and Associates First Capital. Affiliated with the company are JP Stevens, Amfac, and Central Soya. Also part of the corporate family are the Miss Universe and Miss USA beauty pageants. Although a major cement and zinc producer, Gulf + Western is predominantly consumer-oriented. Besides its extensive interests in the Dominican Republic, the corporation has major investments in Puerto Rico (where it employs 3,500), Paraguay, Bolivia, and Thailand.

The people of La Romana live in a company town, where Gulf + Western has a hand in almost everything they do. Employees tell how the company immediately crushed their union in 1967, and ever since has harassed and fired all union leaders that have stood up for the workers. Seventy percent of Gulf + Western's workers at La Romana are unorganized, but even those who belong to the union do not have much recourse to protest wages and conditions because the union lacks militant leadership. For the many people of La Romana who live near the sugar mill, Gulf + Western means the giant stacks that continually belch out a heavy black smoke that covers their homes and fills their lungs with soot. Besides its sugar business, the company has a major role in the tourism, construction, cement, finance, cattle, real estate, and food-processing industries of the Dominican Republic.

Gulf + Western has specialized in creating tourist enclaves removed from the everyday life of the country. About ten miles up the coast from La Romana is the company's exclusive tourist resort of 7,000 beachside acres called Casa de Campo. Maids dressed in "Aunt Jemima" plantation-style outfits of polka-dot dresses and sandals clean rooms and wait on the thousands of wealthy U.S. vacationers who come every year to this luxury enclave. Casa de Campo has its own private jet strip with its own customs and immigration facilities. Guests enjoy two 18-hole championship golf courses, a polo club, and five swimming pools. Nearby, another favorite tourist spot owned by the company is Altos de Chavon, a recreated 16th-century colonial village that features art galleries, shops, and restaurants. According to the company, the village is the "living expression of the cultural and historical values of the Dominican people." Two Gulf + Western subsidiaries, Costasur Dominicana and Corporación de Hoteles, manage the company's tourist industry, which employs 3,000 Dominicans. Besides Casa de Campo, Gulf + Western owns four large hotels, two of which it bought from local owners.

The corporation also offers packaged trips through its subsidiary Camino Tours, and backs a tourist bureau called the Dominican Tourist Information Center, which has offices in Munich, New York, Caracas, and Santo Domingo. A tourist can sign up for a Dominican vacation in New York and pay for the food, hotel, entertainment, and even golf fees before ever getting to the Dominican Republic. The company's own jetport and ground transportation service ensures the tourist's isolation from Dominican life. This monopoly over tourist services means that the flow of in-

come to the Dominican economy is minimal. In the Dominican Republic, Gulf+Western regularly sponsors the Miss Turismo beauty pageant.
The use of the National Theater by Gulf+Western for the 1977 Miss
Universe contest, however, sparked national protests. In the type of co-
incidence that is common in the Dominican Republic, the brother of the
chairperson of Gulf+Western Americas Corporation at one time served
as the country's director of tourism.

More than 9,000 people from La Romana work in a huge industrial
park outside town operated by Gulf+Western under a 30-year tax-free
contract from the government. Rows of factory shells fill the zone, which
is surrounded by barbed wire and guarded at its one entrance by the
company security force. The company claims that its "single benefit in
establishing the free zone has been the sense of achievement in helping
to create much needed jobs for the Dominican people." While the zone
has created employment in the Dominican Republic, some question remains about the quality of that employment and of the motives of the
company. The new employment created by the La Romana industrial
free zone has been the result of the loss of employment elsewhere, as in
Puerto Rico, which lost 1,600 jobs when the assembly plants moved to
Gulf+Western's free zone in the Dominican Republic.[25] The retention
of these jobs in the Dominican Republic depends on low wages and lack
of unionization. About a quarter of the 24 companies operating within
the zone are Gulf+Western subsidiaries, which employ more than a third
of the workforce.[26] The Interfaith Center on Corporate Responsibility
(ICCR) concluded after a lengthy study that the company created the
zone "for its own labor-intensive subsidiaries to operate at low costs and
high profits."[27] In addition to direct benefits to its own manufacturing
firms such as Kayser Roth, Gulf+Western has benefited by contracting
with its own cement and construction subsidiaries to build the zone and
the housing for the workers.

The company's harsh labor policies cause a steady turnover of workers
in the free zone. Firms operating in the zone have been known to fire
pregnant workers. At Romana Athletic Industries, for example, the management laid off six pregnant workers in a little over two weeks in 1978.[28]
Another common practice, according to an ICCR report, is that of firing
workers before completion of their probation period, during which the
workers receive less than the minimum wage. The cycle is repeated over
and over again as those employees are replaced by other probationary
workers. Most factories in La Romana allow groups of unemployed people
to cluster around the doors of the assembly plants as "a reminder to those
inside how easy it is to get replaced."[29] In one celebrated case reported
by ABC-TV, Gulf+Western fired a woman for giving a flower to a politician opposing the company-supported candidate in the national election.
In a report on the conditions for worker organizing at La Romana, the

AFL-CIO concluded that the corporations operating in the free zone "invent their own laws" and "do not permit the workers to organize."[30]

In addition to Gulf+Western's sugar business, it operates Farmers Produce, which the company claims is producing food for local consumption. While the subsidiary does produce a limited quantity of vegetables from its farm, it produces mainly citrus and tobacco for export. It exports lime juice and oil from its 100,000 lime trees to the L. Rose Division of Cadbury Schweppes (UK). In addition, the company has the island's largest cattle operation, which includes a herd of 50,000.

Each year, the Dominican Republic has to import more wheat, corn, beans, and edible oil from the United States. Many Dominicans, especially the local farmers, feel that much of the land Gulf+Western uses for cattle, tobacco, lime trees, and sugarcane would be better used to grow food that the country now has to import. A recent study by the Organization of American States found that sugarcane occupies more than half the country's better agricultural land.[31] In the Dominican Republic, 75 percent of the farmers hold less than 15 percent of the land.[32] Gulf+Western, which owns about 8 percent of the country's arable land, is a major reason for the highly skewed land distribution in the Dominican Republic. Speaking of this pattern of land distribution, Bishop Roque Adames of Santiago said that as a consequence "seventy percent of the country's peasant population live on the border of starvation and misery."[33] Standing in the way of any movement to change the pattern of land ownership, to reverse the direction of agricultural production, to raise wages, or to encourage unions is the conglomerate Gulf+Western.

Soon after the Dominican Republic was shaken by massive popular uprisings and protests against the government's new arrangements with the IMF in the spring of 1984, Gulf+Western shocked the nation with the news that it was selling its sugar holdings and hotel business on the grounds that "sugar no longer fits with the company's long-term strategic plan to concentrate principally on higher-return, consumer-oriented products." Undoubtedly, the falling price of sugar influenced the company's move. Former Dominican president Joaquin Balaguer called Gulf+Western's decision "the coup de grace for foreign investment in the Caribbean."

Grenada

A visitor to Grenada gets an immediate tour of the country while driving from Pearls Airport located on the far side of the lush island. It is a 50-minute drive along a narrow, circuitous road which crosses the island's hilly interior and leads to St. George's, Grenada's major town. Grenada astounds visitors with its natural beauty. The island boasts lush jungle-covered mountains, sparkling waterfalls, an abundance of flowers, and exquisite beaches. Coming out of the mountains, the taxi driver will stop on the road overlooking the city, letting a first-time visitor to Grenada confirm that the tour books are right when they rate St. George's the Caribbean's most picturesque port city. Rows of two-story wooden homes rise on terraces on either side of the calm harbor. On Tuesdays, the Geest Industries banana ship loads up at the port, and twice a week a cruise liner unloads its passengers to shop and dine in St. George's. Down along the Carenage (harbor front), small cargo boats conduct business in the city and rowboat owners ask tourists if they need a ride to the other side of the harbor.

The cafes along the Carenage are gathering places where people discuss politics and business over glasses of flavorful sea moss and spicy Creole dishes. From 1979 to 1983, the talk in the waterfront cafes often revolved around the progress, problems, and future of the "people's revolution." Social activists from all parts of the English-speaking Caribbean traveled to the island to see if the Grenadian model of revolution was relevant to their own countries. Leftists from Canada, Great Britain, and the United States came to Grenada on "solidarity tours" to witness the revolutionary experiment. After October 1983, however, the cafes along the harbor had a new clientele: U.S. Army Intelligence specialists, USAID officials, Caribbean police, American soldiers, and representatives of the World Bank. Instead of talk about the virtues of socialism and state social programs, conversations turned to the virtues of private enterprise.

DICTATORSHIP TO REVOLUTION

The overthrow of the Eric Gairy dictatorship in 1979 radically changed the course of Grenada. Until then, the history of Grenada followed the general course of the rest of the Antilles. For the first hundred colonial years, Great Britain and France played a tug-of-war over Grenada, but they faced unusually strong opposition from the native Caribs. Rather than finally surrender to the French, 40 Carib warriors jumped to their deaths off a shoreside cliff now known as Caribs Leap. In the 1700s, the French surrendered Grenada to the British, who increased the repression of the slaves on the sugar plantations. Because of the island's mountainous terrain, sugar plantations never achieved the production levels of the other Caribbean islands, however, and the tree crops of nutmeg and cocoa took a firmer hold in Grenada's economy. Because the tree crop agriculture was not labor-intensive, landowners regularly shipped their slaves to cut cane for plantations on other islands.

It was not until 1950 that union organizing among agricultural workers started to challenge the colonial structure of power. Leading the movement was Eric Gairy, who later gained political power and directed the independence fight against the colonial rulers. A populist leader, Gairy attracted support because he was the first to confront the large landowners and colonial politicians. Gairy played on his popularity as a labor organizer to win political office in the 1960s. Once in power, he broke the momentum of the union movement and soon established a dictatorship. Repression, sexual exploitation, patronage, corruption, and his personal eccentricities characterized his regime. Gairy created a goon squad called the Mongoose Gang to do his dirty work along with his army, known as the Green Beasts. Gairy believed he ruled by divine mandate. "I feel my assignment is a divine one," he once said, "and I feel that the Master himself is keeping me here and will remove me when he wants me to be removed."[1]

In the early 1970s, two opposition groups formed the New Joint Endeavor for Welfare, Education, and Liberation, commonly called the New Jewel Movement. Besides opposing Gairy, the leaders of the organization espoused anti-imperialist politics and advocated grass-roots democracy, economic self-reliance, and agricultural cooperatives. The Mongoose Gang frequently harassed members of the New Jewel Movement as the main threat to the Gairy dictatorship. In 1973, the goon squad arrested six members (including the late Maurice Bishop), and then beat them and shaved their heads with broken glass. Independence from Great Britain in 1974 meant little to the people of Grenada, who had grown to detest Gairy as much as the appointed rulers from Westminster.

In 1979, while Prime Minister Gairy was away from the island attending a conference on UFOs, the New Jewel Movement thwarted a Mongoose Gang plot to murder their leaders. Rather than let themselves be Gairy's victims, Bishop and the others in the New Jewel Movement seized power in an almost bloodless coup. On the morning Bishop announced the ouster of the Gairy government, thousands of Grenadians went out to the streets to celebrate the end of the dictatorship and the beginning of a new era. The Central Committee of the New Jewel Movement formed the People's Revolutionary Government (PRG) and appointed Maurice Bishop to be the country's new prime minister. Bishop knew he could count on the widespread support of Grenadians, but the new government faced a country in shambles. Political corruption under Gairy had eaten away at the economy, social services were nonexistent, and 50 percent of the workers were unemployed. Remittances from relatives living overseas and a thriving tourist business had barely kept the economy afloat.

YEARS OF REVOLUTION

After it rid the country of its dictator, the New Jewel Movement received the immediate and enthusiastic support of the Grenadian people. Government social programs and attempts to integrate the people into economic and political decision-making deepened that support. Older citizens observed that the "boys are doing a good job," while many young people became directly involved in the militia, youth programs, and educational outreach programs. Not all Grenadians, however, stood behind the revolutionary government of Maurice Bishop. Some, who had initially supported the overthrow of the detested Gairy, felt threatened by the turn toward socialism and were critical of the anti-U.S. tenor of the politics of the New Jewel Movement. Others were bothered by the increasing militarization and politicization of all sectors of Grenadian society. Many among the upper and middle classes worried that the government would eventually threaten their own property and businesses. Despite some grumbling about different policies or practices of the PRG, the majority of Grenadians backed the New Jewel Movement for its economic reforms, its concern for the poor, and its efforts to involve the people in mass organizations and parish councils.

Encouraged by the government to form and join unions, over 80 percent of Grenada's workers became members of labor unions during the Bishop years. The revolution also brought public health care, free secondary education, and free milk for children. New laws particularly transformed the lives of Grenadian women, who under Gairy frequently had to sell their bodies to make a living. Legislation required equal pay for equal work, two months' paid maternity leave, promotion of nontraditional work for women, prohibition of stereotyping of women, and harsh punishment in cases of rape and wife battering.

During the four years of the revolution, Grenada was the target of international and regional criticism for its failure to install a system of representative democracy and elections. Responding to this criticism, the PRG said it was trying to create a participatory democracy in Grenada, not a "five-second, Westminster style" democracy. Prime Minister Bishop charged that traditional parliamentary government divides people rather than unites them. In 1983, the government appointed a five-person commission to draft a new constitution that would institute a form of representative democracy. The constitution was to have been subject to a plebiscite, and elections would have followed in two years.

ECONOMY

At a time when the economic situation in the Caribbean had deteriorated, the economy of Grenada under the PRG government made impressive strides forward. While the rest of the region suffered from growth rates of one percent in 1982, Grenada enjoyed a 5.5 percent increase. Government strategies resulted in decreased food imports, increased exports of nontraditional crops, and rising economic activity. Living standards for Grenadians were improving, while the unemployment rate had dropped. A 1983 World Bank report praised Grenada as one of the few underdeveloped nations to advance economically. It heartily approved of the revolutionary government's program to stimulate growth in both the public and private sectors, maintain sound public finances, and promote agriculture and tourism.[2]

Agriculture constitutes 95 percent of the country's export sector. Its bananas go to Geest Industries, and much of its cocoa harvest is exported to World's Finest Chocolates and other U.S. companies. Its famous nutmeg crop goes chiefly to Holland, where it is processed. To deal with declining prices and shrinking markets for its main export, the Bishop government instituted a three-pronged strategy to revive the country's agricultural sector: a search for alternative markets, the processing of local produce, and the export of nontraditional products. Canada, in spite of U.S. pressure to halt aid to Grenada, had pitched in money to rehabilitate cocoa production and to start a fish-processing plant. The fishing industry holds promise, since the waters of Grenadian dependents Carriacou and Petit Martinique contain some of the richest fishing areas in the Caribbean. Because most fertile land in Grenada had been allocated before the revolution for export-crop production, there was never much local food production in Grenada. Food imports constituted about 40 percent of the annual import bill.[3] Seventy percent of the calories consumed on the island came from imported food.[4] The Bishop government, through an import-control program, had started to reduce costly food imports and encourage more food production and processing for the local market.

THE PRIVATE SECTOR

Even though the economy was improving, the Grenadian business community felt uneasy about the PRG's socialist orientation. Under Bishop, the private sector lost most of the political power it had wielded previously, but it did continue to play an important part in the country's economy. The government emphasized that it wanted a mixed economy with elements of public, cooperative, and private ownership. From 1979 to 1983, the government expanded state ownership in the financial, utility, trade, and tourism sectors. The government nationalized two banks and the electric company in agreements that were satisfactory to their British and Canadian owners. The increase in state participation in the economy came mainly from the start-up of new industries, such as a jam and juice factory.

Although only a few large foreign investors operate in Grenada, those TNCs have been the main influence on the island's economy. Geest Industries, which buys the island's entire banana crop, is the most prominent TNC in Grenada. Barclays and the Bank of Nova Scotia are the island's leading banks, while two other foreign banks, Royal Bank of Canada and Canadian Imperial, decided to sell out to the government during the Bishop administration. Another British firm, Cable & Wireless, owns the communications company. The investors from the United States include the St. George's University Medical School, Continental Grain (which has a joint venture in a feed and flour mill), and several individuals who own a marina and a couple of hotels and restaurants.

In 1983, the PRG passed a new investment code that encouraged additional foreign investment by offering attractive tax exemptions and free trade zone provisions for light manufacturing. Unlike other Caribbean nations, Grenada under Bishop prohibited foreign investment in public utilities, media, transportation, and restaurants that were not part of hotels. The investment code also stipulated that foreign investment must transfer foreign capital to the country, use local raw materials when possible, and positively affect the country's standard of living. The government proposed to insure the investors' interests with regard to takeovers, disputes, industrial unrest, and losses arising from acts of the government.

Not wanting to disrupt the economy, the People's Revolutionary Government took care to consult the local business community about government decisions affecting the economy. In 1982, the private sector enjoyed a 10 percent rate of growth, higher than the public sector and substantially higher than the private sectors in other Caribbean nations. The World Bank report on Grenada noted that the Bishop government "sought to encourage private sector confidence in a number of ways."

While many might have been unhappy about the political direction of the government, the upswing in business during the first four years of New Jewel leadership kept the private sector relatively content.

The PRG was interested in expanding the tourism industry, but it insisted on controlling the direction of its development. It specified that investment in the tourism industry "must provide an effective stimulus for agriculture and agro-industrial production. Local produce must replace imported foodstuffs in our restaurants. Tourism should provide an incentive to our local arts and crafts industries, and tourism must provide an outlet for indigenous cultural expressions and other art forms of our people."[5] The government prohibited high-rise hotels, private ownership of beachfront properties, and tourist enclaves. Instead it encouraged cottage developments more integrated with the local service economy. Although the PRG showed its intentions to aid the tourism industry, as in the construction of the new airport, many hotel owners and shopkeepers blamed the government for the sharp reduction of U.S. tourists to the island.

THE AIRPORT CONTROVERSY

If one issue united Grenadians, it was the need for a new airport. In 1980 the government began the construction of a new airport at Point Salines as its leading public works development project. The airstrip at Pearls has the distinction of being one of the region's few remaining airstrips built during colonial days that is still being used as a main airport. It can only handle small planes, has no night-landing facilities, and is regarded as dangerous because of its location in a narrow clearing among the Grenadian hills. International agencies, including the World Bank, had recognized as early as the 1970s the island's need for a new airport to make Grenada competitive in the Caribbean tourism industry and to facilitate communications and commerce.

Cuban involvement in the airport's construction was no secret in Grenada. Even to those who complained about other government programs, the airport project was a national status symbol and source of pride. Taxicab drivers asked tourists if they wanted to visit the construction site of "our airport." Tourists could wander anywhere they wanted around the construction site and freely talk to the busy Cuban workers. Cuba was not the only country that assisted Grenada with its new airport—Venezuela, Canada, Mexico, France, and the European Economic Community also contributed aid. Several foreign private contractors, including one British firm and two U.S. construction companies, were working on the airport construction and engineering. Before the invasion, U.S. medical-school students at St. George's University, which is located next to the landing strip, used to joke about the purported existence of "clandestine military installations" around the airport construction site that they saw every day.

During the years of the Bishop government, Washington charged that the airport was part of an international communist conspiracy. President Reagan, in a March 1983 speech to the National Association of Manufacturers, asserted that Grenada "is building now, or is having built for it, a naval base, a superior air base, storage bases and facilities for the storage of ammunitions, barracks, and training grounds for the military." According to Reagan, Grenada had become the "virtual surrogate" of Cuba, and its new airport was being constructed with Cuban aid to enhance the flexibility of the Cuban air force. Prime Minister Bishop called the Reagan statements "a pack of lies." "He is stating to the American public," said Bishop, "that Grenada is a threat to the national security of the United States . . . and that it has naval bases, and other sophisticated military installations. Grenada is so tiny, with villages and houses in every nook and cranny that it is not possible to hide anything for more than a few minutes."[6] The late prime minister said that he gave the United States endless assurances that the airport would not be used for Cuban and Soviet aircraft.

As it turned out, the airport was not used for Cuban or Soviet planes but to land the U.S. invasion force. Washington, even after the invasion, could not produce any conclusive evidence to back its claims. Plessey Electronic Systems, the British company that had been in charge of the overall management of the airport construction, said shortly after the invasion that the airport lacked at least a dozen facilities for military use, including radar, fortified shelters for weapons and fuel, and antiaircraft defenses. Plessey offered to continue the management of the project.[7] Underscoring the need for the airport, President Reagan in March, 1984 sent personal assurances to acting head of the island Sir Scoon, that the U.S. government would help complete its construction. Commenting on the need for a new airport in Grenada, John Menz, a former UN worker in Grenada, said, "It's a real bottleneck for the tourist industry. . . . It still takes two days to reach Grenada from the United States, if you don't have the U.S. Navy and Air Force to help you."[8]

THE YANKEES ARE COMING

Grenada in 1983 was a country pervaded by fear. Grenadians heard President Reagan on radio tell the American people that their island was a security threat to the United States. Alarmed by Reagan's bellicose rhetoric, the leaders of the New Jewel Movement called for all Grenadians to join the volunteer militia so they could ward off an attack on their government by U.S. troops. "No Yankee invasion will stop this revolution" was the popular rhythmic chant that supporters of the Bishop government danced to during the mobilization rallies. Guns and the military became an increasing part of Grenadian life in the months before the invasion, which Maurice Bishop said was "imminent."

Bishop and the other members of the New Jewel Movement knew that since 1979 Washington had been considering ways to undermine and destroy the revolutionary government. A series of military and naval war games in the Caribbean confirmed their worst suspicions. One massive exercise called Ocean Venture '81 featured a mock invasion of an Eastern Caribbean island dubbed "Amber and the Amberdines"—widely understood as referring to Grenada and its two dependencies, the Grenadines. In the Pentagon's fictional war-game scenario, Amber was to "seize American hostages," after which U.S. forces would invade the island and set up a government friendly to the United States. The invasion, rehearsed in detail by U.S. Army Rangers on the Puerto Rican island of Vieques, included the actual removal of Americans stationed at the U.S. base in Guantánamo, Cuba, as part of the rescue scenario.[9]

A sense of unreality touched all aspects of life in Grenada. Despite Reagan's belligerence, Grenadians still asked themselves, "Would the U.S. Marines really invade such a tiny nation as ours?" Indeed, it was hard to imagine amphibious landings in front of the Holiday Inn on Grand Anse Beach. It did not seem possible that Washington would risk the international criticism that would result from bullying such a speck of a country. Fear often turned to paranoia. Grenadian youth would occasionally shout at picture-snapping tourists, "CIA out of Grenada." And the leaders of the New Jewel Movement never knew whether to blame economic misfortunes and assorted mishaps on their own failures or on CIA destabilization efforts.

Grenada mobilized to protect itself from a likely Yankee invasion by organizing volunteer militias and increased military strength. But no matter how many people mobilized, no matter how much they trained, there existed the underlying realization that Grenada could never stand up to the might of the United States. What Grenadians had wanted in their revolution were better schools, jobs, health care, the right to organize unions, and a new airport. Within a few years of the New Jewel Movement's taking power, however, the residents of the Spice Isle found that Grenada had suddenly become a hot spot of a new Cold War. In retrospect, neither the people nor their leaders were prepared to handle that kind of pressure.

PARTY BLOODLETTING

The weaknesses of the politics of vanguard parties and democratic centralism became abundantly clear when the New Jewel Movement and the Grenadian revolution came tumbling down in October 1983. During their four years in political power, Maurice Bishop and the New Jewel Movement had earned international respect for their determination to stand up to the Reagan administration and to carry out the experiment in socialism despite constant criticism from their neighbors. "Forward ever, backward never" was the catchy slogan of the party, which called the Grenadian revolution "the Revo."

One had only to observe the spirit of the New Jewel Movement's political rallies to know that the party had successfully touched the popular spirit. Many thousands of Grenadians would march through St. George's, making their own music and singing and dancing to revolutionary calypso. There were also easily detectable strains of cynicism from those who had long ago decided to distrust all politicians and from others who chafed at the abundant party rhetoric. But even the Grenadians who refused to participate in the revolution often expressed appreciation that the new government was improving social services and putting people to work. Maurice Bishop, a member of a leading Grenadian family, was at the center of the Revo. For many, Bishop was both the hero of the revolution and its heart.

There was little warning that something was "rotten" in high places. Party decisions had been unanimous, and to the people of Grenada, the press, and other nations the New Jewel Movement appeared to be a unified team. But personalities and politics collided, as they often do. Minister of Finance Bernard Coard thought that Maurice Bishop was becoming too powerful and popular as an individual figure and that he was drifting away from Marxism-Leninism and toward social-democratic politics. He feared that Bishop would eventually discard the party and rely instead on popular support and elections to guarantee his power. Coard also feared that Bishop might bow to international criticism about Grenada's brand of socialism and the lack of elections and in the process unwittingly allow the country to be destabilized. Several months before the military coup, Coard said he could "no longer work with the group under Bishop's leadership because it was not up to the task of building a true Marxist-Leninist party."[10]

The majority of the Central Committee agreed with Coard that Bishop was becoming too powerful as an individual instead of acting as a representative of the party. From the beginning of the revolution, two groups tended toward two distinct models of decision-making: popular democracy based on mass organizations and the democratic centralism of the party. The Central Committee insisted that Bishop submit to "collective leadership" and share power more fully with the Coard faction. While there was conflict in these two models, never had there been substantial disagreement about the goals of the revolution, which included a mixed economy, the priority of the needs of the poor, and a progressive foreign policy. Describing the conflict within the New Jewel Movement, Tim Hector, a friend of Bishop and the leader of the Antigua Caribbean Liberation Movement, said: "The essence of the dispute between Bishop and Coard turned on the question of whether, as in Bishop's view, the mass organization of workers, students, farmers, women, and youth would be the centers of power, or whether, as in Coard's view, the Party and its Central Committee would be the center of power."[11]

The Grenadian people were not informed of the division in the ruling party until it was too late. The party thought it better that Coard and Bishop work out the leadership differences without alarming the people. Finally, in early October, Bishop decided to defy the party and to discuss openly the party's desire to reduce his power. By that time Bishop apparently felt that Coard did not want to share power but rather to usurp the leadership of the revolution. Prime Minister Bishop told his followers that he feared a coup and a possible assassination attempt by Coard's faction. The Central Committee soon placed Bishop under house arrest, an action that caused an island-wide demonstration of support for Bishop. The Coard group formed the Revolutionary Military Council, headed by General Hudson Austin, to assume control of the government and the military. Fearing an armed rebellion in support of Bishop, the military council seized the arms of the volunteer militias.

On October 19, a crowd of unarmed supporters of Bishop released him from house arrest and then marched to Fort Rupert. Soldiers at the fort fired on the crowd and subsequently executed Bishop and several other leading members of the New Jewel Movement. The last words of the 39-year-old prime minister were, "My God, my God. They have turned the guns on the people."

OFFSHORE STUDENTS

The St. George's University Medical School was an enclave community in Grenada. Located on Point Salines, the school is one of four Caribbean medical schools for U.S. students who cannot pass the admission tests to U.S. medical schools. The life of the students in Grenada was almost totally isolated from Grenadian society. Living in condominiums, guest houses, and dormitories around the medical school, the students spent free time on their own section of the Grand Anse beach, much like other beaches in the Caribbean where black islanders and white tourists do not mingle.

For these Americans, Grenada was their college town. Few of the students knew much or cared about local politics, and many of them scoffed at the concern of locals about a possible U.S. invasion. As it turned out, the security of these American students, who had been so isolated from political and social life in Grenada, became the main reason given for the U.S. "rescue mission."

Shortly after the murder of Prime Minister Bishop, the chancellor of the medical school polled the students and found that 90 percent wanted to stay on the island. Explaining the need for the invasion, President Reagan said the airport had been closed by the Grenadian military, thereby obstructing the departure of students who wanted to leave. But, as was later revealed, the airport had not been closed, and four charter planes had left the day before the invasion. It was the invasion itself that put the students in the most danger when fighting broke out after the Marines landed. The relief the students later expressed at being "rescued" can be understood in this context of the actual danger they experienced when caught in the crossfire at Point Salines on the day of the invasion.

THE MARINES LAND

Neither the safety of the students nor Washington's need to honor a request from the Organization of Eastern Caribbean States (OECS) was the true reason for the Grenada invasion. The arrival of the 82nd Airborne had more to do with Washington's desire to maintain its hegemony in the hemisphere and to stamp out the remnants of a popular socialist experiment. The timing could not have been better for Washington. The military coup had killed off the popular leadership of the revolution and left a dispirited population no longer ready or willing to resist a U.S. invasion. Although they did not anticipate such fierce fighting from the beleaguered Cubans and the Grenadian military, the U.S. invasion force of 6,000 troops had an easy time securing the island and dismantling the Revolutionary Military Council set up by General Austin.

A series of lies and misrepresentations by the Reagan administration shrouded the true circumstances of the invasion. Washington had exaggerated the threat to the medical school students, grossly overestimated the number of Cuban military on the island, understated the role of the United States in formulating the invasion with the OECS, never backed up its allegations that the Cubans and the Soviets were behind the death of Bishop, suppressed news of the assurances by Grenadian military officials and the Cuban government that the students were free to leave Grenada if they wished, and vastly exaggerated the amount of weaponry found on the island. A reporter for the *Chicago Sun-Times* wrote that of the warehouses of weapons the Marines supposedly discovered, one had stacks of rice and cans of sardines, another had truck parts, and a third was filled with canteens and clothing. "As for the three warehouses that did have weapons . . . they weren't stacked to the ceiling, as the president said. They were one-fourth full. Many of the rifles were made in

1871, old breech-loading saddle rifles. Others were World War II vintage. Lots of Saturday Night specials. . . . But very little modern weaponry. It was an arsenal, all right, but you'll find a bigger bang for your buck in any American gun shop."[12]

President Reagan also deliberately ignored pleas by Cuba before the invasion to resolve the crisis peaceably. Instead, Washington authorized the military to attack the barracks of the Cuban construction workers, who were instructed to fight to the death if they were attacked by the Yankee soldiers. One minor casualty of the invasion was the resignation of U.S. Deputy Press Secretary of Foreign Affairs Les Janka, who declared that by transmitting false information to the press he had damaged his credibility "almost irreparably."[13]

Undoubtedly, the Reagan administration considered the invasion as a way to shore up popular opinion in the United States. As a *New York Times* editorial noted: "Most Americans not only approve, but feel positively invigorated. . . . Years of frustration were vented by the Grenada invasion. So the invasion is finally justified because Americans needed a win, needed to invade someone."[14] But President Reagan did not kill a revolution; "the Revo" was already dead. He was merely stomping on its corpse.

A CARIBBEAN PARALLEL

The invasion and occupation of Grenada closely paralleled the invasion of the Dominican Republic in 1965. As in the Dominican Republic, the U.S. Marines landed in Grenada supposedly to "save American lives." Neither in the Dominican Republic nor in Grenada were the lives of U.S. citizens directly threatened by the internal political turmoil that enveloped both countries. In both cases, the United States carted along a regional peacekeeping force to give its intervention an aura of legitimacy. Once order was restored and U.S. citizens were back home, the occupying force stayed in both nations to restructure the economies and politics to reflect the interests of the United States.

In the Dominican Republic, Washington immediately set about reorganizing and training police and military forces. These U.S.-trained security forces then went on to carry out a systematic campaign of repression against the remnants of popular resistance, forcing thousands of Dominicans into exile. In the aftermath of the Grenada invasion, U.S. military police and intelligence teams stayed on to train both Grenadian and Caribbean police forces. Supporters of the Bishop government were harassed, jailed, interrogated, and forced out of the country. The similarities extend to the USAID foreign aid programs that quickly took effect in both countries.

REGIONAL DISPUTES

In the aftermath of the Grenada invasion, it appeared that its main victim may be the Caribbean Community (Caricom). Two of the largest English-speaking Caribbean countries, Guyana and Trinidad, refused to participate in the invasion. Guyana, the seat of Caricom, strongly denounced the invasion, and Trinidad's Prime Minister George Chambers complained that plans for the invasion were hatched behind his back. Relations between the neighboring countries of Barbados and Trinidad became particularly hostile. Joining in the condemnation of the invasion was the influential Caribbean Conference of Churches, which said that there should not be an "externally imposed" solution.[15] Both Jamaica and Dominica began discussing plans for a restructuring of Caricom to exclude Guyana and Trinidad, even though the Caricom treaty has no provisions for the expulsion of or other sanctions against member states. There was talk of replacing the two countries with Haiti and the Dominican Republic, nations that are strongly tied to the United States. Although Barbados gained some temporary prestige for its leading role in the invasion, the country suffered a humiliating setback in the United Nations when it was denied a seat on the Security Council in November 1983 because of international criticism.

DEMOCRACY POSTPONED

The political intrigue in the New Jewel Movement that resulted in the murder of Maurice Bishop disheartened many Grenadians. The course of politics in postinvasion Grenada gave little cause for optimism in the future of the shaken island. The U.S. government chose Sir Paul Scoon, the island's governor-general (appointed to the figurehead position by the Queen of England), to head the interim government. Scoon, however, proved singularly incapable either of sharing authority with his Advisory Council or of running a credible government. Unsuccessful in its attempt to find respected Grenadians to lead a new government, Washington brought in leaders from other Caribbean nations to manage the operations of Grenada's government. Elections, which were initially promised within six months of the invasion, were later delayed for at least a year. Although Washington found friends and allies in the small Grenadian bourgeoisie, it had a hard time finding respected political leaders. When asked who was in charge of politics in Grenada, Roland Kester, a Grenadian worker, answered: "I don't really know. I can't answer that, and I wouldn't even venture to."[16]

The main problem facing Washington in its effort to construct a new government in Grenada will be countering the considerable favorable sentiment that still exists for Bishop and his social programs. The poor and working people of Grenada received many real benefits from the revolutionary government as well as an education in class politics. It is unlikely that the emphasis on private-sector support, the dismantling of social programs, or the removal of price ceilings will be received favorably by those sectors of Grenadian society that benefited from health, education, and economic programs of the Bishop government.

The U.S. military withdrew its combat troops by Christmas 1983 but left 300 "non-combat" troops to maintain order and political stability. It is likely that among these military police were the Army Intelligence and Psychological Operations troops that had been active since the occupation began. Working alongside the U.S. military police was a 329-member Caribbean Peacekeeping Force, which was being maintained by the Pentagon. The United States brought in several non-Grenadians to run a restructured Grenadian police force and prison service. As in other areas, supporters of Bishop were removed from their jobs.

AID TO THE RESCUE

Accompanying the U.S. Marines in their "rescue mission" was a USAID disaster-assistance survey team. USAID Administrator Peter McPherson said that USAID personnel had entered Grenada "almost in conjunction with the troops."[17] He admitted the "Department of Defense people and the AID people have been working closely, really together, as a team." For the four years of the Maurice Bishop government, USAID had refused to channel U.S. development assistance to the revolutionary government. Immediately after the invasion, aid resumed to Grenada at a rate that made it (in late 1983) the highest per capita recipient of U.S. aid in the world. In the two months that followed the invasion, USAID allocated to Grenada $18.5 million (all grants)—an amount equivalent to 20 percent of the island's GNP.

As the U.S. military withdrew, the newly established USAID Mission in Grenada began to exercise more influence in the country's "rehabilitation." The first priority of USAID, to provide food and medicine to Grenadians, demonstrated U.S. goodwill. USAID used an emergency allocation of $3.4 million to rebuild the roads, the water system, and other facilities destroyed by the invasion. Predictably, the major thrust of USAID's long-term development plan for Grenada involves support to the local and foreign private sector. "We are particularly sensitive to the needs of the Grenadian private sector as a central instrument to the recovery process," noted McPherson.[18] He said that USAID was "firmly committed to the economic recovery and long-term development of Grenada."

Immediately after the invasion, several U.S. government's private-sector development organizations began their campaign to increase U.S. investment in Grenada and to boost the position of the island's private-sector organizations. Using USAID funds, the Grenada Chamber of Industry and Commerce went to the Miami Conference on the Caribbean, which took place in late November 1983. Chamber President Richard Menezes presided over the Grenada booth, the busiest exhibition at the annual conference, which is sponsored by Caribbean/Central America Action (CCAA) and funded in part by the U.S. government. Menezes said Grenada needed $50 million in near-term private investment to get the economy moving again, but he stressed that the very first thing that Grenada's private sector needed was to have the new airport completed. "It's a chicken and egg situation," he explained. "Without a modern airport, there's not much point in adding hotel rooms."[19]

In December 1983, a USAID-led interagency team on Grenada published a report entitled "Prospects for Growth in Grenada: The Role of the Private Sector." According to USAID, the virtues of private-sector development were experienced from the first days of colonialism: "The private sector emerged early in Grenada's history when trading ships from Europe brought articles for sale or barter with the islanders in return for products to be taken back to Europe." The report targeted four areas for change in the island's economic structure: (1) revision of investment and tax codes to favor the private sector, (2) formulation of a new labor code that would ensure better labor-management relations, (3) the sale of public-sector enterprises to private interests, and (4) the elimination of the state's role in the marketing of imports and price controls.

Based on interviews with Grenada's business community, which had traditionally made most of its profits in importing and exporting, the report concluded that price controls needed to be lifted on such imports as rice, sugar, powdered milk, fertilizer, and cement. The Bishop government had instituted price ceilings on the sale of many basic commodities, but the report said this practice resulted in "exceptionally thin" profits for the island's private sector. It also said that such state-created industries as the Agroindustry Plant and the Fish Processing Plant infringed on the prerogatives of the private sector. This observation did not explain why the private sector had failed to establish such processing operations in its over 300 years of unfettered freedom. The interagency report recommended that the American Institute for Free Labor Development (AIFLD) be called in to "restructure" the Grenadian labor movement. It acknowledged what the Bishop government had long charged: that AIFLD (although not present in Grenada) had maintained close ties with several Grenadian trade unions throughout the years of the revolutionary government.

According to the findings of the USAID-sponsored interagency report, "The private sector remains suspicious, but understands the necessity of filling the leadership gap to provide for a functional, democratic labor movement and thereby avoid a return to radicalism and business strife." The report noted that "AIFLD of the AFL-CIO is well-equipped to help in this regard."

During the years of the revolutionary government in Grenada, Bishop and other political leaders charged that AIFLD conspired with conservative labor leaders to destabilize the government. The interagency report lends some credence to the charges of the Bishop government. It stated that "AIFLD maintained close contact with these groups during the Bishop years and is on the scene now."

The interagency team recommended that AIFLD take the lead in restructuring and training the unions as quickly as possible and that a U.S. Department of Labor specialist on the Caribbean Basin Initiative begin discussions with the government of Grenada to formulate a new labor code that meets U.S. specifications.[20]

The Caribbean Basin Information Center of the Department of Commerce also began a campaign to promote the private sector in Grenada. Desmond Foynes of the information center said that the state agricultural and industrial enterprises had been "grossly inefficient" and would be replaced by privately owned businesses. "Grenada has been left out of the regional trends in development in the last four years," he said.[21] Foynes cited the trend to diversify the Caribbean economy into light manufacturing, such as the assembly of "ladies' brassieres and electronic components." The Department of Commerce has been using its resources to seek out investors who may be interested in setting up assembly plants in Grenada. One of the early successes of the Department of Commerce was to arrange the purchase of $1 million of Grenada's nutmeg (about one-fifth of annual production) by a little-known U.S. firm based in the U.S. Virgin Islands called Caribbean Corporate Services. Formed to take advantage of the CBI, the company announced plans to market the nutmeg in the United States in the form of a Grenada Nutmeg Cooking Kit. The Department of Commerce denied any financial involvement of the U.S. government in the deal, which was arranged a month after the invasion. "We simply put the buyer and the seller together," Foynes remarked.

Only weeks after the invasion, the White House and CCAA sponsored a trip by a "private-sector survey team" to Grenada. CCAA's Peter Johnson began organizing the island's business organizations to take advantage of the CBI and other Washington programs. In January 1984, the Office of Private Sector Initiatives of the White House sponsored a tour of Grenada by 15 U.S. executives who were considering looking for investment opportunities on the island. James Coyne, who heads the White House office, said that Grenada has good potential to produce

vegetables and flowers for the U.S. market and to establish light manufacturing industries. "If a profitable deal can be struck for both sides,
using credit and technology from America and products and labor in
Grenada, I would not call that exploitation," said Coyne. "It is a two-way
street."[22] Washington also invited representatives of the major cruise-
line and tour operators to see how the U.S. government could foster the
island's tourism sector. Also assisting the private-sector support campaign for Grenada are Eximbank and OPIC, which promised to provide
insurance and start-up capital for U.S. foreign investors on the island.

REVOLUTION BETRAYED

In the Caribbean, revolutionary Grenada invoked the enmity of the right-
wing regimes and newspapers. It also attracted progressives and activists
in the former British territories who felt that Grenada was creating an
example the other impoverished islands could follow. Washington tried
to downplay the achievements of the Grenadian revolution and promote
other Caribbean countries, especially Jamaica, as showcases of democracy and private enterprise. "I think Washington fears that we could set
an example," remarked Prime Minister Bishop. "If we are able to succeed where previous governments following different models failed, that
would be very, very subversive."[23] But, in the end, Grenada did not
succeed. Ultraleftism in the New Jewel Movement, reactionary regional
politics, and U.S. intervention to safeguard its hegemony in the Caribbean were the three elements that joined together to smash the hope of
the Grenadian revolution. It was a severe setback for those who had
hoped that other revolutions would soon burst forth in other parts of the
West Indies. The revolutionary experiment in Grenada was a step forward in Caribbean history. It went beyond the constraints of the past but
failed to establish the political models the Caribbean so badly needs for
its future. The death of the Grenadian revolution and its spirit of "forward ever" was a terrible tragedy for the people of the Caribbean, and a
long step backward.

Guyana

Slavery, sugar plantations, English masters—Guyana shares these elements of its history with most other Caribbean countries. What sets Guyana apart is its relative geographical immensity. The country's coastal plain, although just two to eight miles in width, stretches one hundred miles along the Atlantic Ocean. If Guyana consisted only of this fertile plain, it would still be one of the largest Caribbean nations. But Guyana reaches deep into the interior of the South American continent: an uncharted, roadless land of vast savannah, thick jungle, and majestic waterfalls. The Guyanese call this undeveloped majority of their country "the bush."

The colonial past fashioned the structure of present-day Guyana, which began as an early Dutch trading post in the 1600s. Guyana has maintained a characteristic Dutch look, with its orderliness, the masterly system of dikes and canals, and its distinctive architecture. The country's second-largest city still bears its colonial name of New Amsterdam, while the capital city was named after King George of Great Britain, the country that ruled the territory after 1814. After the abolition of slavery in the mid-1800s, the plantation owners experienced difficulties in maintaining a workforce. Many Afro-Guyanese chose to clear land for their own or cooperative farms rather than remain subject to white overseers of the sugar plantations. The English substituted indentured migrants from British India for the freed black slaves. In India, drought, famine, and strict social stratification enabled the British agents for the sugar companies to lure East Indians into leaving their rural homes and undertaking the journey across what they called the "black water."

While the city of Georgetown is distinguished by a majestic Catholic cathedral, the minarets of Moslem mosques and the domes of Hindu temples rise above the rural villages of Guyana. Today, 52 percent of the country's population is Indo-Guyanese (East Indian), 38 percent Afro-Guyanese, 2 percent Amerindians, and the balance white and of mixed origin. In the bush, the Akawaio, a group of Carib Amerindians, work on cattle ranches or small subsistence farms. Recently, a huge hydroelectric project and the expansion of mining in the interior have threatened the already precarious existence of the Amerindians.

REBELLION AND DICTATORSHIP

Modern political history for the British colony began in 1953 when, in the first elections based on universal adult suffrage, the Guyanese elected the first Marxist government in the British empire. Only 133 days after the election of Cheddi Jagan, however, the British intervened and suspended the constitution to "prevent communist subversion." The People's Progressive Party (PPP), led by Cheddi and Janet Jagan, had succeeded in welding together a multiracial party with strong roots in the working class. In 1961, Jagan and the PPP won national office again. This time, the United States stepped in with a U.S.-orchestrated campaign of destabilization, which toppled the elected government. It ushered in a new coalition government with the right-wing United Force Party and the People's National Congress (PNC), led by Forbes Burnham. The United States, which had feared that Guyana would achieve independence under a Marxist government, cleared the way for an independent Guyana with Burnham in 1966.

After taking power, President Burnham wandered off the course set for him by Great Britain and the United States and assumed a more nationalist political program. Because the only substantial political opposition was leftist, Burnham moved more and more to the left and co-opted his opponents. As a way to broaden his political base and to create an economic foundation for his party, Burnham proceeded to nationalize the leading sectors of the economy: bauxite and sugar. In 1970, Burnham declared Guyana a "Cooperative Socialist Republic" and promised to "feed, clothe, and house" the nation within six years. The rhetorical content of cooperative socialism, however, has far exceeded its real achievements. From 1970 to 1981, government expenditures on education and health actually declined, while during the same period public debt payments tripled.[1] Since 1975, Guyana's per capita income dropped by a staggering 50 percent.

The government's commitment to "make the small man the real man" and to create a socialist society has fallen to dictatorial tendencies. Nothing set the population against Burnham more than his strict import policies. Burnham and the PNC banned the importation of many popular items, including wheat flour and split peas, the staples of an East Indian diet. Explaining that white flour is no good for black people, Burnham advocated that the Guyanese become "rice revolutionaries" by substituting rice flour for wheat flour. The increased reliance on a diet of rice has caused outbreaks of beri-beri, notably among prisoners in Guyana's jails.

Guyanese who have stood in lines all day for food rations have taken exception to the extravagance of their president, who has a plane fitted with a specially made bed with purple trimmings and who traveled to a

Caricom conference with a 46-member entourage including a presidential cook and valet. Meanwhile, the food shortage has increased malnutrition, spurred a huge smuggling business, and spawned an enormous black market. To enforce the ban on imported items, soldiers have inspected students' lunch boxes, raided bakeries, and crashed the weddings of East Indian families. "A large amount of the time of the police force," complained the newspaper *Catholic Standard*, "is now taken up in seizing banned essential items instead of fighting serious crime. It is merely implementing the government's hated food policy and jailing those who oppose it."[2]

While police surveillance escalated, so did crime in Guyana's cities. A Guyana high court judge commented that citizens had become prisoners in their homes. The lack of criminal arrests and the high proportion of crimes against East Indian families created widespread suspicion that the police themselves, who are mostly black, might have been behind the crime wave that swept Guyana in 1983. In addition to the police force, the government maintains 12 different security forces, which have shown their willingness to use brutality to stamp out antigovernment criticism. The Catholic Institute for International Relations said in 1980 that the ratio of military and paramilitary personnel to each civilian is the highest in South America.[3]

DEVELOPMENT OF STATE CAPITALISM

"As economic conditions have worsened," said Clive Thomas, a University of Guyana economics professor, "the minority position of the ruling party can only be sustained by resort to the 'stick,' since there is just no 'carrot' to offer."[4] Cooperative socialism was merely a rhetorical cover for the development of state capitalism, which provided a base for the formation of a new class that benefited from the state industries. State capitalism also supported a small group of indigenous capitalists. Thomas blames the downswing of the economy on "the erratic expansion of state property" and "the absence of a planned framework for economic activity."[5] Rather than emphasize worker self-management, the government used traditional hierarchic methods to run state enterprises. Highlighting the top-down approach of the Burnham government was a Labor Bill passed in 1984 that gave the government the power to declare any strike in the public sector illegal. That put severe limitations on collective bargaining in labor-management conflicts. As one author noted, Guyana has experienced a "profound process of decolonization but not a transition to socialism."[6]

Asked in 1982 about the condition of the country's economy, the administrator of the nation's central bank said that he would rather not discuss it. "The economy is in such a state," he said, "I become sick just talking about it."[7] Increasing malnutrition among children, smuggling along the borders, a wave of urban crime, unemployment, and a decline in bauxite production indicate the country's desperate economic situation. Tens of thousands of Guyanese have migrated out of the country because of the deteriorating economy. Between 1976 and 1981, over 70,000 people left Guyana, or about 70 percent of the natural population increase during that period.[8]

Guyana has a two-crop agricultural economy of rice and sugar. The state-owned Guyana Sugar Corporation, the country's largest employer, sells most of its sugar to the United Kingdom, the United States, and Canada. Many East Indian small farmers make a living from the rice industry, which the government has unsuccessfully tried to control. Forests cover 72 percent of the country's land area, but the lack of roads into the interior has permitted only 20 percent of this to be accessible to commercial exploitation. The government allows private companies to cut timber and to fish the rich Guyanese coastal waters. Most exports from the country's fishing industry, the largest in the region, go to Japanese and U.S. markets.

Sugar dominated the Guyanese economy until the late 1960s, when bauxite became the major foreign-exchange earner. After failing to come to an agreement on royalties and control, the Burnham government nationalized the Aluminum Company of Canada (Alcan) and Reynolds. Inefficient management by the government, lack of skilled personnel, and labor difficulties have debilitated the country's bauxite operations. Industrial unrest has transformed the bauxite towns from strongholds of the ruling party into sources of serious opposition. Workers who originally had supported the nationalization are again open to renewed foreign control of the shaky industry. In 1983, Alcan and Kaiser began negotiating with the government for a possible private takeover of the industry. Burnham's government also invited a number of foreign corporations to explore for uranium, gold, and petroleum. Also interested in Guyana's natural resources is Brazil, which has signed an agreement of economic and technical cooperation with its northern neighbor. On Guyana's eastern and western borders, however, the country faces ongoing territorial disputes with Venezuela and Suriname, both of which claim large slices of Guyana.

A large number of government and international financial institutions have provided grants and loans to Guyana; countries lending Guyana money include Canada, Japan, East Germany, Cuba, Yugoslavia, and the United States. In 1983 the U.S. government used its influence to block two IDB loans for Guyana's agricultural sector. Washington cited the economic instability of the country as its reason, but observers suspected it was the first sign of a Reagan administration plan to destabilize the Burnham government and find an alternative acceptable to the United States. The Guyanese ambassador to Washington characterized the loan veto as "unacceptable meddling" in his country's internal affairs.[9]

In mid-1982, Guyana signed a structural-adjustment loan contract with the World Bank, which, in exchange for financial aid, required that Guyana (1) privatize the bauxite industry and reduce the scope of the Guyana Rice Board, (2) form an investment code, (3) create an industrial development advisory council with strong private representation, (4) limit public-sector involvement in manufacturing, and (5) initiate talks with the IMF. Because Guyana failed to meet the economic growth targets of a previous IMF arrangement, the IMF in 1983 demanded a stricter austerity plan, continued progress on the adjustment program of the World Bank, and a 40 percent devaluation. Burnham initially rejected the IMF demands, saying: "The only thing that they have not proposed is raising the price of air, and God knows they might have it up their sleeves."[10]

PRIVATE INVESTMENT

Government corporations have by no means completely swallowed the private sector. A 1982 study funded by USAID found that the public sector accounted for only 35 to 40 percent of the economy, contrary to the 80 percent figure that the U.S. government had previously cited. [11] The country's private sector, which accounts for 55 percent of the national tax income, is strongest in agriculture (except in the nationalized sugar industry). Although Guyana does have two state-owned banks, the private banks have over 70 percent of the nation's bank assets and deposits.[12] Public enterprises, however, do manage the marketing of the country's exports. While private business complains about the degree of state control, there have been few nationalizations or threats against private business in recent years. In fact, the government requested some corporations to take over projects it mismanaged. Burnham has assured present investors that no enterprise that was established after independence has been or will ever be nationalized.

Most U.S. investments in Guyana enjoy the protection of the U.S. Overseas Private Investment Corporation (OPIC), which offers insurance for risks of nationalization and expropriation. The most prominent U.S. investor is Chase Manhattan; others include Colgate Palmolive, Nabisco Brands, and Sahlman Brothers (shrimp fishing). Exxon, Texaco, IBM, and Singer all have retail operations; and the U.S.-owned Green Construction has been contracted by the government for the engineering and much of the actual mining of bauxite because of the lack of adequate skilled personnel in the Guyana Mining Enterprise.

Great Britain historically has had the most foreign investment in Guyana because of its colonial ties to the country. Before the British sugar giant Booker McConnell sold its operations to the government in 1976, the company exercised pervasive influence in Guyana. Transforming the whole country into one large company town, Booker owned food stores, hardware stores, transportation companies, and the country's largest trading and shipping firm, and it had substantial interests in rum, fisheries, and drug manufacturing. So pervasive was the corporation that many called the country Booker's Guiana rather than British Guiana. The Booker conglomerate, which made its fortune from its sugar plantations in Guyana, still purchases sugar from, and sells agricultural supplies to, the former colony. Other important British investments in Guyana include Barclays, Tate & Lyle, BAT Industries, Taylor Woodrow, and Grand Metropolitan. The major Canadian investment in Guyana was the nationalized Alcan bauxite mine, but Bata Shoes, Seaboard Allied Milling, and Royal Bank of Canada still have operations there.

In its effort to build up the private sector in Guyana, the United States, in 1982 and 1983, sent consultants to Georgetown to advise local and foreign business owners on the creation of a more effective private sector. The U.S.-sponsored "Report on CBI Implementation Plan for Guyana" recommended that USAID directly fund several business organizations, a survey of investment potential and management-training programs, and the activities of the International Businessmen's Executive Corps in the local private sector. The report mentioned the important role business organizations created by USAID could play in providing information to the U.S. government.[13] In line with these recommendations, USAID proposed the implementation of its Private Sector Promotion Program in Guyana. The United States has relied on the World Bank and the IMF to pressure the government to restructure the economy away from its public-sector orientation in the hope that an energized private sector would eventually form a conservative political opposition to the Burnham government.

The combined efforts of the two international financial institutions and the U.S. government have already resulted in increased influence of both foreign and local private businesses. Particularly pleasing to Washington was Burnham's hiring of a prominent U.S. law firm to design the World Bank-required investment code for Guyana. Another U.S. firm was hired to evaluate the performance of the public corporations, and a British investment company started working with the government to assess the external debt situation. The director of the nation's main private-sector organization said in 1983 that the government had begun to consult with the private sector before making any important economic changes. "Current difficulties can be resolved," said the USAID CBI Implementation Report, "through a major transformation of government policies and state corporations to enable the revitalization of the private sector and the attraction of foreign capitalists and management from abroad."[14]

OPPOSITION

Despite the shared problems of the Guyanese people, the widespread repression combined with political bickering and racial animosity have previously prevented the creation of a broad-based coalition to oppose the unpopular government. But one beneficial result of state capitalism has been the increased unity of the Indo-Guyanese sugar workers and the Afro-Guyanese bauxite workers employed by the government. Groups of workers in the two industries have set up "unity committees" to coordinate strikes and distribute scarce food. The Burnham regime has tried to foment racial divisions to prevent unified political opposition, but the economic deterioration of Guyana has worked to build a feeling of solidarity between the two main racial groups. Both have experienced the common problems of unemployment, food shortages, and political repression. In 1983, 8,000 bauxite workers staged strikes to protest food shortages and were joined by taxi drivers, who were angered by incidents in which the police impounded taxis carrying passengers who had wheat flour. Housewives in Georgetown took to the streets beating empty pots and chanting demands for more food.

Human rights violations by the government and the military have been another shared concern of the Guyanese. The Catholic Church, itself a victim of government censorship and repression, has been the leading critic of the regime's repeated violations of human rights. Burnham has prohibited the opposition newspapers, the *Mirror* and the *Catholic Standard*, from importing newsprint. Burnham declared that "open war" existed between the Catholic Church and the government, and his information minister candidly commented in 1983 that it would be political suicide to allow paper to be imported for opposition newspapers.[15]

The main political opposition to Burnham's PNC comes from the Working People's Alliance (WPA) and the People's Progressive Party (PPP), the party of Cheddi Jagan, who has lost some popular backing because of his dogmatic Marxist approach to politics. The fact that both parties are to the left of the Burnham government partly explains the history of tolerance and support to the ruling party by the international financial institutions and the United States. Walter Rodney, founder of the WPA, and a renowned Caribbean scholar, was killed in 1980 when a bomb exploded in his car. The WPA and other observers claim that Rodney was assassinated because he was a political threat. An unsubstantiated report by the U.S. State Department that WPA members received guerrilla training in Cuba gave the government a reason to isolate and suppress the WPA. A multiracial grouping, the WPA is believed to have wide popular support among the Guyanese.

The National Cooperative Socialist government of Forbes Burnham has, among other things, given a bad name to socialism and cooperatives in the Caribbean. But the government has had little to do with either socialism or cooperatives. Rather than promoting workers' control, Burnham built a nationalized economic base for himself and a small group of party followers. In actuality, the cooperatives established have been state-owned corporations that have exploited the workforce through methods not unlike those of capitalist enterprises. While Burnham proclaims the nationalist and socialist character of his government, Guyana has submitted to austerity programs of international financial institutions that directly contradict his rhetoric. Government repression, fraudulent elections, and the absence of a free press have at least temporarily ruled out the possibility of political change in Guyana through a peaceful and democratic process.

Haiti

"This is Haiti," proclaims a government brochure, "a country of incomparable splendor, with brilliant white sands of unspoiled beaches, the peaceful allure of the radiant Caribbean, farmland and markets along the switchback roads, the blue mountains cradling each major port, French and Creole haute cuisine, vibrant open-air bazaars displaying world-renowned paintings and crafts, and a fascinating blend of industrious and hospitable people."

Haiti is a land of startling, shocking contrasts. Jetsetters, a millionaire elite, and luxury tourist resorts are one part of Haiti, but there is also the Haiti of urban squalor, rural destitution, and pervasive repression. Haiti, which means "the land of mountains" in an Amerindian language, is a country of dirt-brown mountains where peasants toil desperately to produce their food from the eroded soil. It is among the poorest and most repressed nations in the world. World Bank figures show that in this country of 6 million residents, only 24,000 people own 40 percent of its wealth. Ninety percent of Haitians earn less than $120 a year and 1 percent of the population owns 60 percent of the land.

Haiti's capital city, Port-au-Prince, has doubled in size in the last ten years to its current 850,000 residents. The city spreads out aimlessly around the bay, and the majestic pink-and-white Cathédrale Trinité dominates the city skyline. A seemingly endless collection of shantytowns stops suddenly at the foothills of the surrounding mountains, where a world of mansions, gardens, and art galleries begins. In Pétionville, an enclave of conspicuous wealth and pleasure, tourists, business executives, and the social elite escape the country's harsh realities. Several hundred Beverly Hills-style luxury homes adorn the wooded hillsides of Pétionville, complete with their own tennis courts, swimming pools, and gardens. Low-paid gardeners water the luxuriant flower beds while down below in Port-au-Prince 96 percent of the population lives without drinking water and waits in long lines for potable water. The poor bathe in an open sewer they call Canal Rockefeller, and hungry human scavengers crowd the city's garbage dumps.

The high life in Pétionville contrasts sharply with the thousands of tin-and-cardboard shacks scattered along the marshy lowland by the bay. In Cité Simone, created by the Duvalier government and named after

François Duvalier, "Papa Doc's," wife Simone, thousands of refugees live in grossly inadequate housing and without services. Infant mortality in Cité Simone exceeds 200 deaths per thousand births, substantially above the 130 per thousand rate for the rest of the country.[1] In comparison, the United States has a rate of 13 per thousand, and nearby Cuba has a rate of 14 per thousand. Death in Cité Simone is as common as the mosquitoes that pervade the community.

RURAL HAITI

The government of Haiti is concentrated in the city of Port-au-Prince, where the Duvalier dictatorship spends almost 90 percent of the national budget, although the city only contributes about 40 percent of the national revenues. Each year, 30,000 rural Haitians come to the big city to seek an education, find a job, and escape the wretched life of the countryside. Although poverty afflicts more than half the urban population, the World Bank estimates that the per capita income in the capital is 10 times that of rural areas. In Haiti, rural poverty refers to virtually the entire population outside Port-au-Prince. Only 3 percent of the rural population has piped-in water, and less than 5 percent has electricity. Government services are almost nonexistent, and only 3 percent of children in rural areas complete primary school.[2] There is only one doctor or nurse for every 30,000 rural inhabitants, and more Haitian doctors practice in Montreal than in all of Haiti.[3] Rural Haiti is a nightmarish land of dusty hills, bloated stomachs, epidemic disease, and utter lack of hope.

In his book *Losing Ground*, Erik Eckholm describes the rural landscape.

> Haiti is among the few countries that already rival or perhaps surpass El Salvador in nationwide environmental destruction. Not coincidentally, Haiti also resembles El Salvador in its inequitable distribution of land ownership, economic opportunities, and social services. Long a consequence of severe poverty, soil erosion has reached the point where it is now a major cause of poverty as well. Wealthy farmers and North American sugar corporations own the best valley lands, crowding peasants onto slopes where cultivation is a futile, temporary proposition.[4]

While population density relative to arable land in Haiti is one of the highest in the world, agricultural experts say that unequal land distribution and improper techniques are the fundamental problems in rural Haiti.

Absentee landowners living in Pétionville depend on the backbreaking labor of Haitian peasants for their income. A small city elite receives the majority of the benefits from Haiti's coffee business, which produces most of the country's exports. An American missionary living in a Haitian village described a scene typical of the rural power structure: "One family controls the community. Besides owning vast tracts of land, the family speculates in coffee and controls the illegal tree-cutting in the area." American and multilateral aid programs have encouraged many small Haitian farmers to switch from producing mostly subsistence and local crops to producing coffee. But promises of increased income have been shattered by high export taxes, the elite's tight control over agricultural production, and inflationary food costs on the local market.

While the population is rapidly rising, annual per capita agricultural productivity is declining in Haiti by 2 percent a year. Since the late 1970s, Haiti has become a net importer of sugar, primarily because the government has done so little to promote research and development of the country's agricultural sector. Food purchases constitute well over half the country's total imports. Because much of this food goes to the tourists and the nation's elite, however, the majority of the population is slowly starving. Almost 90 percent of all children suffer from varying degrees of malnutrition, and only two out of three children survive their first year.[5]

HISTORY

Except for a brief moment of glory in 1803, when armies of rebel slaves succeeded in ridding the country of the French colonizers, Haiti's history is as grim as its present. French pirates used the western part of what the Spanish called Hispaniola as a base for their raids; and in 1697 the Spanish ceded this mountainous part of the island to the French. The French proceeded to fashion what they called St. Domingue into the most productive of the colonial sugarcane territories. Called the "richest pearl in the Caribbean necklace," Haiti in the mid-1700s contributed more to France's revenues than the other French colonies combined. Haiti's productivity of that era, however, depended on the brutal plantation system, and in 1791 the slaves rebelled. After 12 years of bloody war with Napoleon's army, Haitians won their freedom. Haiti, the second country in the Americas to establish a republic, became a symbol of hope to slaves throughout the hemisphere. "No white man," stated the new constitution, "no matter what his nationality, will come to this land to be lord or master, nor will he be able, in the future, to acquire any property."

Twenty-two dictators trampled through Haiti from the 1840s until 1915, when the United States intervened militarily to "protect U.S. lives and property and to prevent invasion by other nations." The U.S. Marines found reason to extend their occupation until 1934, giving them time to build a pro-American militia and to crush an anti-imperialist liberation movement led by Charlemagne Peralte, the Augusto Sandino of Haiti. The popular guerrilla leader, who had the support of a fifth of the population, signed his letters, "Chief of the Revolutionary Army fighting the Americans in the land of Haiti." He was jailed in 1917 and then escaped after killing a Marine who had hit him for refusing to clean the latrines. The U.S. Marines ambushed and murdered Peralte in 1919. His body was exposed to the public as an example of what would happen to other insurrectionists, and the Marines who killed him received medals of honor.

In 1957, François Duvalier, a medical doctor, became president by appealing to the large number of Haitians who resented the control of political and economic power by the minority upper class. After two years as president, Duvalier began to challenge that power. Traditionally, the first sons of the elite inherited the wealth and the second sons joined the military—an arrangement by which the elite protected its financial power through its control of the military. Papa Doc created his own paramilitary force, called the Tonton Macoutes, which struggled with and eventually took over the regular military. Fiercely loyal to Papa Doc, the Tonton Macoutes, trained by former German SS officers, soon brought Haiti firmly under Papa Doc's control, leaving thousands of Haitians missing, tortured, or dead.

With varying degrees of discomfort or embarrassment, most U.S. administrations gave support to Papa Doc's regime, but a general feeling of relief was felt in Washington when the ailing Papa Doc passed on power to his 19-year-old son, Jean Claude "Baby Doc" Duvalier, in 1971, shortly before the elder's death. "The destiny of my country is tightly bound to the American democracy," said Baby Doc, ever conscious of the need to stay on Washington's good side. In a show of Haitian-style democracy, Baby Doc became President-for-Life in 1971 by a vote of 2,391,916 to one.

"BABY DOC'S" TURN

The passing of the dictatorship to Duvalier's son in 1971 also marked the beginning of intensified corporate penetration of Haiti. The industrialized world stepped up its aid programs with the intention of rebuilding the infrastructure of transportation facilities and electricity so necessary for corporate investment. The young Duvalier, who has only once traveled outside the country, has tried to build a coalition of technocrats, foreign businessmen, civil servants, and army officers to support his rule. In 1977, under pressure from the Carter administration, the young dictator made public gestures toward easing the repression. Inside Haiti, however, the complex network of military and paramilitary forces continues to rule the country with an iron hand. Because many of the military personnel volunteer their services, they depend financially on a system of extortion and expropriation of the Haitian people. The security network includes the dread Volunteers of National Security (VSN), a direct descendant of the notorious Tonton Macoutes. Although the regime discarded the infamous name long ago, Haitians still refer to the worst of the security forces as Tonton Macoutes.

For every secondary-school teacher in Haiti there are 189 security-force personnel, and for every secondary school in Haiti there are 35 prisons.[6] Prison conditions in Haiti shock the most hardened human-rights advocates. Lack of food for the prisoners results in slow starvation, clothing is seldom provided, and relatives are not notified of detentions. One survivor of Haitian prisons recounted stepping over skeletons while being pushed into the underground cells. Professionals and peasants alike describe being tied up in excruciating positions and being beaten simultaneously by several people with big sticks. The security forces throw people into these hell-holes on the slightest provocation. The mass executions that made Papa Doc famous no longer occur, but Baby Doc's brand of repression is no less terrifying.

In the last ten years, tensions within Baby Doc's government have increased. Two factions of the power structure have developed among Haiti's economic and political elite. One faction, the old-guard backers of Papa Doc, tend toward a nationalist sentiment. Also known as the dinosaurs or feudals, the old guard has opposed the new industrialization and the diminishing importance of agriculture, since such developments have meant the declining importance of their class. The opposing faction, the technocrats or the liberals, have allied themselves with the new imperialist class of managers that came with the surge of foreign investment in the last decade. Having greatly benefited from the increased circulation of foreign goods and capital, they support measures to liberalize or open up the country to tourists and investors. While they back liberal reforms that enhance the image of a modern Haiti, both they and the dinosaurs share a hard-line position against increased wages and labor unions. The division between the dinosaurs and the technocrats has taken the form of a family fight. Simone Duvalier, who accompanied Papa Doc during the days of undivided power, leads the dinosaurs. The former dictator's wife is widely believed to resent the sudden ascent to power of Michelle Bennett, who married her son in a sumptuous $6 million wedding ceremony in June 1980.

The marriage of Jean Claude and Michelle brought a leading family of the business elite into the National Palace. Michelle's father, Ernest Bennett, controls key sectors of Haiti's export-import trade as well as the flow of such contraband as cars and drugs. Bennett, the country's biggest buyer and exporter of coffee, illustrates the power of Haiti's middlemen, who make huge profits from the exploitative purchasing structure. His power has expanded greatly since he became related to the first family. In the last several years, Michelle Duvalier, who enjoys a $100,000 government salary, has created her own base of power in the regime. While Baby Doc has tried to create a united Duvalierism of the two factions, divisions and bickering still threaten the regime.

In the late 1970s, partially in response to pressure from the Carter administration, Baby Doc allowed the emergence of three moderate political parties, each calling itself Christian Democrat. But when the opposition political leaders and the media began seriously to criticize his regime, he cracked down by arresting and exiling his critics. Baby Doc stepped up the repression in November 1980, shortly after the election of Reagan. The day after the Republican victory in the United States, several members of the old Tonton Macoutes roamed around Port-au-Prince, firing pistols and chanting, "Cowboys are in power; now we rule over human beings." On the night of November 28, the security forces, brandishing machine guns, rounded up 130 people. The 1980 repression targeted journalists, human-rights advocates, and the few lawyers left that would represent clients in politically sensitive cases. In effect, the November 1980 arrests silenced virtually all voices of opposition in Haiti. A year before, Duvalier had warned: "I alone can blow the winds of liberalization. No one else can be put in power to blow the winds more strongly than I do. Never." The political crackdown, while gaining the sympathy of the dinosaurs, has alienated a large portion of Baby Doc's backers. Escalating repression has caused an accelerating flight of capital, a drastic drop in tourism, and increased difficulties in attracting foreign aid, except from the United States.

Despite "human rights abuses," the State Department in February 1984 approved continued foreign aid to the Duvalier government, saying that Haiti "is making a concerted effort to improve the human rights situation." As one indication of Duvalier's efforts to meet U.S. criteria for continued aid, the government sponsored elections in February 1984 for the National Assembly. No opposing political parties were allowed to field candidates, however, and independents who attempted to run quickly withdrew under government pressure.

INDUSTRY

Haiti exports almost 70 percent of its products to the United States and buys half its imports from the United States.[7] France, which buys most of the country's coffee crop, is Haiti's second-largest trading partner. Haiti, the world's largest producer of baseballs, exports 15 million baseballs each year. The material to make baseballs is the largest non-agricultural import from the United States and baseballs are Haiti's largest export to the United States. The country's third-largest corporation, Rawlings Sporting Goods, has an exclusive contract for all the baseballs used by the American and National Leagues in the United States. The company, which has over $60 million in annual sales from Haiti, employs over 1,000 women at its Port-au-Prince factory. Rawlings pays the women $2.70 a day to produce 30 to 40 hardballs. "It would cost a fortune to produce baseballs in this country [the U.S.]," remarked Tim Voss, Rawlings's production manager.[8] To spur production among its Haitian employees, Rawlings once organized the women (who had never seen a baseball game) into competing teams that wore colored uniformlike blouses bearing such names as Tigers, Angels, and Red Sox. Other baseball manufacturers in Haiti include Wilson, Home of Champions, Spalding, Dudley, DeBeer, and Worth.

In the last ten years, Haiti has attracted scores of other assembly industries with its "political stability," lack of unions, and unenforced daily minimum wage of $2.64. These industries include garment, leather goods, shoes, toys, and electronic components. "The organized labor movement in Haiti is almost non-existent," reports the U.S. Department of Labor. "All unions except one, which is directly controlled by the government, are outlawed. There is a long history of government repression of the labor movement in Haiti."[9] A 1982 survey found that 75 percent of Haitian workers did not even know what a union was.[10] In 1980, 40 to 50 labor organizers in Haiti tried to create an informal group to focus on sugar refineries and light industry, but all were arrested, exiled, or forced underground by December of the same year.

In its attempt to induce U.S. firms to move to Haiti, the U.S. government tells investors that Haiti has a "tradition of respect for private property and foreign ownership." Finding the investment climate favorable, about 200 U.S. corporations have settled in Haiti. The founder of the Haitian American Chamber of Commerce, Stanley Urban, concedes that Haiti "has an authoritarian style of government but there are more freedoms and opportunities in private enterprise than in many 'Western style' democracies." The president of Worth Industries was quoted in a publication funded by the U.S. government, An Investor's Guide to Haiti, as saying, "During the past 15 years, we feel the government has been stable and has made a determined effort to improve the conditions of its citizens."

Many subcontracting companies use the cheap Haitian labor mainly to produce textiles for U.S. distributors. Ninety percent of the workers in the assembly industries are women. Most companies, U.S.-owned or subcontractors for U.S. firms, can count on a profit margin of at least 30 percent, and sometimes as much as 100 percent, from their Haitian operations. The major manufacturers include such electronics corporations as Motorola, Bendix, Univac, GTE, and TRW. The plant manager of another electronics company, Argus Industries, said that, thanks to "the trainability and the reliability" of the Haitian worker, "we have been able to manufacture electronic components to U.S. military specifications for the past ten years."[11]

TOURISM

French perfume, voodoo ceremonies, high-quality artwork and crafts, fancy hotels, and curiosity bring tourists to Haiti. Government-licensed taxi drivers await the tourists at the airport, holding out promises to take them to the Cap-Haïtien Castle, to nightclubs, black-magic rituals, and the beach at Jacmel. First-time visitors find Haiti fascinating: a trip into another world far removed from what they know as ordinary. Individually painted trucks called tap-taps serve as public transportation; their bright colors and painted biblical citations command the tourist's attention. Haitian artists and craftspeople have created their own lively and human art. A few nightclubs feature naked dancing girls and voodoo priests eating glass and chomping on burning cinders—all paid $5 a night for their performances for the tourists. The country's tourist association touts Haiti as the "safest country in the world" because of its lack of street crime.

The tourist industry, however, is falling apart in Haiti. The misleading publicity about the feared disease AIDS allegedly in Haiti, the malfunctioning infrastructure, and the hard-to-hide poverty have all hurt Haiti's image of a safe and magical country. Hotel business fell 50 percent from 1979 to 1982, and the Club Méditerranée closed its facility north of Port-au-Prince in early 1983 because of lack of business. Duvalier, concerned about the decline in tourists, tried to present a better picture to the foreign visitors by clearing out obvious slums and creating a rosy picture of the country in expensive tourist brochures.

MIGRATION

Many thousand Haitians cross the border each year to cut cane in the Dominican Republic, where the Dominican people consider work in the canefields degrading and too low-paying. The Haitian government has instituted a program of forced savings whereby Dominican authorities subtract $1 every 15 days from the pay of each Haitian canecutter and then deliver the collected sum to the Haitian Embassy in Santo Domingo. Predictably, not one Haitian worker has received a reimbursement from the government's savings plan. Other Haitians look for jobs far away from the island. From Guyana to Canada, by way of Guadeloupe, the Bahamas, and Florida, Haitian emigrants arrive legally and illegally on many shores in search of ways to earn a living. Usually they find something the Bahamians call "Haitian work"—the dirtiest, hardest employment in the society. The Puerto Rican-based Ecumenical Center for Human Rights says the Haitians "are leaving their country by any route which will take them out, however painful the voyage."[12] An estimated 1 million Haitians live permanently outside their country.

Since 1972, Haitians have been setting out to sea in flimsy, overloaded boats in the hope of sailing 750 miles to Florida. From 1979 to 1982, 40,000 Haitians illegally migrated to the United States. In 1979, the Congressional Black Caucus charged that in contrast to U.S. treatment of refugees from nonblack nations, the U.S. refugee policy concerning Haitians was "tainted with race, class, and ideological prejudice." The U.S. Coast Guard has started patrolling Haitian waters, and the federal government has stepped up military aid to the Duvalier dictatorship. The Lawyers Committee for International Human Rights, based in New York, reported in 1982 that Haitians returned to their country by the U.S. Coast Guard were automatically considered opponents of the Duvalier regime.[13] Called *komokins* (traitors), the few who have been able to recount their experiences report that the security forces routinely beat the arriving returnees and throw them in prison. Many of the *komokins* are never heard from again.

Reporting on the conditions of Haitian refugees who come to the United States, Florida State Representative Reid Moore told the U.S. Senate Committee on Finance: "Unlike the Cubans, who arrived in relatively good health, the Haitians brought a number of medical problems, primarily related to the stresses of poverty, malnutrition, overcrowded substandard housing conditions. . . . The most significant communicable disease of concern has been pulmonary tuberculosis. . . . One half of the Haitians immigrating to Florida have intestinal roundworms and about 10 percent are infested with giardia."

POLITICS AND CHANGE

Change is inevitable in Haiti, but it is hard to predict when or in what form the change will be. "The government could be toppled tomorrow by a gentle breeze," reflected a French businessman who had been living in Haiti for 12 years, "but it could also withstand a decade of hurricanes." It is not that the Duvalier regime has such strong backing by either the rich or the poor. Even the business community would not mind escaping the confines of the feudal-type government, but no one sector can or will join with others to oppose Duvalier.

Years of repression and censorship of the news has obstructed the development of any widespread popular revolutionary movement. Those persons who have resisted are either dead, in jail, or in exile. The almost 30 years of family dictatorship have deepened the isolation of Haiti from the rest of the world. No independent media exist, and the police prohibit the distribution of foreign newspapers and magazines that contain articles critical of Haiti. The 23 percent literacy rate and the language barrier have prevented most Haitians from communicating with their Spanish- and English-speaking neighbors and have contributed to the lack of opposition. The only alternative to the government news is from the informal *telediol*, or word-of-mouth network. Many Haitians, isolated from sources of informed political analysis and news, have as a consequence remained passive in the face of the dictatorship.

In 1983, the Catholic Church surfaced as a major critic of the dictatorship. Criticism of Duvalier by Pope John Paul II during his March 1983 visit released an unprecedented flood of public criticism against the regime. But the ability of the Catholic Church to spearhead a movement against Duvalier is limited by two factors: the archbishop, who was appointed by Duvalier, has traditionally tolerated the government; and many Haitians distrust the church for its often violent campaigns against the popular practices of voodoo.

In a December 1982 government report on corruption, Canada called the Haitian government a "kleptocracy," where almost everything is filched. Haitians have charged that the Duvaliers look forward to hurricanes, because the disasters result in emergency aid. Haitian officials are even known to raid religious relief services and to resell the food for personal gain. Multilateral and bilateral aid provides over 60 percent of the public-works budget of the Duvalier dictatorship. Even with all the aid, Haiti remains the poorest nation in the hemisphere. After almost 30 years of terror and corruption, the Duvaliers have amassed a personal fortune estimated at $400 million from foreign aid and public funds, most of it stashed away in Swiss banks. Baby Doc spends most of his time racing power boats by his seaside villa, occasionally stopping in at the National Palace to oversee the affairs of his fiefdom.

Although foreign donors recognize that a high percentage of their aid never goes for intended purposes, they continue to prop up the regime in fear that the radical opposition would take advantage of a repressive and bankrupt regime to create a left-leaning government. President Reagan, in a letter to Haiti's President-for-Life, praised the Duvalier regime for its "determined opposition" to "Cuban adventurism" and its support for "private enterprise and economic reform."[14] The U.S. president did not address the reasons for the Haitian boat people, nor did he mention that a Haitian child who survives the first five years can expect to live 25 years less than a Cuban child.

Haiti has a favorable investment climate for American business and is a location par excellence for assembly production. The Haitian people suffer in this paradise of profit. It is a world where everything, from the national lottery to the general hospital, bears the Duvalier name. Photos of Jean Claude and Michelle are everywhere. As a safety measure, some Haitian families place them prominently in their homes, and the government displays life-sized images of the Duvaliers in public areas. At night, neon signs bearing the faces of Jean Claude and Michelle light up, a constant reminder of who controls and structures Haitian life.

Jamaica

"Watch Jamaica," said President Ronald Reagan, shortly after taking office. Washington chose Jamaica, the largest of the English-speaking Caribbean islands, to be its showplace to demonstrate the superiority of capitalism to socialism, and the free market to state control. The time was right: Jamaica had just emerged from eight years of democratic socialism under the leadership of Michael Manley.

A mountainous, lush, and picturesque country, Jamaica is the land of saltfish, reggae music, potent ganja (marijuana), Rastafarian cults, and a tradition of violence. Jamaica left the preindustrial era in the 1950s when bauxite was discovered on the island. Manufacturing also developed in the 1950s, and later tourism became an important part of the economy as investors began to realize the playground potential of some of its spectacular beaches. Although the country's economy is based in the canefields, beaches, and strip mines, the pulse of Jamaica is in the city of Kingston, where over 60 percent of its people live.

At the western edge of the city sprawls the urban ghetto called West Kingston, which has a reputation of being the poorest, meanest place in the Caribbean. Unemployed youths play cards and drink Red Stripe beer outside their ramshackle homes. Here, in a section called Trench Town, reggae hero Bob Marley grew up and found a world of "burnin' and lootin'" and "weepin' and wailin'." Each urban slum has its own name, style, and political identity. Whether by work in the garment factories or by drugs and hustling, it is a struggle to make it in West Kingston. Behind the city in the distance, often hidden by fog and smog, the Blue Mountains jut up to form the border of Kingston. On the foothills, the country's elite live in neighborhoods with names like Beverly Hills and look down on miles of urban squalor, small middle-class neighborhoods, and several sections of modern high-rises.

THE MANLEY YEARS

In 1972 Michael Manley became prime minister with the campaign slogan, "Better Must Come." Manley's father, Norman Manley, founded the People's National Party (PNP). The younger Manley won the election as a result of widespread dissatisfaction with the foreign domination, unemployment, and social inequality that characterized the first ten years of Jamaica's independence. From 1972 to 1980, Manley and the PNP sought to move the nation forward under a program of democratic socialism. While social progress did come, Jamaica's economy was torn apart by the flight of capital, IMF austerity programs, the drying up of international loan capital, high oil prices, and the lack of a clear economic management program by the Manley government. In the end, the people of Jamaica rejected Manley and were ready for the "deliverance" that Edward Seaga and his Jamaica Labor Party (JLP) promised in 1980.

The JLP victory ended a long, coordinated, international and local campaign to undermine the progress of Manley and the PNP government. The destabilization was aimed at producing an economic downturn that would undercut the PNP's popularity, push it out of office, or force it to abandon its progressive rhetoric and policies. Washington portrayed Manley's Jamaica as a pawn of the Soviet Union and Cuba, just as it did with Grenada before the invasion. "In the closing days of the Ford Administration," said Larry Birns of the Council on Hemispheric Affairs, "Kissinger had become almost manic about getting rid of Manley."[1] Manley himself believed the CIA was behind efforts by local conservative forces to destabilize the government and deny him reelection.

The United States, foreign investors, and the upper classes in Jamaica took issue with Manley's declaration of support for democratic socialism in 1974. For Manley and the PNP, a combination of public control over the most important means of production, national sovereignty, worker cooperatives, and human dignity constituted their platform of democratic socialism. In his book, *Jamaica: Struggle in the Periphery*, Manley said that his government sought a "third path," a "non-capitalist path of development to distinguish experiments like ours from the neocolonial capitalist model of the Puerto Rican type and the Marxist-Leninist model of the Cuban type." With the slogan "Socialism is Love," the party attempted to soothe the concerns of the middle and upper classes that Jamaican socialism meant class warfare. The PNP government emphasized that the democratic socialist order functioned in countries like West Germany. Under Manley, socialism would mean only the democratic reform of the capitalist system, not its dismantling. The PNP called for state ownership of the economy, worker participation in corporate profits and decision-making, and equitable distribution and productive use of idle lands. Manley repeatedly tried to distance his government from Cuba. "I'm a friend of Castro's," he once said, "but I'm a democratic socialist, and he is an affirmed communist. I'm certain that he views me as a fuzzy liberal."[2] However, friendly relations between the two nations and Manley's failure to condemn Cuba gave Washington the opening it needed to label Jamaica as a communist threat to the hemisphere.

Although the government failed to move the country forward economically, it demonstrated impressive social achievements. It passed laws establishing a minimum wage, maternity-leave rights for women, and severance pay. New programs began to improve literacy, youth employment, and health care, and the government evoked widespread participation in education. Also part of the legacy of the Manley government were public housing programs, rent control, and price controls on basic commodities.

The main destabilizing factor during Manley's incumbency was the flight of foreign investment. Investment dried up during the Manley years not because of dwindling profits but for political reasons. Profits on investment were stable, declining only from 31 percent in 1970–73 to 30 percent in 1977.[3] Investors, however, felt that Manley's embrace of democratic socialism would lead to an unfavorable investment climate. By 1975, new foreign investment had ceased completely, and in subsequent years Jamaica became a net exporter of investment capital instead of a recipient. This marked slowdown in investment deprived the Manley government of desperately needed foreign exchange and convinced many Jamaicans that Michael Manley, despite his good intentions, was leading the country to economic ruin. The flight of capital was accompanied by the flight of thousands of professionals and members of the middle class— a hard blow for the Manley government. Between 1976 and 1980, an estimated 18,000 Jamaicans left for the United States.[4] The PNP felt that the dramatic drop in tourists was attributable to a U.S.-orchestrated campaign to portray Jamaica as a nation torn by crime and violence. Another part of the economic destabilization was the cutoff of multilateral, bilateral, and commercial bank lending. The violence that surrounded Jamaican politics helped persuade many Jamaicans finally to choose Seaga over Manley. Although Seaga's JLP was the leading perpetrator of political violence, many Jamaicans concluded that the violence would cease if Seaga ousted the "socialist" government. In the 1980 elections, 800 people lost their lives in political violence.

During eight years of the Manley government, Jamaica came to be regarded as a pace-setter in the third world. Its bauxite tax and its role in the formation of the International Bauxite Association brought it high acclaim from many other underdeveloped nations similarly subject to TNC domination and uneven terms of trade. Politically, Jamaica also broke new ground trying to institute the politics of democratic socialism in a third-world nation. Jamaica represented the hopes of many third-world nations wanting to pursue a course of nationalism without resorting to socialist revolution and a complete break with the capitalist world order. Around the world, many people closely followed events in Jamaica and admired the way Manley stood up against the United States, the bauxite firms, and the IMF. Finally, though, the Jamaican experiment largely proved a failure.

The middle-of-the-road politics of Michael Manley led to a dead end.

Caught between the demands of the upper and lower classes, the PNP
government could not adequately represent the interests of either group.
The party angered the professionals and the foreign investors but failed
to establish an alternative base of economic support with the lower class.
For all the criticism leveled at it by the United States, the Manley government was never a radical government with a plan for a substantial
restructuring of the economy. The PNP had not formulated an overall
plan to mobilize domestic agricultural and industrial workers. Consequently, it fell helplessly victim to international and local economic pressures.

"DELIVERANCE"

In Jamaica, the politics of the "big man," the leader of the party in power,
dominates the country. Michael Manley is the big man of the People's
National Party (PNP), and Edward Seaga is the big man of the Jamaica
Labor Party (JLP). Seaga, a white man who comes from Jamaica's export-
import trade bourgeoisie, was born in Boston and educated at Harvard.
Neither the PNP nor the JLP has much of an infrastructure, and each
depends on its big man to determine the party's direction and programs.
As a consequence of this reliance on a single figure, the parties are not
very adept at running an efficient government bureaucracy. Prime Minister Seaga has a notoriously difficult time delegating responsibility. Along
with his responsibilities as prime minister, Seaga serves as the minister
of finance, the minister of planning, and the minister of mining. Func-
tionaries in government seldom make any major decisions without his
direct participation. Likewise, Michael Manley retained unquestioned
control of the PNP despite his overwhelming defeat at the polls in 1980.

As the planned 1985 national elections drew nearer, the JLP saw that
its base of support was narrowing. A 1983 poll found that most Jamaicans
were once again lining up behind Michael Manley. Respected Jamaican
pollster Carl Stone reported: "The continued economic crisis, absence of
vital signs convincing the man in the street that the economy was improving, added to the gathering storm of inflation being felt throughout
the economy, have all weakened the JLP's credibility for sound economic
management." Stone said the JLP was increasingly perceived by voters
as unconcerned about the poor and defending only the rich, the business
owners, and the middle class.

Because of his role in the U.S. invasion of Grenada, Seaga experienced a sudden burst of popularity in late 1983. Taking advantage of the
spirit of patriotism in Jamaica created by the invasion, Seaga devalued
the Jamaican dollar by half (a move recommended by the United States).
Before the consequences of the devaluation were felt by the public and

before his renewed popularity subsided, Seaga called for immediate elections in December 1983, two years before his term would have expired. Not having time to prepare for the elections, Manley and the PNP boycotted them. The PNP charged that the election, in which the JLP gained all 60 seats in Parliament, was fraudulent, and that it occurred six months prior to the agreed-upon revision of the voter registration lists.

While the sudden move by Seaga to call elections did have the desired effect of keeping the JLP in control, it was not in keeping with the image of a democratic Jamaica that Washington and Seaga have been promoting. The PNP, with the support of many sectors of Jamaican society, demanded that Seaga hold elections again in 1984, when it will be prepared properly to contest Seaga's hold on power. Until then, Manley has suggested that a series of popular forums be arranged to debate issues usually discussed in Parliament. With the absence of opposition in Parliament and the social problems caused by the failing economy, Jamaica holds the potential for increased political violence.

THE POSTPONED TAKEOFF

When Edward Seaga became prime minister, he found a severely depressed economy. All leading sectors of the economy were in a tailspin, thousands of professional people had left the country, the external debt was unmanageable, the trade deficit was growing, and unemployment had reached an all-time high. Seaga, mimicking the rhetoric of Ronald Reagan, promised to put the private sector to work and to open Jamaica for business and foreign investment. Seaga brought his reputation as a financial wizard to the government's Jamaica House and began making changes: roads were repaired, imports of all types of consumer goods started to flow into the country, professionals began to return, and business owners were talking optimistically again. An atmosphere of prosperity characterized the early part of the Seaga administration. Jamaica lifted most import restrictions as part of its return to a free-market economy and the government's attempt to build public support. No longer did the country's elite need to travel to Miami on weekends for shopping trips. Basic consumer goods from the United States filled supermarket shelves, and more expensive products like cars and video equipment were readily available.

The temporary economic euphoria experienced in Jamaica was not due to any burst of private-sector activity or TNC investment. Rather, it was bilateral aid (mainly from the United States) and a flood of multilateral aid from the World Bank that brought the immediate yet superficial results. Economic aid from the United States jumped from $38 million in the last two years of the Manley government (1978–79) to $208 million

TABLE II C
JAMAICA'S ECONOMIC PERFORMANCE

Indicator	1980	1982
Balance of trade	$ − 75 million	$ − 476 million
Current accounts balance	$ 166 million	$ 426 million
Public external debt	$1,634 million	$2,060 million
Public external debt as % of GDP	54%	65%
Unemployment	26%	26%
Debt service as % of exports	20%	29%
Total Exports	$ 963 million	$ 726 million

Sources: *Economic and Social Progress in Latin America*, IDB, 1983; *Congressional Presentation Fiscal Year 1984 Annex III*, AID, 1983; *The World Factbook*, CIA, 1983

for the first two full years of Seaga's term in office (1981–82). In that same time frame, multilateral aid went from $174 million to $302 million. The World Bank especially favored Jamaica with its loans. Over 67 percent of its lending to the Caribbean went to Jamaica in 1981–82. In contrast to the increased flow of bilateral and multilateral capital, private foreign investment and private capital formation remained relatively static.

"Jamaica is open for business" is the slogan of the country's campaign to attract foreign investors. Jamaica receives a lot of help from its friends in the international corporate world in this effort. Shortly after Seaga became prime minister, President Reagan asked David Rockefeller to form a committee to promote foreign investment in the country of his new friend, Edward Seaga. Rockefeller formed the U.S. Business Committee on Jamaica, whose corporate members include United Brands, Chase Manhattan, Kaiser Aluminum, Anaconda, Reynolds Metals, Control Data, BankAmerica, Gulf + Western, WR Grace, Culbro, Eastern Airlines, and Alcoa. Following the creation of the U.S. committee, similar committees of representatives from major foreign corporations with interests in Jamaica formed in Canada, Great Britain, and West Germany. Rockefeller said, "We have worked hand-in-glove with the State Department, the Commerce Department, the AID administrator, and the National Security Adviser and, indeed, the President himself. I have never seen a case where there has been better private/public cooperation."[5] The cooperation, however, remains in the form of conferences and business committees rather than actual investment.

AGRICULTURE

Once a large Caribbean sugar and banana producer, Jamaica lately has had problems meeting its European production quotas. Banana production is only about a third of the output of several years ago, and the sugar industry is in a severe slump. The Seaga administration has used the economic downturn in both industries as an excuse to turn over portions of banana and sugarcane production to private industry. The Jamaican government has invited corporations like Tate & Lyle, United Brands, Booker McConnell, and Gulf + Western to own, manage, or restructure the country's two main export industries.

Government plans to "privatize" the sugar industry, the country's second-largest source of income, have met with the opposition of the Jamaican sugar workers, who constitute the island's largest workforce. Seaga has called for a moratorium on all wage increases and is pursuing other recommendations from Gulf + Western, which the government said was providing the country with free technical consulting. The workers claim the government pays more attention to foreign consultants than to the workers. The fate of the sugar industry in Jamaica has great significance because of the large number of workers employed in the industry and because sugar workers have traditionally been the base of worker militancy on the island. "If the sugar industry dies, the country folds," warned the public relations director of the National Sugar Company.[6]

As part of its campaign to attract foreign investors and increase foreign-exchange earnings, the government has advertised the country's potential to produce nontraditional agricultural exports. Only a handful of new investors, however, have come to Jamaica to grow flowers and vegetables for the U.S. market. One of the nontraditional producers has been Kaiser Aluminum, which started Jamaica Floral Exports. Not only has Jamaica been unable to expand its export agriculture, but it faces a major food crisis because of declining production of staple foods for the local market. In the last ten years per capita food production has dropped over 10 percent, yet Jamaica is the largest exporter of processed food in the Caribbean. Although Jamaica hosts several large locally owned food processors like Desnoes & Geddes and Grace Kennedy, TNCs have gained a stronger grip on this sector in the last several years through joint ventures with local firms. Prominent transnational food processors include Nestlé, Beatrice, Kellogg, Culbro, BAT, Unilever, Central Soya, Pillsbury, and Ralston Purina. TNCs dominate the production of flour, feed, liquor, milk products, coffee, chocolate, tobacco, and soft drinks.

INDUSTRY

Seaga's policies have split the local industrial sector into two camps: those that have experienced a boom in business due to the new export incentives, and those that cannot compete with the flood of lower-priced imports. The high tariffs that were established in the 1960s and continued during the Manley government were lowered by the Seaga government in keeping with his free-market philosophy and in consonance with IMF and World Bank demands. According to the Jamaican Manufacturer's Association, government deregulation and liberal import policies have forced 33 Jamaican factories (mostly shoe and garment manufacturers) to close. Many other factories were operating at only 40 percent capacity in 1982. Outraged at the attention and favors lavishly given foreign investors, the association demanded that Seaga "stop and examine" the situation before proceeding too far with his free-market program.

The presence of TNCs in the industrial sector, though by no means as pervasive as in the food-processing sector, is sizable. TNCs from the United States dominate the industrial sector, but there is a strong representation of Canadian and European TNCs in the import-substitution sector. Foreign investors frequently have joint ventures with the leading local manufacturing and industrial firms or arrange for production of their products through licensing or subcontracting. Incentive legislation in Jamaica has virtually eliminated corporate taxes, income tax, and customs duties for foreign investors. Major British firms include Berger Paints, Kier Holdings, and Metal Box. The leading Canadian firms in manufacturing are Diversey Chemicals and Bata Shoes; West Germany's Henkel and Denmark's Rentokil have major chemical-manufacturing operations.

U.S. firms that use Jamaica as a base for manufacture and distribution of pharmaceuticals and home products include Procter & Gamble, Bristol-Myers, Johnson & Johnson, Colgate Palmolive, Gillette, Sterling Drug, and Richardson-Vicks. The other major import-substitution sector with major U.S. TNC involvement is production and distribution of chemicals and gas, and includes the following firms: WR Grace, Transway (Tropigas), Wyandotte Chemicals, Houston Natural Gas (Liquid Carbonics), Sun Chemical, and Signal Oil & Gas. Two communications TNCs, Continental Telephone and Cable & Wireless (UK), also do business in Jamaica. Commenting on the role of foreign investment, former prime minister Manley said: "You need to identify the areas where foreign capital can genuinely assist you, but never see it as the linchpin, as Seaga does."[7]

MINERALS

Internationally, the bauxite industry is in the doldrums, a serious setback for Jamaica's national recovery plans. Despite measures by the U.S. and Jamaican governments to help the industry, production of bauxite and alumina dropped steadily during Seaga's first three years. While the industry expanded at a rate of 9 percent in 1980, it had shrunk by 26 percent in 1982. A major problem with the alumina industry in Jamaica is the high cost of fuel needed to run processing plants.

Recognizing the importance of the bauxite/alumina industry to Jamaica's economy, Washington took several extraordinary steps to aid the depressed market. It authorized two direct U.S. government purchases totaling 2.6 million tons of Jamaican bauxite in 1982, sidestepping regulations for competitive purchases. The federal government also approved a tax deal that allows bauxite firms to offset part of the production levy they pay the Jamaican government as a foreign tax credit on their U.S. income taxes. Jamaica, under pressure from the aluminum industry, reduced taxes in a futile attempt to spur production. The Seaga administration also negotiated two barter deals with General Motors and Chrysler, exchanging bauxite for vehicles—not a priority in an economy already highly dependent on imported supplies.

MIGRATION

More than half the world's 4.4 million Jamaicans live outside Jamaica, mainly in Great Britain, Canada, and the United States. As in other Caribbean islands, the migratory trend is a result of the declining need for agricultural labor and the failure of new sectors like tourism, light manufacturing, and mining to provide a sufficient number of jobs. Many Jamaicans who have left their rural parishes to find work in crowded Kingston later decide that their chances of landing a job are better outside the country, even as illegal workers.

Migration, however, is not a recent phenomenon. In the early part of this century, Jamaicans helped build the Panama Canal and the railroad in Costa Rica. United Fruit brought them in to cultivate bananas on its mango plantations in Central America. The main migration flowed to Great Britain, where Jamaicans could enter freely as citizens of the British Commonwealth. When Great Britain imposed immigration controls in 1964, the pace of Jamaicans entering the United States and Canada increased. More than 10,000 Jamaicans leave the island each year to work in the sugarcane fields of Florida and the apple orchards of New England under a temporary work program of the U.S. Department of Labor.

PAWN OF THE UNITED STATES

It would be hard to overstate the contributions of the Reagan administration to the government of Prime Minister Seaga. In Seaga's Jamaica, U.S.

ideology, capital, and government support are the critical influences on just about everything that happens in the country. From the beginning of President Reagan's term, Seaga was given special treatment. In fact, he was the first foreign official to visit President Reagan in the White House. Neither leader tires of praising the virtues of private enterprise and foreign investment. Seaga's cooperation with U.S. politics and corporations proved fruitful: in 1982, Jamaica was the third-largest per capita recipient of U.S. aid. At the urging of Washington, multilateral aid poured into the island. Several U.S. agencies, like the General Services Administration and the Overseas Private Investment Corporation (OPIC), even violated their own regulations (on open bidding and insurance limits) to support Seaga's private-enterprise government. In May 1983, Seaga thanked the National Security Council for its role in pushing for additional balance-of-payments support for Jamaica. "Whether we like it or not," commented a Jamaican business owner, "the United States has become a partner in most everything we do."[8]

In return for this financial aid, Jamaica has been turned into a tool of U.S. foreign policy in the region. Embassy officials in Kingston say Washington is making Jamaica into its showcase of democracy and free enterprise. But Jamaica is more than window dressing. It was in the forefront of the U.S. campaign to destabilize the Grenadian government of Maurice Bishop and was the regional leader of the invasion force that occupied the island in October 1983. In the words of Jamaican singer Harry Belafonte, "Jamaica has become the new pawn of the United States." For his services, Seaga was honored in 1982 when President Reagan presented him with the American Friendship Medal of the Freedom Foundation for his "furtherance of democratic institutions" and "courageous leadership in the cause of freedom for all people."[9]

Jamaica's special relationship with the United States has angered other Caribbean nations, which felt it was undermining the movement for regional integration. Caricom members had decided beforehand that they would consult each other and formulate a joint reaction to Reagan's CBI proposals, but Seaga jumped the gun in his approval of the initiative— which he helped design—and in doing so tied the hands of the other members. Most Caribbean nations felt that they should not appear to be at odds with one another, squabbling for the crumbs from Washington's table. Jamaica—which got a piece of the cake instead of crumbs—decided that its interests lay more with Washington than with the region. "If it weren't for U.S. foreign policy," remarked a U.S. banker in 1982, "the country would be bankrupt."[10]

By 1983, the promise of an economic miracle had burst. The promised economic takeoff has failed to happen despite generous injections of loan capital into the economy. Seaga's globetrotting to find new investors and lenders has produced few results. Rather than attracting large TNCs,

Seaga's plan attracted only small corporations, like Affordable Custom Dental Appliances, which uses cheap Jamaican labor to manufacture dentures. Seaga's financial wizardry could not attract the private bank loans that the country sorely needed to build its foreign-exchange reserve. The government could not keep its promises to maintain wages and jobs in the public sector and in state industries like sugar. Social-service programs and funds for education and medicine have been cut. "Education is again becoming the privilege of the rich, instead of a right for all," said a spokesperson for a Jamaican women's group.[11] Schoolchildren have no books, school buildings and fixtures are falling apart for lack of maintenance, and there is not enough medicine or hospital staff for the sick.

The early period of free-flowing imports ended because of scarce foreign-exchange reserves and a growing trade deficit. Many bigger companies are exempt from import restrictions on raw materials because they are exporters. Exporting firms, which are often TNC subsidiaries, benefited from a unique program set up by the World Bank that provides credit for buying raw materials intended for processing for the export market. Smaller businesses, which produce only for the local market, have had a much harder time importing the materials and components they need. The infusions of international aid and the consequent improvement in investor confidence led to a very temporary rebound of the Jamaican economy. But Jamaica sank back into the quicksand of debt and foreign-exchange difficulties. By early 1984, the external debt had risen to $2.8 billion, or more than $1,000 for every Jamaican. Commenting on the country's difficult economic straits, one Jamaican said, "Seaga's no good for the people. He's brought all the capitalists down here with their money. But we don't see any of it."[12]

St. Kitts-Nevis

St. Kitts and Nevis gained independence from Great Britain in September 1983, and it is likely that their independence day was the last one the Commonwealth Caribbean will see for some time. Bermuda and Montserrat may begin the independence process in a couple of years, while the others have no plans to change their status as colonies.

Two miles of sea separates St. Kitts from the smaller Nevis to the south. Because the English settled St. Kitts before any other island in the British West Indies, they called it the "mother colony" and "cradle of the Caribbean." From their base on the island, the British colonized Antigua, Barbuda, Tortuga, and Montserrat. St. Kitts-Nevis maintained jurisdiction for a hundred years over Anguilla, which seceded from the island union when the British declared the three islands an Associated State. Anguillans earned meager incomes from fishing and small-scale farming during the 1700s and early 1800s, while the landowners of St. Kitts-Nevis grew rich from the canefields. The affluence of the islands' colonial economy continued until 1834, when slavery was abolished.

Political independence has not freed St. Kitts-Nevis from its dependence on the traditional sugar industry. The industry accounts for 70 percent of the country's exports, occupies 90 percent of the cultivated land, and employs almost half the labor force. Steadily declining since 1961, the sugar industry will fall further due to new, restrictive sugar quotas. The slowdown of the regional sugar industry has affected hundreds of workers from St. Kitts-Nevis who can no longer find work as migrant canecutters in Trinidad. A canecutter in St. Kitts earns an average of $50 to $75 per week, a relatively high wage for the Caribbean, which results in high production costs. Six prominent families owned all the country's sugar estates until the government nationalized them several years ago. Although some farmers grow groundnuts and raise cattle, the economy relies chiefly on the sugarcane crop. The Ministry of Agriculture estimates that agricultural production satisfies 30 percent of domestic food requirements and could be expanded easily to meet over 65 percent of those needs, which would reduce the new nation's heavy reliance on food imports.[1]

FOREIGN INVESTMENT

Offshore assembly operations, particularly in garments, shoes, and electronics, have expanded rapidly in the last few years. A resident adviser from USAID encourages U.S. firms to establish operations at one of the country's two industrial parks. Wage rates average 67 cents per hour for trained workers in the apparel industry, and 88 cents per hour in the data industry. Trainees on the assembly line get only 52 cents per hour. The electronics companies that establish plants in St. Kitts often start their operations by using a local subcontractor, Electrofab, which sets up the initial labor contracts.

Among the U.S. firms in the country are Exxon's Tranducer Systems, Bowmar Instrument, Coca-Cola, Fashion Trading, Kellogg, and Analysis Programming Corporation. Two corporations, Coopers & Lybrand and Louis Berger International, are designing a program for the government to improve the country's infrastructure and to attract foreign investment. One of the development consultants described St. Kitts-Nevis as a "small country with a small government, and you can come in and easily manage the situation."[2] Referring to the U.S.-sponsored growth in offshore industries, Prime Minister Dr. Kennedy Simmonds said: "I do not believe the future of this country lies in enclave industries, which bring things in for manufacture to simply send them out. They are useful and provide employment, but when there are problems in the markets abroad, we suffer immediately. I believe that if we are able to develop that natural resource which we have, our soil, and use it to feed ourselves, and ultimately to export to other countries, then we are building an economy on a sound base."[3] Despite the government's commitment to this approach, its representatives attended the CBI seminar in Washington, D.C., in October 1983 and met with manufacturers in Puerto Rico regarding the possibility of twin plants and joint ventures.

Kittitians have always regarded tourism uneasily but in recent years have made more efforts to please tourists, including dredging the deepwater harbor and refurbishing the airport. St. Kitts has also instituted the Conference to Commemorate Christopher Columbus' Founding of the New World as a gimmick to attract tourists. In February 1983, the main building of the Royal St. Kitts Hotel, the country's largest hotel, burned down. The government sold the smoldering remains to Transamerica Investments for $7 million, with the agreement that the huge TNC will collect the benefits from the insurance claim when settled. In Nevis, USAID has provided funds for the first phase of converting the Hamilton House, the birthplace of Alexander Hamilton, into a museum.

POLITICS

Party squabbles and union rivalries are a staple of Kittitian conversation. The issue of independence sparked a controversy between the administration and the opposition Labour Party. The opposition favored independence only after a general election and criticized the country's new constitution because it gives Nevis the option to secede. More importantly, the new constitution heavily favors the smaller Nevis in the apportionment of the legislature, which has made many Kittitians unhappy with independence in its present form. On September 1, 1983, when fire destroyed the historic Basseterre building that housed the Supreme Court, the registry, and the public library, Dr. Simmonds blamed the Labour opposition. "LABOUR MADMEN BURN DOWN COURTHOUSE," screamed the headline of the government newspaper. Two other fires followed, in which the home of an opposition supporter and a building owned by the widow of former Labour Party Premier Robert Bradshaw were burned down. A month after independence, St. Kitts was thrown into international politics as orchestrated by the Reagan administration. Although it initially did not give its support to the invasion of Grenada, the Kittitian police later joined the Caribbean Peace Force stationed in Grenada.

St. Lucia

Blown off course on their way to the Guianas, a ship of English settlers washed ashore on the island of St. Lucia in 1605. During their first months on the island, they lived in huts provided by the native Carib Indians. In the next 150 years, St. Lucia changed hands 14 times in bloody battles between French and English colonizers. Finally, in 1814, the Treaty of Paris gave the island to Great Britain, but evidence of former French control remains in the common French place names and the lilting French patois spoken by St. Lucians.

BANANAS AND SUGAR

Filling the valleys and climbing the hills, bananas are everywhere in St. Lucia. The island has always depended on agricultural export, but it used to be sugarcane that covered the island. In the 1950s, the colonial government decided that bananas would be a better bet and mandated the island-wide switch. Farmers sell all their bananas to Geest Industries through the St. Lucia Banana Growers Association. At one time, Geest owned 40,000 acres of choice farmland on its two estates on St. Lucia.[1] Although it has relinquished most of its land, the banana conglomerate still buys, ships, and markets the country's entire banana crop. In 1980 Hurricane Allen struck the banana industry hard, giving the government reason to think it should have retained at least part of the sugar industry. The country now pays millions of dollars each year to import sugar, but will probably begin to reestablish the crop. "Sugar has bad connotations," said a government official, referring to the history of slavery, "but we would produce a syrup for local consumption and use it in food processing."[2]

After Jamaica, St. Lucia has been the largest banana-exporting island in the Commonwealth Caribbean. Yet the banana industry on the island has experienced extreme economic difficulties. A multimillion-dollar debt hangs over the growers' association, and the small banana farmers receive only about 10 cents a pound for their bananas—a price that does not even cover their production costs. In 1982, the United States stepped in to help the country's agricultural sector with a $7 million loan under the CBI program. The loan provided credit for purchases of U.S. fertilizers and pesticides and is being used to restructure the industry to encourage more involvement by private entrepreneurs. Another change in the island's agricultural scene was the founding of St. Lucia Model Farms, a joint venture among Geest, the island's government, and the Commonwealth Development Corporation. In a fertile valley owned by Geest, the new corporation is cultivating mangoes, passion fruit, avocados, limes, and bananas. Geest not only stands to profit directly by the venture (funded in part by the European Development Fund[3]), but it will also indirectly benefit because of its position as the island's major shipper.

FOREIGN INVESTMENT

St. Lucia wants to industrialize in order to reduce its dependency on agricultural exports. Supporting the government's attempts to attract foreign investors, the United Nations Development Project (UNDP) initiated a feasibility study for an industrial zone, and USAID financed the construction of five factory shells. The industrial sector began in the 1970s with the establishment of a carton-manufacturing plant (a joint venture among the four Windward Island governments and a Venezuelan paper firm called Papelería Industrial). Seventy manufacturing operations in St. Lucia produce garments, plastic products, and soft drinks. Booker McConnell (UK) owns a bottling company; Heineken (Netherlands) operates the Windward and Leeward Brewery; and Clevepak (U.S.) has its Equality Specialties Division in St. Lucia. Two U.S. agribusiness corporations active in St. Lucia are Universal Flavors and World's Finest Chocolates.

Foreign investors have clashed with the strong unions in St. Lucia, and the International Labor Organization has listed St. Lucia as one of the countries in the world that has an above-average loss of working time due to strikes.[4] Union leaders in St. Lucia cite the case of the Milton Bradley Corporation—whose assembly plant pulled out of the island when workers started complaining about wage levels—as a prime example of foreign investors' treatment of St. Lucian workers. The island's government, in an attempt to create a better investment climate, has been pressuring the unions to sign a social contract that would modify their wage demands.

Private direct investment in 1981 was estimated at $41.6 million, $34.1 million of which was accounted for by the Amerada Hess transshipment terminal.[5] In 1977 Amerada Hess said it would build an oil refinery and a terminal, but needed the unanimous approval of the legislature as one of its conditions for investing in St. Lucia. The privately owned oil company also received guarantees of holidays from all income, sales, property, and franchise taxes, as well as waivers of import duties, licenses, and fees on equipment. The company's promises of a refinery and jobs for thousands of St. Lucians have fallen flat, since the oil refinery was never built. It constructed the transshipment terminal on the prime agricultural land it bought from Geest Industries. Only 300 workers have ever worked at the terminal at one time, and the current Amerada Hess payroll covers only 40 employees. St. Lucia earns a mere two cents on every barrel of crude oil passed through the terminal and four cents on barrels exported for refining. There is widespread speculation in St. Lucia that the government is not even getting this agreed-upon payment, because only the company monitors the quantity of oil handled by the terminal.

Even more than in other Caribbean locations, tourism in St. Lucia is an enclave industry. Fancy hotels on hilltops or isolated beaches are a world away from the rundown tenements and urban destitution in the capital city of Castries. The luxury of the new Couples resort, with its romantic beachfront bungalows, contrasts sharply with the life led by St. Lucians. Rain forests, secluded harbors, British culture with a French flair, and a renowned Creole cuisine have made tourism a leading foreign-exchange earner. Because the hotels and restaurants are mostly foreign-owned, however, the real benefits of the industry are few. Since the tourist trade depends on charter flights for the major stock of its visitors, it experiences severe setbacks when the foreign agencies shut down or change destinations.

Political slogans splatter the downtown buildings in Castries. Epigraphs supporting one candidate are invariably crossed out and painted over with mottos of another. After an internal political struggle, the St. Lucia Labor Party lost to the right-wing United Workers Party (UWP) in 1979. In his campaign for prime minister, UWP's John Compton paraphrased revolutionary Grenada's saying, "Forward Ever, Backward Never," with "Christians Ever, Communists Never." The landslide victory of Compton, an outspoken advocate of foreign investment, put St. Lucia firmly in the U.S. camp.

At the time of its independence in 1979, St. Lucia was commonly regarded as the best equipped of the smaller Caribbean islands to withstand the economic rigors of nationhood. Since then, the economy of St. Lucia has begun a downhill slide. The Compton administration has adopted the fashionable Reaganesque rhetoric extolling the virtues of private enterprise. Having laid out the red carpet for foreign investors who have never come, it now has to deal with an increasingly restless and unemployed population.

St. Vincent and the Grenadines

From the air, St. Vincent and the Grenadines resemble a kite: a roughly oval-shaped island outlined by its black volcanic sand beaches, followed by a tail of the tiny Grenadines. Although their natural endowments make St. Vincent and the Grenadines a yachting paradise and an exclusive retreat for wealthy travelers, nature struck the islands with a volcanic eruption of La Soufrière in 1979 and with Hurricane Allen, which devastated the agricultural sector in 1980.

ECONOMY

Agriculture accounts for a quarter of St. Vincent's export earnings.[1] Bananas, grown mainly on farms of less than one hectare, are the most important crop. Geest Industries purchases and exports the entire banana crop through its contract with the St. Vincent Banana Growers Association. The island also produces coconuts and nutmeg and has begun to cultivate sugar again after several years of inactivity. St. Vincent is a major supplier of arrowroot, a starch used in food processing and the production of computer paper; it is the island's second-largest export crop. When arrowroot production stagnated, the government established a program to increase the yield. It hopes to some day locally manufacture the finished product St. Vincent now exports unprocessed. The United States and the United Kingdom buy 95 percent of St. Vincent's arrowroot crop.[2]

Manufacturing may surpass agriculture in importance to St. Vincent's economy. For the island's stage of development, and in comparison with other Caribbean countries, the manufacturing sector is quite large. The U.S. State Department called the growth of this sector "remarkable" and credits the U.S.-based consulting firm of Coopers & Lybrand with the achievement. The company assisted Devco, St. Vincent's development agency, with several industrial projects, including a fiberglass-boat factory, a foam-rubber plant, and an electronics-assembly plant. A flour mill built in 1978 in a joint venture with a Canadian company, a St. Vincent private firm, and the government produces flour and feed for the Eastern Caribbean market. Neither agriculture nor manufacturing have provided enough work for the island, however, and every year hundreds of Vincentians leave to cut cane in Trinidad and Barbados.

The tourism industry in St. Vincent is small but growing. The well-appointed yachts in the harbors, however, contrast with the poor living conditions of the local population, which has one of the highest mortality rates of any in the Caribbean due to protein-calorie malnutrition, intestinal diseases, and a severe shortage of potable water. Like most other Caribbean islands, St. Vincent suffers from a lack of water, and even imports some of its water supply.

Because of local political differences, St. Vincent took ten years longer to become an Associated State of the Commonwealth, which it did in 1969. Leading a nation independent since 1979, St. Vincent's government faces opposition from a diverse array of seven political parties, a surprising number for a country of only 124,000 inhabitants. In 1981, workers issued a call for a general strike, and 15,000 people demonstrated in response to two antidemocratic bills that have since been dropped because of popular opposition. One bill proposed jail terms of up to seven years for doing "anything that can have an adverse effect on the democratic process," or for promoting "hostility between different classes of persons."[3] Before the Grenadian coup, a reporter for the Grenada weekly newspaper *Free West Indian* was refused entrance to St. Vincent in 1981 on the grounds that he was "undesirable and a revolutionary."[4]

The current administration in St. Vincent supports the injection of foreign capital and the expansion of export-oriented industry to support its economy. The government advertises its low wages ($5 per 8-hour day for men, $3.85 for women), its duty-free arrangements, its plans for a free zone, and its eagerness to increase offshore banking and assembly operations.

Suriname

Suriname, one of the three Guianas on the northeast shoulder of South America and the continent's smallest independent state, shares a similar past with its closest neighbors and with many Caribbean islands. The Dutch colonized Suriname as part of their sugar empire after acquiring it from the English in exchange for what is now Manhattan, New York. In a region where slavery was the norm, the Dutch became legendary throughout the Caribbean for their cruelty to the slaves, causing even many French and British slave owners to shudder. Many slaves escaped the horrendous conditions of the plantations by disappearing into the dense forest interior of Suriname (an Amerindian word meaning "rocky rapids"). The so-called Bush Negroes created villages and lifestyles safe from the feared Dutch slave masters.

Once slavery was abolished, blacks refused to stay on the plantations. The Dutch imported laborers from India, Java, and China. Consequently, the country boasts a rich mixture of ethnic heritage, with a third of the population black, a third East Indian, and the other third a variety of ethnic backgrounds. The population of 376,000 speaks several languages: Dutch, English, Hindi, and Sranang Tongo or Taki Taki, a type of English Creole.

AN ISOLATED COUNTRY

The variety of languages isolates Suriname from the rest of the continent and the Caribbean. Because English is the base of Taki Taki, its most common language, the government plans to establish English as the official language in an attempt to improve international relations. Other factors isolating the sparsely populated country are the jungle that covers 90 percent of its surface and a clock setting that keeps it at a half-hour variance with its Latin neighbors.

Surinamers also live isolated from each other. At the time of independence from the Netherlands in 1975, over 40,000 Surinamers lived in Holland; by 1980 the figure jumped to more than 150,000. This emigration has become a major obstacle to overall growth, since it has caused a severe lack of trained workers. Suriname, which has long had its own law and medical schools, has more physicians, engineers, scientists, and lawyers living in Holland than at home. Dutch labor-union leaders have called for the severing of political ties to Suriname and other territories to curb the flow of immigrants.

In Suriname, the government is developing programs to lure its citizens back to their homeland. More than half the 350,000 Surinamers who do live in Suriname are under 17 years of age. Other residents of the former colony include over 30,000 Guyanese who work in the skilled or semiskilled jobs previously held by native workers.[1] Because of increasing illegal immigration from strife-filled Guyana, Suriname's government began a deportation campaign that expelled 3,600 undocumented Guyanese in its first two months.[2]

POLITICAL TURMOIL

Suriname's transition to independence in 1975 went smoothly, with the Dutch promising an extensive aid package of $1.5 billion over 15 years. The first government after independence was protective of the heavy Dutch corporate investment in the country and kept the former colonial power happy. The Dutch have been less satisfied with the current government of Desi Bouterse, who took power in 1980 in a relatively bloodless coup. In December 1982, the military defended the Bouterse government against a coup attempt the government claimed had been planned with CIA assistance. In that incident the military executed 15 Surinamese opposition leaders, including conservative union leader Cyril Daal, who had helped organize antigovernment demonstrations earlier in 1982 and who was said to have connections with the CIA through his Moederbond Union's association with the American Institute for Free Labor Development (AIFLD).[3] In the first part of December 1982, the CIA devised a plan for a mercenary overthrow of Bouterse, but Congress voted against it on the grounds that the new government had not proven to be a threat to U.S. interests.[4]

The Bouterse regime suffered severe adverse consequences from the December 1982 killings. The Dutch suspended all aid, the U.S. government temporarily suspended its assistance, and rumors began to fly about Suriname's possible connections with Cuba. The Bouterse regime admitted that the 1982 killings were an "overreaction," and emphasized its intention to "regionalize" and improve its relations with all countries in the Caribbean, including, but not especially, Cuba.

Suriname's South American neighbor, Brazil, has approached the Bouterse regime with offers of military and civilian assistance. Because the United States prodded Brazilian officials to make this move, two Suriname cabinet members opposed the acceptance of Brazilian aid; they were later dismissed.[5] In mid-1983, a joint Suriname-Cuba commission met for the first time and signed an agreement covering cooperation in various areas, including agriculture, education, health, culture, economic planning, and people's mobilization. Since the U.S. invasion of Grenada, however, Bouterse succumbed to Brazilian and U.S. pressure and expelled the Cuban ambassador and approximately one hundred Cuban diplomats and advisers from Suriname.

In order to offset the cutoffs in aid, Suriname secured large loans from the Central Bank and from the Inter-American Development Bank (IDB). In 1983, the IDB expressed approval of Suriname's investments in high-return, rapid-gestation projects and its general development program. Bouterse commented in a 1983 interview, "In just three years we have built 10 times more houses and 10 times more roads than the previous government did in four years."[6] The government enforced previously ignored price controls on basic commodities such as flour, meat, and bread. Contrary to early expectations from international observers, Suriname's balance of payments has held up well.[7]

Touted by the *Wall Street Journal* as "one of the most affluent countries in the third world,"[8] Suriname produces many agricultural staples for its local market and is self-sufficient in rice, edible oil, citrus fruits, coffee, and bananas. Rice, the main agricultural crop, constitutes the second-largest source of foreign-exchange earnings. Mechanization has improved the rice industry, making it the most productive of that of any underdeveloped country. The government has sponsored palm oil plantations that supply 90 percent of Suriname's edible-oil needs, and has opened an experimental cattle ranch to help decrease meat imports. Two companies dominate the shrimp industry: Suriname American Industries (owned by Castle & Cooke, with a small interest held by the government) and Sujafi (a Japanese and Surinamese-owned firm). The industry suffered a 25 percent decline in 1981, and 20 fishing vessels were consequently transferred to French Guiana. Bruynzeel, a Dutch company, founded the major firm in Suriname's forest industry and now owns the firm jointly with the government. Suriname's vast forests are mostly unexploited and to a large extent inaccessible. Other Dutch corporations still operating in Suriname include Heineken, Hagemeyer, Algemene Bank, and Royal Dutch Shell.

Close to half the manufactured goods consumed by the average Suriname family are imported, mostly from the United States. The U.S. Department of Commerce says that this "assures price stability for U.S. purchases, sales, and contracts." In a 1982 report, the U.S. Department of Labor commented that Suriname has "looked increasingly to the United States as a source of supply, and the buy American mentality has taken root."[9]

BAUXITE AND ALUMINUM

Suriname sells over half its exports to the United States and the European Economic Community. The main export, representing 80 percent of all exports, is bauxite with its related products, alumina and aluminum. The country's bauxite deposits are believed to be the richest in the world. The U.S.-owned Alcoa, through its subsidiary Suralco, and Royal Dutch Shell's Billiton control Suriname's bauxite industry. Alcoa also built a huge dam in Suriname, creating one of the largest artificial lakes in the world.

Although the Bouterse government increased taxes on the bauxite industry, it intends to leave it in private hands because nationalization would be difficult given the industry's elaborate operations and the lack of alternative markets. Bauxite created a flow of wealth for the Netherlands, particularly before Suriname's independence, and for the two major corporations. The industry also provided Suriname with a definite advantage over most of its Caribbean neighbors, and despite its decline continues to be the backbone of Suriname's economy. Looking for new industry, the government plans to undertake an oil pilot-research project in an area where Gulf Oil recently discovered petroleum-bearing sand.

The stability of the Bouterse regime has been buffeted on all sides. The controversial Bouterse charged that the United States, the Dutch government, and unnamed Communist nations have attempted "to influence our political development and our internal affairs."[10] The anti-U.S. rhetoric of Bouterse quieted down, however, after the Grenada invasion, at which time Suriname expelled the Cubans in the country. The main threat to the survival of the military government, though, has not been outside forces but has come from inside Suriname. An impressive strike victory by 4,000 aluminum and bauxite workers in January 1984 showed that the Bouterse grip on the country was steadily slipping. Despite the government's condemnation of the strike and its military intervention, the strikers gained the support of other workers and much of the discontented population. All signs indicate that the days of the frenetic Bouterse government are numbered.

Adding to the problems facing the Bouterse government is the threat of armed resistance from a group of rebel forces based in French Guyana and the Netherlands Antilles. Called the Council for the Liberation of Suriname, the group is headed by former Surinamese President Henk Chin A. Sen. According to COMA's May 1984 *Washington Report*, the CIA in 1983 proposed to Congress that it arm the insurgents, which include a small number of U.S. mercenaries.

Trinidad & Tobago

A country of limbo, calypso, and steel-drum bands, Trinidad & Tobago is also the land of "capitalism gone mad." All over the English Caribbean in 1983, people were singing along with a calypso number by Trinidad's Mighty Sparrow called "Capitalism Gone Mad." "It's outrageous and insane, those crazy prices in Port of Spain. . . . It's sad, and getting so bad, Oh Lord, capitalism gone mad."

Prices are among the highest in the Caribbean, and the service is the very worst at restaurants and hotels. The latest in styles from the United States immediately catches on in Port of Spain, with the unspoken assumption that everyone else in the Caribbean is hopelessly behind the times. An editorial in an Antiguan paper described Port of Spain as a "hustler's paradise, a fairground with pirates at large, music booming, New York trinkets on the sidewalk, everybody on a hustle. . . . Our diseased and destitute sprawled on the roadsides, our mad directing traffic or otherwise engaging with their demons [and quoting the song] 'Capitalism gone mad.'"[1]

PETRODOLLARS AND POLITICS

Trinidad possesses the worst aspects of both the developed and underdeveloped world. Crime, alienation, decadence, and consumerism of the industrial world exist alongside the economic dependence, the foreign domination, and the desperate poverty common to other underdeveloped nations. The reason for the striking differences between this country and the others of the West Indies is its wealth of oil and natural gas. For over 70 years, Trinidad & Tobago has been a major Caribbean refining center and the region's largest oil and gas producer. This petroleum wealth catapulted the country ahead of the other Caribbean nations. When oil prices shook the economies of other island nations in the 1970s, Trinidad & Tobago was enjoying a period of unprecedented wealth. The wealth, however, is unevenly distributed: the top 10 percent of households receive about a third of the income, while the bottom 40 percent get only 10 percent.[2] That is about the same distribution ratio that existed before the oil boom even began.

The flood of petrodollars came more from taxation and production-sharing contracts than from direct ownership of the industry. But the rush of foreign exchange into the economy has been largely wasted on lavish import bills rather than transformation of the economy. "There's no morality left," wrote one Caribbean commentator. "It is now a free for all. The paramount value today is money."[3]

The country is physically divided between the two islands of Trinidad and Tobago, which some call the Yin and the Yang of the Caribbean. While constant hustling and industrial pollution characterize Trinidad, Tobago is supremely quiet, with all the beauty of the tropics. In 1888, Great Britain united the two islands into one colony. The Tobagans have always resisted the association with Trinidad, and its house of assembly passed a resolution in 1983 that referred to the union as "colonial and contrary to the will of the people of Tobago." Depicting the island as being "forcefully kept in subjugation to Trinidad by neo-colonial policies," the statement called for either more autonomy or complete independence for the island of Tobago.[4]

A prominent feature of Trinidad & Tobago has been its political stability. In 1956, the British-trained "island scholar" Eric Williams and his People's National Movement (PNM) won their first elections. Williams led the nation to independence from Great Britain in 1962 and ruled the country singlehandedly as prime minister until he died in 1981. The major challenge to Williams's political power came in 1970, when black-power riots broke out around the country and the army mutinied. As a result of the pressure, Williams agreed to nationalize the leading sectors of the economy. Anxious not to scare off foreign investors, Williams yielded to the high compensation demands of the sugar and oil companies and subsidized the new joint ventures with state funds.

Under Williams, nationalization in Trinidad & Tobago was a very amiable affair between the government and the corporations. In 1978, when the black-power unrest had subsided and high oil prices were moving the economy forward, Williams reversed the nationalizing trend and invited foreign governments to oversee large development and construction projects for their own corporations. By 1982, the open invitation for foreign control of the country's major development projects was regarded as a complete flop. A report by the Ministry of Foreign Affairs showed that outside corporations had uniformly exploited the situation by pushing out local contractors, dictating costs and terms, and performing shoddy work.

Williams, an authoritarian, anti-working-class politician, did nothing to hide his subservience to international capitalism. Barely able to conceal his contempt for the regional integration movement, Williams refused to attend Caricom summit meetings. Williams died in 1981, a sullen, uncommunicative, and dictatorial leader who had lost most of the respect he had gained while leading the country to independence. In the end, despite his impressive achievements, Williams left as his legacy only the results of the country's sad transition from the confines of the colonial world into the cold, competitive neocolonial world.

ECONOMY

"The fête is over," said Prime Minister George Chambers in his 1983 budget report. Chambers, successor to Williams, is a PNM politician who, unlike Williams, has given strong support to the regional integration movement. Chambers was displeased, however, when other members of Caricom did not consult him before the invasion of Grenada. The golden days of expansion in Trinidad & Tobago have ended as the prices and demand for the country's black gold have shrunk on the world market. In 1982, for the first time in eight years, the country suffered a trade deficit which amounted to over $200 million.

Visitors as well as residents commonly complain that Trinidad "doesn't work." In the rush to industrialize, the government failed to create an adequate infrastructure to handle the growth. As a result, the highways are constantly jammed, the phones are unreliable, constant water shortages plague the country, blackouts are a way of life, and public transportation is a poor joke. Because of a shocking inadequacy of housing, many Trinidadians simply rent plots to build their own small homes. Squatters have taken over public land around Port of Spain and have resisted government attempts to remove them. Finding itself short of revenue, the government has cut back social services, lifted price controls on basic consumer items, and allowed higher utility charges. King Austin, a popular calypsonian, summed up the state of the country in "Progress," a biting and bouncy commentary on the cost of affluence: dirty rivers, no jobs, and drug abuse.

Total trade amounts to about $3 billion a year, and the United States is far and away the country's largest trading partner. The United Kingdom, Japan, and Canada are its secondary trading partners, whose combined exports equal the U.S. exports to the country. On a per capita basis, Trinidad ranks among the best international customers of the United States. The country also leads the Caribbean with the most U.S. direct investment, and U.S. firms overrun Trinidad with consultants and contractors. In addition to the more than 200 U.S. firms doing business in the country, more than 40 nonprofit U.S. organizations have activities or operate in Trinidad. Commenting on the nature of the nation's relationship with the United States, a representative to the European Economic Community (EEC) compared Trinidad's relations with the United States to those of a person who has to share a bed with an elephant and spends all night worrying about getting squashed.[5]

AGRICULTURE

Tate & Lyle of Great Britain dominated the agricultural sector with its Caroni sugar company until 1971, when the government acquired 51 percent of the firm. During this time Caroni enjoyed good relations with the government and faced no strong union opposition. Five years later, however, Tate & Lyle divested its direct interests in sugarcane production in favor of providing technical, advisory, and marketing services. In that way, it reduced its risks in agriculture while retaining much of its control over the industry. Several Tate & Lyle subsidiaries have kept their interests in the country's sugar industry: Sugar Lines and Anchor Lines (shipping companies), Tate & Lyle Refineries, Dominion Sugar, and United Molasses.

As in the entire Caribbean, sugar has fallen upon hard times, but in Trinidad it still provides between 65 and 80 percent of the value of total agricultural exports. The world market plus local conditions added up to make sugar production drop to a 40-year low in 1981. Production of the other leading export crops—cocoa, citrus, and coffee—has also suffered from low market prices and reduced demand. Landholdings in Trinidad tend to be either large estates producing export crops or small family farms. The historic disinclination toward agriculture of the black Trinidadians is one reason for the lack of strong pressure for land reform.

Although the country has available land for agriculture, it imports more food than any other Caribbean nation. Per capita consumption amounts to $800 worth of imported food each year. Twenty years ago, Trinidad & Tobago was a net exporter of food but now produces only about one-quarter of its requirements. Agriculture accounts for just 2 percent of the gross domestic product. Meat production is on the upswing, and the country is nearly self-sufficient in poultry production. But even this small success story has a dark side: imports of animal feed have risen to over $20 million annually.

Foreign firms dominate the local food-processing sector. Borden and Switzerland's Nestlé have affiliates in the dairy and milk sector; while three U.S. firms, Central Soya, International Multifoods, and Pillsbury, control the feed- and grain-milling industry. Other major food processors are Unilever (UK/Netherlands), Cannings Food (U.S.), and Nabisco Brands (U.S.). Foreign corporations like Guinness (UK), Heineken (Netherlands), and PepsiCo are the major drink manufacturers and bottlers. More than most Caribbean states, Trinidad & Tobago has attracted U.S. fast-food restaurants like McDonald's, Pizza Hut, Tastee Freeze, Tennessee Foods, and Kentucky Fried Chicken.

PETROLEUM

Petroleum production and refining account for over 90 percent of the country's export earnings and about 60 percent of the government's revenues. Trinidad's 100-acre asphalt bog—the largest in the world—was an early indication that the country has expansive underground oil and gas reserves. British Petroleum and Shell, the first companies to set up refineries in Trinidad, at first processed only Venezuelan oil but later included Trinidadian production. British Petroleum and Shell operated in Trinidad for close to 50 years before selling out to the government in 1968 and 1974, respectively. Increased profitability elsewhere, particularly with the discoveries of oil in the North Sea, persuaded the companies to phase out their operations in Trinidad. The government contracted with Tesoro Petroleum of Texas to own and manage British Petroleum's former assets, with the government controlling 50.1 percent of the equity. Shell Trinidad became the government-owned Trinidad and Tobago Oil Company (Trintoc).

Texaco and Amoco, the two mighty TNCs, control most of the oil industry in Trinidad. Texaco Trinidad owns the major refining capacity in the country and produces about 20 percent of the nation's crude petroleum. Amoco Trinidad, the major oil and gas producer in Trinidad, sends most of its production to the United States for refining. Another major producer, Trinmar, is a joint venture in offshore production between Amoco, Trinidad Tesoro, and Trintoc. The country has only 30 years of reserves left, and the production of crude oil has steadily declined since 1979. The country is now relying on its more extensive reserves of natural gas to funnel into the Point Lisas Industrial Estate in the hope of building an industrial sector that will strengthen the economy.

When the government in 1975 asked Texaco to sell its operations to the government, the company answered with an emphatic no. Several years ago, the Oilfield Workers Trade Union (OWTU) demanded that the government nationalize Texaco without compensation. The union claimed that the company had not maintained the refinery properly and intended to dump the deteriorating operation. "So we are saying, before Texaco goes, let's take it over," remarked a union official in 1981, "so that we get something that is at least worth taking over."[6] Texaco proved the union right in 1983 when it proposed that the government buy 75 percent of the refinery. The company, claiming that it was losing money, also demanded higher tax concessions from the Chambers government and threatened to close down the refinery if its conditions are not met. The

Tesoro Petroleum Company also wants to sell out. The sales offers have put the government in the uncomfortable position of either risking the closure of two refineries or putting yet more government money into the rehabilitation of two money-losing operations.

At a solidarity march of the OWTU in April 1983, Errol McLeod, deputy leader of the union, recalled that the government failed to heed the repeated warnings and advice from the union as far back as 1974. The union says the government should take complete control over the country's petroleum sector rather than rely on the good intentions of Texaco, Amoco, and Tesoro. "If this had been done," he said, "our reserves would have been in such a healthy state that Trinidad & Tobago would have been able to face the international capitalist crisis with a smile."[7] The union claims that foreign oil companies that are interested primarily in exporting have prevented the country from establishing linkages with other sectors of the economy. Such linkages could have created an "internal dynamic" propelling the country through a strong period of economic development.[8]

INDUSTRY

A number of U.S. and British corporations use Trinidad & Tobago as a base to distribute to the entire Caribbean market. Bristol-Myers, Chesebrough-Ponds, Colgate-Palmolive, Johnson & Johnson, Pfizer, Sterling Drug, and Crown Cork & Seal have manufacturing operations in Trinidad. IBM, 3M, Xerox, and Singer Sewing Machine have distribution operations. Other large U.S. corporations doing business in Trinidad include Westinghouse, GTE, Digital, Maidenform, and Manhattan Industries. Many U.S. construction firms establish joint ventures with local firms to get government construction contracts. One U.S. construction company, Sam P. Wallace, allegedly bribed the director of the Trinidad & Tobago Racing Authority with $1.4 million to obtain the contract to construct a new race track. Once made public, the affair challenged the government of George Chambers, which had already been under criticism for failure to take effective action in other cases of possible corruption. One such case involved alleged payments by Tesoro Petroleum to the government during negotiations for the sale of its minority holding in Trinidad-Tesoro.

Firms from the United States have overtaken corporations from the United Kingdom as the major foreign investors, but a sizable British investment remains in the country, including such firms as Berger Paints, Dunlop Tires, Metal Box, Imperial Chemical, BAT Industries, and Cable & Wireless. As the government has assumed more control over the economy, U.S. suppliers have won out over British firms through lower prices and faster deliveries. The tourism industry, the country's second-largest foreign-exchange earner, relies for 20 percent of its business on visiting businessmen, who lighten their work in Port of Spain with a vacation in Tobago.

Trinidad's wealth of hydrocarbons has resulted in a flourishing fertilizer industry. Three large U.S. firms—Amoco, WR Grace, and the Williams Companies' Agrico—have extensive interests in the fertilizer business. WR Grace's Fedchem has been the target of widespread resentment because of the special exemptions from income taxes the company has enjoyed.

In its campaign to nationalize Fedchem, the Oilfield Workers Trade Union has charged that Fedchem receives water and electricity at much cheaper rates than average householders, that it disposes of the poisonous chemical hydrazine each day into the Gulf of Paria, and that it provides no special protection for employees who work with hazardous chemicals. The union in 1981 charged that WR Grace was selling ammonia to buyers at rates as much as 6 times higher than rates charged to its own subsidiary. WR Grace has vigorously opposed the organizing by the Oilfield Workers, and the union complains of frequent harassment and firings of union organizers. Along with their paychecks, workers often receive friendly reminders saying, "Aren't you glad you don't have a union?" The company, besides owning Fedchem, jointly owns Trinidad Nitrogen with the government. For the last several years the government has repeatedly promised, but made no move, to buy 51 percent of Fedchem, which has been enjoying attractive concessions in the country since 1958.

The desperate state of the economy has threatened the government's plans for an industrial park in southern Trinidad. The government planned the project as a base for a number of new government-owned heavy industries, such as an aluminum smelter, liquefied natural gas (LNG) production, and methanol and urea production. These petrochemical and LNG plants will be operated mainly by U.S. corporations. Critics have charged the government with mismanagement and corruption in the industrial park project, however, which thus far has been a money-losing venture. Others say that the government should be putting money into building labor-intensive industries that produce consumer products for the local and regional markets. Possibilities include plastics, pharmaceuticals, and petrochemicals for synthetic textile production.

A key part of the Point Lisas project, the government-owned Iron & Steel Company (ISCOTT), has had a difficult time finding export markets. Some skepticism exists about ISCOTT, which exports steel when the United States is closing down its own industry. Five U.S. companies have tried to block further iron and steel imports from Trinidad on the grounds that ISCOTT benefits from large capital and operating subsidies from the government. Many citizens of Trinidad & Tobago claim the subsidies are used simply to keep the company's international creditors, like Citibank and the Bank of Tokyo, satisfied. While the government does have oil and gas for the time being, it is having a hard time finding guaranteed sources of water for the planned petrochemical plants. Referring to the government's planned $380 million joint-venture methanol plant with Borden, the Oilfield Workers asked in an editorial: "Are we going to divert 730,000 gallons of fresh water per day to that white elephant?"[9]

In Trinidad, the government has been manipulated and reportedly bribed by TNCs, and development has overtaken the society. Each year, the calypsonians harp on the shortcomings of progress and development in their country, and each year the politicians reply that Trinidad is moving forward. In 1983, Mighty Sparrow sang a catchy calypso about the direction in which the country is moving.

> If you tell them that the economy
> is no longer in full bloom,
> Then you become a prophet of doom and gloom.

Even though the calypso artists of Trinidad & Tobago do not offer many answers, they certainly are in touch with the pulse of the people. As their bards have dramatized in their songs, many of the citizens of this "industrialized" country have lately grown less appreciative and understanding of their nation's rush to development.

Tom Barry, Deb Preusch, and Beth Wood are founders and directors of The Resource Center in Albuquerque, New Mexico, an independent research organization that produces films and educational materials on foreign economic and political control in third world regions. They are the authors of *Dollars and Dictators: A Guide to Central America*, published by Grove Press in September 1983.

Reference Notes

Sources on the Caribbean

The best regular source of news on the Caribbean comes from the reporters of the Latin American Weekly Newsletters in London, which publishes the *Latin American Regional Report* (Caribbean) and *Latin America Weekly Report*. Another publication from Great Britain, the monthly *Caribbean Insight*, provides a factual account of the month's events and good statistical information. *Caribbean Business* from Puerto Rico gives its readers up-to-date news on the Caribbean from a straightforward, business perspective. For a general overview from within the region, there is nothing better than the *Caribbean Contact*, published by the Caribbean Conference of Churches in Barbados. Two magazines cover the region—the *West Indies and Caribbean Chronicle* from London and the *Caribbean Review* from Florida. The latter offers essays on culture, history, and political issues. For solid political analysis and the best in-depth examination of the Caribbean and Latin America, the bi-monthly *NACLA Report on the Americas*, published in New York, is highly recommended. Canada's Latin American Working Group (LAWG), which publishes *LAWG Letter*, is in the same company as NACLA. Washington DC hosts several top-notch groups that provide timely analysis and background reports on the region: Council on Hemispheric Affairs (which produces *Washington Report*), the Institute for Policy Studies, and EPICA (Ecumenical Program for Interamerican Communication and Action). The books and reports by EPICA are important reading for those interested in understanding Caribbean issues. In Oakland, the Data Center offers a valuable clipping service on Latin America and the Caribbean. The Resource Center also relied extensively on the work of Caribbean scholars, Clive Y. Thomas, Gordon K. Lewis, Norman Girvan, Hilbourne Watson, Trevor M. A. Farrell, and Maurice Odle in the preparation of *The Other Side of Paradise*.

Three sources used frequently in the book are identified within the reference notes in abbreviated fashion. *Latin America Regional Report* is listed as *LARR*, *Latin America Weekly Report* as *LAWR*, and *NACLA Report on the Americas* as *NACLA*.

PART ONE

Introduction

1. *Wall Street Journal*, January 7, 1983.

2. Inter-American Development Bank (IDB), *Economic and Social Progress in Latin America*, 1983.
3. The Caribbean Group of Experts, *The Caribbean Community in the 1980s*, (Georgetown: Caricom, 1981) p. 29
4. IDB, *Annual Report*, 1982, p. 108.
5. "Should the U.S. Be Prohibited From Intervention in the Western Hemisphere?" Intercollegiate Topic 1982–1983, Compiled by the Congressional Research Service, House of Representatives, Document 97–226.
6. The Caribbean Group of Experts, *The Caribbean Community in the 1980s*, pp. 41–42.
7. *Caribbean Review*, No. 4, 1982.
8. Trevor M. A. Farrell, "Decolonization in the English-Speaking Caribbean," *The Newer Caribbean*, (Philadelphia: Institute for the Study of Human Issues, 1983) p. 10.
9. Martin Carter, "I Come from the Nigger Yard," *Caribbean Voices: An Anthology of West Indian Poetry*, (London: Evans Bros., 1970)

Transnational Corporations: The Strangers in Paradise

1. *Fortune*, August 22, 1983.
2. U. S. Department of Treasury, *The Operation of the Possessions Corporation System of Taxation*, 1983.
3. Marc Herold, "Worldwide Investment and Disinvestment by U.S. Multinationals: Implications for the Caribbean and Central America," (paper presented at El Segundo Seminario Centroamerica y el Caribe, February 9–12, 1983, Managua, Nicaragua).
4. U. S. Department of Commerce, *U.S. Direct Investment Abroad, 1977*, April 1981.
5. "Canadian Investment, Trade and Aid in Latin America," *LAWG Letter* (Toronto: Latin American Working Group), May–August, 1981, p. 4.
6. U. S. Department of Commerce, *U.S. Direct Investment Abroad, 1977*, April 1981; U.S. Department of Commerce, *Survey of Current Business*, August 1983.
7. InterAmerican Development Bank (IDB), *Annual Report*, (Washington: IDB, 1982).
8. U. S. Department of Commerce, *U.S. Direct Investment Abroad*, 1977 and 1981.
9. Clive Y. Thomas, *Dependence and Transformation: Economics of the Transition to Socialism*, (New York: Monthly Review Press, 1974) pp. 95–96.

Agriculture: The New Plantation

1. Gordon K. Lewis, *Growth of the Modern West Indies*, (NY: Monthly Review, 1968).
2. *New Internationalist*, February 1982.
3. Robert H. Girling, "The Caribbean Basin in the 1980s: Notes on the Current Economic Crisis," (unpublished paper).

4. *Commodity Review and Outlook*, Food and Agriculture Organization (FAO), (New York: United Nations 1982).
5. AID, "Caribbean Agriculture Trading Company," Project Paper #538–0080, July 28, 1982.
6. Judy Whitehead, "Select Technological Issues in Agro-Industry (2)," *Social and Economic Studies*, Vol. 28, No. 1, March 1979, p. 161.
7. Frances Moore Lappé, Joseph Collins, *Food First*, (New York: Ballantine, 1977) p. 109.
8. InterAmerican Development Bank (IDB), *Social and Economic Progress*, 1982.
9. Testimony by Dr. Robert E. Culbertson, International University of Florida, before Subcommittee on Inter-American Affairs, Committee on Foreign Affairs, U. S. House of Representatives, July 20, 1982.
10. J. W. Delimore, "Select Technological Issues in Agro-Industry (1)," *Social and Economic Studies*, Vol. 28, No. 1, March 1979, p. 56.
11. Curtis McIntosh and Patricia Manchew, "Nutritional Needs, Food Availability and the Realism of Self-Sufficiency," (Jamaica: Caribbean Food and Nutrition Institute, 1982).
12. *U.S. Foreign Agricultural Trade Statistical Report*, 1982.
13. Testimony by Robert A. Pastor, University of Maryland, before Subcommittee on Inter-American Affairs, July 20, 1982.
14. Ibid.
15. Ibid.
16. Ibid.
17. *UNEP/ECLA Report 1982*, cited in *Earthscan*, Briefing Document No. 34A, (London: International Institute for Environment and Development, 1983)
18. Ibid.
19. Maurice Foley, UNESCO *Courier*, September/October 1982.
20. *Wall Street Journal*, November 17, 1982.
21. *Courier*, No. 75, September/October 1982.
22. Testimony by Robert Pastor, Subcommittee on Inter-American Affairs, July 20, 1982.
23. *Caribbean Contact*, April 1983.
24. *LARR*, August 20, 1982.
25. *Courier*, September/October 1982.
26. Gulf + Western, *Annual Report*, 1982.
27. Testimony by Arthur Lee Quinn, before Subcommittee on Inter-American Affairs, July 20, 1982.
28. *NACLA*, November/December 1977.
29. *Courier*, September/October 1982.
30. *Workers Times*, (newspaper of Jamaican sugar workers), January 1982.
31. *Multinational Monitor*, April 1982.
32. AID "Regional Profile of Barbados," 1982.
33. *Journal of Commerce*, December 14, 1982.
34. *NACLA*, March/April 1982.
35. *Miami Herald*, August 8, 1982.
36. *Courier*, March/April 1983.
37. Testimony before the Foreign Affairs Committee of the United Kingdom, April 19, 1982.
38. *Insight*, April 1983.

39. British Development Division, "Plan for Restructuring of Windward Islands Banana Industry, Discussion Paper," December 1981.
40. Interview by Tom Barry, May 1983.
41. British Development Division, December 1981.
42. Arthur D. Little Inc., "Review of Windward Islands Banana Industry's Financial and Economic Status," August 1981.
43. Interview by Tom Barry, May 1983.
44. AID, "Dominica Banana Company Project," Project Paper #538–0083.
45. *Multinational Monitor*, October 1980.
46. Dominica Liberation Movement, 1982 (press release).
47. Interview by Tom Barry, May 1983.
48. Ibid.
49. United Nations Commission on Trade and Development (UNCTAD), "Marketing and Processing of Coffee: Areas for International Cooperation," 1983.
50. *New Internationalist*, February 1982.
51. *Advertising Age*, August 29, 1983.
52. Testimony by Dr. Robert Paarlberg of Harvard University before Committee on Inter-American Affairs of U. S. Senate Committee on Foreign Affairs, July 20, 1982.
53. *Jamaica National Industrial Promotion News*, April 1982.
54. Interview by Tom Barry, March 1983.
55. William R. Finger, "Making the Third World Marlboro Country," *Tobacco Industry in Transition*, (North Carolina: Lexington Books, 1981) p. 155.
56. *Development Forum* (Switzerland: United Nations), June/July 1983.
57. *LARR*, August 21, 1981.
58. Figures from the World Health Organization (WHO), cited in *Cultural Survival Newsletter*, Summer 1981.
59. *Hold the Fort*, (newspaper of the Committee for Labor Solidarity, Trinidad), February 1983.
60. Whitehead, "Select Technological Issues," March 1979, p. 161.
61. Caricom Member Countries, "Observations and Recommendations on Import Procurement of Grain."
62. United Nations Center on Transnational Corporations (UNCTNC) *Transnational Corporations in Food and Beverage Processing*, (New York: United Nations, 1981) pp. 32, 36, 50, 72.
63. *Third World Quarterly*, Vol. 4, No. 4, October 1982, p. 768.

Island Factories: Industry and Commerce in the Caribbean

1. Interview by Tom Barry, April 1983.
2. Interview by Tom Barry, March 1983.
3. ONAPI (Office National pour la Promotion des Investissements), "The Textile Industry in Haiti," 1983.
4. John Cavanagh and Joy Hackel, "Multinational Corporations in Central America and the Caribbean," (Institute for Policy Studies, August 1983).
5. *Caribbean Contact*, July 1983.
6. Figures from the U. S. Department of Commerce, November 1982.

7. Interview by Tom Barry, February 1983.
8. Clive Y. Thomas, "Neo-colonialism and Caribbean Integration," *Contemporary International Relations of the Caribbean*, (Institute of International Relations, University of the West Indies, Trinidad, 1974).
9. Ibid.
10. *Caribbean Contact*, July 1983.
11. *Caribbean Business*, March 9, 1983.
12. *Caribbean Business*, October 27, 1982.
13. Interview by Tom Barry, April 1983.
14. *Multinational Monitor*, June 1982.
15. Ibid.
16. Philip E. Wheaton, *Report on the Miami Conference on the Caribbean*, (Epica Task Force, November 1979).
17. B. Zorina Kahn, "Foreign Direct Investment From a Public Policy Perspective," (University of the West Indies, May 1983), p. 9.
18. Norman Girvan, "The Approach to Technology," *Social and Economic Studies*, Vol. 28, No. 1, March 1979, p. 3.
19. Ibid.
20. Interview by Tom Barry, April 1983.
21. *Atlantic Monthly*, September 1983.
22. *Wall Street Journal*, January 7, 1983.
23. *Forbes*, February 1982.

Tourism: The Sun-Lust Industry

1. Neil D. Sealy, *Tourism in the Caribbean*, (London: Hodder and Stoughton, 1982) p. 24.
2. *Moody's Industrial Manual*, 1983.
3. *Transnational Corporations in International Tourism*, (New York: United Nations Center on Transnational Corporations [UNCTNC], 1982) p. 10.
4. UNCTNC, *Transnational Corporations in International Tourism*, p. 25.
5. Ibid., p. 29.
6. *Moody's Industrial Manual*.
7. UNCTNC, *Transnational Corporations in International Tourism*, p. 63.
8. Ibid., p. 41.
9. Sealy, *Tourism in the Caribbean*, p. 50.
10. Ibid.
11. *Caribbean Tourism*, (newsletter of the Caribbean Tourism Research Center), June 1983.
12. Sealy, *Tourism in the Caribbean*, p. 50.
13. *Caribbean and West Indies Chronicle*, October/November 1982.
14. Robert Chodos, *The Caribbean Connection*, (Toronto: James Lorimer & Company, 1977) p. 179.
15. *The Travel Agent*, June 16, 1983.
16. Angela Bishop, *Caribbean Tourism in the 80s*, "Tourism in the Context of Economic Development Strategies," (Canada: Ryerson International Development Center, 1982) p. 19.

17. "Fighting Blight in Paradise," *Time*, April 4, 1983.
18. "Cruise Ship Visitors Spend Freely in St. Thomas," *Caribbean Business*, June 1, 1983.
19. "Tourism in the Caribbean: Impacts on the Economic, Social, and Natural Environments," *Ambio: A Journal of the Human Environment*, Vol. 10, No. 6, 1981.
20. Bishop, *Caribbean Tourism in the 80s*, p. 19.
21. Shirley B. Seward and Barnard K. Spinard, eds., *Tourism in the Caribbean: The Economic Impact*, (Ottawa: International Development Research Center, 1982)
22. Bishop, *Caribbean Tourism in the 80s*, p. 19.
23. Seward and Spinard, *Tourism in the Caribbean*.
24. *LARR*, September 25, 1981.
25. Jan S. Holder, *Caribbean Tourism Policies and Impacts*, (Barbados: Caribbean Tourism Research Centre) p. 251.
26. Herbert L. Hiller, "Tourism: Development or Dependence?" in Richard Millet and W. Marvin Will, eds., *The Restless Caribbean*, (New York: Praeger, 1979) p. 53.
27. Interview by Tom Barry: April 1983.
28. Herbert L. Hiller, "Escapism, Penetration and Response: Industrial Tourism and the Caribbean," *Caribbean Studies*, Vol. 16, No. 2, p. 113.
29. "Notes of the Conference: Tourism and Jamaica Today—Perspectives," (Kingston, Jamaica: October 5–7, 1972) p. 143.
30. Hiller, "Tourism: Development or Dependence?" in *Restless Caribbean*, p. 56.
31. *LARR*, September 25, 1981.
32. Alister Hughes, "National Inferiority," *The Sunday Gleaner* (Kingston, Jamaica), June 30, 1974, p. 10.

Oil and Mining: Control of Natural Resources

1. "Focus on Trinidad," *NACLA*, October 1976, p. 18.
2. Caribbean Central America Action, *Caribbean Databook*, (Washington: 1983) p. 272.
3. *NACLA*, October 1976, p. 26.
4. *Courier*, May/June 1982, p. 2.
5. *NACLA*, October 1976, p. 17.
6. "Oilfield Workers Trade Union," (40th Anniversary Report by the Oilfield Workers Trade Union in Trinidad), September 1982, p. 10.
7. Trevor M.A. Farrell, "A Tale of Two Issues: Nationalization, the Transfer of Technology and the Multinationals in Trinidad & Tobago," *Social and Economic Studies*, March 1979, p. 276.
8. "Confronting the Multinationals: Trinidad Workers on the Lines," *Multinational Monitor*, January 1981.
9. George Beckford cited in Farrell's "A Tale of Two Issues," *Social and Economic Studies*, p. 279.
10. *Business Latin America*, February 14, 1979.

11. "The Caribbean Export Refining Center," *NACLA*, October 1976, p. 10.
12. "Hess' Twin Tactics: Play Island Against Island, Bypass U.S. Shipping Costs," *Multinational Monitor*, April 1981.
13. Doris M. Hyde, "The Mineral Industry of the Islands of the Caribbean," *Minerals Yearbook*, 1981, p. 1236.
14. *Caribbean Monthly Bulletin* (Caricom Secretariat), April 1979, p. 2.
15. M. Desmond Fitzgerald and Gerald Pollio, "Aluminum: the Next Twenty Years," *Journal of Metals*, December 1982, p. 37.
16. Thakoor Persaud, *Conflicts Between Multinational Corporations and Less Developed Countries*, (Texas Technical University, 1980) p. 23.
17. *Journal of Metals*, December 1982, p. 38.
18. UN Center on Transnational Corporations (UNCTNC), "Transnational Corporations in the Bauxite/Aluminum Industry," (New York: 1981) pp. 1, 5.
19. *Journal of Metals*, December 1982, p. 39.
20. "Bauxite: A Buyer's Market," *Multinational Monitor*, February 1981, pp. 18, 19.
21. Cited in *Multinational Monitor*, Ibid.
22. Ibid.
23. IDB, *Economic and Social Progress in Latin America*, 1983.
24. Stafford Wesley Cargill, *The Impact of Direct Foreign Investment on the Jamaican Labor Movement*, (University of Notre Dame, April 1982).
25. Robert Chodos, *The Caribbean Connection*, (Toronto: James Lorimer & Co., 1977) p. 139.
26. *Multinational Monitor*, February 1981.
27. Persaud, *Conflicts Between Multinationals*, p. 57.
28. *NACLA*, May/June 1978, p. 19–22.
29. Ibid.
30. Ibid.
31. Ibid.
32. "The Giants Are Vulnerable," *The New Internationalist*, No. 94, December 1980, p. 15.
33. "Statement by President, November 24, 1981," U. S. House of Representatives Committee on Armed Services, December 9, 1981.
34. "Reagan's Jamaican Push Helps U.S. Industry," *New York Times*, April 27, 1982.
35. Ibid.
36. Ibid.
37. *The New Internationalist*, p. 15.
38. Persaud, *Conflict Between Multinationals*, p. 56.
39. Quoted in Chodos, *The Caribbean Connection*, p. 141.
40. Persaud, *Conflict Between Multinationals*, p. 108.
41. Ibid., p. 90.
42. AID, *Congressional Presentation Fiscal Year 1984, Annex III*, 1983, p. 172.
43. *Caribbean Contact*, September 1982.
44. Fred Goff, "Falconbridge—Made in U.S.A.," *NACLA's Latin America Report*, April 1974.
45. *Caribbean Business News*, February/March 1982, p. 17.
46. Falconbridge Dominicana, *Annual Report 1982*, p.3.

47. *NACLA*, April 1974.
48. Falconbridge Dominicana, *Annual Report 1982*, p. 13.
49. *NACLA*, April 1974.
50. Falconbridge Dominicana. *Annual Report 1982*, p. 13.
51. *NACLA*, April 1974.
52. Earthscan, "The Improbable Treaty," *Briefing Document No. 34A*, (London: International Institute for Environment and Development, 1983) p. 3.
53. Peter Hulm, "The Regional Seas Program: What Fate for UNEP's Crown Jewels?" *Ambio*, Vol. 12, No. 1, 1983.
54. Earthscan, *Briefing Document No. 34A*, p. 41.
55. *Development and Environment in the Wider Caribbean Region: A Synthesis*, UNEP (United Nations Environment Program Regional Seas Reports and Studies), 1982, p. 13.
56. *NACLA*, October 1976, p. 10.
57. Persaud, *Conflict Between Multinationals*, p. 139.
58. Trevor M.A. Farrell, "Decolonization in the English Speaking Caribbean," *Newer Caribbean*, (Philadelphia: Institute for the Study of Human Issues, 1983) pp. 8–9.
59. *Multinational Monitor*, January 1981, pp. 12–16.
60. *NACLA*, May/June 1978, p. 23.

Caribbean Finance: Laundering Money in the Sun

1. Federal Reserve Bank of Atlanta, *Caribbean Basin Economic Survey*, March 1981.
2. Hearings before Subcommittee on International Finance, U. S. Senate, 1977, p. 144.
3. *Caribbean Basin Economic Survey*, May 1979.
4. Maurice Odle, *Multinational Banks and Underdevelopment*, (London: Pergamon, 1981).
5. Richard Swift & Robert Clark, *Ties That Bind, Canada and the Third World*, (Toronto: Between the Lines, 1982) p. 112.
6. *New York Times*, October 18, 1982.
7. Maurice Odle and Norman Girvan, *Transnational Corporations in the Caribbean*, unpublished manuscript, May 1983.
8. Odle, *Multinational Banks and Underdevelopment*.
9. Howard M. Wachtel, *The New Gnomes: Multinational Banks in the Third World*, (Washington: Transnational Institute, 1977).
10. Staff Study of Crime and Secrecy, Permanent Subcommittee on Investigations, "The Use of Offshore Banks and Companies," February 1983, p. 1.
11. Ibid., p. 2.
12. "International Banking Facilities," *Federal Reserve Bulletin*, October 1982.
13. *Transnational Banks*, (New York: United Nations Center on Transnational Corporations, 1981).
14. *Bahamas Handbook*, (Nassau, Bahamas: Dupuch Publications, 1982) p. 155.
15. *Caribbean Dateline*, Vol. 3, No. 10.
16. Staff Study of Crime and Secrecy, p. 10.
17. *Caribbean Business*, October 1979.

18. Staff Study of Crime and Secrecy, p. 26.
19. *New York Times*, September 13, 1982.
20. *Multinational Monitor*, October 1982.
21. *Euromoney*, April 1983.
22. *Wall Street Journal*, October 11, 1982.
23. *LARR*, May 1981.
24. *Institutional Investor*, June 1983.
25. *Wall Street Journal*, May 5, 1983.
26. *Offshore Financial Centres*, (London: London Times Business Publishing, 1981).
27. Ibid.
28. Staff Study of Crime and Secrecy, p. 45.
29. Ibid.
30. R. Ramsaran's study cited by Staff Study of Crime and Secrecy.
31. Jane Little, *Euro-dollars: the Money-Market Gypsies*, (New York: Harper and Row, 1975).
32. Staff Study of Crime and Secrecy, p. 59.
33. Ibid., p. 63.
34. Staff Study of Crime and Secrecy, p. 50.

Debt For Development

1. Robert Girling, "The Debt Crisis and Human Development in the Caribbean" (unpublished paper by Research and Training International in Washington, 1983).
2. IDB, *Economic and Social Progress in Latin America*, 1982, 1983; IDB, *Annual Report*, 1982.
3. Organization for Economic Cooperation and Development, *External Debt of Developing Countries*, 1982.
4. Girling, "The Debt Crisis and Human Development."
5. IDB, *Economic & Social Progress in Latin America*, 1982, p. 166.
6. Ibid., p. 389.
7. Anthony Sampson, *The Money Lenders*, (New York: Viking Press, 1981).
8. Economic Policy Council, "U.S. Policies Toward the World Bank and the IMF," August 1982.
9. Federal Reserve Bank of Chicago, "International Letter #503," July 1, 1983.
10. Federal Reserve Bulletin, "Private Bank Lending," October 1981.
11. Organization for Economic Cooperation and Development, *External Debt of Developing Countries*, 1982.
12. "International Banking Developments, First Quarter 1983." Bank for International Settlements (Basle, Switzerland).
13. Federal Financial Institute Examination Council, "Statistical Release," June 1, 1983.
14. Ibid.
15. Richard Bernal and Norman Girvan, "The IMF and the Foreclosure of Development Options: The Case of Jamaica," *Monthly Review*, February 1983, pp. 34–48.
16. "MacNeil/Lehrer Report," October 30, 1980.

17. *Guardian* (New York), June 8, 1983.
18. Bernal and Girvan, "The IMF and the Foreclosure of Development Options."
19. Ibid.
20. "Senate Approves Increase in IMF Funding," *Congressional Quarterly*, June 11, 1983, p. 1167.

The Multilateral Lenders: Structuring Caribbean Development

1. World Bank, *Assault on World Poverty*, (Johns Hopkins University Press: 1975) p. 143.
2. Robert Carty, Virginia Smith, Latin American Working Group (LAWG), *Perpetuating Poverty*, (Toronto: Between the Lines, 1981) p.46.
3. Cheryl Payer, *World Bank, A Critical Analysis*, (New York: Monthly Review Press, 1982) p. 20.
4. Frances Moore Lappé, Joseph Collins, *Food First*, (New York: Ballantine Books, 1978) p. 395.
5. Richard Swift and Robert Clarke, eds., *Ties That Bind: Canada and the Third World*, (Toronto: Between the Lines, 1982) p. 198.
6. *Multinational Monitor*, October 1981.
7. World Bank, *Annual Report*, 1982.
8. International Finance Corporation (IFC), *Annual Report*, 1982.
9. Washington Report on the Hemisphere, (Washington: Council on Hemispheric Affairs), January 26, 1982.
10. *IDB News*, February 1982.
11. "CDB: Its Purpose, Role and Functions—20 Questions and Answers," (Barbados: Caribbean Development Bank) March 1983, p. 2.
12. CDB, *Annual Report*, 1982.
13. GAO, "AID Assistance to the Eastern Caribbean," July 22, 1983.
14. GAO, *AID Assistance to the Eastern Caribbean: Program Changes and Possible Consequences*, July 22, 1983.
15. Carty, Smith, LAWG, *Perpetuating Poverty*, p. 154.
16. Economic Policy Council, "U.S. Policies Toward the World Bank and the International Monetary Fund," August 1982.
17. Lappé and Collins, *Food First*, p. 402.
18. *Multinational Monitor*, October 1982.
19. *Multinational Monitor*, February 1982.
20. Organization for Economic Cooperation and Development, Press Release, December 15, 1982.

Million Dollar Diplomacy: U. S. Government in the Caribbean

1. *Multinational Monitor*, March 1983.
2. LARR, January 15, 1982.
3. Jorge I. Dominguez, *U. S. Interests and Policies in the Caribbean and Central America*, (American Enterprise Institute, 1982) p. 21.

4. AID, *Congressional Presentation Fiscal Year 1984, Latin America and the Caribbean*, 1983, p. 105.
5. Department of Commerce, *Survey of Current Business*, August 1983, p. 24; Department of Commerce, *U. S. Direct Investment Abroad, 1977*, April 1983, p. 6.
6. IMF, *Direction of Trade Statistics Yearbook 1983*.
7. U. S. Department of State, *Bulletin*, September 1982.
8. Interview by Tom Barry: David Ryback, AID Development Officer, Jamaica; February 1983.
9. *Caribbean Business*, December 21, 1983.
10. *Forbes*, February 1, 1982.
11. *Caribbean Business*, December 21, 1983.
12. AID, *U. S. Overseas Loans and Grants*, 1983.
13. AID, "Productive Infrastructure Rehabilitation Project Paper," AID Project Paper #538–0082.
14. Ibid.
15. Hearings before the Subcommittee on Foreign Operations of the Appropriations Committee, House of Representatives, March 9, 1982.
16. Ibid.
17. *LARR*, March 31, 1983.
18. *Los Angeles Times*, January 30, 1983.
19. Heliodoro Gonzalez, "The Caribbean Basin Initiative: Toward a Permanent Dole," *Inter-American Economic Affairs*, 1982, p. 484.
20. Robert Pastor, "Sinking in the Caribbean," *Foreign Affairs*, Summer 1982, p. 1045.
21. *Economic Impact*, (U.S. Department of State Bulletin), #39.
22. Interview by Deb Preusch: James Holtaway, AID; September 1983.
23. AID, "Loan Agreement Between the Government of the USA and the Government of the Dominican Republic for Private Sector Development," Loan #517–K–039, September 30, 1982.
24. *Economic Impact* (U. S. Department of State Bulletin), #39.
25. Interview by Deb Preusch: John Gelb, Liaison Officer for Private Enterprise, Bureau for Private Enterprise; September 1983.
26. Ibid.
27. "Caribbean Investment: Following the Flag?" *Multinational Monitor*, November 1980.
28. Ibid.
29. Ibid.
30. Interview by Deb Preusch: Robert Jordan, OPIC Public Relations; September 1983.
31. Council of the Americas, *Annual Report*, 1980.
32. *Calling the Caribbean*, (Barbados: Newsletter of the Caribbean Association of Industry and Commerce) October 1982.
33. Interview by Tom Barry: David Ryback, AID Development Officer, Jamaica; February 1983.
34. *Calling the Caribbean*, October 1982.
35. AID, "Private Sector Investment Assistance Program," Project Paper #538–0043.

36. *Calling the Caribbean*, March 1982.
37. *Caribbean Journal*, (Caribbean Center) Spring 1982.
38. Jenny Pearce, *Under the Eagle*, (London: Latin American Bureau, 1982) p. 83.
39. AID Mission Barbados, "CBI Implementation Plan, Eastern Caribbean," July 1, 1982.
40. Ronald Radosh, *American Labor and United States Foreign Policy*, (New York: Random House, 1969) p. 395.
41. Ibid.
42. Ibid.
43. Ibid.
44. Pearce, *Under the Eagle*, p. 83.
45. Radosh, *American Labor and United States Foreign Policy*, p. 405.
46. Ibid.
47. Ibid.
48. Ibid.
49. Ibid.
50. Ibid.
51. "The AFL-CIO in Latin America: The Dominican Republic—A Case Study," *Viet Report III*, September/October 1967.
52. AIFLD, *Annual Progress Report 1962–1982, 20 Years of Partnership for Progress*, 1983.
53. Interview by Tom Barry: Julio de Peña Valdez, CNTD Director, Dominican Republic; March 1983.
54. AIFLD, *Annual Progress Report 1962–1982, 20 Years of Partnership for Progress*, 1983.
55. Interview by Tom Barry: Tim Hector, ACLM, Antigua; May 1983.
56. Catherine Sunshine and Philip Wheaton, *Grenada, the Peaceful Revolution*, (Washington: Epica Task Force, 1982) p. 63.
57. *AIFLD Report*, November/December 1982.
58. Interview by Tom Barry: Laurel Shea, Jamaica Political Officer, U. S. Embassy; February 1983.
59. Interview by Tom Barry: Debbie Coates, Jamaica Commercial Officer, U. S. Embassy; February 1983.
60. *AIFLD Report*, May/June 1981.
61. *Miami Herald*, October 30, 1982.
62. Hearings before the Committee on Foreign Affairs, U. S. House of Representatives, April 29, 1982.
63. Food for Peace, *Annual Report*, 1981.
64. AID, *U. S. Overseas Loans and Grants*, 1983.
65. Joint Hearings before the Subcommittee on Inter-American Affairs of the Committee on Foreign Affairs and the Subcommittee on Department Operations, U. S. House of Representatives, *Agriculture Development in the Caribbean and Central America*, July 20, 22, 1982.
66. *Multinational Monitor*, January 1981.
67. *Miami Herald*, December 19, 1982.
68. Ibid.

REFERENCE NOTES · 385

69. AID Mission Office Haiti, "Agriculture in Haiti," p. 211.
70. Ibid.
71. AID, "Haiti Country Development Strategy Statement Fiscal Year 1984," 1982, p. 92.
72. AID, "Agriculture in Haiti," p. 211.
73. Ibid.
74. AID, USAID Strategy Statements, "Dominican Republic" and "Jamaica," 1983.
75. *Multinational Monitor*, January 1981.
76. OPIC, *Annual Report*, 1982.
77. OPIC, *Annual Report*, 1980 and 1981.
78. *Topics*, (OPIC Newsletter) May/June 1982.
79. *Miami Herald*, October 10, 1982.
80. Hearings before the Subcommittee on International Finance and Monetary Policy of the Committee on Banking, Housing, and Urban Affairs, Senate, September 14 and 16, 1982.
81. Interview by Tom Barry: David Ryback, AID Economic Officer, Jamaica; February 1983.
82. AID, *U. S. Overseas Loans and Grants*, 1983.
83. Interview by Tom Barry: Debbie Coates, Jamaica Commercial Officer, U. S. Embassy; February 1983.
84. Memorandum from Talbot Penner, "USAID Programs and Activities Which May Be of Assistance to U. S. Businesses," January 21, 1983.
85. Interview by Tom Barry: Richard Mangride, AID Agricultural Office, Jamaica; February 1983.
86. AID, *U. S. Overseas Loans and Grants*, 1983.
87. GAO, *Assistance to Haiti: Barriers, Recent Program Changes, and Future Option*, February 22, 1982.
88. Church World Services, *Refugees and Human Rights Newsletter*, Summer 1983.
89. GAO, *Assistance to Haiti: Barriers, Recent Program Changes, and Future Options*, February 22, 1982.
90. *LARR*, January 15, 1982.
91. IDB, *Annual Report*, 1982; IMF, *Direction of Trade Statistics*, 1982.
92. GAO, *Assistance to Haiti: Barriers, Recent Program Changes, and Future Options*.
93. AID, *Congressional Presentation Fiscal Year 1983, Latin America and the Caribbean*, p. 178.
94. AID, "Haiti Country Development Strategy Statement Fiscal Year 1984."
95. *Caribbean Business*, June 29, 1983.
96. IDB, *Economic and Social Progress in Latin America*, 1982, p. 346.
97. AID, "Haiti Country Development Strategy Statement Fiscal Year 1984."
98. AID, "CBI Implementation Plan, Eastern Caribbean," 1983.
99. *Calling the Caribbean*, January 1982.
100. GAO, *AID Assistance to the Eastern Caribbean: Program Changes and Possible Consequences*, July 22, 1983, p. 16.
101. Ibid., p. 31.

Caribbean Alert: The Militarization of the Region

1. *Miami Herald*, May 18, 1983.
2. Michael T. Klare and Cynthia Arnson, *Supplying Repression: U. S. Support for Authoritarian Regimes Abroad*, (Washington, DC: Institute for Policy Studies, 1981).
3. U. S. Department of Defense (DOD), *U. S. Department of Defense Congressional Presentation Fiscal Year 1983*, 1982.
4. Committee in Solidarity with the People of Guatemala, "Update on Guatemala," November 22, 1982.
5. Hearings before the Subcommittee on Foreign Operations of the Committee on Appropriations, U. S. House of Representatives, *1983 Security Assistance Request*, 1982.
6. John Enders, *United States Military and Puerto Rico*, (San Juan, Puerto Rico: Instituto Caribeno de Justicia y Paz, 1977) p. 23.
7. *Caribbean Contact*, August 1983.
8. *LAWR*, May 13, 1983.
9. *Guardia Nacional*, (newsletter of the Puerto Rico National Guard) July 1, 1980, p. 3.
10. *Caribbean Business*, May 18, 1983.
11. *LARR*, September 25, 1981.
12. *Caribbean Business*, October 19, 1983.
13. DOD, "DOD Presence in Puerto Rico," March 1983.
14. Ibid.
15. Norman Gall, "How Trujillo Died," *New Republic*, April 13, 1963; Philip Agee, *Inside the Company: CIA Diary*, (Harmondsworth: Penguin, 1975) p. 425; *Washington Post*, March 16, 1975.
16. Ibid.
17. *NACLA*, November/December 1982.
18. *Wall Street Journal*, January 7, 1983.
19. *LAWR*, September 9, 1983.
20. DOD, *Congressional Presentation Fiscal Year 1983*, p. 469.
21. Ibid.
22. *LAWR*, September 9, 1983.
23. *Caribbean Contact*, April 1983, p. 13.
24. DOD, *Congressional Presentation Fiscal Year 1983*.
25. Interview by Deb Preusch: Chris Webster, Grenada Task Force, Department of State; January 3, 1984.
26. Interview by Deb Preusch: Harvey Lampert, Political-Military Affairs, Department of State; December 30, 1983.
27. Interview by Deb Preusch: Harvey Lampert.
28. Committee on Foreign Affairs, House of Representatives, *Staff Study Mission Report*, June 22, 1983.
29. *Struggle*, (newspaper of Workers Party of Jamaica) July 23, 1982.
30. *Caribbean Review*, Spring 1982.

PART TWO

Great Britain and the Caribbean

1. Data obtained from *The Reverse Transfer of Technology: Its Dimensions, Economic Effects and Policy Implications*, TD/B/6.6/7 UNCTAD 1975, Annex A.
2. *Insight*, July 1983.
3. Interview by Tom Barry, April 1983.
4. Bank of London and South America, *Quarterly Economic Review*, Spring 1983.
5. *Wall Street Journal*, January 11, 1983.

Canada and the Caribbean

1. Robert Chodos, *The Caribbean Connection*, (Toronto: James Lorimer & Co., 1977) p. 67.
2. Canadian International Development Association, (CIDA), *Canadians in the Third World—CIDA Year in Review Statistical Annex 1981–1982*, 1983, pp. 55–56.
3. Ibid.
4. Neil S. Sealey, *Tourism in the Caribbean*, (London: Hodder & Stoughton, 1982) p. 50.
5. *Latin American Working Group (LAWG) Newsletter*, Vol. VII, No. 1/2, 1982, pp. 4, 5.
6. Ibid.
7. Ibid.
8. Robert Carty, Virginia Smith, & LAWG, *Perpetuating Poverty: The Political Economy of Canadian Foreign Aid*, (Toronto: Between the Lines, 1981) p. 52.
9. Ibid., p. 53.
10. Tim Draimin, "Canada's Policy Toward Central America," *Canada-Caribbean-Central America Policy Alternatives*, (Toronto: 1983).
11. CIDA, *Canadians in the Third World*, p. 21.
12. Canadian Association Latin America and the Caribbean, *Annual Report*, 1980.
13. IT&C official at meeting of business owners in 1973, cited in *Ties That Bind: Canada and the Third World*, (Toronto: Between the Lines, 1982) p. 169.
14. *Caribbean Business News*, February/March 1982.
15. Ibid.
16. CIDA, *Annual Report*, various years.
17. Carty, Smith, & LAWG, *Perpetuating Poverty*, p. 53.
18. Organization for Economic Cooperation and Development Press Release, Paris, December 15, 1982.

France and the Caribbean

1. *LARR*, Jan. 16, 1981.
2. Interview by Tom Barry: Richard Dwyer, U. S. Embassy, Martinique; April 1983.
3. Institut National de la Statistique, Paris, *Bulletin de Statisques*, January 1983.
4. *Washington Post*, February 28, 1981.
5. *Bulletin de Statistiques*, January 1983.
6. *National Geographic*, January 1975.
7. *Washington Post*, February 28, 1981.
8. Ibid.
9. "Guadeloupe Departamiento Frances en el Caribe," *Pensamiento Propio*, (Managua, Nicaragua), April 1983.
10. *National Geographic*, January 1975.
11. *LARR*, May 8, 1981.
12. *LARR*, January 16, 1981.

Netherlands Antilles

1. *LARR*, July 16, 1982.
2. U. S. Department of State "Airgram," October 10, 1978.
3. *LARR*, April 22, 1983.
4. Bank of London & South America, *Quarterly Economic Report*, Spring 1983.
5. *Caribbean Business*, October 20, 1982.
6. *Albuquerque Journal*, March 13, 1983.

Puerto Rico

1. U. S. Jenny Pearce, *Under the Eagle*, (London: Latin American Bureau, 1982) p. 49.
2. U. S. Department of Commerce, *Economic Study of Puerto Rico*, December 1979.
3. *Caribbean Business*, August 10, 1983.
4. *Quarterly Economic Report*, Puerto Rico, No. 1, 1983.
5. *New York Times*, July 3, 1983.
6. Department of Commerce, *Economic Study of Puerto Rico*.
7. U. S. Department of Treasury, *The Operation of Possessions Cooperation System of Taxation*, February 1983, p. 102.
8. *Puerto Rico Business Review*, March 1983.
9. Ibid.
10. "Interview with Dr. Neftali Garcia," *Multinational Monitor*, February 1980.
11. "Puerto Rico: End of Autonomy," *NACLA*, March 1981.
12. U. S. Department of Treasury, *The Operation of the Possessions Corporation System of Taxation*, p. 5.
13. *Caribbean Business*, April 13, 1983.

14. U. S. Department of Treasury, *The Operation of Possessions Cooperation System of Taxation*, February 1983, p. 2.
15. *Caribbean Business*, March 2, 1983.
16. *Puerto Rico Business Review*, March 1983.
17. Department of Commerce, *U. S. Quarterly Financial Report*.
18. *U. S. Treasury Report*, p. 90.
19. *Business Facilities Magazine*, February 1983.
20. *U. S. Treasury Report*, p. 8.
21. *LARR*, March 26, 1982.
22. U. S. Department of Commerce, *Survey of Current Business*, various issues, 1983.
23. Ibid.
24. Statement of Dr. Larry Simon of OXFAM/America before the Subcommittee on Inter-American Affairs, U. S. House of Representatives, July 20, 1982.
25. *Multinational Monitor*, February 1980.
26. *Caribbean Business News*, April 27, l983, p. 16.
27. *Puerto Rico Industrial Development Company Annual Report 1942–1982— The First Forty Years*, 1982.
28. *NACLA*, March 1981, p. 28.
29. Ibid.
30. *Caribbean Business*, May 4, 1983.
31. *Mision Industrial Informa*, "Humacao." No date.
32. Aristalco Calero, "Letter to the Senators and Representatives of the Congress," January 20, 1980, (photocopy).

U. S. Virgin Islands

1. *Multinational Monitor*, April 1981.
2. *Business Facilities Magazine*, May 1983.
3. *NACLA*, November 1977.

Antigua-Barbuda

1. U. S. Department of State, "Antigua Bulletin," August 25, 1982.
2. *Outlet* (newspaper of the Antigua-Caribbean Liberation Movement), April 5, 1983.
3. *Insight*, December 1982.
4. *Insight*, January 1983.
5. Interview by Tom Barry, May 1983.
6. *Caribbean Business*, December 14, 1983.

The Bahamas

1. Anthony Thompson, *An Economic History of the Bahamas*, (Commonwealth Publications, 1979).

2. Robert Chodos, *The Caribbean Connection*, (Toronto: James Lorimer & Co, 1977) p. 90.
3. Department of Commerce, *Foreign Economic Trends*, January 1983.
4. Testimony by Alexander Peters before the U. S. Senate Committee on Finance, August 11, 1982.
5. *LARR*, September 25, 1981.
6. *Ambio*, 1981, p. 290.
7. Ramesh Ramsaran, "External Dependence and National Development—Case Study of Bahamas," 1974, p. 212.

Barbados

1. *Insight*, March 1983, p. 3.
2. USAID, Bridgetown Mission, "Barbados Profile," 1982.
3. *Caribbean and West Indies Chronicle*, August/September 1982.
4. Jean Crusol, "Impact of International Subcontracting on the Integration of the Caribbean," (photocopied report).
5. *Business Latin America*, April 4, 1983, p. 32.

Cuba

1. Arthur MacEwan, *Revolution and Economic Development in Cuba*, (New York: St. Martin's Press, 1981) p. 13.
2. U. S. Department of Commerce, "Investment in Cuba," 1956.
3. *Counter Spy*, November 1981; *Newsday*, January 9, 1977.
4. MacEwan, p. 14.
5. Fidel Castro, *History Will Absolve Me*, 1956.
6. MacEwan, *Revolution and Economic Development in Cuba*, p. 159.
7. *LARR*, January 21, 1983; Ministry of Public Health, United Nations; *LARR*, September 30, 1983; *New York Times*, October 31, 1982.
8. *LARR*, August 20, 1982.
9. Ibid.
10. Caribbean/Central American Action (CCAA), *Caribbean Datebook*, 1982, p. 81.
11. *Los Angeles Times*, August 13, 1982.
12. *Insight*, March 1983.
13. Testimony by U. S. Department of Commerce before Joint Economic Committee, Summer 1982.
14. *Insight*, February 1983.
15. MacEwan, *Revolution and Economic Development in Cuba*, p. 17.
16. Francis Moore Lappé and Joseph Collins, *Food First*, (New York: Ballantine Books, 1977) p. 198.
17. Arthur MacEwan cited in Frank Fitzgerald's "Direction of Cuban Socialism: A Critique of the Sovietization Thesis," *Caribbean Sociological Reader*, p. 264.
18. Ibid.

19. *LAWR*, May 6, 1983.
20. Jay Mandle, *Patterns of Caribbean Development*, (London: Gordon and Beach, 1982).
21. *LAWR*, May 6, 1983.
22. Ibid.
23. Barry Sklar, "Cuban Exodus—The Context," *Political Economy of the Western Hemisphere*, (Washington: Government Printing Office, 1981).
24. *Insight*, October 1983.
25. *Miami Herald*, August 23, 1982.
26. *Multinational Monitor*, June 1982.
27. *Multinational Monitor*, March 1983.
28. *Insight*, April 1983.
29. *Miami Herald*, July 7, 1983.
30. *Miami Herald*, January 12, 1983.
31. Department of State, "Cuba's Renewed Support for Violence in Latin America," December 14, 1981.
32. *Granma* (Havana, Cuba), January 14, 1973.
33. *Caribbean Contact*, June 1983, p. 13.
34. Wayne Smith, "Dateline Havana: Myopic Diplomacy," *Foreign Policy*, Fall 1982, p. 157.
35. Ibid., p. 174.
36. U. S. Department of State, "Cuba, Background Notes," April 1983.
37. William M. LeoGrande, "Cuba Policy Recycled," *Foreign Policy*, Spring 1982, p. 109.
38. Wayne Smith, *Foreign Policy*, Fall 1982.
39. *Los Angeles Times*, July 1, 1983.
40. Richard R. Fagen, "The Real Clear and Present Danger," *Caribbean Review*, Spring 1982.
41. Bank of London and South America, "Quarterly Economic Report," No. 1, 1983.
42. *Inter-American Economic Affairs*, Summer 1982, p. 67.
43. *Defense 1982* (magazine of U. S. Department of Defense), March 1982.
44. Nita Rous Manitzas, "Cuba and the Contemporary World Order," *Newer Caribbean*, (Philadelphia: Institute for the Study of Human Issues, 1983) p. 153.
45. Ibid., p. 157.

Dominica

1. *Courier*, January/February 1982, p. 24.
2. Cathy Sunshine and Philip Wheaton, *Death of a Revolution*, (Washington DC: Epica), November 30, 1983.
3. Dominica Farmers Union, "What Is To Be Done?" 1982, p. 4.
4. *Courier*, January/February 1982.
5. Dominica Farmers Union, "What Is To Be Done?" 1982, p. 4.
6. Ibid.
7. AID, "Regional Profile of Dominica," 1982.

8. *Caribbean Business*, November 2, 1983.
9. *Courier*, January/February 1982.
10. *Harvard Business Review*, July/August 1981, p. 6.

Dominican Republic

1. *LARR*, August 26, 1983.
2. USAID, "Health Sector Assessment for the Dominican Republic," 1976.
3. Bernardo Vega, "The Dominican Economic Moment," Speech delivered before the American Chamber of Commerce, 1983.
4. *NACLA Report on the Americas*, November 1982.
5. *New York Times*, August 30, 1982.
6. Interfaith Center on Corporate Responsibility, *Gulf+Western in the Dominican Republic: An Evaluation*, October 1979, pp. 24–27.
7. Ibid.
8. Ibid.
9. Interview by Tom Barry, March 1983.
10. *El Nuevo Diario* (Santo Domingo), March 14, 1983, p. 4.
11. *El Nuevo Diario* (Santo Domingo), March 15, 1983, p. 15.
12. UN Center on Transnational Corporations, *Transnational Corporations in Food and Beverage Processing*, 1981, pp. 31, 36, 50, 72.
13. *El Nuevo Diario*, August 2, 1982.
14. *Listin Diario* (Santo Domingo), February 15, 1983.
15. U. S. Embassy, Dominican Republic, "Investment Climate for the Dominican Republic," January 1983, p. 10.
16. Lic. Manolo Dominquez, "Consideraciones Sobre Las Zonas Francas en La Republica Dominicana," (unpublished paper, 1983).
17. Economic Commission for Latin America, "Industrial Development Strategies in Caribbean Countries: Dominican Republic," April 10, 1981.
18. Information from U. S. Embassy, Dominican Republic, April 1983.
19. AID, *Congressional Presentation Fiscal Year 1983, Annex III*, 1982, p. 93.
20. G. Pope Atkins, *Arms and Politics in the Dominican Republic*, (Boulder: Westview Press, 1981) p. 32.
21. Interview by Tom Barry, March 1983.
22. "International Marketing: You've Got to Know the Territory," *Business America*, September 20, 1982.
23. Statement by Gulf+Western, submitted to the Committee on Foreign Affairs, April 29, 1982.
24. Milton Moskowitz, Michael Katz, and Robert Levering, eds., *Everybody's Business*, (New York: Harper & Row, 1980), p. 819.
25. AFL-CIO, "U. S. Firms Flee to Caribbean," *American Federationist*, 1973.
26. *Gulf+Western in the Dominican Republic: An Evaluation*, p.55.
27. Ibid.
28. "Cancelan Trabajadores Zona Franca," *La Noticia* (Santo Domingo), July 30, 1978.
29. "What is Gulf and Western to the Dominican Republic?" *Christian Science Monitor*, January 17, 1979.

30. *El Caribe* (Santo Domingo), January 16, 1977.
31. Organization of American States, "Estado Nutricional en la Republica Dominicana: Informe Sobre la Encuesta Nacional de Nutricion," 1969.
32. Ibid., p. 43.
33. *El Caribe*, November 8, 1976.

Grenada

1. Robert Chodos, *The Caribbean Connection*, (Toronto: James Lorimer & Company, 1977) p. 50.
2. *Insight*, February 1983.
3. Anthony Boatswain, "Industrial Development Strategies in Caribbean Countries," Economic Commission for Latin America, January 29, 1981.
4. *Report on the National Economy for 1982*, Ministry of Planning, Finance, and Trade.
5. Grenada Ministry of Tourism, *Tourism in the Context of Economic Strategies*, 1982.
6. *LARR*, March 31, 1983.
7. *LAWR*, November 4, 1983.
8. *International News*, October 31, 1982.
9. Cathy Sunshine and Philip Wheaton, *Death of a Revolution* (Washington, DC: Epica) November 30, 1983.
10. *Washington Post*, November 9, 1983.
11. *Outlet* (newspaper of the Antigua-Caribbean Liberation Movement), October 21, 1983.
12. *Chicago Sun Times*, November 1, 1983.
13. *Los Angeles Times*, November 17, 1983.
14. *New York Times*, November 10, 1983.
15. *Caribbean Contact*, November 1983.
16. *New York Times*, December 26, 1983.
17. *Multinational Monitor*, December 1983.
18. *Horizons*, (monthly magazine of AID), December 1983, p. 5.
19. *Caribbean Business*, December 7, 1983.
20. InterAgency Team on Commercial and Private Sector Initiatives "Prospects for Growth in Grenada: The Role of the Private Sector," December 5, 1983, p. 20.
21. Interview by Tom Barry with Desmond Foynes, Caribbean Basin Information Center, January 1984.
22. *Washington Post*, December 7, 1983.
23. *New Internationalist*, December 1980.

Guyana

1. Clive Thomas, *Guyana: The World Bank Group and the General Crisis* (Guyana: University of Guyana, 1983) p. 37.
2. *Caribbean Contact*, July 1983, p. 5.

3. *Comment*, Catholic Institute for International Relations, 1980, p. 9.
4. *Caribbean Contact*, July 1983.
5. Thomas, *Guyana: The World Bank Group and the General Crisis*, p. 36.
6. J. R. Mandle, *Patterns of Caribbean Development*, (London: Gordon and Breach, 1982) p. 72.
7. *LAWR*, May 6, 1983.
8. Thomas, *Guyana: The World Bank Group and the General Crisis*, p. 42.
9. *LAWR*, August 19, 1983, p. 7.
10. *LAWR*, May 6, 1983.
11. R. D. Associates, "Report on CBI Implementation Plan for Guyana," January 1983.
12. Ibid.
13. Ibid.
14. Ibid.
15. *LARR*, May 13, 1983.

Haiti

1. AID, "Country Development Strategy Statement: Haiti, FY1984," January 1982.
2. AID, "Food and Agriculture Strategy for Haiti," December 23, 1981.
3. GAO, "Assistance to Haiti: Barriers to Recent Changes and Future Options," February 22, 1982, p. 1.
4. Erik P. Eckholm, *Losing Ground*, (New York: W. W. Norton, 1976) p. 169.
5. Gino Lofredo, "Transnational Subcontracting: An Assessment of the Impact of Export-Oriented Assembly Industries on Social and Economic Development in Haiti," Johns Hopkins University, School of Advanced International Studies, Washington, December 1980.
6. Michael S. Hooper, *Violations of Human Rights in Haiti: A Report to the Organization of American States*, (New York: Lawyers Committee for International Human Rights, November 1982, pp. 42, 54.
7. U. S. Embassy, Haiti, "Haiti Fact Sheet," 1982.
8. *Multinational Monitor*, August 1982.
9. U. S. Department of Labor, "Labor Conditions in Haiti," 1982.
10. Lofredo, "Transnational Subcontracting: An Assessment of the Impact of Export-Oriented Assembly Industries on Social and Economic Development in Haiti."
11. *An Investor's Guide to Haiti*, 1982.
12. *Food First News* (Institute for Food and Development Policy), Summer 1983.
13. Hooper, *Violations of Human Rights in Haiti: A Report to the Organization of American States*, p. 52.
14. *LARR*, January 15, 1982.

Jamaica

1. "Jamaica," MacNeil/Lehrer Report, July 11, 1980.
2. *Washington Post*, August 25, 1980.

3. Jay R. Mandle, *Patterns of Caribbean Development*, (London: Gordon and Breach, 1982) p. 100.
4. *Washington Post*, July 1982.
5. "Jamaica: A Striking Turnaround," *Institutional Investor*, 1981.
6. *Courier*, #75, September/October 1982.
7. *Atlantic Monthly*, September 1983.
8. *Sunray's Sunday Sun Magazine*, June 13, 1982.
9. *Multinational Monitor*, March 1983.
10. *Sunray's Sunday Sun Magazine*, June 13, 1982.
11. *Caribbean Insight*, October 1983.
12. *Atlantic Monthly*, September 1983.

St. Kitts-Nevis

1. "St. Kitts," supplement to the *Caribbean Chronicle*, September 1983, p. viii.
2. *Caribbean Business*, September 28, 1983.
3. *Caribbean Chronicle*, September 1983, p. iii.

St. Lucia

1. Interview by Tom Barry: David Dimark, St. Lucia Ministry of Agriculture; May 1983.
2. *Courier*, January/February 1982.
3. Ibid.
4. *Insight*, May 1983.
5. Department of Commerce, *Foreign Economic Trends, St. Lucia*, March 1983.

St. Vincent and the Grenadines

1. Department of Commerce, "Foreign Economic Trends and Their Implications for the United States, St. Vincent and the Grenadines," March, 1983.
2. *Caribbean Business News*, February/March 1982.
3. *LARR*, July 17, 1981.
4. *LARR*, August 21, 1981.

Suriname

1. *Foreign Economic Trends*, September 1982.
2. *Caribbean Contact*, October 1983.
3. *Sobernia* (Managua, Nicaragua), February/March 1983.
4. *LARR*, June 17, 1982.
5. *LAWR*, June 9, 1983.
6. *Sobernia* (Managua, Nicaragua), February/March 1983.
7. Bank of London and South America, *Quarterly Economic Report*, Spring 1983.

8. *Wall Street Journal,* January 26, 1983.
9. *Foreign Economic Trends,* September 1982.
10. *Sobernia* (Managua, Nicaragua), February/March 1983.

Trinidad & Tobago

1. Earl Lovelace, "We Need Courage to Go From Corruption to Regeneration," *Outlet* (newspaper of Antigua-Caribbean Liberation Movement), April 4, 1983.
2. *New Internationalist,* #94, December 1980.
3. *Outlet,* April 4, 1983.
4. *Caribbean Contact,* May 1983.
5. "EEC-Trinidad & Tobago Cooperation," *Courier,* May–June 1982.
6. "Confronting Multinationals: Trinidad Workers on the Lines," *Multinational Monitor,* January 1981.
7. *Vanguard,* April 8, 1983.
8. *Multinational Monitor,* November 1982.
9. *Hold the Fort* (newspaper of the Committee for Labor Solidarity, Trinidad), January 21, 1982.

Selected Name Index

GROVE PRESS BOOKS ON LATIN AMERICA

Barnes, John / EVITA—FIRST LADY: A Biography of Eva Peron / The first major biography of the beautiful and strong-willed leader of the impoverished Argentina of the 1940's. / $2.95 / 17087-3

Barry, Tom, Wood, Beth, and Preusch, Deb / DOLLARS AND DICTATORS: A Guide to Central America / "A thorough and comprehensive study of the effect the ubiquitous corporate presence in the region has had on its politics and on American foreign policy."—*The Progressive* / $6.95 / 62485-8

Borges, Jorge Luis / FICCIONES (ed. and intro. by Anthony Kerrigan) / A collection of short fictional pieces from the man whom *Time* has called "the greatest living writer in the Spanish language today." / $6.95 / 17244-2

Borges, Jorge Luis / A PERSONAL ANTHOLOGY (ed. and frwd. by Anthony Kerrigan) / Borges' personal selections of his work, including "The Circular Ruins," "Death and the Compass," and "A New Refutation of Time." / $5.95 / 17270-1

Fried, Jonathan, et al., eds. / GUATEMALA IN REBELLION: Unfinished History / A sourcebook on the history of Guatemala and its current crisis. / $8.95 / 62455-6

Gettleman, Marvin, et al., eds. / EL SALVADOR: Central America in the New Cold War / A collection of essays, articles, and eye-witness reports on the conflict in El Salvador. "Highly recommended for students, scholars, and policy-makers."—*Library Journal* / $9.95 / 17956-0

Neruda, Pablo / FIVE DECADES: POEMS, 1925-1970 (Bilingual ed. tr. by Ben Belitt) / A collection of more than 200 poems by the Nobel Prize-winning Chilean poet. / $12.50 / 17869-6

Neruda, Pablo / NEW DECADE: POEMS, 1958-1967 (Bilingual ed. tr. by Ben Belitt and Alastair Reid) / $5.95 / 17275-2

Neruda, Pablo / NEW POEMS (1968-1970) (Bilingual ed. tr. and intro. by Ben Belitt) / $3.95 / 17793-2

Neruda, Pablo / SELECTED POEMS (Bilingual ed. tr. by Ben Belitt) / A selection of Neruda's finest work. Intro. by Luis Monguio. / $6.95 / 17243-4

Paz, Octavio / THE LABYRINTH OF SOLITUDE, THE OTHER MEXICO, AND OTHER ESSAYS (New preface by the author. Tr. by Lysander Kemp, Toby Talbot and Rachel Phillips) / A collection of Paz's best-known works and six new essays, one especially written for this volume. / $9.95 / 17992-7

Paz, Octavio / THE OTHER MEXICO: Critique of the Pyramid (tr. by Lysander Kemp) / Paz defined the character and culture of Mexico in what has now become a modern classic of critical interpretation. / $2.45 / 17773-8

Rosset, Peter and Vandermeer, John / THE NICARAGUA READER: Documents of a Revolution Under Fire / A sourcebook of articles on the Nicaraguan revolution and U.S. intervention / $8.95 / 62498-X

Rulfo, Juan / PEDRO PARAMO: A Novel of Mexico (tr. by Lysander Kemp) By the Mexican author whom the *New York Times* says will "rank among the immortals." / $2.45 / 17446-1

Thelwell, Michael / THE HARDER THEY COME / The "masterly achieved novel" (Harold Bloom) by Jamaica's finest novelist. Inspired by the now-classic film by Perry Henzell, starring Jimmy Cliff, it tells the story of a legendary gunman and folk hero who lived in Kingston in the late 1950's. / $7.95 / 17599-9

Books may be ordered directly from Grove Press. Add $1.00 per book postage and handling and send check or money order to: Order Dept., Grove Press, Inc., 196 West Houston Street, New York, N.Y. 10014